THE ZULLIGER INDIVIDUAL AND GROUP TEST

THE ZULLIGER INDIVIDUAL
AND GROUP TEST

Hans Zulliger

Edited by FRITZ SALOMON

Translated by DUSYA T. DUBROVSKY

INTERNATIONAL UNIVERSITIES PRESS, INC.
NEW YORK

Library of Congress Catalog Card Number: 69-19369

Manufactured in the United States of America

Contents

v

Contents

Contents

PART II

THE TEST EVALUATION

vii

Contents

Contents

THE ZULLIGER INDIVIDUAL AND GROUP TEST

Foreword to the English-Language Edition

In 1948, the late Dr. Hans Zulliger published in German his form-interpretation test for group testing, "The Zulliger Group Test" (second enlarged edition published in 1959); in 1954, he published "The Zulliger Individual Test" (second enlarged edition published in 1962), a version of the previous test adapted for individual testing. Both volumes were published by the Hans Huber Publishing House, Bern and Stuttgart. Following the second edition of the individual test, the name of the test was changed from "Z-Test" to "Zulliger Test," by analogy with the Rorschach and Behn-Rorschach Tests. (The French translation of both these books still bears the title "The Z-Test.") Zulliger created the group test in his capacity as psychologist within the framework of the Swiss Army during the Second World War.

After conferring with both the Swiss publisher, Hans Huber, and the American publisher, International Universities Press, it was decided to publish both books in one volume. The main reason for this decision was the fact that some chapters—especially the purely theoretical ones—are in part the same in both volumes; furthermore, the technical aspects of evaluation remain almost unchanged in both versions of the test. Dr. Zulliger and the Huber Publishing House then entrusted me with the preparation of this combined edition for the American publisher.

In combining the textbook and the manual for the two versions, it was my task to avoid unnecessary repetitions as much as possible. In a supplement to the "Zulliger Individual Test," the author had published a number of separate articles, which dealt with certain aspects of the test that, in his opinion, had

1

not been sufficiently discussed in the original edition. I have incorporated these articles into the general text. In so doing, I have found that some material could be left out, since it is covered in the original text. Slight changes of the text, which thus became necessary, have not been specifically credited to me, except in instances where they were somewhat more extended, or constituted outright additions. Moreover, some of the original test samples have not been presented here. Instead, Dr. Zulliger placed at my disposal several new tests, along with their psychological evaluations, especially intended for the American edition.

The first part of this book, then, is devoted to the general theoretical foundations, and instructions for the evaluation of the Zulliger Test, as well as to examples derived from the individual test. In the second part, instructions are given for the administration of the group test; this is followed by a number of interpretations of group test records.

Since it was first published, the Zulliger Test has been widely and enthusiastically used in most European and many non-European countries. Studies about the test have already been published in a great many languages, some in book form, some as articles in psychological and psychiatric periodicals. Whenever it has come to the attention of the Huber Publishing House or myself, original research dealing with the test has been included in the bibliography added to this volume. I should like to express my gratitude to Dusya T. Dubrovsky, Ph.D., for her translation of this book, and to Harold Collins for his painstaking editorial assistance in preparing the manuscript for publication. I am grateful to International Universities Press for their helpful assistance.

Primarily, however, I am grateful to my personal friends, the late Dr. Hans Zulliger and the Swiss publisher, Hans Huber, for their trust in giving me the assignment of preparing and editing the combined edition of the two Zulliger Test books. Dr. Zulliger in particular was always willing to give me his advice and support in this work, both by personal communication and by correspondence.

New York, 1968   FRITZ SALOMON

Some Biographical Remarks about the Author

Originally, Hans Zulliger, a Swiss, who died in October 1965, at the age of 72, was a schoolteacher. In spite of many other professional and scientific activities he remained faithful to this profession until his retirement a few years ago. While he was still studying at a teachers college, Zulliger was attracted to Freud's psychoanalysis. For this, the influence of his teacher and subsequent friend, Pastor Oskar Pfister, was primarily responsible. Oskar Pfister, an early and life-long intimate friend of Freud, had introduced psychoanalytic theory into the service of religion and education. His immediate influence resulted in the fact that Hans Zulliger, after having undergone psychoanalysis himself, became the first to introduce psychoanalysis into schoolteaching. In addition, he was one of the pioneers in the field of child analysis. His first case (1913) was a stuttering schoolboy, whom he succeeded in freeing from his affliction; it has not recurred to this day. Later, after the First World War, he began to develop his own play technique for the therapy of children, using interpretations only very sparsely. At the same time, he increasingly employed psychoanalytic theories and his own related experiences in school instruction. This he applied in two ways: first, in shaping the work of the entire class work; second, in helping individually slightly neurotic pupils. In this way, he protected these pupils from becoming more seriously neurotic, and also made it possible for them to profit from lessons more than they would have otherwise. His first book in this field was entitled: *Psychoanalytische Erfahrungen aus der Volksschul-*

3

praxis (*Psychoanalytic Experiences in Elementary School Practice*), 1921. About 20 books followed this publication, and many more than one hundred articles appeared in the most diverse scientific periodicals. They all deal with child analysis and the general application of psychoanalysis to educational problems and mental hygiene. Soon after the publication of the above-mentioned work, Zulliger became a member of the Swiss Psychoanalytic Society; he held the post of secretary for many years.

Through his friend, Dr. Emil Oberholzer, Zulliger met Dr. Hermann Rorschach at the Swiss Psychoanalytic Society. He soon became his student and friend. He was probably Rorschach's only surviving immediate disciple and friend, to the end of his life engaged in further elaborating on the latter's test and developing it. His first publication in this field dates back to 1932, *Der Rorschachsche Testversuch im Dienste der Erziehungsberatung* (*Rorschach's Test Experiment in the Service of Educational Counseling*). A large number of other publications followed; there are four books among them. *Jugendliche Diebe im Rorschach-Verfahren* (*Young Thieves in the Rorschach Technique*) was published in 1938 by the Paul Haupt Publishing House, Bern and Leipzig. In 1941, *Einfuehrung in den Behn-Rorschach Test* (*Introduction to the Behn-Rorschach Test*) was published by the Huber Publishing House; the English translation appeared in 1956, also published by Huber. (The Behn-Rorschach Test is the parallel series, created by the Swiss psychiatrist Behn-Eschenburg with the direct collaboration of Rorschach himself; frequently, it has proven more valuable for use with children than Rorschach's original series.) In 1948, and again in 1954, Zulliger's books about his own test, the Zulliger Test, were published.

In the entire international Rorschach literature, there is hardly any writer who contributed more than did Zulliger to the further development and deepening of this excellent psychodiagnostic instrument. Remaining to the end of his life faithful to the creator of psychoanalysis, Sigmund Freud, in the application of his theories to the analysis of children and to the general problems of mental hygiene, be behaved in the same way toward his teacher, Rorschach. The formal psychogram remained for

4

him the basis of the test evaluation. The practical samples presented in this book provide excellent proof of his exceptional ability to evaluate psychologically the various formal factors in their infinite combinations.

Starting very early, Zulliger has continued the work that Rorschach, who unfortunately died quite young, had begun—namely, to integrate successfully psychoanalytic insights into test theory and practice. Some of the special circumstances of his own psychoanalytic and psychological work served him particularly well in this endeavor. After 1912, he lived in Ittigen, a suburb of Bern, and was thus able to observe, often for several decades, the further development of subjects whom he had once tested. In addition, he himself treated, psychoanalytically or psychotherapeutically, many children and adolescents whom he had previously tested. There is hardly any psychologist who worked with the form-interpretation test under such exceptionally favorable conditions. Thus, whenever the need arose, he was always able, both directly and indirectly, to re-examine and correct his diagnoses and his newly acquired insights by way of longitudinal observations. If he believed that he had discovered new diagnostic possibilities, he often waited for years for their confirmation before he finally published them, in the form of a case history or a theoretical study.

There is probably no single area in the utilization of the form-interpretation test to which Zulliger did not make his own personal contribution. The Zulliger Group Test, for example, served him in the application of the test to sociological research. In all his publications, however, regardless of whether they were devoted to the test or remained within the framework of psychoanalysis, the simplicity of his language is quite astonishing. He was able to present the most complicated material in a simple way. Purely abstract conceptualizations were alien to his creative nature; he made use of them only when he deemed them to be absolutely necessary. In all his scientific publications, didactics—teaching and helping to understand—remained his most important goal. The reader, in his view, must not merely comprehend the material from a purely intellectual point of view; he must also *feel* everything presented to him by the written word. Only in this way will he be in a position simultaneously to cathect it by libido as well, and thus to make it his own for the purpose of practical application. Here Zulliger followed the same principle that he had successfully developed and applied during a period of more than 40 years as a teacher.

Zulliger had a valid reason for not giving up his teaching activity. He wished to maintain continuous contact with healthy children, in whom normally, and at different stages of their development, one may always observe some merely transitory neurotic phenomena. Such constant comparison makes it possible to judge correctly the degree of psychological disturbance, to avoid overestimating it. In each case, and especially when dealing with young patients, it was Zulliger's primary objective to understand as fully as possible the healthy part of their structure, as well as the ailing ego functions, in order to arrive at a correct prognosis and to be able to recommend the most suitable psychotherapeutic treatment. Many diagnoses in this book will bear out this approach.

In addition to all his scientific publications, Zulliger wrote a large number of books and essays in the field of literature, in both poetry and prose. A number of them were composed in the Swiss dialect.

Especially after the end of the Second World War, Zulliger was very active lecturing in German speaking countries. In addition, he taught at various universities and scientific institutes, both in Switzerland and in Germany. He held membership in a number of Swiss and international scientific societies, and was the joint editor of scientific periodicals and books. Many of his books and papers have been translated into a number of languages.

In 1952, in appreciation of his scientific works, he was awarded an honorary doctor's degree by the historical-philosophical faculty of the University of Bern. In 1958, the medical faculty of the University of Heidelberg, Germany, bestowed upon him the honor of making him a *Doctor medicinae honoris causa*. In addition, he was the recipient of some renowned Swiss literary prizes. On the occasion of his seventieth birthday, the Huber Publishing House published a volume entitled: *Hans*

Zulliger, Eine Biographie und Wuerdigung seines Wirkens (*Hans Zulliger, a Biography and Appraisal of His Work*), edited by Professor Werner Kasser. In this book, his disciples and friends honored him and expressed their appreciation of his multidimensional scientific and literary activities.

FRITZ SALOMON

Author's Introduction

THE ZULLIGER GROUP TEST

The Zulliger Group Test was originally created in 1942 for the Swiss Army Psychological Service (*Generaladjutantur*, Section 2). At first, the Army Psychological Service had intended to use the existing form-interpretation tests, such as the Rorschach and Behn-Rorschach card series. However, this meant that if, for instance, 60 officer candidates were to be tested, the test had to be administered to all 60 candidates individually. This would have required too much time—about 30 hours for the recording of the test alone. Therefore, the attempt was made to test simultaneously entire groups of officer candidates, etc. The possibility was discussed of projecting a card series upon a screen and also of a method that would permit the recording of the answers. However, the cards proved to be too complicated for such an undertaking. The objection was further raised that the methods prescribed by the creators of the tests could not be changed without leading to serious errors. Therefore, the plan to project some of the cards in the existing picture series was abandoned.

We were in need of a form-interpretation test which, while not drawn from the existing series, would lend itself to the testing of groups consisting of as many as 30-60 subjects. For this purpose,

---

Translated from the Introduction to the first edition of *The Zulliger Group Test* (Bern: Huber, 1948) and from the Foreword to the first edition of the *Zulliger Individual Test* (Bern: Huber, 1954).

8

I selected four ink blots from among 600 ink blots that I myself had made. They were tried out on a large number of subjects, and compared with the corresponding individual tests Rorschach or Behn-Rorschach Tests) for the respective subjects. Certain flaws were then discovered in the series. Thereupon, from some 400 additional ink blots, two more were selected that stimulated the kinesthetic responses particularly well. This series of six was again tried out on a significant number of subjects, just as the series of four had been.

The series of six proved to be usable. The attempt could be made to reduce it to three pictures; and in its practical application the reduced series also proved to be usable.

Thus, at present, the final test apparatus consists of three pictures. They have been standardized with a large sample (800 subjects) and they have proven to be reliable.

THE ZULLIGER INDIVIDUAL TEST

While it is true that occasionally short individual diagnoses were prepared, based upon the examination with the three plates, I had never imagined that these three pictures could be developed into a useful individual test; it was the good fortune of the Institute for Psychology and Characterology at the University of Freiburg in Breisgau to make this discovery, and we owe a debt of gratitude to its director, Prof. Robert Heiss, for his suggestion to the publishing house that it publish the test in the form of *cards*. Subsequently they were so published, and it became necessary to provide a special introduction.

Accordingly, the *individual* test developed from the original "group test." Very lengthy preliminary research was necessary in order to write this book. A great deal of comparative study was required, comparing the results on Rorschach and Behn Tests with those on the Zulliger Test, administered to the same subjects. Although one could indeed rely in part on the results of the Zulliger Group Test, it was discovered soon enough that it is an entirely different matter whether the subject interprets slides projected upon a screen or produces his responses to cards presented to him individually. The way of perceiving is different, and accordingly the subject produces different interpretations.[1]

This research was not carried out by myself alone. The results obtained by many of my co-workers have been at my disposal, among others those of the University Institute of Freiburg in Breisgau, Professor Hans Biaesch of the Institute for Applied Psychology in Zürich, Professor A. Friedemann, M.D., of the Institute for Mental Hygiene in Biel, Fritz Salomon, psychoanalyst in Paris, Professor Zietz of the Teachers College in Braunschweig, etc., to all of whom I am profoundly grateful. I also wish to express my gratitude to the Publishing House of Hans Huber in Bern, which has always been helpful to me.

At the present time, we have at our disposal a large number of tests that examine innate ability, character, intelligence, affectivity, talents, and the entire emotional structure of a subject. The drawback of most of these tests is the fact that they require a *great deal of time*. It has therefore been the goal of psychological research to find some means that are less time-consuming and yet will produce useful results. The Zulliger Individual Test should represent *one* of these means. It is obvious that it should be used together with other such means and that other tests should hardly ever be used by themselves. It is—at least it seems so to me—a daring, a hardly permissible undertaking to attempt to give a valid diagnosis about a human being by using but one single test; it is imperative to use a *"test battery"* which allows us to compare with one another the results obtained through various sources in order to weigh, to verify, and to correct our findings.

Experience with the Zulliger Individual Test has proven that, in their scope, its results are frequently entirely in keeping with those produced by the Rorschach (Ro) and the Behn-Rorschach (Bero) Tests. From time to time, it even produces them in a much more concentrated form. The three cards contain all the essential elements of the Ro and the Bero.

---

[1] Similar differences were discovered when the Ro- or the Bero-series was used in a projective procedure; experiments have been performed to that effect.

Occasionally, however, the test is "unproductive." In that case, there is still enough opportunity later to use one or both of the other form-interpretation tests. Moreover, experience has shown that both the Rorschach and the Behn Tests may also be "unproductive" at times. Other projective tests may be unproductive too: it depends on the extent to which the test has the ability to appeal to the subject. This is another reason why it is advisable to use a "test battery": if not all the tests, then perhaps one or the other of them will appeal to the subject.

However, at this point a qualifying remark seems in order: there are some psychologists who use a great many tests. I do not believe that this is necessary. On the contrary, I am of the opinion that it is better to limit oneself to a few tests with which one is quite familiar, and of which one has a *profound* knowledge. I feel impelled to make this remark because I have seen psychologists using a dozen or more tests, none of which they have studied minutely enough; they maintain that this is unimportant, because whatever they do not discover in one test, they are sure to find in another. I would rather that the practicing psychologist should be well acquainted with a small number of tests, representing a selection from among an infinite variety; that he should familiarize himself with these tests more and more thoroughly, and then use them exclusively. It seems to me that, in this way, the work carried on with tests would be much more fruitful and, above all, more exact.

In order to employ a test more profitably, one must, so to speak, "fight" over a test. This takes *endless practice, painstaking absorption,* and *empathy.*

A single test does not reveal everything about a subject; it has its *limitations.* Yet the final limitations are the ones imposed by the *broad* or *narrow consciousness* of an examiner: here there is either understanding or misunderstanding; here the poet's words come alive: "You bear a likeness to the spirit that you grasp. . . ."

The Zulliger Test is a form-interpretation test. The creators of form-interpretation tests were Hermann Rorschach and his predecessors (Alfred Binet, Victor Henry, Rybakow, and especially Whipple).

Anyone who knows how to handle the Rorschach Test or the Behn-Rorschach Test will find it very easy to work with the Zulliger Test. However, it is the aim of this book to supply a complete manual for the Zulliger Test.

The experts who have been working with the form-interpretation test have particularly urged me to write a textbook "at last" for the Zulliger Test. These practitioners of the form-interpretation test come from many different countries; among them are physicians, psychiatrists, psychotherapists, remedial teachers, guidance counselors, and vocational counselors.

Thus, may this book be a guide to, and serve well, not only the beginners but also all those who have already been trained in other card series (Ro and Bero)!

Bern, 1954   HANS ZULLIGER

PART I

The Test Apparatus

1. The Cards

The Zulliger Group Test was first used in the Psychological Service of the Swiss Army. Later, we prepared a photographic three-card series, since we wished to find out whether the test pictures would yield the same results whether projected upon a screen or handed singly to a subject. We soon discovered certain differences. If picture I was projected onto a screen, we quite often obtained the interpretation "a bedbug," "an insect," etc. If the same card was handed to a subject, however, the response "a bedbug" was given much less frequently; instead, it was more often "a crab," "a fat beetle," etc. When the picture was projected upon a screen, "bedbug" or "insect" occurred three times for every 10 subjects, "crab" and "beetle" not more than once; this ratio was reversed for the individual test. As we shall see later, this fact has a certain significance in the scoring of test results.

A large number of similar differences could be enumerated for picture I as well as for all the other pictures. I do not want to dwell on this, since at this point I wish only to demonstrate that different interpretations occur, depending upon whether we project the Zulliger Test upon a screen, or hand it to the subject in the form of cards.

In the following discussion, I shall refer to the *card* pictures as the *"Zulliger Individual Test."*

CARD I

The first card is executed in shadings of gray, white, and black; it permits a great many different concepts and interpretations. These include all the possibilities implicit in the corresponding color values of the Rorschach and Behn-Rorschach tests. The present picture has been selected, on the basis of many experiments, as the most useful in that it warrants many possible interpretations. (We shall discuss these later.) For certain subjects, this card is highly inciting to chiaroscuro shock.

Some subjects interpret the *whole picture* without any difficulty at all. Should this fail to occur immediately, we at once suspect the presence of temporary or even chronic disturbance of intelligence. Mention is made here of this fact because we wish to point out that it is important whether an interpretation initially has to do with the whole picture or only its details. Such a *detail*, for instance, is the dark blot in the center of the picture, or the "skull" in its upper center portion, with the two round "eye sockets" and a round "mouth."

At the start, still other subjects are influenced by small details—such as, for instance, the picture's lower diagonal portions, which resemble poles. After these subjects have interpreted the periphery or inner parts of the picture, they may succeed in integrating some larger portions or the whole. Yet sometimes they do not get to do this at all.

From time to time, some subjects will conceive a detail with accuracy; for instance, the "poles" at the bottom. Proceeding from this detail, they then interpret the whole picture: "This is a pile of wood," etc.

Other subjects try to avoid *chiaroscuro tonality*, and therefore interpret the white spaces in the center and on top of the picture: "Here is a lake—perhaps it is the Walen Lake—and above there are three round ponds."

Subjects who give the interpretation: "An X-ray picture, inside one can easily see the lungs [the darker part in the center of the picture]," or subjects who think that the whole may be a "cloud," are also influenced by chiaroscuro tonality.

Once an adolescent girl gave the following interpretation: "A nude woman lying on her back." It emerged that this girl had had a comparable experience, and one could recognize that she was identifying herself with the "movement" of the figure in the picture. The following interpretation concerning the left upper portion of the picture belongs to a similar response category: "An Indian woman sitting there with a feather in her hair holding her little child on her lap." Here too *movement* has been perceived.

It ought to be mentioned that occasionally the subjects turn the cards around as soon as they are handed to them. They contemplate the picture first from the side, or else they turn it into the reverse position, so that the "skull" (the top center part) appears at the bottom.

CARD II

This card is in color.

The following explanation must be given to those who are already familiar with the Ro (Rorschach Test) or the Bero (Behn-Rorschach Test):

I have been frequently asked why I selected a *colored* card as the second card. In both the Ro and the Bero tests, colored cards do not appear until the end of the series, and therefore it is "wrong" to present a colored card as the second one. To correspond with the Ro and Bero series, no other colors than black and red should be represented in Card II.

Extensive experiments have been carried out to establish whether Card II should follow Card I, or whether Card III, which is black and red, should be presented prior to the colored Card (II).

Experience with the Zulliger Test has proven that there are definite diagnostic advantages in the present order of the cards.

The relatively large red blot and the inner white space in its center are most conspicuous in the colored card of the Zulliger Test. As the only colored card, Card II has among other things the purpose of finding out whether the subject produces a so-called "color shock": Is he startled by the colors? is he confused by them? irritated by the red blots? "Color shock" has a very specific diagnostic significance. When Card II of the Zulliger Test is presented to the subject, color shock becomes apparent in his initial avoidance of response to the red color. If one is dealing here with a true color shock, then the subject escapes by interpreting the inner white space, the "intermediate form": "This is a potted plant"; "The spinal cord"; "The spine"; "A bird" (a portion of the white inner space on top), etc. Other subjects avoid the problem by interpreting the green and orange blots. Not until the very last do they give an interpretation of the red blots.

If, however, Card III of the Zulliger Test is presented to the subject as the second one, color shock—assuming that it is experienced by the subject—is far less readily apparent. It may perhaps appear indirectly in the form of prolonged reaction time, or of the subject's failure to produce kinesthetic responses. The examiner is uncertain, or not quite certain, whether or not color shock has been experienced. If the Zulliger Test is used as a group test, color shock cannot be determined unless Card II is presented in the second place. For if Card III is used as the second card, the subject may have already become accustomed to the presence of red blots, so that, when he is later confronted with the multi-colored picture of Card II, color shock does not appear.

Subjects do not find it very easy to produce a whole response for Card II. If a subject succeeds nevertheless, we may assume that he has a definite ability for abstraction or combination. Depending upon the elaboration of his interpretation, either one of these traits may be diagnosed. A performance in which quality remains high and at the same time form is accurately perceived, while details leading to perception of the whole are sharply seen, clearly indicates substantial comprehension and intelligence. This may be exemplified by a response such as: "A Chinese water fountain; a pagoda surrounded by bushes, with a sandy path in the foreground." Occasionally, however, infantile abstractions of little value are submitted ("a triangle," for instance). Also, the response may have a confabulatory flavor, and contain a DW as well. Under these or similar conditions, we may be dealing with nothing but an effort to demonstrate the positive characteristics mentioned above. Actually, such a subject lacks these intellectual qualities, or else they are prevented by a psychoneurotic condition from being realized positively.

We have intentionally chosen the second picture in such a way as to make interpreting the whole difficult, yet not entirely impossible. The different color blots are symmetrical; but they are clearly separated from one another, at the same time that they are united with one another.

Primarily, Card II stimulates detail responses.

Frequently these are form perceptions; for example, the red area: "A mask," "The head of a monkey," "A paper cut-out," or the green blot: "A polyp," "A necklace," or the orange area: "A fly."

Much more frequently, however, color is included in the interpretation: red area: "Flower petals"; green area: "Moss"; orange area: "Plough furrows."

Less frequently, we encounter a movement response; for example, red area: "Two women leaning their heads against each other, engaged in conversation"; green area: "A dwarf strolling along carrying a shield"; placing the card on its narrow side, orange area: "A man wearing a beret and a cape, leaning against a dry fir tree."

Occasionally the shading of the individual blots influences an interpretation. For instance, holding the card by its narrow side, red area: "An animal with a bushy tail standing before a forest"; green area: "Grass of different shadings of green," or "Thunder clouds."

On the other hand, a large number of small-detail responses may also be given for Card I. The periphery of the various blots may especially be selected for such interpretations. Now and then, miniature animated scenes are seen; for instance, at the rim of the picture's upper orange part: "People climbing a hill." If the subject holds the card by its narrow side, the green area of the picture's upper portion may be interpreted as "a small rearing horse with a rider on its back," or as "a woman who flings herself upon her husband."

CARD III

Card III is black, gray-black, and red in color. In addition to kinesthetic responses, it readily lends itself to three popular responses. By analogy with Card III of the Ro and Bero, we consider it to be a whole response, if it is evoked by all the dark blots (without the red areas). For instance: "These are two men." On obtaining the following interpretation, "Two men are warming themselves in front of a fire, and two Indian boys come running from the distance," we know that all the blots on the card have been united into one scene, and we may again assume that such a "whole response" is indicative of high intellectual achievement (combinatory ability).

It is easier to interpret Card III as a whole than Card II, yet a whole response is more difficult to produce for Card III than for Card I. Combinatory ability, possibly already diagnosed in Card II, will either be confirmed or its degree will be somewhat reduced. A subject who has presented an inaccurate, "ill-defined" interpretation in Card II will hardly produce a well-defined one in Card III. In other words, some specifically neurotic or other emotional disturbances have effected the subject's whole response in Card II. Thus, the three cards supplement one another, and provide a means of checking the individual findings for each one of them. At any rate, if no "whole response" is produced in Card III, the indications are that the subject's intellectual activity is in some way disturbed. This is the case, for instance, if "human heads," "arms," or "legs" are seen instead of whole "men." In such cases, the aftereffect of color shock experienced in Card II may still be in force.

The different picture parts provoke detail interpretations. The larger dark blots may be seen as "a goose," for instance (holding the card by its narrow side), the smaller dark blots as "a gnome," the red area in the center as "a butterfly," and the red areas at the periphery as "dancing boys." By way of interpreting a tiny detail, the response "a snake" may occur. It is seen in the uppermost portion of the "men." Another response may be "a devil's head with two horns," which is seen in the same portion of the "men," etc.

It is also quite possible to render an interpretation of a miniature animated scene. A 40-year-old man, after placing the card on its left narrow side, interpreted the portion of the larger dark figure that extends from within the red area towards the pistol-like protrusions, in the following manner: "Little men with fur caps sliding upon a glacier. The last one of them (towards the red area) is just about to cross a crevasse."

The large inner white space in the center may be seen as a "mushroom" or a "cactus." Holding the card by one of its bottom corners, one can see between the two dark blots that form a "man's trunk and leg," a "sitting or walking lady, with a feather hat and a tight waistline." Sometimes a subject, turning the card in such a way that the picture is reversed, interprets the large inner white space between the two dark blots and the red blot as a "flower pot with a bushy plant," etc.

Each of the cards presents some characteristic challenge. In the response to each one of them, all sorts of variations may occur, with the exception of color responses to the first card (unless one considers black a color). This does occur, however, in responses such as "a black ink spot," or "an X-ray picture." The latter response is the result when the interpretation has been affected by chiaroscuro tonality.

In general we may state:

a. At least one "whole response" should be given for Card I.

b. Card II should provoke color responses—in other words, such responses as include color.

c. Card III has been selected so that movement is experienced in at least *one* response.

With regard to contents, interpretations may pertain to human beings, human details, animals, animal details, objects, plants, maps, etc. There are no limits to the conceivable responses.

2. Instructions to the Subject

The subject must not be "attacked" with the test. I would never test anyone who had not agreed to being tested or who showed constraint.

It is particularly important to keep this in mind with *children*.

Before one begins the test, it is necessary to *prepare* the subject well. With children, it is advisable to begin with "small talk," choosing a totally innocent topic such as discussing their toys with them, talking about their trip to the examiner, etc. Occasionally, if a child is withdrawn, I offer him a piece of fruit or a candy. Another time, I might let him draw freely with colored crayons or suggest to him: "How would you like to draw a village or a tree for me?" "How would you like to draw your family for me?"

Only when I have gained the impression that the child is not afraid any longer, that he is not concerned and has lost his embarrassment, do I ask him whether he is ready to play a game with me, explicitly giving him permission at the same time to refuse.

If the child agrees, I then proceed to explain to him what he is expected to do.

INSTRUCTION I

"I will show you three pictures. As you see, they are printed on cards [the cards are placed in such a position that the pictures can not be seen]. The pictures have no fixed meaning. I want you to tell me what they could mean—what they remind you of, what they are like, or whom they resemble. Tell me everything you can see. It is very simple. Anything you tell me will be right. This is not as it is in school, where there is only one correct answer. All your answers will be correct, and I shall write them all down on a sheet of paper here in front of me. I am curious to know all you may see.

"You may use either the whole picture for your answers or only portions of a picture. You are completely free to do as you please. I shall hand you a card, and you may even turn it around [I demonstrate with a sheet of paper what I mean, otherwise the child might think that *turning* means reversing the cards]. Do you have any questions?"

Usually the child or adolescent does not have any questions. Then I say: "All right, let us start! You will see, it is not difficult. Take your time. Whenever you are finished with a card, give it back to me and I shall hand you another one!"

If a child looks at me uncertainly after the very first interpretation, I nod to him in a friendly manner and say: "You see, it is really very easy!"

The instructions are shorter for more mature or adult subjects. Most of the time, they know why they have come to the examiner. A 16-year-old, let us say, has come for vocational guidance; he understands very well that he must be tested. Yet in such a case too the subject must be informed that this is not an "examination," and that all his "interpretations" are "correct." Occasionally I add: "The more you tell me, the more I shall be able to find out, in order to help you!"

The examiner should try to create the impression that he wants to *help* the subject, especially if the subject has been sent to him for testing by the juvenile court or some other authorities, or by angry or concerned parents. Let us assume that the subject has committed a crime: he has stolen something, or has been involved in sexual delinquency. His delinquencies have been reported to the juvenile court, and the juvenile delinquent has been referred to the psychologist and counselor. The "sinner" went reluctantly; he does not at all wish to expose himself.

23

Under these circumstances, it is necessary to proceed with twice as much caution. It would be wrong to play the role of judge, or to act morally offended. One should avoid giving the impression of a "soul detective," who wants to return the subject to the path of "righteousness." It is much better to address the juvenile delinquent in some such manner: "You know very well why you have been sent to me by the juvenile court, don't you? Well, I would like to see whether I can help you. In order to be able to, however, I shall perform certain tests, which will help me find out about you and show me what should be done with you now. Perhaps I might be able to help you to decide which vocational training would be indicated for you. It is perfectly all right for you to say 'no' if you do not want to be tested!"

Occasionally, I pass a cigarette to an adolescent, or offer him something to eat, before beginning a conversation with him. At times, however, I am compelled to leave the formation of *rapport* to good luck or to my premeditated planning.

I shall always remember how I once came to "grips" with an 18-year-old boy who, I was told, would never utter a single word to me. I thought about how to make him talk. When he arrived, I busied myself with cleaning my army pistol. I let the youth sit on a bench opposite me and excused myself, saying that I had to finish something first. At the beginning, he sat there without looking at me; I, in turn, did not look at him. Secretly, however, I told myself that this boy would not be a real boy if he was not interested in an army pistol. I was not wrong. Soon the boy began to watch all my manipulations with great interest. Observing his interest, I intentionally dropped one of the weapon's parts onto the floor. He picked it up and handed it to me. After thanking him, I continued putting the pistol together. Presently I asked the youth: "Did you ever hold such a 'piece of furniture' in your hands?" When he answered in the negative, I gave him the weapon and showed him how to tighten it. I cocked the hammer and closed the lock, and he followed my example. The ice was broken. We discussed army weapons and officer pistols. Twenty minutes later, the youth had become convinced that he could trust me. I could see it in his attitude and in his behavior. It was not difficult then to induce him to be tested.

I have related this little episode in order to show that now and then one must proceed with ingenuity. Something must be found that would be interesting to the subject and would make it possible to enter into a conversation with him. However, there is no one set formula to be passed along.

Frequently, puppets can be employed successfully with smaller girls and boys, in order to begin a conversation. Talking to the subjects usually relieves their tension and the game is won.

I advised one of my co-workers, who wished to test whole schools and classes, to first pay a visit to the school so that the children might meet him, and after that to participate actively in one of their play sessions. For when one tests a whole class, the children should not be treated like customers in a barber shop: "Next, please!" Children and adolescents cannot be given orders to take a test. If this is done, the test results become of doubtful value, because they were obtained in a situation in which the subjects offered a great deal of inner resistance. Despite the statistics, such results are incorrect, if not altogether deceptive.

Frequently, it is possible to overcome the children's resistance by asking whether any of them would want to help with a scientific study. Are there any volunteers among them? Then, being curious, all the other children follow suit. (It is needless to say that the children are made to promise not to disclose to the others what they have "seen" on the cards after taking the test.) One explains to them why they should not talk about it, or else one avoids, by proper planning, their influencing one another.

Both the preparation and the instructions are simpler and shorter for adults. Since they have come to be tested, they know what to expect.

INSTRUCTION II

"I have here three cards with some pictures printed on them. They have no fixed meaning. Please tell me what you think this may be!" With these words, I hand the subject the first card. If the subject produces a "whole response" and wants to relinquish the card, I interject: "You may also interpret some of the picture's *parts!*" After the subject has finished, and is again about to relinquish the card, I interject once more: "You may also turn the card!" On the record, I make note of everything that the subject has himself chosen to do, as well as of all the instructions that I have given him *during the testing*. Also, I write down all the subject's exclamations, in addition to his questions and any other occurrences, such as sighs, wrinkling of the forehead, etc.

ADDENDUM

FRITZ SALOMON'S DOUBLE PRESENTATION OF THE TEST

Immediately after completion of the three-card test, Salomon hands the cards to the subject once more, remarking: "Sometimes people [or "children," if children are being tested] see some additional things when they look at them for a second time." "Sometimes" and "additional things" are emphasized by the tone of the examiner's voice, in order to avoid exerting pressure upon the subject such as would make it difficult for him to find new responses and at the same time to exclude his repeating the responses already given at the first presentation. By the use of this technique, some extremely important facts often come to sight. These facts may then become essential for the diagnosis of possible psychopathologic conditions, and may also assist in determining their severity (Salomon, 1962).

3. Recording of the Protocol and Inquiries

After the instructions have been given, everything that the subject, or perhaps also that the examiner says, is recorded strictly in order of its occurrence. The following three examples show how this should be done:[1]

Martin Balz, 12 years old, son of Anton, businessman.

Recorded: February 14, 1950
Start: 4:30 P.M.

I.
A kind of butterfly (whole area)
There again is a butterfly (dark area within blot).
A cow (whole area)
Snakes (at the top, adjoining the "head")
Clouds (left bottom portion)
Holes, four of them (white inner spaces)
Map of Europe (b-position)

II.
Two sitting butterflies (red area)
A tulip (red area, b-position)
Leaves (green area, b-position)
Wood (orange area, b-position)
A cat's eye (inner white space within the green area, a-position)
Rose tree (inner white space within the red area)
Willow bush (green area)

[1] All names used in this book are fictitious.

III.

Men with their legs cut off
Butterfly (center red area)
They shoot at each other (refers to "men").
Snail (dark blot in the center of the small lower black blot, its middle portion)
There again is a butterfly (red area at the outer rim).
There too (on the opposite side)
And here again are clouds (dark area, right picture part, larger blot).

End: 4:41 P.M.

[If it is not otherwise indicated, the card has been held in an upright position (*a-position*); *b-position* indicates that the subject has turned the card clockwise and placed it on its narrow right side; *c-position* signifies that the card has been turned 180°; *d-position* shows that the card has been scrutinized while being held on its narrow left side.]

Inquiry: The examiner obtains information about the various interpretations. For instance, Card I, third response: "Where did you see a cow here?" *Response:* "There is the udder (bottom left and right, outer rim) and there is the head (upper center), and here are some kind of horns (protrusions, curving around the 'head')." Presently it becomes clear to the examiner that the subject has seen details that reminded him of a cow, and that he has "made" them into a whole "cow" by confabulation. The subject has proceeded from one or more accurately perceived details in the picture and has arrived at a "whole interpretation" by confabulation of the remaining parts.

Card I, last response. "What made you think of a 'map of Europe'? What was it that reminded you of it?" The card is once more presented to the subject in the b-position. The subject points to the lowest part of the picture: "There one can clearly see the boot of Italy!" Again the examiner recognizes that this is confabulation.

Card II, first response: "Did you ever see such butterflies before?" "Yes, the way they are sitting here; only usually they are not red. There are some reddish butterflies, but they are not of the same red color as here on the card!" Thus the examiner comprehends immediately that this is a form interpretation and not an interpretation that has been determined by color.

28

Card II, second response: "How did the 'tulip' come to mind?" "The form is the same and also the color. The green petals are too high up, though!"

The examiner realizes that, although form is the primary determinant for the second interpretation, color has played a secondary role. Simultaneously, the subject has given the answer as to the origin of the "leaves." They were produced by confabulation, as part of the "tulip." The green color has helped, of course. Had there been black blots instead of green ones, the subject hardly would have seen and interpreted them as "leaves."

Card III. No inquiry.

Luise Roth, 15 years old, daughter of Bendicht, foreman.

Recorded: December 12, 1949
Start: 2:15 P.M.

I.

The whole is some kind of crab.

Here is a human head with evil eyes (top center).

A pansy (center, dark area) or an ivy leaf.

(The subject laughs merrily.) Hey, here is a little girl. She is wearing a feather in her hair and she is talking with her doll, holding it on her lap (left upper outer rim); I see it less clearly on the opposite side.

And here (bottom left, darker shaded area) one can see a man looking down at him. He looks up and waves with his cane.

II.

Two sisters kiss each other good night (red area).

A gnome striding along with a sack in his hand (green area).

There at the bottom—a large mole (orange area). The color is just about right.

This green here could also be some bushes. Twigs are jutting forth.

And in the brown area one can see shadings, like on maps (inner orange portion).

III.

Two men carry a large, strange-looking butterfly.

Outside are some strange-looking small boys approaching on the run (red areas). (Turning the card into c-position): And here is a man sitting on a rock smoking his pipe. He is wearing a beret on his head (upper portion of left black blot, toward the center of the picture).

29

These are two horse or dog heads (red center area, c-position).

I think I do not see anything any more—oh yes, I do. Here are some pliers, perhaps, or scissors (c-position, top of the smaller black blot, gray area). No inquiry.

End: 2:27 P.M.

Hanni Steinmann, 21 years old, office worker.

Recorded: November 16, 1950
Start: 3:45 P.M.

I.

(Breathes heavily, loudly.)

(Turns the card, hesitates.)

A skull, already decayed on the right side. Here are the eyes and the mouth.

Perhaps an X-ray photograph, inner part of the body

A tree leaf (black center area)

A small lonely fir tree hanging over a slope (at the outer periphery, center)

Fists holding knives or curved daggers (outer top, adjoining the "skull")

II.

(Hesitates; prolonged reaction time. Sighs; wrinkles her forehead.)

The colors are—well—real pretty.

Spine (white space within the red area)

There on top is a little white dove—like the Holy Ghost (inner white space at the very top of red area).

Fox fur-pieces, like the ones ladies wear in winter around their necks (orange area)

A bundle of grass (green area)

And the red—well, it looks very much like dried blood.

III.

(Bites her lip. "Ah well!")

These are two women; they are quarreling (the larger black blots without the detached "legs").

Butterfly (red center area)

A "piggy" (c-position, a portion of the smaller black blot facing the large black blot)

Icebears or dogs (b- and d-position, outer red area).

End: 4:00 P.M.

Inquiry: "What was it you said about the little dove?" (Card II, second interpretation). "Such white doves really exist. And

30

on some pictures the Holy Ghost is often painted as a little white dove." The examiner now knows that the white color contributed to the interpretation.

The preceding three examples ought to make clear *how* a record is taken.

4. Location Sheets as Aids in Recording

When one takes a record, the location at which something has been "seen" on the test card must be noted precisely. This will make it possible later to check and score the subject's interpretations.

In the beginning, we proceeded with the individual test, as we had done earlier with the group test, by imagining a circle around each test picture, equipped with the numerals of a clock. We then indicated the spot that had been interpreted by the corresponding numeral of the clock. Let us assume that somebody has interpreted the lowest blot portion in Card I, b-position, as "Italy." On the record we would note in this case: = b 6, specifying that the indicated spot is to be found "at 6 o'clock."

Since then, the Hans Huber Publishing House in Bern has printed a location-sheet blank, which greatly simplifies the recording of interpreted locations. The responses, or rather their corresponding locations, are encircled on this sheet. If it becomes necessary to determine a certain location even more exactly, the pre-printed letters and numerals may be used. Thus, in the example mentioned above, D 9 would be recorded for "Italy," AB 5/6 for the "dove" in Card II, E 5/6 for the "bird of prey" in Card II, b D 5/6 for the "flower" in Card II, b EDC 7/8 for the "pipe-smoking man" in Card III, etc.

5. The Scoring of Interpretations

After one has finished the record as well as the subsequent inquiry (which should not be attempted while one is recording, in order not to influence the subject by suggestion), the subject may be dismissed. All further work can be carried out without his being present.

We have now arrived at a discussion of the so-called scoring technique. During the experiment, most subjects feel that their imagination is being put to a test, and that it is therefore extremely important *what* they have seen in the pictures. They assume that the *content of their responses* is of prime significance for the subsequent psychological evaluation. The truth of the matter is, however, that it is not imagination that is being tested but *perception*. The subject is faced with the task of adjusting his memory images (engrams) to the blot pictures, or rather of using the blot pictures for the re-awakening (ecphoria) of corresponding memory images. It is much less important for the examiner's aims to establish how a subject interprets than what his interpretation is. Therefore, the examiner first evaluates the interpretations that he has obtained, according to the formulae created by Rorschach, and only then according to their content. Thus we write down the scores—in other words, the formula-like symbols that are attached to all individual interpretations—in the reserved space at the right side of the record sheet.

33

The symbols and their meaning:

W = "whole response." The entire picture has been perceived.

D = "detail response." A portion of the picture that hits the eye has been perceived. Such portions are usually situated in the center of the picture or at its radius, or else they form large conspicuous portions at its periphery.

Dd = "small detail response." A tiny or unusual detail has been perceived.

S = "space response." A white space has been perceived.

The following differentiations must also be made:

DW and DdW = confabulatory W. The subject perceives a part of the picture, a D or a Dd, and confabulates a W with it. We have seen such interpretations in the record of Martin Balz.

A DdW interpretation is one in which, for example, a subject calls Card III "a herd of swine." He has seen a "little tail" protruding from the smaller of the black shapes and then, perhaps, other similar formations in the dark and red blots. The whole has been perceived on the basis of one or several Dd.

SW = confabulatory space-whole response. An S has been accurately perceived; the remainder of the picture is then united with it by confabulation. Card III, for example: "A mushroom surrounded by a dark forest and small red animals."

WS = a space is made a component part of the whole. The black picture or the colored one *and* S have been perceived with accuracy. This is not an achievement of confabulation. Nothing has been added "by way of pretense" or "by imagination." The S has been organically incorporated into the whole. In presenting the interpretation of a "nude woman lying on her back," the adolescent girl mentioned earlier organized all four of the card's S into a whole.

DS = an S combined into a detail S. It is analogous to a WS.

SD = S to which D has been added, as, for instance, in Card II: "A plant standing before an evening cloud," or the S within the green area: "A snow spot on a lawn." From the diagnostic point of view, an SD has the same significance as an SW; it is also confabulatory.

W = as a rule, this is an abstractly conceived interpretation, such as "a bat" in Card I.

WM = this W is not derived primarily by abstraction. It originates in perceiving movement by empathy. For example, Card III: "Two men warming themselves in front of a fire; two boys come running from the distance." There is a trace of awareness of perspective in this concept: since the boys come "from a distance," the depth of the picture's expanse has been "seen."

A constructive W in Card II is, for instance: "A Chinese pagoda; close by are some bushes, and there is a sandy path in the foreground."

D = attention must be paid here to whether it has been achieved by abstraction or by some other means.

Do = "oligophrenic details." These are interpretations in which a detail is extracted from the commonly seen larger area. Some examples of this are: Card III: "A face" (usually a whole human being is seen here); "Butterfly wings" (Card III, red center area; as a rule, a whole "butterfly" is perceived.)

The term "oligophrenic detail" was devised by Hermann Rorschach. Originally he found such responses in oligophrenics. Later, it was established that Do are produced by anxious individuals, as well as by compulsive neurotics. Therefore, it cannot be inferred with certainty that oligophrenia is present if a subject produces Do interpretations. The test record must show several other appropriate indications if oligophrenia is to be diagnosed. (We shall discuss this problem later.)

After finding out whether the subjects have given W, D, Dd, Do, or S interpretations—that is, having ascertained their spatial perception—we then proceed to uncover the *quality* of the subjects' responses. We designate these as follows:

$F+$ = accurately conceived form responses. What do we mean by "accurately conceived," however? I myself think that the picture in Card I is not at all "bat"-like. Yet the interpretation "bat" is produced with such frequency—namely, about 30 times per 100 subjects—that I am forced to score it as an "accurate form" ($F+$).

We must regard those interpretations as "accurate forms" ($F+$) which, because of their outlines, may be produced by all subjects with ease. The "maple or ivy leaf" in the center of the blot in Card I, the "human, monkey, or dog head," and the "skull" at the top center of Card I are examples of such interpretations. If one is uncertain about evaluation, it is advisable to refer to statistics. An interpretation that occurs with relative frequency must be scored $F+$, even though this particular "accuracy of perception" may not be at all evident to the examiner himself.

In order to facilitate scoring for students, I shall affix scoring tables to this chapter. They are based on statistical material comprising approximately 800 subjects of both sexes and all ages. These scores should not be simply used as a "key," however, and they should not exempt the examiner from the necessity of performing his own evaluation and using his own reasoning. They are nothing but suggestions, which every examiner must verify with his own material.

$F-$ = inaccurately perceived forms, as, for instance, in Card I: "A cross section of an apple."

$F\pm$ = interpretations that are quite accurate, yet not accurate enough to deserve an $F+$. For example: Card I in b-position, top left half of the picture: "An elephant's head with a raised ear. Underneath there is the tusk."

M = an interpretation arrived at by "empathy" with movement. Unconsciously, the subject identifies himself with a figure that he sees as moving. This figure is not seen merely as a picture; it does not evoke an optical image, but rather empathy with movement. We again

remind the reader of the adolescent girl who has interpreted the picture in Card I as "a nude woman lying on
her back." This interpretation represents a real WM
response (whole response and movement; kinesthesia).
M responses are given most easily to Card III. The subject who is capable of ignoring the spaces between the
two black blots—the larger one, as well as the smaller
one, which resembles a leg—and of combining these
blots into "two men" has produced an M. Hermann
Rorschach used the corresponding formation in his
card series (Ro Card III) as a criterion for determining
whether a response implies an M or an F. Rorschach
says that a subject who interprets the upper part of the
picture as a "man" has seen a *form* (F+). If, on the other
hand, a subject regards the unattached dark blot as a
"leg" of a "man," we may assume that he has em-
pathized with a *movement,* and has produced an M.

A subject who interprets Card I as "a *flying* bat" has not *felt*
the movement's characteristic qualities. Such an interpretation
is based on an *optical* impression alone, and therefore, the score
is not an M but an F.

Yet if someone sees the small red outer configurations in Card
III as "dancing bears," he has produced an original M, even
though his interpretation does not refer to human beings. We
are confronted here with a fact whose meaning is rather difficult
to grasp. Some animals have a very close relationship to man. A
child regards a cat, a dog, or a teddybear as his playmates; in his
imagination, he endows these animals and their cloth-made
likenesses with human traits. To the child, the little dog with
whom he plays is not an animal, but rather a brother; the same
thing holds true for the Teddy bear. We are touching here upon
totemistic thinking. Many primitive tribes designate a wild animal as their forefather, their tribe's ancestor. In this connection, we may mention that "leopard people" of the Congo, who
claim to be descended from a leopard and behave just as these
wild beasts do. (There also exist tribes with plant totems. However, we have succeeded in proving that, at the very beginning,

37

a fierce animal has played the role of a "totem animal" for these peoples too. Their conversion to a plant totem took place much later and then finally became predominant).

Thus, not all animal responses may be simply scored as F in our form-interpretation test. On the other hand, an M appears most often in the interpretation of human figures. To repeat: when we are confronted with an M, the determining factor remains whether or not there exists an *empathy for human motion,* and not only an optical impression of it.

Many students find it difficult to score M with accuracy. I know quite a few experts on the form-interpretation test who, although they have had a great deal of experience, are nevertheless incapable of differentiating between an M and an F with confidence. "Since the bat is 'flying'," they say, "movement has been seen!" "It has been *seen* indeed," I would like to answer them, "but it has not been felt, it has not been experienced!" Yet they would not understand me; it would be just as if I were talking to them in a foreign language.

As the result of experiments, I began to suspect that individuals who fail in their efforts to determine M in others unerringly, are unable to produce M, when they themselves take the form-interpretation test, or else they produce only one single M (Card III). Their personality is lacking in the inner ability to feel M. They are almost completely extratensively oriented and therefore have no understanding of introversion (as indicated by M). They are deficient in introversive capacity and in introversive characteristics.

Therefore, it is desirable that individuals who wish to study form-interpretation tests (Zulliger, Ro and Bero Tests) should be uncoarctative by nature, and yet ambiequal, with a capacity for being coarctative. Their own form-interpretation test ought to show at least a number of M and several color responses. This would prove that they possess sufficient introversive substance and would be in a position to recognize M in a form-interpretation test, when they were functioning as examiners.

MC = kinesthetically perceived configurations, in which color also plays a determining role. Intuitive subjects give

MC responses. For instance, Zulliger Test, red area, Card II: "Two dancers illuminated red by floodlights." Or Card III, red outer area: "Two little devils jump around in their red clothes!" (Lucifer)

MCh = kinesthetic responses codetermined by chiaroscuro. For example, Card I: "A man who has been injured in war is sitting here. His arms are badly crippled, and his thighs are fleshless."

Ms = diminutive animated scenes. For example, Card III, d-position, larger dark blot, portion leading from the red inner area toward the center of the picture, upper periphery: "Some little men, wearing fur caps, who are sliding over a glacier. The last one is just about to cross a crevasse." Another example, Card III, c-position, portion of the large dark blot, upper lateral protrusion: "A woman is sitting here. Behind her stands a fir tree and still further away, next to a precipice, towers a tree trunk."

FC = color responses in which the form has been accurately perceived. For instance, Card II, green area: "Hazel bush," "Grass tuft." Or Card II, orange area: "A mole," "Fox fur," "Tawny-colored cattle, fighting."

CF = color responses in which form is of much less importance, although it is still suggested. The interpretation is primarily based on color. As an example, let us again refer to the green and orange areas in Card II: "Moss patch" (green area); "A pond with algae" (green area); "Earth clods" (orange area).

C = color responses in which color alone has stimulated the interpretation. There is no indication at all of form. If the red blots of Card II are interpreted as "blood *spots*," for instance, form has still been suggested, to a small degree. We score it CF. If, however, this red area is interpreted simply as "blood," this score must be a pure C. Further examples are: "Moss" (green area); "Water" (green area); "Earth" (orange area); "Filth" (orange area).

CCh = interpretations effected by both color and its shading. For instance, Card II, orange area: "Two islands on a geography map. There are mountains on it."

FCh = Form as well as chiaroscuro impressions have determined the interpretation. For example, Card I: "A wilted tree leaf." (Compare with FC!)

ChF = Chiaroscuro tonality has been mainly responsible for the interpretation, while form has played a secondary role. For instance, Card I: "A thunder cloud," "Fog formations." (Compare with CF!)

Ch = Chiaroscuro impressions alone have been decisive for the interpretation. For example, Card I: "Fog," "Steam," "Haze." (Compare with C!) All Ch interpretations include depth and perspective, while ChC (see below) is seen superficially, merely as color shadings.

F(C) = interpretations in which light and dark tonalities are sharply separated from each other. For example, Card I: "A pile of rotten tree leaves. There is a dark leaf in the middle of it." Or Card I, center portion: "A bearded Alpine cheese maker wearing a *Kuchermutz* [a cap]" (the dark shading in the center is designated as a piece of clothing—namely, the *Kuchermutz*).

In his excellent work on chiaroscuro interpretations, Binder has pointed out that sometimes colors also play a part in perception, and that this fact should be taken into consideration in evaluating. For the sake of simplicity, I would make the following suggestion to the student: only four Ch categories (FCh, ChF, Ch, and F (C)) should be scored. The examiner must take care, however, to find out whether the subject's interpretations imply understanding of plasticity and perspective. While scoring, the examiner should make a note of it by some additional remark.

ChC = Primarily chiaroscuro, secondarily black, plays a role.

Thus we have enumerated the qualitative possibilities of interpretations. Therefore, after having scored the three sample records according to W, D, Dd, Do, and S, students, in order to exercise their skill, may now proceed to add these scoring symbols of quality.

In scoring, we place the symbols that represent the *content* of responses in a third column.

H = humans

Hd = human details, as for instance, "arms," "legs," "heads," etc.

anat = anatomy responses. Hermann Rorschach has stated that anat that are not produced by physicians, general nursing personnel, midwives, or nurses should, as a rule, be scored with an F—. Thus we would score the S situated between the red blots of Card II as SF— anat, although it is interpreted quite frequently as "spinal column." (A healthy physician would hardly ever interpret this S as "spinal column.")

bl = blood

cl = clothing

fd = food, edibles

Sc = scene

A = animals

Ad = animal detail

obj = objects

pl = plants

nat = nature. For instance, Card II, c-position, orange area: "A forest landscape destroyed by war."

geog = geography responses (maps)

cld = clouds

vol = volcanoes

One can find abbreviations oneself. Nevertheless, it is important to score according to the above instructions. Thus, "clothing" must not be scored as objects; food or edibles must not be scored as plants or animal details; responses pertaining to maps must not be scored as nature.

41

The fourth column should contain the scores for "popular" and "original" responses.

P = interpretations that appear at least 33 times per 100 persons. (See table of contents for responses and scores in the next chapter.)

O+ = *good* original responses. They usually contain a creative element; frequently they are surprising. An O should be scored with caution. A response is not an O simply because it is rare, or occurs but one single time in 100 subjects. In addition, it must "display" some intuition. If, for instance, a subject should interpret the orange area in Card II as an "anteater," it cannot be regarded as an O response, even though such a response occurs but once in 100 tests. On the other hand, the two "chatting women" (red area) or "dancers," etc., which appear on the same card, deserve an O+, although in one form or another ("little girls who whisper into each other's ear," "Chinese people who greet each other by rubbing their noses together," etc.) they are given with equal frequency—namely, once per 100 subjects.

O— = are interpretations that should be regarded as "original" by definition; their originality is of such a nature, however, as to indicate a strange person, an "eccentric," frequently an abnormal individual. Let us assume, for example, that a schizophrenic has called Card II an "owl tree." We are dealing here with an O—, for the subject has perceived the red blots as "owls," and the green and orange areas as a "tree," and he has thrown them together into a concept of an "owl tree."

"Shocks" must be noted if a subject, upon being presented with a card, appears startled or hesitant, becomes frightened or confused, or suffers "association stupor."

"Rejection." If subjects assert that they are incapable of "making anything" of a card, one has to mark their reaction a "rejection."

Hermann Rorschach had stated that a rejection, even a single one, is always "suspicious."

A child who presents a rejection must be encouraged: "Look at the picture well! You will surely see something there just as well as other children do!" etc. Such suggestions are permitted, but they must be recorded. It was Rorschach who once advised me to proceed in this manner.

Frequently, encouraged by his success, a subject will go on to produce a number of responses.

Similarly, adult subjects who are about to "reject" must also be encouraged: "Please try again, it will be all right. I should get at least one response from you!," etc.

"Rejections" *are* suspicious. Yet, frequently, it is the examiner rather than the subject who ought to be under suspicion. For perhaps the examiner has not prepared the subject correctly, or sufficiently well, for his test (see the discussion on "instructions").

According to my very long experience, there are very few "rejectors," especially when the Zulliger Test is used.

At this time, using our three sample records, we shall give an illustration of how scoring should be carried out.

Martin Balz, 12 years old, son of Anton, businessman.

Recorded: February 14, 1950
Start: 4:30 P.M.

I.

A kind of butterfly (whole area)	WF + A
There again is a butterfly (black area within blot)	DF + A, tendency towards perseveration
A cow (whole area)	DWF − A
Snakes (at the top, adjoining the "head")	DdF + A
Clouds (left bottom portion)	DCHF cl
Holes (four white inner spaces)	SF ± holes
Map of Europe (b-position)	SWF − geog

II.

Two sitting butterflies (red area)	DF ± A
A tulip (red area, b-position)	DFC Pl
Leaves (green area, b-position)	DCF Pl

43

Wood (orange area, b-position) .... DC Pl
A cat's eye (inner white space within the
   green area, a-position) .... SF — Ad
Rose tree (inner white space within the
   red area) .... SF + Pl
Willow bush (green area) .... DFC Pl

III.

Men .... {W → DF + H/(P)
with their legs cut off .... {Do → DF + Hd (P)
Butterfly (center red area) .... DF + A P
They shoot at each other (refers to "men") .... DM + H (P)
There again is a butterfly (red area at
   the outer rim) .... DF — A (confabulatory,
                                        because of the red)
There too (on the opposite side) .... DF — A (does not
                                        see symmetry)
And here again are clouds (black area,
   right picture part, larger blot) .... DChF Cl, persp.
                                        End: 4:41 P.M.

Remarks: I score a tendency with the corresponding scoring symbol, and add an arrow. A (P) suggests that although a P would be indicated, the given P is not the usual one (P-tendency).

Luise Roth, 15 years old, daughter of Bendicht, foreman.

Recorded: December 12, 1949
Start: 2:15 P.M.

I.

The whole is some kind of crab .... WF + A P
Here is a human head .... {DF + Hd
   with angry eyes (top center) .... {SF + Hd
A pansy (center, dark area) .... DF + pl
   or an ivy leaf .... DF + pl "or"
(Laughs merrily): Hey, here is a little girl; she.. DM + H O+
   is wearing a feather in her hair .... DdF + obj
   and she is talking with her doll, holding it
   on her lap (left outer upper rim) .... DF + H
I can see it less clearly on the opposite side .... object criticism
And here (bottom left, darker shaded
   area) one can see a man looking at him. He
   looks .... DM + H O+
   and waves with his cane .... DdF + obj

44

II.

Two sisters kiss each other good night .... DM + H O+

A gnome strolling along .... ⎰ DMs H O+

with a sack in his hand .... ⎱ DdF ± obj

There, at the bottom, a large mole (orange

area). The color is just about right .... DFC A

This green here could also be some bushes.

Twigs are jutting forth .... DFC pl

And in the brown area one can see shadings,

as on maps (inner orange area) .... DdCCh geog

III.

Two men carry a large, strange-looking

butterfly .... ⎰ WM + H P

⎱ DF + A P

Outside are some curious small boys

approaching on the run (red area) .... DM + A P

combinatory tendency +

(Turning the card into c-position): And here ⎰ DM + H O+

is a man sitting on a rock smoking his pipe. ⎱ DF ± obj

He is wearing a beret (upper portion of left

black blot toward the center of the ⎰ DdF + obj

picture) .... ⎱ DdF + cl

End: 2:27 P.M.

Remarks: It is advisable to score single details separately in the Zulliger Test. The various segments may then be joined by a bracket indicating their being of a larger D or W.

Hanni Steinmann, 21 years old, office worker.

Recorded: November 16, 1950
Start: 3:45 P.M.

I.

(Breathes heavily, loudly. Turns the card,

hesitates) .... initial shock

A skull, already decayed on the right side ...... ⎰ DFCh Anat

here are the eyes and the mouth .... ⎱ SF + Hd

Perhaps an X-ray photograph, of the upper

part of the body .... WChC Anat

A tree leaf (black center area) .... DF + PL

A small *lonely* fir tree hanging over a slope

(at the outer periphery, center) .... DdF + Pl

individual interpretation

45

Fists holding knives or curved daggers (outer
   top, adjoining the "skull") .... DF + Hd
                                                    DdF + Obj "or"

II.

(Hesitates, prolonged reaction time. Sighs,
   wrinkles her forehead .... color shock!
The colors are—well—real pretty .... description
Spine (white space within the red area) .... SF — Anat
There on top is a little white dove, like the
   Holy Ghost (inner white space at the very
   top of red area) .... SFC Relig O+
                                                    white seen as color

Fox fur-pieces like the ones that ladies put
   around their necks in winter (orange area) .. DFC Ad Cloth
Tuft of grass (green area) .... DFC Pl
And the red—well, it looks very much like
   half-dried blood .... DC bl

III.

Bites her lip .... after effect of shock
Ah well! These are two women, *they are*
   quarreling .... DM + H (P)
   (the larger black blots without the detached
   "legs") .... aggression
Butterfly (red center area) .... DF + A (P)
A piggy (c-position, a portion of the smaller
   black blot facing the large black blot) ...... DF + A
Icebears or dogs (b- and d-position, outer
   red area) .... DF + A "or"
                                                    End: 4:00 P.M.

Remarks: When presented with the first card, the subject is confused
about the task confronting her; the engrams do not appear until later.
Some time elapses before the subject produces her first interpretation. In
this case we speak of "initial shock."

Response 5 to Card I is an "individual response." In other
words, it is a response that only this particular person could have
produced. Even an inexperienced examiner understands immediately that the *lonely* fir tree hanging over a precipice is a
description of the subject's life situation. The fact that the subject is startled by the colors is clearly apparent from her hesitancy, prolonged reaction time, and mannerisms. It is equally

characteristic that, initially, the subject presents a description instead of a response (which is her task). Finally the first response follows, and it is an evasion into an S. Considering that the red color is responded to at the very onset, and that it is a pure C ("blood"), we deduce that the shock has been primarily a "red shock," produced by the presentation of Card II. Its aftereffect is seen when Card III is presented. The subject is incapable of producing the usual WM + H P response. Nevertheless, an M is produced (after the shock has been quickly overcome). With regard to its content, an aggressive scene attracts our attention.

When a subject produces two responses for one picture blot, connecting them with "or" (as we have observed above in Luise Roth's record), it must be so scored. The subject is uncertain; he does not wish to "give himself away." He wants to leave a door open to other possibilities. He does not wish to commit or to restrain himself; he does not wish anybody to "look at his cards." But with these statements I am ahead of myself, and I am encroaching upon the discussion of some of the psychodiagnostic "values" of responses. Nevertheless, I thought it wise to indicate at this point that all such "small details" (they are not small) must be precisely recorded and noted in scoring.

6. List of Responses and Scores

The list of responses and their scores is based upon material consisting of about 8,000 subjects of both sexes and various age groups, drawn from the most diverse categories. It includes normal people, as well as subjects suffering from neurotic and psychotic disorders. Inasmuch as the list is based solely upon Swiss subjects, it is perhaps incomplete. It is quite possible that some of the popular responses would not be considered as such in another country; there might be some other small differences, too. At any rate, it should be pointed out that this list before us should not be considered inviolable. It is not to be used as a "key," in the sense of a "genuine Egyptian dream book." This list is primarily an auxiliary instrument.

A generally valid standardization of the responses is impossible to achieve. It has proven impossible even with the Rorschach test, no matter how hard people have tried. Human beings are human beings and not automatons. Inquiry remains necessary in each individual case. Under certain circumstances, the same response may have been seen differently by different people. Moreover, it should be remembered, in this connection, that many persons, especially mental patients, frequently find it extremely difficult to tell how they have arrived at a certain interpretation. In any event, a comparison with the examples listed below will reveal to some extent whether or not one has scored correctly.

Many similar interpretations occur in practice, such as, for instance, the whole response to Card I: "crab, shrimp," etc. If one were to attempt to list all these variants, an infinitely long index would result. Thus, whoever expects to find all possible interpretations of the individual test, as well as their scores, in the following list of responses, will be disappointed. The cards offer unlimited possibilities for producing interpretations. Time and again, the tester will be surprised, even after working with the test for many years. He will constantly obtain interpretations that he has never met before.

CARD I

Dancers, a fairytale figure, a				
man crawling	W	M	H	O
A man with raised arms	W	M	H	O
Three dancing couples	W	M	H	O
Two fighters with drawn sabers ...				
	DW → W	M	H	O
Devil, ghost, witch, elf-king				
	FCh → W	M	H	O
Monster	FCh → W	F+	H	O
Advancing monster, death	W	MCh	H	O
Devil surrounded by flames,				
threatening	S → W	MCh	H	O
A crouching monkey	W	M	A	O
Advancing bear	W	M	A	O
Two women in the arms of a				
monkey	S → W	M	H	O
A nude woman lying on her back .	WS	M	H/sex	O

Editor's note: The original list of responses has been greatly expanded. It now contains a number of responses based upon approximately 5,000 tests administered to Frenchmen in Paris as well as some 1,000 tests recorded in the U. S. The scoring of all these responses was discussed with Dr. Zulliger, both by correspondence and in person. It appeared quite clear that the scores obtained in the above-mentioned countries did not differ from those obtained in Switzerland. Even the popular responses proved to be the same. There are, to be sure, some responses that occur with more or less frequency in one or the other country. Yet, despite extensive statistical research, new popular responses could not be established. A few responses are determined by the cultures of the particular countries; they are almost never found in any other country. Thus, such responses occasionally seem to be more original in one country than in another.

A witch with threatening eyes				
FCh → WS	M	H/eye	O	
A fight .... W	M	scene/ abstraction	O	
c Somebody crawling on his belly ... W	M	H	O	
a Two people embracing each other DW	M	H	O	
Two dancers .... DW	M	H	O	
Two bears fighting .... DW	M	A	O	
A man sitting on a chair .... DW	M	H	O—	
Two monkeys standing back to back .... W	M—	A	O—	
(DW	M—	H	O—	
Two men sitting at a table .... {D	F—	obj		
Two people lying on top of each other as if they were having sexual intercourse .... DW	M—	H	O—	
c Conductor of an orchestra .... DW	M—	H	O—	
(DdW	F—	obj		
a Two hands holding a globe ...... {Dd	M—	Hd	O—	P
Beetles .... W	F+	A		P
Crab, crayfish .... W	F+	A		P
Louse, bedbug .... W	F+	A		
Insect .... W	F+	A		
Turtle .... W	F+	A		
Spider .... (possibly FCh) W	F+	A		
Bat .... (possibly FCh) W	F+	A		
Bee, bumblebee .. (possibly FCh) W	F+	A		
Frog .... (possibly FCh) W	F+	A		
Two mice close to each other .... W	F+	A		
The shell of an animal ... FCh → W	F+	Ad		
An animal's fur, a bedside carpet.. FCh → W	F+	A		
The magnified head of an insect.. FCh → W	F+	Ad		
A tree leaf, a plane-tree leaf ..... W	F+	pl		
A wilted tree leaf, a torn tree leaf.. W	F+	pl		
The astrological sign of the zodiac W	F+	symbol		
A sculpture .... FCh → W	F+	obj		
A scarecrow .... S → FCh → W	F+	obj		
		H and M repression		
Two bumblebees fighting with each other (because of the prickles and wings) .... FCh → DW	F+	A/sex		
A caricature of the devil .... S → ChF → W	F+	devil/M repression		

A mussel	ChF → W	F±	A	
c A shield	FCh → W	F±	obj	
a A tree	ChF → W	F±	pl	
A flower, a pansy, an orchid				
	ChF → W	F±	pl	
A nut	FCh → W	F±	pl	
A butterfly	DW → W	F±	A	
c A butterfly	W	F—	A	
a The head of an elephant with				
tusks	W	F±	Ad	
Clouds, cloud formation ..	ChF → W	F±	cloud	
An X-ray picture	ChF → W	F±	anat	
An ice-flower on a window pane..				
	ChF → W	F±	ice	
A cave or a tunnel	ChF → WS	F±	nat	
An abstract painting				
	ChF → CF → W	F±	painting	
A human being who has been				
cut open	ChF → DW	F±	H/anat/O—	
An animal cut open or cut into				
parts	FCh → DW	F±	A/anat	
A beetle on a tree leaf	DW	F±	A/pl	
	D	F±	A	
	combinatory-confabulatory			
A spider on a plant leaf ...	ChF → DW	F±	A/pl	
	combinatory-confabulatory			
A bee drinking from a flower	DW	F±	A/pl	
	ChF → combinatory-confabulatory			
A mask costume with the head of a	WS	F±	mask	
dancer	ChF → combinatory-confabulatory			
A mask that you can look through				
	ChF → W	F±	mask	
c A mask	ChF → DW	F—	mask	
c The heart of a human being	W	F—	anat	
c A bat	W	F—	A	
c The head of an animal	W	F—	Ad	
			(children: F±)	
Coat of arms	DW → W	F—	coat of arms	
Fish	DW → W	F—	A	
A polyp, a cuttlefish	ChF → W	F—	A	
A vase, a jug	W	F—	obj	
Footprint of a cat's paw ..	ChF → W	F—	Ad	
A skull seen from above ..	ChF → W	F—	anat	
A roasted chicken	ChF → W	F—	food	

A fish lying on the shore and covered with algae ..... ChF → W	F—	A	
Smoke .... Ch → W	F—	smoke	
Fog .... Ch → W	F—	fog	
A puddle .... Ch → W	F—	puddle	
A bird (because of the wings) .... DW	F—	A	
A dog (because of the head) .. S → DW	F—	A	
c An elephant (because of the tusks) DW	F—	A	
a A scorpion .... DW	F—	A	
An animal's head .... DW	F—	Ad	
Two birds with long beaks ...... DW	F—	A	
A cow .... DW	F—	A	
A cello .... DW	F—	obj	
Fans .... FCh → DW	F—	obj	
An armchair seen from the back .. DW	F—	obj	
Several plant leaves, one on top of the other .... FCh → DW	F—	Hd	
The palm of a hand with lines ... FCh → DW	F—	pl	
A bird's nest .... ChF → DW	F—	nest	
The skeleton of an animal .... ChF → DW	F—	A/anat	
Cross section of an apple .... WS	F—	pl/food	
b,d An island with lakes .... WS	F—	geogr	
A volcanic island .... ChF → WS	F—	geogr	
An owl nailed to the wall . ChF → SW	F—	A	O—
A flag .... DdW	F—	obj	
b,d Europe: down below is Italy ..... DdW	F—	geogr	
Dried blood .... ChF → W	CF	blood	
The vagina with hair .... ChF → SW	CF	sex	
An Indian with a feather on his head kissing his child (BC 4, 7) D	M	H/scene	O
A woman holding a child on her lap (BCD 3/4; 7/8) .... D	M	H/scene	O
A man taking a woman into his arms (BCD 3/4; 7/8) .... D	M	H/scene	O
A girl is sitting there with her doll (BCD 3/4; 7/8) .... D	M	H/scene	O
A stooped warrior with a shield and a knife (entire center portion) .... D	M	H/scene	O aggression
A woman with raised arms is calling for help (entire center portion) .... D	M	H	O

A cripple with a wooden leg (DEFG 3/4/5 .... (FCh ➜)	D	M	H	O
A man with a cane in his hand (seen from above) (DEFG 3/4/5)	D	M	H	O
c A boy defending himself with a stick (GFED 5/4/3)	D	M	H	O
a A monkey crouching in a tree (DEF 3/4)	D	M	A	O
c A farmer with a hump blowing his nose (GFED 8/7; 3/2)	Dd	M	H	O
a A man is standing there, one can see his arms and his feet ("head" and dark portion)	DdD	M—	H	O—
A face, a head (upper center portion) .... S ➜	D	F+	Hd	
An animal's head, a dog's head, a monkey's head (upper center portion) .... S ➜	D	F+	Ad	
A skull .... FCh ➜ S ➜	D	F+	anat	
Mask (upper center portion) . S ➜	D	F+	mask	
An owl (upper center portion)... S ➜	D	F+	A	
A fist or hand with knife, dagger, sickle (BA 4/5; 6/7) ... (Do ➜)	D	F+	Hd	
Raised hand, fist with knife (BA 4/5; 6/7)	D	M	Hd	
A human head (B 4 and 7) . Do ➜	D	F+	Hd	
A cat's head seen from the back (B 4 and 7)	D	F±	Ad	
A blouse, pullover, etc. (dark center portion)	D	F+	clothing	
A butterfly (dark center portion)..	D	F+	A	
A bat (dark center portion)	D	F+	A	
A tree leaf, a maple leaf (dark center portion)	D	F+	pl	
A pansy, a violet (dark center portion)	D	F—	pl	
A cat's head (dark center portion)	D	F—	Ad	
c A cat's head (dark center portion)	D	F±	Ad	
a Lungs, heart	D	F—	anat	
			(➜ position)	
An X-ray picture of the lungs .... ChF ➜	D	F±	anat	
A dog's head (DEF 3/4)	D	F+	Ad	
Mask (DEF 3/4) .... FCh ➜	D	F+	mask	

Skull (DEF 3/4) .... FCh → D	F+	Hd/anat	
A hand reaching (DEF 3/4) ..... D	F+ (→ M)	Hd	
An elephant's head (D 2/3; 8/9).. D	F+	Ad	
b,d Italy (D 2/3; 8/9) .... D	F±	geog	
c A bat (EF 3/4/5/6/7/8) .... D	F+	A	
b,d Rhinoceros, bull elephant (one half of the blot) .... D	F+	A	
b,d Mountains and forest .... ChF → D	F±	nat	
a A human head (BC 3/4) .... Dd	F+	Hd	
A doll (ECD 3/4) .... Dd	F+	obj	
Three little people stepping into a ditch (C 5 and 6; above the center dark portion) .... Dd	Ms	scene	O
A plant leaf, the dark lines are the arteries (C 5/6) .... Dd	F (C)	pl	
A hand with its fingers (C 5/6) ... Dd	F+	Hd	
A cross (C 5/6) .... Dd	F+	religious obj	
Sickle, knife (A 5 and 6) .... Dd	F+	obj	
Snake (B 5 and 6, small ramification next to the "head") ...... Dd	F+	A	
A jumping deer, chamois, stag, goat (D 2 and 9) .... Dd	F+	A	
A human profile (C 3 and 8) ..... Dd	F±	Hd	
b,d A fir tree, a group of trees (D 2 and 9) .... Dd	F+	pl	
b,d A fir tree covered with snow (D 2 and 9) .... FCh → Dd	F+	pl	
a An animal's horn (D 3 and 9) .... Dd	F+	Ad	
b,d A cat lying down (CD 4/5; 6/7) .. Dd	F±	A	
b A hedgehog, a pig lying (EF 3 and 8) .... Dd	F+	A	
c A head with peaked cap (GF 8)... Dd	F+	Hd	
A lace kerchief (EFG 3/4; 7/8) ... FCh → Dd	F±	clothing	
A butterfly (EFG 3/4; 7/8) ...... Dd	F±	A	
Wilted tree leaves (EFG 3/4; 7/8) .... ChF → Dd	F±	pl	
Animal testicles (FG 3/4; 7/8) ... Dd	F+	sex	
A cow's udder (FG 3/4; 7/8) .... Dd	F+	Ad/sex	
An icicle (FG 3/4; 7/8) .. FCh → Dd	F+	ice	
A water drop (FG 3/4; 7/8) .... ChF → Dd	F+	drop	
A breast nipple (FG 3/4; 7/8) .... Dd	F−	sex/Hd	
c Penis (FG 3/4; 7/8) .... Dd	F−	sex	

54

Antiaircraft guns (FG 4/5; 6/7)... Dd	F+	object, aggression	
a Sticks (FG 4/5; 6/7) .... Dd	F+	obj	
c A drawbridge (FG 4/5; 6/7) ..... Dd	F+	obj	
a Penises (FG 4/5; 6/7) .... Dd	F—	sex	
Animal testicles (FG 5/6) .... Dd	F+	sex	
Male or female sex organ (FG 5/6) Dd	F—	sex	
Shoes (FG 5/6) .... Dd	F±	obj	
A crab's pincers, insect feelers (A 4/5; 7/6) .... Do	F+	Ad	
A woman's head, the head of an Indian woman (B 4/5; 7/6) .... Do	F+	Hd	
A crab's head, a beetle's head (B 5/6) .... Do	F+	Ad	
Holes (all S) .... S	F±	holes, description	
A wood beetle (S, E 5/6) .... S	FC	A, white as color	
Vagina (S, E 5/6) .... S	F—	sex	
Female sex organ with hair (DE 5/6) .... ChF → DS	F—	sex	
Eyes and mouth (upper S) . Do → S	F+	Hd or Ad	
An oblong lake (S, E 5/6) .... S	F±	geog	
A lake with dark forests, seen from an airplane (DE 5/6) .. ChF → DS	F±	nat	
A duck with head and beak (E 2/3; 8/9) .... S	F+	A	
c A fairy striding (card held by its rim, BA 5 and 6) .... S	Ms	H	O
a A harp, a lyre (G 5 and 6) .... S	F+	obj	O

CARD II

Two women gossiping with each other in the back of a garden ... W	MCF	scene	O
A ballet with people in costume .. W	MCF	scene	O
A giant with legs spread out and a hat upon his head .... W	M—	H	O—
The Holy Ghost rides in the shape of a white dove from a pink cloud down to earth .... WS (white dove, AB 5/6) white as color	CF	religion	O
A Chinese painting, a pagoda within a landscape ...... WS → W	CF	obj	O

A chapel, in front of it is a path with bushes .... W	CF	landscape	O
An Indian burial place ... WS → W	CF	architecture	O
A scene sketch by a theater painter, two women greet each other amidst scenery .... W	CF	obj	O
An altar with plants and flowers .... WS → W	CF	obj, relig	O
An aquarium .... W	CF	obj	
Ornament .... W	CF	ornament	
The upper part of a flowerpot with flowers .... W	CF	pl	
A piece of wallpaper .... W	CF	ornament	
A multicolored church window ... W	CF	obj	
A butterfly .... W	CF	A	
The bottom of the sea with plants and animals .... DW → W	CF	nat	
An owl on a tree branch .... DW	CF	A	O—
An animal taken apart .... DW	CF	A/anat	O—
A plate with various fruits or vegetables .... DW	CF	food	
The various colors make me think of corals .... DW	CF	nat	
A bee in a plant .... DW	CF—	A/pl	
c A coat of arms .... W	F— or CF	heraldry	
a A triangle .... DW	F—	infantile abstraction	
Fire in a forest .... DW	C	fire	
A flower vase with painted pictures WS	CF	object	

figure-ground fusion

c The head of a bull . DW → FC → WS	F+	Ad/heraldry	

figure-ground fusion

c A mask .... WS	CF	Hd/mask	
c A chandelier .... WS	CF	obj	
A face (red = nose; green = eyes; brown = moustache) .... WS	F—	Hd/infantile abstraction	
Human pelvis .... WS	F— or CF	anat/sex	

THE DARK RED PORTION:

Two women kissing each other; dancers .... D	M	H	O

Two girls chatting with each other, putting their heads together .... D	M	H	O
Two women kissing each other, their shadow is behind them (light red area) .... FCh → D	M	H	O, schizoid
Two women are standing there with a floating veil (light red area) .... D	MFC	H	O
c A man smoking a pipe .... D	M	H	O
c Two bears greeting each other ... D	M	A	
A penguin .... (→ M) D	F+	A	
b,d A polarbear .... D	F+	A	
b,d A squirrel .... (in children) D	F+	A	
(in adults) D	F±	A	
b,d An anteater .... D	F+	A	
a Mosquito, fly .... D	F±	A	
Kidneys .... D	F— or CF	anat	
Beans .... D	F—	pl	
A butterfly .... D	F—	A	
A butterfly (red area and S) ...... DS	F±	A	
A bird .... D	F—	A	
A lobster in its shell .... DS	CF	A/food	
Lungs .... D	CF	anat	
Heart .... D	CF	anat	
Embryo .... D	CF	H/sex	
A blood stain .... D	CF	blood	
Blood .... D	C	blood	
Part of the chest with spinal cord.. DS	CF	anat	
Vagina .... DS	CF	sex	
Penises .... D	CF	sex	
A leech .... D	CF	A	

RED AND LIGHT RED AREAS:

Strawberries .... D	CF	pl/food
Rose, tulip, flower petals .... D	CF	pl
Cross section of a tulip .... DS	CF	pl
A sliced tomato, apple .... DS	CF	pl/food
Fire .... D	C	fire
Flames .... D	CF	flames
A face .... DS	F—	Hd
A monkey's head .... DS	F—	Ad

A Chinese lantern .... DS ➜ D	FC	obj/—CF	
A magnified head of a fly ... DS ➜ D	F±	Ad	
The shell of an animal .... D	F—	Ad	
A pagoda (together with S) ...... DS	F+	architecture	
A house or a pagoda (without S).. DdD	F—	architecture	
A cooking pot .... D	F—	obj	
A fir tree, tree .... D	F—	pl	
A coat of arms .... S ➜ D	F—	obj/heraldry	
The human brain .... FCh ➜ D	F—	anat	
	or CF		
An X-ray picture of the lungs .... FCh ➜ D	CF	anat	
Clouds in the setting sun . ChF ➜ D	CF	clouds	
c A mill .... DS	F—	obj/ architecture	
a A mask .... DS	CF possibly F—	mask	
A paper kite .... DS	F— possibly CF	obj, infantile	
Two farmers greeting each other (upper dark-red area) .... Dd	Ms	H/scene	
An elephant, an animal in profile (only the light dark area) ...... DdD	F—	A	
An elephant's head, a dog's head (B 4 and 7) .... Dd	F+	Ad	
A face (BC 4 and 7) .... Dd	F—	Hd	
b,d The head of a man with a cap (C 3 and 8) .... Dd	F+	Hd	
b,d A duck flying upward, a bird ..... Dd	F+	A	
b,d A father speaking to his children (small details, light-red blob)... Dd	Ms	scene	
A traveling caravan with people and animals (small details, light-red blob) .... Dd	Ms	scene	
a Snakes (D 5 and 6) .... Dd	F+	A	
Human legs (C 5 and 6) .... Dd	F+	Hd	
Anus (B 5 and 6) .... Dd	CF	sex	
A woman's head (AB 5 and 6).... Do	F+	Hd	

BROWN AREA:

b,d A man is standing there, wearing a beret and a cape .... D	M	H	O

b,d	A monk wearing a brown overcoat, praying .... D	MFC	H	O	
a	Two people swimming in the water .... FCh → D	M	H	O	
b,d	An ape, gorilla or bear out for a walk (or seen moving in some way)	D possibly MFC	M	A	
	Insects .... D	F+ possibly FC	A		
	A buffalo, bull, ox .... D	F+ possibly FC	A	P	
	Bulls fighting .... D	F+ possibly FC	A	P aggression	
	Flies .... D	F±	A		
	Centipedes .... D	F±	A		
	A wasp .... D	F— possibly CF	A		
	Fishes .... D	F— possibly FC	A		
	Frogs .... D	F—	A		
d	A vessel, barge, ship (both brown blots) .... D	F—	obj		
a,c	A moustache .... D	F— possibly CF	Hd		
a	Beetle, ants .... D	FC	A	P	
	A drawing of prehistoric animals.. D	FC	A/drawing		
	Caterpillars, larvae .... D	FC possibly CF	A		
	A mole .... D	FC	A		
	A bee, bumblebee .... D	FC	A		
	A fox drinking .... D	FC	A		
	A fox fur, a lady's fur .... D	FC	A/clothing		
	Roots, carrots .... D	FC	pl/food		
	Sheep .... D	FC	A		
	A grasshopper .... D	FC	A		
	A pig .... D	F— possibly CF	A		
c	Animal horns, antlers .... D	FC possibly F—	Ad		
a	A bedbug .... D	CF	A		
	A worm, worms .... D	CF	A		
	A butterfly .... D	CF	A		
	A bat .... FCh → D	CF	A		
	A sea animal in a shell .... D	CF	A		
	A fossil .... FCh → D	CF	obj		

Sand dunes .... D		CF	nat	
Clods from a farm field .... D		CF	nat	
Foaming sea .... ChF → D		CF	nat	
Sea algae .... D		CF	pl	
Wilted tree leaves .... D		CF	pl	
Embryo .... D		CF	embryo/ anat/sex	
Dried-out blood .... ChF → D		CF	blood	
An island with mountains, on a map .... FCh → D		CF	geog	
Feces .... D		C	feces	
d A scorpion (because of the stings; FG 1/2; 9/10) .... DdD		F—	A	
a Butterfly wings (F 3/4; 7/8) ..... Dd		CF	Ad	
A mask with a long nose (F 3/4; 7/8) .... Dd		F+	mask	
A human head (F 3/4; 7/8) ...... Dd		F+	Hd	
A caterpillar; one can see its bands clearly (EF 2/3; 8/9) .... Dd		F (C)	A	
A mountain range, the dark places are the high points and the light ones are the valleys (EF 2/3; 8/9) .... Dd		F (C)	geog	
Breast nipple (G 1 and 10) ...... Dd		F+	Hd/sex	
A fox' head (FG 1/2; 9/10) ...... Do		F+	Ad	
A lion's head (EF 5 and 6) .... Dd		F—	Ad	
A bull's head (EF 5 and 6) .... Do		F+	Ad	
An eye (dark blot EF 5 and 6) .... Dd		F—	Ad/eye	
c A landscape shot to pieces; an autumn forest ("abdomen of the animal") .... Dd		CF	landscape	
c A howling dog (FG 3 and 8) ..... Dd		F+	A	
c A horse-drawn coach; the driver is swinging a long whip (FG 5/6) .... Dd		Ms	scene	
c A group of people with animals marching in the mountains ("abdomen of the animal") .... Dd		Ms	scene	

GREEN AREA:

A rider upon a rearing horse .... D	Ms	scene	O
Dwarfs striding along carrying shields .... Ms → D	M	H	O
b,d A pair of lovers kissing each other D	M	H	O

b,d	A stooped man (S=head), a running man .... DS	M	H	O
b,d	A stooped monkey (S=head) preparing to jump .... DS	M	A	O
b,d	A woman greeting her husband, the children come running ..... D	M	scene	O
b,d	A large animal drawing a carriage of state with people in it .... D	Ms	scene	O
a	A baby with outstretched arms and legs .... D	M—	H	O—
	Somebody spreading the fingers of his hand wide out .... DdD	M—	Hd	O—
	The snake god with observing eyes DdDS	M—	H/God/eye (→ contamination)	
	A fish, South Sea fish, ornamental fish .... D	F+	A	
	A fish with a large eye .... DS	F+	A	
	Cuttlefish, polyp .... D	F+	A	
	A coral .... D	F+	object	
b,d	A stag .... D	F+	A	
b,d	A cock .... D	F+	A	
a	An eye .... DS	F—	Hd/Ad/eye	
	A bumblebee .... D	F—	A	
	A scorpion, beetle, insect .... DdD	F—	A	
	A butterfly .... DdD → D	F—	A	
	A shell .... DS → D	F—	A	
	A beetle, bedbug on its back and with its legs in the air .... DdD	F—	A/sex/O—	
b,d	The head of a Cyclops with one eye DS	F±	Hd	
	Bushes, grass tufts .... D	FC	pl	
	A cactus .... D	FC	pl	
	A jellyfish, sea animal .... D	CF	A	
	Grass tufts .... D possibly CF	FC	pl	
	Trees .... D possibly CF	FC	pl	
	Moss, lawn, algae, herbs .... D possibly C	CF	pl	
	A forest .... D	CF	pl	
	A pond .... D	CF	nat	
a	A stag coming out from the bushes (C 2/3; 8/9) .... Dd possibly FC	F+	A	
	The pupil of a cat's eye (dark-green area in front of the S) .... Dd	F—	Ad/eye	

The pupil of a human eye (dark-green area in front of the S) .... Dd	F—	Hd/eye	
b,d A cactus; the crown of a tree (DE 2 and 9) .... Dd	FC	Hd	
Two human heads (DE 2 and 9) .... Do → Dd	F+	Hd	

WHITE SPACE INTERPRETATIONS:
LARGE S WITHIN RED AREA:

A man standing upright .... S	M	H	O
A baby lying on a red pillow .....{ S	M	H	O
{ D	FC	obj	
Christ on the cross .... M → S	F+	H/religion	
A plant in a pot, an exotic plant .. S	F+	pl	
A totem pole .... S	F+	obj	
A plastic figure, decorative form .. S	F+	obj	O
A silhouette cut from red paper ..{ S	F+	obj	
{ D	CF	paper	
A water fountain .... S	F±	fountain	
Spine .... S	F—	anat	
The spine of an animal .... S	F±	A/anat	
Insect larva, scorpion .... S	F±	A	
A caterpillar .... S	F—	A	
A tree .... S	F—	pl	
A cross .... S	F±	religious obj	
Don Quixote's head (BC 5/6) .... S	F+	Hd	
A human head (BC 5/6) ... Do → D	F+	Hd	
A flower (BC 5/6) .... S	F+	pl	
A white rose, flower (BC 5/6) .... S	FC	pl	
		white as color	
A mushroom (BC 5/6) .... S	F—	pl	
A butterfly (BC 5/6) .... S	F+	A	
A tooth (BC 5/6) .... S	F+	tooth	
A dove (B 5/6, small S) .... S	F+	A	
The Holy Ghost as a white dove (B 5/6, small S) .... S	FC	religion/A	
		white as color	
A pilot's insignia, airplane (B 5/6, small S) .... S	F+	obj	
A butterfly (C 5/6) .... S	F+	A	
A dancer in a white dress, bowing (D 5/6) .... FC → S	Ms	H	O
Pinocchio with two heads (D 5/6) S	F—	Hd	
A bird of prey (S between the red and brown areas) .... S	F+	A	

An airplane (S between the red and brown areas)	S	F±	obj	
b,d An infant in diapers (S within the green area)	S	Ms	H	O
b,d A sitting woman in a robe with a white veil (S within the green area)	S	Ms FC	H	O
				white as color
a A fir tree (S within green area) ...	S	F+	pl	
A dog sitting there (S between the green, red, and brown areas, DE 3/4; 7/8)	S	F+	A	

CARD III

The scoring of this card proceeds according to the method used in scoring the third card of the Rorschach Test. If all dark parts are included in an interpretation, it is scored as a whole response.

All the variations of human forms that are perceived in such a way that the lower separate dark blots represent the legs of these human figures are scored as .... W   M   H   O

In addition to P, these responses are frequently also O+—namely, in those cases where:

1. they are combined with all the other blots of the cards;
2. the figures which are interpreted as M are provided with special features.

Often an entire scene is described. If this is the case, all additional details should be scored separately.

Two people greeting each other ..	W	M	H	P
Two men fighting over a piece of meat, tearing at it; a part of it they have thrown behind them combinatory	W	M	H	P O
				aggression
	D	CF	meat/food	
A dance by two funny chimney-sweeps	W	MCF	H	P O
Two men with Janus heads threatening each other with pistols ...	W	M	H	P O
combinatory	Dd	F+	obj, aggression	
Two fellows fighting over an exotic butterfly and two Indian boys come running in order to see				

what is happening there	W	M	H	P	O
					aggression
combinatory	D	FC	A	P	
	D	M	H	P	
Men warming their hands at a fire	W	M	H	P	O
combinatory	D	C	fire		
Devils fighting over a soul (the "soul" is the red area in the center)	W	M	H	P	O
combinatory	D	CF	soul		
A diver surrounded by corals	W	M	H	P	O
combinatory	D	CF	nat		
Two skiers in snow	W	M	H	P	O
confabulatory	S	CF	snow (white as color)		
Two women holding a red scarf ...	W	M	H	P	O
combinatory	D	FC	obj		
A naturalist in an ice-cold country	W	M	H	P	O
confabulatory	S	CF	nat		
Two men in diving suits	W	M	H	P	O
Two dancing witches	W	MFCh	H	P	O
Mystical ballet, a fire dance	W	MCF	scene	P	O
People moving from light into darkness .... ChF →	W	MCF	H	P	O
People meeting at night under torch light .... ChF →	W	M	H		O
confabulatory	D	CF	torches		
Ghost fight, ghost meeting	W	MChF	H	P	O
Human shadows fighting with each other	W	MChF	H	(P)	O
					aggression
A devil in a purple cape	W	MFC	H/clothing	P	
Men upon horses; one sees only one leg, the horses are not there	W	M	H	P	O—
					confabulatory
Dancing or fighting monkeys	W	M	A	(P)	
Two large animals dressed like people, dancing and laughing ..	W	M	A	(P)	
				H repression	
Caricatures	W	F+	drawing		
			M and H repression		
A scarecrow .... FCh →	W	F+	obj		
			M and H repression		
Skeletons	W	F±	anat		
			M and H repression		

Response	Loc	Det	Content	
a,c Trees	W	F—	pl	
c A man, wearing loose pants, and bending his knees	W	M—	Hd	
			confabulatory	
c A conductor conducting an orchestra, a music stand is standing in front of him (red center area) . { DW	M—	H	O—
combinatory and confabulatory { D	F—	obj	
a Animals from fables	W	F—	A	O—
A gathering of animals .... DW → W	F—	A	O—
Undersea landscape with corals ... FCh → DW → W	CF	nat	
Color stains	W	CF	description	
A group of islands .... DW → W	F—	geog	
A victor's wreath with red ribbons DW	CF	obj	O—
A vase with two handles	DW	F—	obj	
c A house, cottage	DW	F—	obj, infantile abstraction	
c A grotto	SW	F—	anat	
a A human head, here is the mouth (red center area)	DW	F—	Hd	
			CF, if mouth is seen as being red	
c Crab or shell animal	DW	F—	A	
a The shadow of laundry on a wash line .... ChF → W	F—	shadow	O—
Paper painted in two colors	DW	CF	drawing, infantile	
Two women wearing old-fashioned hats (larger dark blot) .. Do → D	F+	H (Hd)	
Two women, old aunts, pointing at each other (larger dark blot) ... Do → D	M	H (Hd)	
Sitting girls (larger dark blot) .... D	M	H	
Two men without legs (larger dark blot)	Do	F+	Hd	
A tree (larger dark blot) .. FCh → D	F±	pl	
c A man sitting there smoking a pipe (EDC 4/3; 7/8) { D	M	H	O
combinatory { Dd	F+	obj	
c A man walking along carrying another one on his back (EDC 4/3; 7/8)	D	M	H	O
Two men standing opposite each other (whole larger dark blot) .. DdD	M—	H	O—

b,c A dragon (EDC 2/3/4; 7/8/9) belching forth smoke (light-gray area, EF 4; 7) and fire (red center area) .... combinatory ChF →	D	F+	A	
	Dd	F±	smoke	
	D	CF	fire	
b,c A burning ship enveloped by smoke (larger dark part) ChF →	D	F—	smoke, obj	
b A dragon, some sort of antedeluvian animal (EDC 1/2/3; 8/9/10)	D	F+	A	
a A cat (larger dark blot)	D	F—	A	
c A cat (larger dark blot)	D	F±	A	
c A hippocampus (larger dark blot)	D	F—	A	
c A sea-horse (" " ")	D	F—	A	
b,d A swan, duck (CDE 1/2/3; 10/9/8)	D	F+	A	
a A human head (AB 3/4; 7/8) .... Do →	D	F+	Hd	
a A mask (dark part of the "head"; B 4/3; 7/8) .... FCh →	D	F+	mask	
c A cat (dark part of the "head"; B 4/3; 7/8)	D	F+	A	
a A hand, arm (CD 1/2; 9/10) ..... Do →	D	F+	Hd	
b,d A bird's head (CD 1/2; 9/10 .... Do →	D	F+	Ad	
b,d A human head and neck	D	F+	Hd	
A hand holding forks (CD 1; 10) ..	D	F±	Hd	
The paw of a large bird (CD 1; 10)	D	F±	Ad	
b,d A candle with a smoking flame (CD 1/2; 9/10) .... ChF →	D	F—	obj/flame	
b,d A flower, plant (CD 1/2; 9/10) ...	D	F±	pl	
b,d A windblown tree (CD 1/2; 9/10) FCh →	D	F+	pl	

DETAIL RESPONSES PRODUCED FOR THE SMALL BLACK-GRAY BLOT, THE "LEG" OF THE PEOPLE

A little man with hair on his head, lying on his back .... Ms →	D	M	H	O
Embryo	D	F—	H/anat/sex	O—
c A hand with a finger outstretched	D	F+	Hd	
a Viper's grass	D	FC	pl	
A carrot	D	F+	pl	
A cactus branch, tree root	D	F—	pl	

66

An earwig, centipede	D	F+	A
A crab's pincers, beetle feelers	D	F+	Ad
A caterpillar, forest snail, larva ...			
FCh →	D	F+	A
A scorpion	D	F+	A
A sea crab in an elongated shell, ex-			
tending its claws	D	F (C)	A
An instrument for pulling out			
thumbtacks	D	F+	obj
Pliers	D	F±	obj
A candle	DdD	F—	obj
A hissing snake	DdD	F—	A
A crocodile	DdD	F—	A
A worm	DdD	F—	A
The foot of a donkey	D	F—	Ad
Sausage	D	F±	food
A mouse, rat, piggy, dog (EF 2/3;			
8/9, mostly seen in c-position) ..	D	F+	A

SMALL DETAIL RESPONSES PRODUCED FOR THE BLACK-GRAY BLOT

A devil's head (A 4 and 7)	Dd	F+	Hd
Snakes (on the "head")	Dd	F—	A
Horns (" " ")	Dd	F±	Ad
A human head in profile (AB 3 and			
8)	Dd	F+	Hd
Mask (A 3 and 8)	Dd	F+	Hd/mask
The neck of a giraffe and its head			
(B 4; 6/7)	Dd	F+	Ad
An elephant's trunk (B 4; 6/7)	Dd	F±	Ad/sex
A horn (B 4; 6/7)	Dd	F±	Ad
Revolver (C 4 and 7)	Dd	F+	obj, aggression
c A foot (C 4 and 7) .... Do →	Dd	F+	Hd
a Horns (C 4 and 7)	Dd	F—	Ad
a A little dog extending its paw (C			
1 and 9/10)	Dd	F+	A
c Three small fir trees standing on a			
rock (CD 1/2; 9/10)	Dd	F+	pl
c A finger (blobs of the "hand," CD			
1 and 9/10)	Dd	F+	Hd
a A hand (light gray, toward the red			
center area)	Dd	F+	Hd

b,d	Three little men striding over a glacier, the last one of them jumps over a crevasse .... Dd	Ms	scene	
a	A dragon's head, bull's head, dog's head (DE 3/4; 7/8) with an eye .... Do → S → Dd	F+	Ad (eye)	
b,d	A crocodile's head with open jaws (D 2 and 9) .... Dd	F+	Ad	
	Tree leaves (blobs at the larger dark blot) .... Dd	F—	pl	
c	A human head .... Do → Dd	F+	Hd	
c	Hair (E 2 and 9) .... Do → Dd	F+	Hd	
a	The head of a fish (small dark blot in the "leg") .... Dd	F+	Ad	
	Cheese (small dark blot in the "leg") .... Dd	F—	food	
	A crocodile's head (mostly in c, light-gray area at the "foot"; (G 6 and 7) .... Dd	F+	Ad	
	A crab's claw (G 6 and 7) ... Do → Dd	F+	Ad	
	A donkey's foot (G 6 and 7) ...... Dd	F+	Ad	
	A shoe with a high heel (G 6 and 7) Do → Dd	F+	clothing	

RED BLOTS:

Bloodstains	(all red blots) .. D	CF	blood
Blood	" " " .. D	C	blood
Color stains	" " " .. D	CF	color/stains
Red ink, red paint " " " .. D		C	paint/color

RED CENTER AREA:

	A female dancer in a flowing gown D	MFC	H	O
	Icarus with outstretched wings ... D	M	H	O
	Butterfly, moth, insect, fly .... D	F+	A	P
	A red butterfly from a foreign country .... D	FC	A	P
	A top .... D	F+	obj	
	An airplane .... D	F±	obj	
	A basket .... D	F±	obj	
	A road sign .... D	F±	obj	
	A technical object .... D	F—	obj	
	A weather vane .... D	F—	obj	
c	A flying stork .... D	F±	A	

a	A bat .... D	F±	A	
	A warrior's hatchet .... D	F±	obj, aggression	
	A torture wheel .... Dd ➔ D	F—	obj, aggression	
	A plant leaf .... D	F—	pl	
	A bow .... CF ➔ D	FC	clothing	
	A basket with red fruit .... D	CF	obj/food	
	A red scarf .... D	CF	obj	
	Vagina .... D	CF	sex	
	A wound, the location of an operation .... D	CF	anat, sex	
	An airplane (lower part of the red area and center lines) .... Dd	F+	obj	
	A lion's head (one half of the red area) .... Dd	F+	Ad	
c	A sheep's head (one half of the red area) .... Dd	F+	Ad	
b,c	A face (one half of the red area) . Dd	F+	Hd	
a	Two heads kissing each other .... Dd	M—	Hd	
	Two heads in profile hanging on two sides of a wall .... Dd	F+	Hd	
	Two pencils (center line) .... Dd	F+	obj	
	A bridge (" ") .... Dd	F—	obj	

OUTER RED AREA:

	Dancing, jumping, running little men, children, dwarfs, devils .. D	M	H	P
		(in dwarfs, devils—Ms tendency)		
	Indians wearing a feather on their heads come running .... ⌠D	M	H	P
	combinatory ⌡Dd	F+	Ad	
	Children, playing, in red clothes .. D	MFC	H	P
	Dancing bears .... D	M	A/H repression	
	Puppet, doll, Teddy bear .... D	F+	A/toy	
			M and H repression	
b,d	Dog, bear, camel, bird, elephant .. D	F+	A	
b,d	A butterfly .... D	F—	A	
b,d	A horse .... DdD ➔ D	F—	A	
a	Embryo .... CF ➔ D	FC	H/anat/ O—/sex	
	Human head seen in profile (profile turned inwards) .... D	F—	Hd	
	A head (upper part) .... Do	F+	Hd	

69

INNER WHITE SPACE RESPONSES:

A mushroom with a decayed head and stem (between the large dark blots)	S	F+	pl (defective)	
A cactus, flower in a pot (between the large dark blots)	S	F+	pl	
c A girl's head (between the large dark blots)	S	F+	Hd	
c A lady striding through the night .	DS	MCh	H	
a A girl with a small waist, striding (holding the card by its corner, between the two dark blots)	S	M	H	O
The torso of a polar bear (underneath the "arms")	S	F±	Ad	
Eyes (E 4 and 7)	S	F+	eye	

7. The Psychogram

A psychogram is the tabulation of scoring symbols.

It may be carried out by two different methods.

1. One can establish certain *vertical* columns (apperception, determinants, content, percentile, other factors).

2. One can use a *horizontal* method, which permits one to see at a glance in what manner apperception took place for the individual cards and what determining criteria were disclosed in them.

Moreover, we must note on the scoring sheet the following:

A. SEQUENCE

Here we examine the regularity or irregularity of apperception modi.

RIGID

A sequence is "rigid" if, for all pictures, first a W, then several D, and finally 1–2 (or more) Dd are produced.

ORDERLY

A sequence is "orderly" if it is neither rigid nor loose (see below), nor irregular. The following is an example:

Card I	II	III
W	D	W
W	S	D
D	D	D
Dd	Dd	D
D	Dd	Dd

71

LOOSE

A sequence is "loose" if the lack of order of the apperception modi increases:

Card I	II	III
W	S	W
Dd	Dd	Dd
D	D	D
Dd	D	Dd
D	Dd	Dd

IRREGULAR

A sequence is "irregular" if there is no order at all of apperception. For instance:

Card I	II	III
D	DW	Dd
W	Dd	W
Dd	D	Dd
W	S	D
D	Dd	Dd

INVERSE

A sequence is "inverse" if a subject first looks for Dd in a picture, then arrives at a D, and finally produces a W, thus reacting "inversely," as compared with rigid or orderly sequences.

B. EXPERIENCE BALANCE

This indicates the relationship between M (kinesthetia) and colors. An M equals CF, FC is evaluated as ½, and C as 1½. Depending on its evaluation, CCh is included either as 1 or ½, and ChC as 1 C value. (Usually, CCh corresponds to FC).

EXAMPLES:

Subject A produced 4 M, 4 FC, 2 CF, 1 CCh. I score:

$$4 \text{ FC} = 2 \text{ C}$$
$$2 \text{ CF} = 2 \text{ C}$$
$$1 \text{ CCh} = \tfrac{1}{2} \text{ C}$$

and I obtain the following formula: 4 M : 4½ C.

Subject B produced 1 M, 3 FC, 1 CF, 1 C. I score:

3 FC $= 1\frac{1}{2}$ C
1 CF $= 1$ C
1 C $= 1\frac{1}{2}$ C

and I obtain the following formula: 1 M : 4 C.

Subject C produced 3 M, 3 FC, 2 CF, 1 C, 1 ChC. I score:

3 FC $= 1\frac{1}{2}$ C
2 CF $= 2$ C
1 C $= 1\frac{1}{2}$ C
1 ChC $= 1$ C

and I obtain the following formula: 3 M : 6 C.

C. THE APPERCEPTIVE TYPE

I note every one of the subject's modes of perception, and underline the two that occur with the greatest relative frequency. (The *average scores* serve as the criterion.) In 15 interpretations or responses, they amount to 3 W, 10 D, 1 Dd, 1 S; in 25 responses, 4 W, 18 D, 1–2 Dd, 1 S.

In a case like this, I would note for the apperceptive type: W — D — Dd — S, indicating that relatively many D were produced, followed in number by W, but fewer Dd and S.

D. REMARKS

In our "remarks" column, we note everything concerning the subject that has attracted our attention while we were administering the test, including any special forms of test behavior. These must be taken into consideration at the time of psychological evaluation (diagnosis), and we therefore do not wish to overlook them.

Some scoring examples based on the sample record of Luise Roth follow (Tables 1 and 2).

$F+\%$ is computed by the following method:

Total number of responses minus number of F— responses. The difference between these two figures is then multiplied by 100 and divided by the total number of responses.

TABLE 1

Scoring Sheet

Subject: Luise Roth, 15 years old; daughter of Benedicht, foreman.   Date: December 12, 1949

Time: 12 minutes

Total number of responses: 23/6 (23 responses, 6 of which were produced for the colored Card II)

DW	= —	F+	= IIIII IIIII I ⎫ 13(−1)	P	= IIII	4
SW	= —	F−	= — ⎬	O	= IIIII	5
WS	= —	F±	= II ⎭	H	= IIIII III	8
W	= II 2	M	= IIIII I 6	Hd	= III	3
D	= IIIII IIIII IIII I 14	MC	= —	anat	= —	
Dd	= IIIII I 6	MCh	= —	blood	= —	
Do	= —	Ms	= I 1	scene	= +	(=tendency)
S	= I 1	FC	= II 2	cloth	= I	1
		CF	=	food	= —	
F+%	= 91	C	=	A	= II	2
A%	= 9	CCh	= I 1	Ad	= —	
P%	= 17	FCh	=	obj	= IIIII	5
O%	= 21+	ChF	=	pl	= III	3
anat%	= —	Ch	=	geog	= I	1
H%	= 50	F(C)	=	nat	= —	
obj%	= 21			cloud	= —	
				arch	= —	
				etc.	= —	

Sequence: orderly-loose

Experience balance: 6 M : 2 C

Apperceptive type: W − D − Dd/S

Shocks: − (= none)

Remarks: "or"; object criticism; combinatory tendency, strongly stereotyped with H.

74

TABLE 2

Scoring Sheet
Subject: Luise Roth, 15 years old; daughter of Bendicht, foreman.

Time: 12 minutes
Responses: 23/6

Date: December 12, 1949

	P	DW	SW	WS	W	D	Dd	Do	S	F+	F−	F±	M	MC	MCh	Ms	FC	CF	C	CCh	F(C)	P	O
I	—	—	—	—	1	6	2	—	1	8	—	—	2	—	—	—	—	—	—	—	—	1	2
II	—	—	—	—	—	4	2	—	—	—	—	1	1	—	—	1	2	—	—	—	—	—	2
III	—	—	—	1	1	4	2	—	—	3	—	1	3	—	—	—	—	—	—	1	—	3	1
	—	—	—	—	2	14	6	—	1	11	—	2	6	—	—	1	2	—	—	1	—	4	5

F% = 91
A% = 9
P% = 17
O% = 21+
anat% = —
H% = 50

obj% = 21
H = 8
Hd = 3
anat = —
blood = —
scene = tend

clothing = 1
food = —
A = 2
Ad = —
obj = 5
pl = 3

geog = 1
nat = —
cloud = —
arch = —
others = —

Sequence: orderly—loose
Experience balance: 6 M : 2 C
Apperceptive type: W—D—Dd/S.

Shocks: none

Remarks: "or"; object criticism; combinatory tendency +, strongly stereotyped with H.

75

For example, Luise Roth's record:

13 F responses minus two times $\frac{1}{2}$ F$\pm$ ($= 1$ F$+$) $= 12$ times $100 = 1200 : 13 = 91\%$.

The other percentages are computed by multiplying the particular number of responses by 100 and then dividing the sum by the total number of responses.

For example, Luise Roth's record:

A$\%$ $=$ number of A and Ad $= 2$; times $100 = 200$; divided by number of responses $= 200 : 23 = 9\%$

P$\%$ $=$ number of P $= 4$; times $100 = 400$; divided by number of responses $= 400 : 23 = 17\%$

O$\%$ $=$ number of O $= 5$; times $100 = 500$; divided by number of responses $= 500 : 23 = 21\%$

Since we are dealing here throughout with well perceived O(O$+$), I mark O$\% = 21+$. If 1–2 O— had been produced, I would have had to mark it O$\% = 21\pm$; if 3 or 4 O— (among the 5 O) had been produced, I would have had to note it as O$\% = 21\mp$. If all O had been O— (5 O—), I would have had to write O$\% = 21-$.

Thus, later on, when preparing the diagnosis, I shall be able to see at a glance whether, in a given case, "originality" is, in a positive sense, the originality of a creative human being or that of an ingenious individual who possesses an "original mind." On the other hand, such "originality" may indicate a person who is more or less defective in his mental and imaginative abilities, and in his ways of perceiving and understanding. He may be an "eccentric" or a "crank" (an individual who tries to build things that are impossible to build, for instance, or who makes all sorts of "discoveries," such as the *perpetuum mobile*, etc.)—or he may even be a psychotic.

All the other percentages are calculated by the same method as A$\%$, P$\%$, and O$\%$.

For the sake of practicing, students are advised first to carry out the scoring of the sample records of Martin Balz and Hanni Steinmann, and then to score the records of a number of other subjects.

For the same purpose, it is also recommended that one perform the scoring by using the two different techniques mentioned above.

Each scoring method has its advantages. The method that we have first discussed serves extremely well the purpose of comparing the results of the Zulliger Test with those of Ro, Bero, or both. I shall exemplify it in parts II and III of this book.

The second scoring method has advantages for the evaluation of a Zulliger Test (not for any other form-interpretation test).

In working with the Zulliger Test, it has proven practical to score FCh as such and simultaneously to score them F+ as well. Correspondingly, ChF are scored as F± and pure Ch as F—.

This procedure may be justified by the fact that Hermann Rorschach usually scored all "animal skin" responses WF + A P and not WFCh Ad P.

If a subject produced an "animal skin" response for Card I of the Zulliger Test, I would score it FCh ➔ WF + A. In addition, I would mark the response as both FCh and F+ on the scoring sheet.

Moreover, with reference to Rorschach, I should score A in this instance (instead of Ad, which "skin" actually is). Such a step has been approved by experience. Proceeding in this manner we do not, under certain circumstances, run the risk of obtaining too few A in proportion to Ad.

One can work very well indeed with arrows (➔) and with advance scoring. For instance, if a subject interprets the upper center part in Card I as a "human head," a "monkey head," "dog head," or a "skull," S are always included, although they may not be specifically mentioned, but are interpreted as "angry eyes," "a round mouth," etc. It would never enter the subject's head to interpret this portion of the picture as a "human head," etc., if there were no S. Therefore, I compute or rather score it as S ➔ DF + Hd. By scoring in this fashion we obtain, by adding the totals of the three columns (apperception column, determinants column, content column), dissimilar results. Accordingly, as the "total of responses," I use the sum of all response contents (third column). In particular, an account is given

TABLE 3

PI	SW	DW	W	D	Dd	Do	S	F+	F−	F±	M	Ms	FC	CF	C	FCh	ChF	Ch	P	O
I	—	—	2	2-3	1	—	1	5	1	1	↑	—	.	—	—	↑	—	—	1	—
II	—	—	—	3-4	1	—	↑	1	1	—	—	—	1-2	1	—	—	—	—	1	—
III	—	—	1	4	↑	—	1	3	—	—	2	—	↑	—	—	↑	—	—	3	1

Time: 8-10 minutes

F+% = 70-85-90 Number of responses = 15/5—20/6-7
A% = 30-50 Sequence = orderly, occasionally inverse
P% = 25-35 Experience balance = 2 M to more C, mostly rather ambiequal
O% = 6-10 Apperceptive type = W: D: Dd: (S)
H% = 15-25 Number of H larger than number of Hd
anat% = — Number of A larger than number of Ad

of all the responses produced for Card II. See, for example, the responses of Luise Roth: 23/6, namely, 23 responses have been made by the subject, of which 6 refer to the colored Card II.

AVERAGE SCORES

These scores are expressed in numbers that are based on nearly 1,000 experiments with "normal" subjects. Approximately, we obtain the above table (Table 3).

In children, and in well-trained or openly cautious and shrewd adults, 1–2 FCh occur with almost certain regularity. According to my observations, DW replace M responses in young children, 4–7 years old. This phenomenon is frequently found in 8-year-olds as well (whether it should be considered a "rule," must be verified on the basis of larger statistical material). DW produced by small children are clearly in accordance with their "fairy-tale age," and their still greatly marked "magic" way of thinking. Thus, a part is taken for a whole (*pars pro toto* law). A child sees a dog's head (Card I, top center) quite clearly and says immediately: "Here is a dog!" He then points to the whole picture blot. Consquently, we are dealing here with a DW response. The child's thinking is still confabulatory in accordance with his age. He is not yet capable of differentiating completely between his imagination and reality—something that every adult, however, should be quite capable of doing. The child combines fantasy with reality; he mistakes imagination for reality, and succumbs to illusions. At his stage of mental development, this is entirely natural and "normal." In an adult or an adolescent subject, the situation is different. Both should be able to think rationally and in terms of "reality." Therefore they should not produce DW, DdW, or DdD (corresponding with DW) any longer.

In an average record, M are M P; they are as a rule extensor kinesthesias.

8. Psychological and Characterological Significance of the Factors

A. AGE AND SEX OF THE SUBJECTS

As a rule, factors that could give cause for concern should be judged much less severely in children and youths under 16 years than in adults. In this connection some specific instances will be pointed out in the course of the following discussion.

Subjects over 50 years of age quite often show an "impoverishment" of experience balance. Nevertheless, one would be greatly mistaken if one ascribed to them emotional apathy and creative incapacity. It is merely that they have become much more well-balanced than the younger age groups and, in general, have grown more reserved.

The occurrence of CF more than once or twice in an adult male must give cause for concern. In females, however, these may not carry quite the same weight. Females *are* more easily aroused; they are more emotional and usually more impulsive than the average male. Thus, one would be well-advised to evaluate the CF produced by female subjects more liberally, especially if they are accompanied by the same number of FC.

In short, in diagnosing it is essential to take into consideration the age and sex of the subjects.

B. REACTION TIME

The average reaction time for one response is approximately 1/3 to 1/2 minute. The average time for the entire form-interpretation test of about 15 responses thus amounts to 5-8 minutes.

Dull people have a longer reaction time and a smaller number of responses. Those who stay with the test for up to 20 minutes, producing during that time the average number of responses (15–20 responses with a high F+%), must be credited with *persistence* and *diligence*. Frequently these are people who try stubbornly to solve a task that has been set for them. Despite many failures, they persistently keep in mind the goal that they themselves have chosen and work toward it, slowly but steadily. They are often *cautious, self-critical,* and *introverted* individuals (with many M); but, then again, they may be *distrustful, cautious,* and *timid* people (with DS, Do, and an inverse sequence).

Occasionally, retarded persons also prove to have a long reaction time with a small number of responses. However, they can be more easily recognized by other factors—such as, for example, DdW, their more awkward than anxious Do, etc. In addition, their F+% is low.

In order to determine a personality trait with some certainty, the examiner should not ever depend upon one single factor for his diagnosis. He should rather try to reach the goal of combining harmoniously certain groups of factor relationships, all of them indicating a definite ability, characteristic trait, etc.

Thus, it is quite certain that a subject with a long reaction time and many exact responses (including numerous Dd) is a person who goes through life with an inclination toward *thoroughness, conscious effort, dependability,* and *eagerness for quantity.* If he produces too many Dd, however, all these basically valuable characteristics tend to acquire a somewhat distressing overtone of *pedantry.* If W are absent, then the subject belongs in the category of people who can easily become fearfully perturbed and upset, who like to do everything just "right," who refuse to ignore the "other side" of things, and who, often unnecessarily, worry too much, work too hard, and take too many pains. Moreover, if M are absent and color responses (coarctated experience balance) are but few, these are individuals who have no sense of humor; they seem arid and shallow, and it is not exactly pleasant to live with them.

If the reaction time proves to be prolonged, while the responses are of poor form quality but numerous, we may conclude that the subject's attitude is somewhat *"indifferent"* (superficial, careless), even though he may appear to be rather interested. His effort is more pretended than real. He is quite *active,* yet he is at the same time *careless* in his work, the quality of which is not high.

In the form-interpretation test, a temporarily or persistently *depressive* mood finds its expression in a long reaction time, with only a few responses; these are always well perceived, however. The color responses but not W and M are absent in this case. Depressed persons have a strongly coarctated experience balance. Often, moreover, they do not produce any M.

People with great *verbal needs* and an *ability for easy expression* have a short reaction time and produce many responses. They are enterprising and *delight in creating.* If, in addition, a high F+% is present, *unconscious diligence* may be attributed to them. They are intelligent and their work bears the mark of quality. On the other hand, if F+% is low, these people *talk a great deal;* they *like to talk.* Children who fall into this category are chatterers, even *babblers.* If, in addition, there appear numerous color responses and 1–3 M, these individuals are jolly and carefree, endowed with a gay (although not very "profound") disposition.

C. NUMBER OF RESPONSES

The number of responses is related directly to the subject's *verbosity,* his *desire for expression,* and his *eagerness for quantity.*

Industrious, "well-behaved" students often stand out by their large number of responses. Primarily, they produce numerous Dd. They are driven by conscious and unconscious diligence, often by ambition (anatomic and geographic interpretations), which they substitute for their insufficient, neglected, or "inhibited" productive intelligence. However, if they succeed in producing an imposing number of W and D, in addition to some M and FC, they turn out to be *gifted workers,* often tending to possess *creative ability.*

A small number of responses may be indicative of people with the following character traits:

Reserved individuals. They show a high F+%, several M, and only a few FC.

Ill-tempered individuals. Color responses are absent; FCh, ChF, and ChC are produced instead.

Quality-ambitious individuals. They offer many WM and a high O+%.

Critically suspicious, stubbornly uncommunicative, noncompliant individuals; these produce several S.

Anxious, self-conscious individuals, who "do not want to have said anything." Although they show a high F+%, they produce only a few W and often several Do. Their sequence is inverse. In many instances they produce a chiaroscuro or color shock. They often combine their responses with an "or."

If, when a card is handed to him, a subject asserts that he "cannot do anything with it," some prodding by the examiner is indicated, encouraging him to try once more. Usually the subject then produces at least *one* response. *Rejection* suggests a mental block. In a real-life situation, a rejecting subject will on occasion react unreasonably, in a similarly unpredictable manner, "losing his head completely."

Even one single "rejection" of one of the cards should make the examiner apprehensive. Should several rejections occur, it may be assumed that the subject is emotionally unbalanced and to a greater or lesser extent "peculiar." The actual degree will be revealed by further examination of the test factors.

A refusal to give a response to a card does not always mean that the subject is a "rejector." It may be that the subject has discovered something in the cards that he does not want to mention, or is not able to mention, because he is embarrassed.

A 12-year-old girl rejected Card I. Such suggestions as: "Come on, you certainly see something! Other girls of your age can, and you are no less smart than they are!" proved fruitless. By the manner in which the girl stared at the picture, I could surmise, however, that she had "seen" something. Thereupon, I handed the girl a piece of paper, saying: "Write down for me what you have seen. I shall turn around in the meantime. Then you may lay the sheet of paper face down, which will prevent me from reading what you have written there. I shall not read it until after you have left." The girl wrote down: "At the bottom of the picture are two formations like the ones that bulls have and that they put into the cows to make them have calves." Thus, it turned out that this pre-adolescent girl had interpreted the stick-like protrusions at the lower rim of the picture as penises. She was too embarrassed to communicate to me in spoken words what she had seen. But she could very well write it down, provided I would read it later when the subject herself was no longer present!

Another girl, 14 years old, was about to reject Card II. I proceeded in the same manner as with the 12-year-old girl mentioned above. The girl wrote down: "Menstruation blood." Later, she produced five additional responses to Card II, but still shrank from referring to the red blots.

A 26-year-old woman rejected Card II. Once more, I induced the subject to write down her response. She gave the following interpretation: "Female sex organ." After writing down this response, the subject produced three further responses to Card II.

A 16-year-old boy was about to reject Card I. Yet, on a sheet of paper, he wrote: "A part of the female body between the legs." Later, he refused to give any more responses to Card I, and sighed with relief when I handed Card II to him. To this card he gave six responses.

An examiner should not lose his patience too quickly, if a subject seems to "reject" in responding. Moreover, one should be capable of mustering enough intuition to be able to provoke "just one more" (or several more) responses.

Rejectors are extremely rare when the Zulliger Test is used. In the 12 years during which I have worked with the Zulliger Individual Test, I have very rarely observed a real rejector. Once a 15-year-old girl had been sent to me for psychological examination by the court. She had accused her uncle of having had sexual intercourse with her. A medical examination has proven, however, that the girl was a *virgo intacta*. There were two possibilities: either the girl was lying, or else something illicit had been done to her, and she believed (by mislocating physical stimuli) that sexual intercourse had taken place, although an *immissio penis* had not actually occurred and the coitus attempt had been merely an *"inter femores"* incident. The examining judge had asked me to try to throw some light upon the facts of this case. The girl rejected all three cards; she also refused to submit to further attempts with other tests. In the pyramid color test, for instance, she merely put down four pegs into the first pattern and then, after asserting that the task was too "difficult" for her, refused to continue. In the Wartegg Test, she completed only the first symbol, by enlarging the dot and adding radiating lines to it. Later, she maintained that she could not "do" anything with the other seven symbols. In reality, she was afraid to expose the fact that she had lied. In further interventions by the examining judge, she became involved in a net of contradictions, and finally confessed to merely having dreamed once that her (beloved) uncle had had sexual intercourse with her. After that, she had boasted to a "false snake" of a friend—first making her promise to keep her mouth shut— that her uncle had slept with her. The friend had then spread the "secret" about. When the village policeman came to the girl's house and questioned her, she was very much ashamed; since she did not want to be taken for a liar, she had continued to accuse her uncle of having made illicit attacks. We can understand why this girl "rejected" all tests.

Once, a 21-year-old paranoiac produced the following response to Card I: "This is an evil spirit, a tempter; it flies toward me. Well, yes, this is a picture of you, you are trying to lead me into temptation!" It was impossible to move him into giving any further responses. He rejected all other cards.

Thus, we cannot deny that "rejections" do occur. They are extremely rare, however, and rejecting subjects are usually abnormal. The example of the 15-year-old girl who had become a liar and slanderer has demonstrated that now and then rejections may occur in normal persons, too. Nevertheless, the rule remains that invariably a rejecting subject is highly suspicious.

There is one strange and psychologically still unexplained fact that prevails in testing. After one has worked with the Zulliger Test for some length of time, one obtains many more responses than one did in the beginning. This phenomenon has come to the attention of other test users as well. Even though one has obtained only 12–15 responses in the beginning, one later averages 15–25 responses, and usually several more.

Perhaps, once one is well acquainted with the Zulliger Test and feels confident, one gives the instructions more calmly, in a different tone of voice. The examiner's "frame of mind" communicates itself to the subject and effects a greater productivity. There is a case of a 42-year-old college graduate who produced 86 responses.

D. THE FIRST SCORING COLUMN (APPERCEPTION COLUMN)

WHOLE RESPONSES, W

In general, these correspond to the *need for unification,* uniformity and a large scale conception. The relative number of such responses (2–4 W are the norm in 15 responses) is a measure of these traits.

It is of great diagnostic significance to note which cards evoke W responses. As a rule, one W is given for Card I and one for Card III. Often 2–4 W are produced for Card I and another W for Card III. For the most part, these are WP and not WO. If a subject is capable of uniting the diffusely plotted multicolored blots in Card II into a W, this represents an especially intelligent achievement, as long as it is a WO+ (not too rarely, schizophrenics also produce a W in Card II, but it is a WO−. For instance: "This is a colored sky"; "This is love"; "A toilet with excrement, bile, and blood").

The horizontal "scoring" of signs permits us to see at a glance for which card W were produced.

The production of many W+ always indicates people who distinguish themselves by a certain energetic associative activity. They have surprisingly good ideas, and are capable of organizing and arranging. They are usually characterized by an unconscious, often even a conscious, ambition for quality.

If the W+ are of an abstract nature (for instance, "crab," "bat," "toad," in Card I)—if the blot is conceived in its outlines all at once—then the subject is readily capable of conceptualizing and organizing abstractly; he thinks scientifically. If the W+ are more combinatory in character (for example, Card III: "Two men warming themselves in front of a fire"; or even: "Two wild creatures fighting over a piece of meat and they have torn off a slice and have thrown it behind them," in which all the blots of Card III are combined, composed into an interpretation), and furthermore if the record shows a large number of M responses and good original responses, then the subject must certainly possess artistic abilities of a productive and reproductive nature, often both. On the basis of other factors, it may then be usually determined which of the abilities predominate; in other words, whether one is dealing with an actively creative artist and in which artistic field he works or has talent.

If the majority of the W are not sharply seen (W—), this means that the need for unification is not supported by an adequately specified ability for its realization. The subject would really *like* to organize and to plan, but he is not capable of doing so. There is a lack of creative ability in his integrative capacity; his intellect is weak, dull (few responses; a small total number of responses). The indifferent person reacts in a similar manner (a great many or very few responses with a short reaction time), as do superficial and lazy people (high A% and a large number of P are added here). People who finish things fast, who are flighty, careless, and inconsiderate, belong in this category, as well as those "optimists" who like to take things "in one lump," and are not wholly reliable either in their thinking or in their work.

We shall now discuss a number of special cases of W interpretations; while these are given more rarely, they are extremely characteristic of the subjects in question.

Certain people are characterized in their W+ responses not only by combinations but also by their producing *"constructive W."* Upon being presented with Card II, for example: "There is a Chinese pagoda in the background. It is built of marble stone, and it is illuminated by the sun. Close by, there is a projection of bushes; in the foreground, a sandy, mushy path winds its way." One senses in such an interpretation an undoubted integrative creative ability; our attention is drawn to the perception of perspective. A marked ability to construct and to compose is characteristic of such subjects. Often engineers and architects react in such fashion, as well as painters, sculptors, and playwrights, or people with similar capabilities. These are people with much higher than average ability, as is corroborated by the other findings of the experiment. They are outstanding in creative tendency.

Still other subjects—usually, highly educated intellectuals—produce so-called "W impressions." For example, Card II: "These are rich midsummer colors; they arouse a festive impression"; or in Card I: "Something melancholy, sad, like fog or snow, an ice-flower, winter, cold." These subjects always give evidence of very differentiated moods. They are sensitive and impressionable, and focus upon the esthetic. Their capacity for empathy is quite high; they are refined and delicate in their behavior. If, however, there is an abundance of such W impressions in a record, then the subjects are hypersensitive: they often do not get down to doing things because of their moods, or they "talk away" everything in order not to let things come close to them, because of their painful sensitivity. They therefore appear over-intellectual and arid in their overall attitude, since they immediately find a word for every impulse, pinning down their emotions as if they were butterfly collectors, and killing them. They are reaction types; their skin being too thin, it is shielded by an intellect that tears everything apart.

W impressions should not be mistaken for "contaminated W." These are W responses in which a number of single impressions are condensed and brought into association with other impressions. A subject may glance at Card II and immediately remark: "The animals' Mardi Gras in Heaven." Asked how he ever arrived at this strange interpretation, he explains: "These are animals (subject points to the red outer blots), and here is the bear ditch (the subject indicates the orange and green areas), and here is the sky (the subject points to the inner white space at the upper rim of the card), and the bears are wearing red costumes." Not all subjects who produce contaminated W are capable of explaining later how they arrived at their response. Whether or not the subjects are able to offer an explanation, however, it is obvious that their thinking processes do not function altogether properly. Thus, although such subjects may seem to react strangely only because they have chosen to "make fun" of the examiner or the experiment, on the basis of their interpretations it must be deduced that their mental productivity is largely devious. In most cases, such individuals cannot be considered normal.

Confabulatory W (DW, DdW) are presented by subjects who are deceiving themselves about reality. Their observations are superficially formed, and they substitute fantasies for their deficiency in observation. These are people who like to indulge in self-deceit, who believe that what they have themselves imagined is objectively "true." Numerous DW are found in people who are inclined to confabulatory manipulations. They also occur frequently in the mentally retarded, as well as in flighty and boastful individuals, and in braggarts.

Subjects with DdW are always of inferior intelligence. Frequently, DdW appear in retarded children.

Subjects who produce SW or WS are in conflict with something that touches them deeply. Often they know what constitutes their contradictory impulse, which is more permanent than sporadic. They may be discontented with their profession, for instance; they believe that they have missed their vocation; they feel antagonistic toward their fate in that it allegedly has not conferred the right place in life on them; they are disappointed in their marriage partner; they oppose their parents or teachers; they think that they have been slighted like Cinderella, and react like a "Kohlhaas type."[1] Thus an abundance of SW and WS indicates subjects with a permanently hostile and depressive attitude, which has become an integral part of their personality. They are the pessimists, convinced that everything will turn out badly for them; they may also be people who are completely resigned to their fate.

WS are analogous to W. Ordinarily, an S is included in the response that is well perceived, as if it were a dark or colored blot. It is organically enclosed in the whole. On the other hand,

---

[1] Kleist, *Michael Kohlhaas.*

an SW corresponds more closely to a DW or DdW; it is formed by confabulation. The subject has perceived S accurately, and has then united the dark or colored blot with S into a confabulatory relationship. Here the dark or colored blots themselves are not well perceived, for the subject proceeded from S as he was giving the response.

From the point of view of a differentiated psychological diagnosis, it is essential to determine whether a response is WS or SW. WS are produced by people who try to conceal their feelings of hostility, their discontent, or even their intelligent and justified criticism. They disguise all of these for the sake of conciliation. Although their opposition may be directed toward their own self, "inward," in the form of self-criticism and self-doubt, these subjects do not show it externally. On the contrary, publicly they "pretend" to be sure of themselves, completely composed.

On the other hand, SW responses are given by individuals who persistently expect to find the proverbial "hair in the soup." On general principles, they face the external world with distrust, and tend to express their criticism loudly. They make an insurmountable mountain out of a molehill, and always see things and situations in a rather unfavorable, evil, imperfect light, never with an eye for the good. These are people who are not capable of "appreciating" anything. They look for an "if" and a "but" in every situation, even though their critical objections may be completely unjustified and there may be absolutely no grounds for criticism. Like DW and DdW, SW contain a confabulatory element.

DETAIL RESPONSES, D

A number of keenly perceived D+, accompanied by some M, lead us to the conclusion that there exists a well-formed sense for the evident, the objective and the tangible. People who are distinguished by "common sense," those who are neither generous nor petty, produce many D+ when tested with the form-interpretation test. Skilled craftsmen, for instance, as well as expert housewives and experienced mothers who are, however, without intellectual ambitions, may be D types.

If M is absent in D types, then these are the "petty official" types of personality. Such individuals are too "impractical" for regular artisan's work; they are much better suited for subordinate office work, such as (copying) typists perform, for example. Or they may fill the position of a registrar, work at selling in a store, or find employment in a factory, at a stamping machine, or on an assembly line.

D— are produced by less practical persons, and also by those of lesser ability, people who are dull in their thinking and acting. Not infrequently these people approach a task from its wrong end; they try to "tame a horse by its tail."

Unsophisticated and stereotyped individuals are prone to producing many D which are P at the same time.

SMALL DETAIL RESPONSES, Dd

A large number of Dd always points to the characteristic of adhering to the unessential (with the exception of industrious students under the age of 13; in their case, an abundance of Dd+ means conscious effort and ambition).

Professional people who must deal with minute objects—as, for instance, watchmakers, workers on precious stones, and dentists—produce many Dd+ (in addition to W). It seems that Dd+ indicate an interest in small things. These people are exact, conscientious, and dependable, even in the smallest matters.

A large number of D— appears in absent-minded people, or in those who are greedy in a petty way. It is also present in pedantic persons, as well as in those who perpetually claim to know everything better, or in nagging and petty individuals.

Some exceptions follow:

If there is a tendency to combine Dd+ and Do into D+, that indicates anxious and indecisive individuals.

A mixture of Dd+ and Dd—, perceived similarly as to their size, form, and sequence, is found in mental defectives and in retarded individuals of every possible degree.

Where there exist many Dd+ and Dd— of unequal size and form, in a confused sequence, the subject's entire prognosis must become a matter for concern. For frequently these people are altogether unpredictable in their mental and emotional behavior. They are unstable, flighty, and cannot be depended on. It would be, for instance, an extremely precarious and dubious undertaking to advise them on the basis of a psychological examination. Since a fully normal person does not react as they do, it would be best to refer them to a psychiatrist, should they need psychological advice. Not infrequently, such individuals are schizophrenics.

OLIGOPHRENIC DETAIL RESPONSES, Do

The term "oligophrenic ("feeble-minded") is somewhat unfortunate, since one might be tempted to rate subjects with Do as if they were mentally retarded.

Some mentally retarded subjects do produce Do (but not all oligophrenics do so). Moreover, one should never draw the conclusion that mental retardation is present on the basis of Do alone, since some highly intelligent people may present Do in a form-interpretation test.

Do are either the symptoms for an attitude of anxious apprehension and uneasiness, or else they reflect an inability to grasp large relationships.

Some isolated Do, together with an orderly or rigid sequence and a high F+%, are presented by intelligent individuals who are given to self-distrust and are "afraid of their own courage."

Do with an inverse sequence are found in cautious, mistrustful persons.

Pedants produce many Do and Dd, along with isolated W or no W at all.

Several Do, together with very few or no color responses, indicate an anxiously depressed basic disposition.

SPACE RESPONSES, S

More than 1–2 S in 15 responses is too large a number. They suggest the presence of emotionally determined antagonism. This becomes all the more apparent, the fewer M are present and the more CF.

One to 2 S is characteristic of the ability to assert one's opinion firmly, to think critically, and to be capable of looking at "the other side of things."

Several S, in combination with an extratensive experience balance, are produced by people with a strongly pronounced impetuous willfulness, to which they give the external expression that is consistent with their own temperament and vitality. These are the "fault-finders"; they may be aggressive. If they are intellectuals, then they have the tendency to debate endlessly every problem.

If they are endowed with superior intelligence, they may become excellent lawyers—but only if they produce in addition several M and more FC than CF (introversion; the inner ability for circumspection, including circumspection directed towards oneself), and if furthermore they possess adaptive tendencies.

If several S appear, in combination with an introversive experience balance, the subjects have extreme doubts as to their own personality, their own "productive sphere of activity." These people are characterized by a lack of confidence, an inability to make decisions. They are haunted by mistrust concerning themselves, and by hesitancy. They belong in the category of people with perennial bad luck, and are tormented by feelings of inferiority. Frequently these people, after making an excellent start, discover all too soon that their endeavors have evaporated into thin air. They are plagued by the painful question: "Is it possible for me to accomplish anything at all?", and they abandon all their energetic efforts prematurely, disregarding the fact that they will still need them in order to succeed. Among the artistically gifted, they are the "inwardly inhibited" ones.

The presence of several S and pure C in a record indicates individuals who are hot-tempered, who constantly keep themselves in readiness for arguments and fist fights. They are quarrelsome and belligerent.

In ambiequal experience types, several S indicate simultaneous hostility toward both the inner and outer worlds. Usually, such people grumble against themselves, as well as against the external world around them. They are pessimists who "predicted that misfortune a long time ago."

Among *young* children (4-8 years old), one must employ caution in evaluating S responses. Among them are subjects who are actually in no way more obstinate than their peers, even though they do produce a great many S.

Children often use the white inner spaces in some kind of stereotypy and occasionally for perseveration. For instance, having discovered in Card I that S may also be interpreted, with each new card they are on the alert for more of them. With small children, it is the low number of S that warns the examiner about the possibility of antagonistic attitudes, such as stubbornness, resistance, reticence, etc.

In cases in which all signs and factor relationships point to superior intelligence, it follows almost "causally" that some S must occur as well. They are the indicators of the subject's critical thinking and self-criticism.

When all other signs point to mental deficiency, and there are some S present, a basically "hostile" attitude is suggested. These subjects are easily irritated and, being provoked, tend to open defiance and acts of violence—especially if their test shows some pure C.

There are some subjects who combine S with D or Dd. This is carried out in a manner very similar to that of people with SW and WS.

Some examples follow:

Card II, b-position: "A woman is sitting on a patch of lawn wearing a baggy skirt." S is seen in combination with the green blot. I would score this: DSMsCF Sc O.

Card II, a-position: "A dove flying through reddish evening clouds." This subject has been more strongly affected by S. The "reddish evening cloud" is added by confabulation. I score: SD CF A/cloud.

The confabulatory element is even more clearly expressed in the following response to Card III: "A lady walking through the night." The "lady" is the S between the two dark blots (EF 3/4); the "night" has been perceived because of the dark background. The score is: SD MCh Sc O.

Subjects who produce SD or DS strive for and have a potential for combination. Those who produce DS responses think more clearly and observe more keenly than those who offer SD (compare with the difference between WS and SW).

A person who produces WS and DS responses is trying to manage his opposition tendencies somehow, and to make an effort not to show them to the external world (if that is possible). Subjects who produce SW and SD, however, tend to hunt everywhere for things that may be criticized. They are the people who nag, are distrustful, like to quarrel.

FIGURE-GROUND FUSION (BOHM)

Among others, Ewald Bohm has paid special attention to the above variety of responses. Here inner white spaces (S) are treated as if they did not exist at all; they are placed on the same plane as all other colored blots. Therefore, figure-ground fusion must be differentiated from ordinary SW, WS, or DS responses, in which the white inner spaces as such have been observed by the subjects and have contributed to their responses. The following responses to Card II, c-position, represent figure-gound fusion, for instance: "A bull's head," "An aurochs," "Head of a monster." Responses such as these are found most frequently among children, people with intuition, and artists, as well as among epileptics and schizophrenics. Originally, Hermann Rorschach had noted them. He thought them unusual, and saw a wish or anxiety fantasy hidden behind them. In one of his unpublished test evaluations, he made the following statement with regard to such a response, produced by a subject in Card X of the Ro ("monster with yellow eyes"):

"One of the last responses, namely the monster with yellow eyes, is typically infantile. It is quite obvious that, in a person with such large experience balance (8 M : 2 FC : 2 CF : pure C tendency), such impulsive affectivity would be permeated with infantile propensities. Yet the residue of these infantile elements seems to be the condition for uninhibited intuition. The fact that he (the subject) designates it as a 'monster' signifies, perhaps, that the subject does not want to acknowledge the existence of infantilism in himself or refuses to exhibit it to his environment. . . ."

Bohm believes that figure-ground fusion is a complex response, in some way connected with the deepest layers of man's unconscious mind.

According to my own experience, such responses represent primordial anxieties. Either they are expressed in totemistic fantasy creations (for example, "an aurochs" in Card II, c-position, Zulliger Test) or, after they have become further transformed, one figure representing anxiety is replaced by another, antithetical one. A subject interpreted Card II, c-position, Zulliger Test, as "Moses' head." When the subject was later questioned as to how he had arrived at this response, he answered: "Moses led the Jewish people out of Egyptian oppression and bondage over the Red Sea and into the Holy Land!" Thus Moses was perceived as the liberator from fear and peril, and became the antithetical figure to the anxiety figure of a "bull's head."

Furthermore, the totem animal always occupies an ambivalent position in the minds of primitive peoples, who still live at a totemistic developmental stage. It is simultaneously feared and loved adoringly. It destroys its followers and, at the same time, protects them. Therefore, in an interpretation such as "aurochs" or "bull's head," metaphoric expression is given not only to physical fear, but also to liberation from it. The totemistic "aurochs" symbol contains both impulses—that of fear, as well as that which is directed towards the liberation from fear.

All this is not exact knowledge, since we can rely only on analogies derived from anthropology and depth psychology, or on the slightly more thoroughly studied responses of figure-ground fusion, and the generalizations drawn from them. These findings should be verified by further experimental data.

E. THE DETERMINANTS

FORM RESPONSES, F AND F+%

F+% is the criterion for the accuracy of engrams and for sharp and rational thinking. We obtain in

pedantics and individuals of superior intelligence	very intelligent or highly intelligent individuals	individuals of medium to average intelligence	individuals of low intelligence, careless, gay, shallow, mentally confused or feeble-minded
100%	90% and more	90-70%	70-65-40%

KINESTHETIC RESPONSES, MOVEMENT RESPONSES, M, Ms

M are the criteria for inner personality factors (introversive powers and capabilities), and for creative imagination.

Numerous M are characteristic of introverts, of circumspect, reflective, prudent individuals, and of individuals who behave rather awkwardly, who do not move quickly and are phlegmatic. M types always possess creative powers, although these may remain latent and unable to be realized and utilized. Under certain circumstances, they may be introverted to such a degree as not to be capable of taking a work of art, for instance, "out of themselves," of "liberating" it from their own self. It remains in their imagination and never reaches the stage of an externally tangible manifestation.

In addition to poor motility, introversive characteristics include equally limited motility needs. They show a rather phlegmatic attitude, a strong tendency toward intense observation and contemplation, and an internally oriented reactivity. The inner experience is more important to them than the need for expression; there is a higher degree of intensive than extensive rapport. The formation of new friendships and relationships is difficult for them, while human ties of long duration prevail. There is a tendency to experience the world passively, and an inclination to pessimistic mood changes.

Flexor kinesthesias are responses in which a moving figure is perceived as bending, almost rolling inward. For example, in Card III: "Two men bending over a fire." Flexor kinesthesias imply a tendency to a rather passive attitude of "enduring" one's environment. One "retires into oneself," one "hides in a snail's house." Usually such responses are characteristic of people who autistically "nurse their own fantasies." People with flexor kinesthesias are less easily influenced by others than those who produce extensor kinesthesias (see below). Children with flexor kinesthesias prove to be more difficult to raise (which does not mean that they are problem children; nevertheless, it does mean that educators may not be able to find an approach to them without a great deal of difficulty). Individuals with flexor kinesthesias tend to become secluded, isolated; a great many of these people are either morose or eccentric.

Extensor kinesthesias are responses in which figures, perceived in motion, stretch themselves as if they were growing out of themselves. There is, for example, the following response to Card III: "Men pointing to something with their hand," or "Men threatening each other with their fists," etc. Highly active individuals produce extensor movement responses, as do creative persons with a rather aggressive basic disposition. These are enterprising human beings. They try to "come out of" themselves; they are ambitious; they have the desire to fulfill themselves.

All kinesthetically oriented people are intensively rather than extensively affected by suggestions. It is easier to influence people with extensor kinesthesias than those with flexor kinesthesias.

M have a stabilizing effect upon affectivity. Highly intelligent people with kinesthetic responses perceive forms accurately; yet they produce only a small number of original responses (M+ and O+). On the other hand, inhibited people with many M are more successful in producing original responses. The difference is based upon the instinctive attitudes of the two different human categories: the highly intelligent individual habitually activates his thinking, his acute mental processes, his "functioning in reality,"while the inhibited individual activates his inner self, the introversive content of his experience apparatus. He is fixed in the principle of wish-fulfillment and not very well adjusted to reality. He is ignorant of the world, a dreamer. Kinesthetic responses often reveal the deepest unconscious attitudes, especially if they are original responses. Frequently they are self-portraits. Most "individual" responses are at the same time M.

Precision and quality workers need to possess introversive tendencies.

If an M implies a *dual meaning*—such as, for instance, in this response to Card III: "Two men want to extend their hands to each other *or* they are both withdrawing"—it signifies hiding, a concealing tendency toward one's own inner self. While such subjects give of themselves freely to the outer world, they "shy away" from their own inner depths. They refuse to think about themselves and try to overcome by an extreme amount of activity the impulse that is driving them to it. The same may be said of individuals who repress their M (individuals, for instance, who instead of M produce F or Do responses or, in Card III, replace "men" and "jumping boys" by some caricatures).

Unusual M responses are found in intuitive and artistic persons with manifold talents. At times, their tests show M combined with color responses. Consequently, these become MC, as, for instance, in Card II, red area: *"Two dancing girls wearing red dresses."* The experience of such people includes both extremely intense introversive and extraversive tendencies. It is of the "dionysian" kind.

Similarly, intuition exists when a subject produces WF+ and WM responses with ease and skill. Kinesthetic, combinatory, constructive, and abstract abilities are in effect here. They alternate freely and occur haphazardly in many diversified forms, thus permitting these subjects to produce some of the responses mentioned above with extraordinary speed.

Some of the MC responses are produced in combination with *body sensations.* For instance, in Card III: "Two poor, freezing chimney-sweeps in rags, warming themselves in front of a fire." We must acknowledge that subjects with such responses are prone to occasional outbursts of enthusiasm, which lead to emphatic and ecstatic states.

"Happy-go-lucky" types, and people with many talents, produce a balanced mixture of M and FC. Several M, in addition to only a few FC and no further color responses, make these subjects outstanding for their serene, contemplative attitude, which permits them to look upon the world without ever becoming perturbed.

In Card III, a completely normal individual produces WM+ HP or DM+ HP; emotionally tense persons, on the other hand, usually produce WF, DF, or even Do. Frequently we notice that the latter hesitate when they are confronted with cards that suggest kinesthetic responses. Rorschach spoke in cases such as these of an "M repression." Loosli-Usteri used the term *le choc kinesthétique* in characterizing this phenomenon, evaluating it in the same manner as a color or chiaroscuro shock. People who show M repression in the form-interpretation test latch tight onto everything visual and auditory during the course of the experiment, just as they do in real life. They mistrust their own inner self, but not so much their intelligence as their affectivity. They are afraid of their unconscious forces, expecting harm and distress from them. Consequently, they persist in a state of instinctive defense against their fantasies, warding off their creative qualities and preventing both from becoming effective. Frequently M repression is clearly evident in adolescents who are oppressed by sexual fantasies and are struggling to repulse them.

M repression may also occur in subjects who experienced an intensive color shock when Card II was presented to them. As a result, they cannot produce kinesthetic responses to Card III, of if they do produce them, it is only after having given 2–3 other responses first. Because of the emotional irritation caused by Card II, they become subject to a temporary inhibition of their mental processes.

Frequently, M repression is encountered in introversive persons who are engaged in an "extraversive" profession.

The so-called "secondary, poor M," which are evaluated as M—, occur when a subject who is familiar with the technique of the experiment tries very hard to see in all cards as many M as possible. Otherwise, M— are found only in individuals who are in a state of agitated gaiety or in those who are slightly intoxicated, alcoholics, or epileptics. If one desires to find out about M— and to understand their origin, one may observe them very clearly in epileptics, who will contemplate a card and then begin to twist their body until they have found the position that they imagine corresponds to the card's picture. Finally, much relieved, they proceed to interpret the M that they have found.

Feeble-minded subjects often lie about having experienced kinesthetic perceptions. In this respect, they behave as they do when they lie about F; later, they are not able to show the examiner the spot on the card where they have seen one or the other response.

Further reference to M and their relationships with other factors of the experiment will be found in the section on experience balance.

Ms must be differentiated from *M*. This differentiation was originally introduced by Behn-Eschenburg. The content formulation of Ms clearly suggests that subjects who produce them are inclined to elaboration and ornamentation: they are fond of details and of fabulation. Frequently they offer responses that describe miniature animated scenes, often with fairy-tale motives. Such desire for fabulation, which finds its expression in Ms, is more closely related to imagination than it is to confabulation. It signifies pleasure derived from relating fantasies. It is an act of "abreaction of kinesthetic sensations," and thus does not indicate a potential for imaginative creation as such (thus it is necessary to distinguish between Ms and M). As a rule subjects with Ms produce M as well; nevertheless, there are people who offer Ms but not M.

COLOR RESPONSES, C, CF, FC

Pure C are rare in normal subjects. When they occur, they must be understood in terms of highly egocentric affectivity. They are found in very impulsive, "explosive," impressionable individuals, as well as in reckless people and people who become easily but passingly enthusiastic about certain things. More than one C is a warning signal: subjects with several C are unpredictable, as the result of their egocentricity. They lack understanding for their fellow man, for anything living and outside themselves. They behave as if nobody exists but *they* alone. Depending on their mood, they may be extremely sentimental, almost bursting with enthusiasm at one moment, yet emotionally completely uninvolved at another, acting as if they did not care for anybody or anything except themselves. If the form-interpretation test of such individuals shows more than two, or perhaps several S responses, then they are quick-tempered. Under the impact of their feelings of hate, they are quite capable of committing some "foolishness," or even a criminal act.

The number of CF responses is a criterion for affectivity that has not been adapted and is not adaptable, although there does exist a willingness for adaptation. CF types are also egocentric human beings, although to a lesser degree than C types. Every variety of self-centered behavior may be discovered in them. They are irritable, sensitive, enthusiastic, impressionable. At one moment, they may be "happy as a lark"; at another, "down deep in the dumps." They are moody and an easy prey to suggestions (although not lastingly). They regard themselves as the center of the world, and try to treat their fellow human beings as their servants. They would like to be loved, yet they do not love anybody except themselves, with a "narcissistic" love.

On the other hand, the number of FC responses indicates adapted and adaptable affectivity in a measure and proportion that correspond to all the other color factors. This means that emotion is adjusted to reality: it is appropriate to the realistic occurrence or experience that causes such emotion. Grief and anger, as well as desire, joy, etc., are proportionate to the significance of the given situation. There is neither emotional dullness nor exaggeration. FC suggests direct, natural, authentic adaptation; it is straight-forward, without intellectual elaboration, and thus different from all forced and more or less artificial *pseudo-adaptation* (on the basis of "proper" education and training, for instance).

Direct naming or enumerating of colors, as, for instance: "Here is red, here green . . . ," etc., is never found in individuals with normal intelligence. It occurs, however, in feeble-minded persons who wish to impress the examiner with their knowledge of colors. Normal young children may react very similarly: they too are proud of being able to communicate to the examiner their familiarity with colors, and they do not want to miss this opportunity to do so. Color naming may also occur in epileptics. In the majority of cases, a response such as "a red butterfly" to Card III, for example, hardly suggests an FC response, but rather an F+ response. Here the color designation has the significance of an orienting or descriptive characterization. The subject wishes to indicate to the examiner the blot that he is interpreting, by naming its color. The subject may even have the more or less pedantic desire to make a statement about the red color intimating that, in reality, *he* has never observed butterflies of this color. Rorschach has stated that such responses indicate "a diluted or dutiful adaptation." After having completed the record, the examiner must often try to establish by inquiry whether or not a response has been affected by color admixtures.

People with primitive impulsivity almost "plunge" into the red blots. On the other hand, some other subjects show a conspicuous "red shyness." They are rather partial to the orange and green colors. Their attitude may have been determined in one of two ways: either calmly and naturally, or tensely. In the former case, they are human beings who have trained themselves to appear emotionally well-balanced and are consequently self-controlled; in the latter case, they are individuals who have succeeded only partly in achieving such self-control. As a result, their conscious affectivity control is somewhat constrained.

Individuals who show a special likeness for the orange blots have succeeded in taming their affects with the aid of their mental and intellectual mechanisms.

An absence of color responses, only a few WF, and some very keenly perceived forms are characteristic of human beings whose affectivity is extremely restricted. Their basic disposition is sober, arid, formalistic. They are not energetic, although they are industrious. Quite often, they are sorely distressed by some experience that has left a permanent mark upon them.

Absence of color responses and inaccurate perception of forms are indicative or individuals who are apathetic, inactive, or feeble-minded.

Subjects who are without color responses but show many varied WF+ are capable of skillful abstraction, strongly associative combinations, and well-joined constructions. At the same time, this picture may be characteristic of those who are pessimists, not as the result of some sad experience, but by nature. Such subjects are also phlegmatic and may be fond of solipsistic ideas and speculations.

A record with several FC, one CF, no C, in addition to a high F+%, suggests individuals who are capable of a good rapport. It is easy to approach them; they are vivacious but not fickle. Although they are easily distracted, such persons show presence of mind and are capable of concentration. They are energetic rather than industrious.

Several diversified color responses and a low F+% are characteristic of subjects who are thoughtless, unstable, quick-witted but superficial, agitatedly gay, and given to confabulation.

Several color responses (primarily FC), in addition to numerous diversified WF, are produced by people whose associative activity functions with great energy. They handle mental and imaginative processes skillfully, and they possess a strong need for unifying and generalizing ideas. They maintain a "sanguine" position in all real-life situations.

Many FC, one CF, many DF+, and few WF+ indicate individuals with a very active personality structure: they adjust easily; they are quick, energetic, effective, prompt; they are the "practical opportunists."

It seems that subjects who perceive S as a color (they see white as C) are human beings with great sensitivity and inner vulnerability. Making an effort to cover up these traits, they often appear quite consciously rough and irritable in their behavior. In this way, they try to protect themselves from their own "inner peril." In any event, during a period of many years, I have time and again seen this diagnostic value of SC confirmed in children and adolescents.

Further references concerning C, in terms of its relationship to other factors, are to be found in the chapter dealing with experience balance and color shock.

CHIAROSCURO RESPONSES, F (C), (C)F, Ch

Rorschach made the distinction between F (C) and (C)F, or between those chiaroscuro responses in which form has been more accurately F (C) or less accurately (C)F perceived.

He spoke of the following diagnostic values: these were persons with a generally depressed affectivity, often individuals who *pretend* to have attained a better affective rapport than is actually true. They are subjects who have consciously "tamed" their instincts. Their affectivity rapport is characterized by intense participation of the intellect. People who produce conspicuous chiaroscuro interpretations conceal important *complex symptoms* within the content of their responses. These complex symptoms appear in the form of *corrections* or *wish-*

fulfillments. In cases in which chiaroscuro responses are conceived as architectural landscapes, castles and towers, temples and archways, one may indeed conclude: "This subject feels himself to be going to pieces inwardly. He is in disharmony with himself; he believes himself to be weak, 'out of harmony.' Thus he projects his feelings in the form of wish-fulfillments onto buildings and highways, temples and archways that he has constructed or rather interpreted." An exceptional vision for space, as well as for depth and distance, and three-dimensional understanding, lead us to the quite certain conclusion (assuming that we find them to be O+), that there exists a fine ability for spatial perception and a talent for constructive planning. This is correlated with certain feelings of insufficiency. A sense of instability and inconsistency, a feeling of "going to pieces"— these are the fundamental features of such contents. Affectivity is here characterized by a slightly fearful, self-protective and somewhat depressive orientation.

The more F (C) approach (C)F, the more the characteristics described above become apparent within a subject's general attitude. The talent for constructive planning lessens with the increase of (C)F.

In his very meritorious essay, Binder has not only made an attempt to *substantiate our form-interpretation experiment theoretically,* at least to some extent, but has also devoted a detailed study to *chiaroscuro responses and their diagnostic significance.*

To begin with, he differentiates F (C) from Ch.

As we have already mentioned, F (C) are interpretations in which the various delineated portions of a dark-gray blot have stimulated the response. For the most part, these are D. The various shadings are sharply delineated; yet, as in combinatory responses, they are blended together into a broader context.

On the other hand, Ch responses are primarily whole responses. They are effected by the total sensory impression, based on the blot's gray tonality. Frequently, larger D stimulate such Ch responses.

For instance, the following is an authentic Ch in Card I: *"This here is a cloudy, foggy formation."* .

Binder subdivides F (C) into two varieties. In order to differentiate between them while recording, one must pay attention to *emotional emphasis,* which may be tinged by either pleasure or unpleasure. In those cases in which blot perception is determined by "emotional signs of pleasure," responses frequently contain lovingly described and intimate landscape images, which suggest an idyllic atmosphere. Often there also occur finely shaped human and animal heads, which may strike the subject as being either appealing or amusing. Next the subject proceeds to interpret imposing buildings, describing them with ease, and observing all the shadings with care. Finally, he offers some responses pertaining to cuddly material and to varieties of fur which he seems to enjoy greatly. Some examples follow: Card III, lower dark blot: "A hare would like to play with his young. But it has slipped into the stovepipe."

Card I, c-position, top left: "The head of a good-natured farmer who is wearing a transparent nightcap."

Such responses are *indicators of a loving and pleasure-accented peripheral and sophropsychic emotional readiness.* They indicate an intimately obliging and gently submissive adaptation of the kind that may be found in normally sensitive people. People like these are distinguished by their capacity for devotion, their gentleness, pliant kindness, tact, etc. They are capable of establishing a differentiated syntonic rapport; theirs is the quality of a "fingertip sensitivity." Yet they are not artificially hypersensitive in their inner participation. They are lovingly devoted to individuality and to detail. They enjoy chiefly the intimate fine points of art and nature, and to a very high degree.

Other subjects, too, search in the dark blots for distinctly shaded and sharply delineated parts, which they then interpret as "serious trees," "gloomy towers," etc. However, these are F (C) that have not been perceived within a "pleasure-accented emotional state." For instance, Card I, b-position, at the very top: "In front of a small windblown fir tree, across a snow-covered flower field, a bear is advancing toward a wild boar."

Such responses represent cautiously conscientious absorption of sensory impressions. These impressions are related to *peripheral emotions, with slight depressive and anxiety traces; they are formed by strongly predominating and finely modulated sophropsychic control tendencies.* The adaptation to the environment is awkward, cautious, painfully conscientious and group-oriented, fearful and timid. Self-control approaches self-concealment. Rapport is a mixture of a good-natured warmth and a sensibly engaging attitude, implemented by a somewhat sluggish temperament.

A distinctly different mode of perception and a different "stratum" of emotional reactivity form the basis for *Ch responses.* Invariably they suggest that a *basic emotion* is at play, that a mood reaction has taken place. Both make themselves felt when an authentic total impression has been experienced as emanating from a fundamental stimulus.

F (C) responses are characterized by the fact that an isolated blot area has been viewed with an attitude that aims at perceiving every single detail. Thus, each conspicuous individual shading is set off separately, and interpreted according to its delineating form and chiaroscuro value. Each particular light- or dark-shaded area is treated as a shading of color. On the other hand, in Ch responses, the shadings of a dark-gray card are perceived as diffuse variations. Since they are of uniform quality, they represent valid whole impressions. By perseveration, they finally extend to the details of the blots as well (provided that details are interpreted and not W).

By taking Ch responses into account and differentiating between them, one may examine the *reaction capacity* of a subject's *basic emotions.* Ch responses are related to *dysphoric mood reactions.* The less the responses lean upon accurately perceived forms in approaching pure Ch impressions, the stronger and more inclusive are these mood reactions.

We differentiate as follows:

FCh: These are Ch responses in which form has been accurately perceived.

Symptomatic value: The subject does not wish to be "carried away." He controls his moods sophropsychically, and his control mechanism is highly differentiated.

When a subject produces three and more FCh+, for instance, we may assume that dysphoric mood changes, which represent either a labile or prolonged condition, are characteristic of him. They are troublesome for the subject, in that they cannot be concealed from his environment. Nevertheless, the subject makes every effort to keep himself under control.

ChF: These are Ch-responses in which the form has been less accurately perceived, although traces of form still remain.

Diagnostic value: failure of the sophropsychic control mechanism. Mental processes do not function with sufficient differentiation. Subjects with these symptoms have the desire to control and to adapt themselves, yet they are incapable of realizing this desire or else succeed only partly in doing so. They are governed by depressive, essentially dysphoric moods.

Pure Ch: These are Ch responses which (by analogy with the "pure" C in color responses) are produced without any reference to form. However, they must be differentiated from intellectual descriptions (such as, for instance: *"The whole thing is gray, blotted down in gray."* Card I). The following responses are pure Ch, for example: *"Foggy stuff," "Dirty water,"* etc.

Diagnostic evaluation: Subjects with "pure" Ch responses succumb to depressive moods to an extreme degree; they possess pronounced depressive tendencies. They are soft and impressionable by nature, being mournfully poetic and sorrowfully romantic. They try to escape from the world that surrounds them, although their disposition is rather calm. Distant journeys are characteristic daydreams for them.

Binder differentiates three *dysphoria forms* with corresponding reactions:

a. Anxious dysphoria ➔ readiness to escape
b. Depressive dysphoria ➔ readiness to become paralyzed
c. Irritable dysphoria ➔ readiness for aggression

The presence of one to two FCh responses occurring in a test, in addition to several different color responses (for instance, 3 FC, 1 CF, and about 15-20 responses), warrant the conclusion that qualities of slyness are present, especially if the subjects are youths or adolescents. These subjects appear to be affectionate and kind; they are charming in their external behavior; they carefully test every situation beforehand in order to behave properly, and wherever they go one can observe the effects of their "good breeding." They *know* how to behave. Yet, affectively, they are one step behind this knowledge. They are aware of this discrepancy and are therefore slightly depressed, unless they succeed in keeping themselves in steady readiness, prepared to take advantage of their partner, to subjugate him. By seeming to be servile, they manage to turn an unsophisticated stronger individual into their servant. They convert everything to their own advantage. If there also appears some S, then we may be sure that these subjects are secretly vindictive and react with resentment.

ChC and CCh: Subjects who produce ChC responses tend to be guided by depressive reactions, "losing their heads" as a result, since they do not fight these reactions but assume a passive attitude toward them.

Subjects with CCh are individuals who make an attempt to tame and adapt their moods and emotions (in terms of FC). They strive not to become subdued by their moods; they wish to control themselves; and they would like to remain self-controlled, instead of "losing their heads." They want to give themselves over to their ideas, to surrender to their own conscious desires.

COLOR SHOCK AND CHIAROSCURO SHOCK

The reaction of hesitancy, which occurs upon the presentation of the colored cards (Rorschach defined this as "color shock,") is rather infrequently expressed by some definite verbal remarks. For instance: *"These colors! I do not like them at all!" "Well!"* or, after a lengthy indecision: *"These colors, see here now, they have really selected them quite well to harmonize with each other!"* (In the last case, the original rejection, the fright at the sight of the colors, the brief confusion of associative processes effected by the colors have all been mentally absorbed, and therefore the remark sounds "appreciative." However, one should not commit the error of overlooking the original emotional condition by assuming that a color shock has not occurred, on the grounds that the subject "definitely does not reject the colors. On the contrary, he has found them appealing!" The very fact that the subject has allowed himself to become diverted from the task of interpreting the blots and, instead of a response, has produced a description or some similar statement, clearly indicates that the appearance of colors has inhibited the free flow of his associations and has caused a conflict—namely a color shock).

Much more frequently "masked color shock" shows itself in a stupor that lasts for a more or less prolonged period of time, and a suspension of associations, caused by the colors. In other words, it is suggested by some other indications, and the examiner must be capable of recognizing a masked color shock.

At this point, I should like to describe a few of the various attitudes encountered in subjects, which may help us in the determination of a masked color shock. At the same time, we must add that frequently color shock cannot be positively recognized on the basis of one *single* indication alone. It can be established only by referring to an entire *group of phenomena* all of which point to the fact that color shock has been experienced. These phenomena are listed below:

a. prolonged reaction time, upon presentation of the colored Card II;

b. rejecting or confused gestures or facial expressions, such as sighs, contemptuous movements of the hand, wrinkling of the forehead, head-shaking, etc.;

c. change in the sequence of the modi of perception—especially, avoiding color blots by interpreting white inner spaces (S);

d. M responses cease, although originally they were produced freely (for the dark-gray card);

e. initial rejectors: the subject asserts that he is not capable of doing anything with the colored card. Only after being prodded does the subject succeed in producing a response;

f. sudden deterioration of form accuracy which, at the onset, was adequate;

g. obvious decrease in the number of responses for the colored card, making the sum of responses produced for this card smaller than one-third of the total number of responses. (Therefore, in evaluating, we note not only the total number of responses, but also the number of responses produced specifically for the colored card.) If the subject holds on to Card II, after having hesitated initially, we may also take this as reason to suspect the presence of color shock. After finally giving a response, these subjects produce many more responses, and are reluctant to surrender the card; they try to cover up the previous inhibition of their associative process;

h. clearly exclamations of embarrassment, upon being presented with Card II or III; "This is a bloody affair!" (because of the red color); or merely "blood," "blood stains," accompanied by a tone of voice or a facial expression that reveals the embarrassment caused by the sight of blood;

i. W are missing in Card III. Instead of a WM, a DF or some Do are produced.

Rorschach found that subjects who produce a color shock invariably "repress their affectivity."

Naturally, the form-interpretation test provides still other signs that indicate repression of affectivity in these particular subjects. Not every individual with repressed affectivity reveals that fact by color shock. A similar psychodiagnostic "value" may be ascribed to "chiaroscuro shock," which frequently replaces color shock. (Binder has made this point.) Chiaroscuro shock is expressed in a manner similar to color shock: by embarrassment, hesitancy, impoverishment of associations for Card I.

It is not possible, except in a minority of cases, to make a definite statement about the psychological and personality effects of affectivity repression, solely on the basis of an existing color or a chiaroscuro shock. For this purpose, a number of other indices must be present in the form-interpretation test. *Experience balance* must be especially taken into account.

In general, it may be said that individuals with "affectivity repression" make a conscious or unconscious effort to protect themselves against anxiety. These individuals may be "afraid of life," or else fear the demands that life, or their environment,

111

makes upon them. They may be afraid of the responsibilities they must carry. Such fears may also imply fear of one's own inner self, of the "dark, inner, unconscious elements of life itself." Anxiety may manifest itself simply as anxiety, or else it may become converted until it cannot even be recognized any longer. When this is the case, then only an exact psychological analysis can once again uncover anxiety.

There are people who evade everything that may in some way trigger their affective reactions; they are afraid of their own affects, or rather of their violence, which may cause danger. These are the people who, according to Rorschach, "shy away from emotions." Within a form-interpretation test, they are characterized by a color or chiaroscuro shock of the following variety: their responses seem flighty and fantastic.

Persons with "affectivity control" behave differently. When they are confronted with the colored card, their responses grow less numerous. Moreover, the subjects avoid interpreting the red blots, and instead show a great liking for the orange and green areas.

It is interesting to note that mentally retarded subjects of all categories do not reveal shock effects in the form-interpretation test. This may be explained by the fact that such individuals do not repress their affects at all. The absence of color shock in mentally retarded subjects may be of importance to the examiner who is administering the form-interpretation test. For instance, a pupil may have been brought to the examiner for testing because, on the basis of his performance, his teachers believed him to be retarded. If there appears a definite color shock, or its equivalent, in the form-interpretation test of such a person, in addition to a F+% amounting to over 75, then the examiner may rest assured that the subject's mental inhibition is caused by something other than inferior or deficient learning ability. The examiner is then in a position to advise both parents and teachers to send their "pseudo-retarded" child to a specialist. The task of the specialist now becomes to remove the emotional causes of the child's "stupidity." (As a rule, students like these also present several Do in their form-interpretation test. This phenomenon too is indicative of the fact that unnatural embarrassment, timidity, anxiety, and other similar traits —perhaps, even a neurosis—are inhibiting the child's intelligence and his attitude toward life.)

Some subjects do not produce a color shock initially. However, after they have been presented with the colored card, they suddenly begin to offer abstract, conceptual, and symbolic responses (originally, they had given only concrete and good responses). People in this category have at their disposal a talent, which they have carefully cultivated and trained, for transforming their disturbing emotions by sublimation. At least within the realm of the abstract, they succeed in adapting to reality their non-adaptable egocentric emotions. They "cultivate" emotional control with the assistance of intellectual or esthetic aloofness, and thereby transform their original emotions into abstract, secondary, greatly diluted, and watered-down emotional reactions. These, then, are presented in a humorless manner, merely as statements and definitions of experiences. An immediate emotional reaction is no longer experienced. Instead of "experiencing," there is only contemplating and registering. (At the opposite extreme, we find those subjects, driven by instincts and emotions, who almost "plunge" themselves into the red blots without any inhibition and color shock. For instance, in Card II they immediately discover: "Beefsteaks," "Slices of ham," and more of the same.)

When a color shock occurs in the third card, indicating that it has been "delayed" (coming to the surface, for example, with an exclamation such as "Hey, this red does not match the other one!" or some other shock symptom), it characterizes human beings who are distinguished by a certain insecurity in their emotional reactions. They are embarrassed because they fear that their emotions may "run away" with them (Rorschach). We recognize in them an impulse directed toward control. As soon as their affectivity comes into play, they strive to "come to their senses." In addition to colors, they are also disturbed by the diffuseness of the entire configuration of Card II. This reaction corresponds with a strong need for completeness and uniformity, symmetry and compactness. On the other hand, such need for stability in oneself is again related to the more

113

or less strong feeling of inner insecurity, lability, inconstancy. In general, the search for symmetry and stability is closely linked with the fear of impulsiveness, formlessness, and emotional insecurity, which loom uncannily.

A subject who pays attention to symmetry and makes a statement about it, or who, in Card I, for instance, becomes irritated by the symmetry of the "skull" (top center), is searching for stability because he is tormented by the feeling that, within himself, he does not have any stability, or only very little of it.

People with artistic talent frequently try to communicate their own impression, their own *emotional reaction*, instead of producing a color shock: "The colors are fragrant, delicate," etc. They are impressionable and express reactively their emotional instability and impulsiveness; they are used to paying active attention to the interplay of their emotions. In this fashion, they seek to transform and control them, while other more ordinary subjects display a more passive attitude toward emotional experience.

If a definite color shock occurs in Card II or III, in conjunction with an immediately following response, such as "blood," free-floating anxiety underlies the personality. People with such reactions are generally apprehensive; they are continually in a state of fearful readiness, and neither think nor act freely. They have a "crippled" personality, a fact that affects their way of experiencing and living. Often these people reveal hypochondriacal personality traits.

The relationship between color shock (or chiaroscuro shock) and experience balance will be discussed later (in the section of the book that deals with "experience balance").

Here we can already begin to understand what subtle psychological and characterological insights the color shock enables us to gather about a human being.

Finally, one other peculiarity. It has frequently been observed that people who have red and green color-blindness nevertheless experience color shock at the appearance of the red blots or colored cards. Thus, they too are capable of producing a color shock.

F. THE CONTENT COLUMN

When Rorschach wrote his *Psychodiagnostics,* he did not put a great deal of emphasis on the "content column" of his test. He restricted himself to merely pointing out, for instance, the relationship of A and Ad to the total number of responses (A%) and to each other. In addition, he established the relationship between H and Hd, and directed our attention to the significance of anatomical responses.

In unpublished diagnoses, which Rorschach worked out in 1921 as "blind diagnoses," he proceeded to explore the backgrounds of certain contents *psychoanalytically,* mentioning, for example, "individual" and "complex" responses. Rorschach was himself a member of the Swiss Psychoanalytical Society, whose chairman was his friend, Emil Oberholzer; Hans Behn-Eschenburg was also a member. Rorschach not only "leaned upon" psychoanalytic literature, but treated his patients according to the theories of Sigmund Freud. Thus he was able to gather practical experience, and as a result, certain responses attracted his attention when he used his test. Recognizing these as symbols of the unconscious, he utilized them in making his diagnoses.

However, such an evaluation of the "content series," or rather of certain responses contained in it, is permissible only in an examiner who is familiar with depth psychology, and who is especially well acquainted with dream symbolism.

We have touched here upon a problem of great importance. If one wishes to work with the form-interpretation test, it is not sufficient to be familiar with its technique. One must also have studied theoretical and clinical psychology, including depth psychology and psychopathology.

At the time when I was able to publish Behn's Parallel Test (Behn created it with the cooperation and under the supervision of his teacher, Rorschach), I warned against the too extensive use of the "content series." "It seems dangerous to me to look upon and to evaluate the contents as 'symbols' because one might easily succumb to 'projecting oneself,' I wrote (*The Behn-Rorschach Test*: [Textbook], p. 65).

At the present time, one must still have nothing but scorn for the bungling pseudo-depth-psychological attempts made by insufficiently informed or misinformed workers, who are likely to substitute their own "symbolism" for the responses obtained from their subjects on the form-interpretation test.

Nevertheless, there is nothing to be said against the true experts in the field of psychoanalysis and depth psychology, who skillfully evaluate all those responses of the form-interpretation test that are without any doubt both individual and complex responses.

There is also this to say about the "content column":

Normally, most responses are either A or Ad. The numbers fluctuate between 40% and 55%. When they are larger, we are dealing with individuals whose thinking is highly stereotyped. Their way of thinking and their capacity for perceiving is "one-track"; they are without initiative and of low intelligence. A% is the indicator for stereotyped thinking. If it remains within the norm, this means that the subjects are still capable of both forming and dissolving their stereotyped associations in very much the same way as any person with a healthy mind would. If A% falls below the norm, however, there exists a certain lack in the associative thinking process. This trait may be observed in artists, but also in distracted individuals. If, however, form shows a great degree of accuracy, and if the test contains several O+ and a high A%, it follows that these are not mentally slow people or people with a narrow horizon, but rather persons who are mentally tired and overworked.

People with a practical mind, who grasp at once how to handle a thing or a situation, etc., invariably produce more A than Ad, and usually (proceeding in a parallel fashion) more H than Hd. (Only anxious subjects present a higher number of Hd than of H, in addition to the usual relationship of A to Ad.)

People with superior intelligence, who derive pleasure from imagination, who conceive with courage, and show a vivid interest in "all that is human"—such people produce many H in addition to a few Hd, as do people who are capable of compassion and of a sympathetic understanding of others, who feel pity for others, and are able to identify themselves with others.

116

Individuals with a great deal of empathic understanding and compassion for others, and an ability to identify themselves with others, achieve an H% of over 30 in the Zulliger Test.

Anatomical responses are typical for persons who are greatly interested in medicine, anatomy, and psychology. Often, however, these interests are related to hypochondriacal ideas, if the subjects are not professionally involved with medical information (physicians, nurses, general nursing personnel, midwives, baby nurses, etc.). These subjects are afraid of falling ill or of injuring themselves. They are hypersensitive to pain, and touchy and sentimental toward their own body. Frequently, several anat are found in women during the climacteric period—which means that, for one reason or another, they are not happy with the bodily changes that are taking place.

Not infrequently, subjects conceal sexual interpretations in anat. These subjects are plagued by sexual fantasies, which they try to push away because they experience them with displeasure.

In cases in which the Zulliger Test presents a perfectly "normal" picture, with only 1-2 additional anat, we have before us subjects who are suffering from feelings of inferiority in regard to their intellectual ability. Rorschach speaks in cases such as these of an "intelligence complex." People with an intelligence complex believe that their intelligence has been "blocked"; they are convinced that, intellectually, they are not appreciated enough and do not occupy a position in keeping with their intelligence, etc. They believe strongly in educational values and knowledge, even though they themselves may not have "absorbed" any of it and, intellectually, they may be hardly capable of carrying out such a process. Inasmuch as they have little education, overestimate themselves, and like to show off, they are frequently characterized by the continuous and incorrect use of foreign words, sometimes altogether misusing them.

From time to time, we encounter subjects who replace stereotypy in A by stereotypy in anat. These are often cases of hysteria; sometimes they are epileptics. At any rate, they are individuals who are not fully "normal," who are somehow mentally disturbed.

Coarse *sexual responses* are rare. If within a test there occurs more than one response referring to sex, this indicates that sexual needs play an excessive role in that particular subject's life. Individuals of this order are frequently tormented by sexual fantasies. For the most part, they do not find pleasure in them and repulse them; in other instances, they accept them arrogantly.

A large number of *object responses* is often found in children. As Loepfe has established, these are equivalent to thinking processes that are concrete and objective, tending toward factual evaluations and estimations. In adults, such responses are generally rather symptomatic of infantilism or dullness; not infrequently, however, they indicate an "escape" from oneself and one's fellow human beings into the world of inanimate matter. When this is the case, then the subjects also produce numerous nature responses, which are also characteristic of children. In general, both obj and nat are related to infantile animistic thinking.

Persons of a model student type, as well as subjects who only pretend to be such and are not really so at all, ordinarily produce several *land map* responses. In children, these are indicative of the ambition to *excel in school*.

Large *content variety* in a form-interpretation test is characteristic of subjects who have at their disposal a wealth of ideas. In particular, this holds true if forms are accurately perceived, and if a number of well-defined original responses have been included.

There are cases in which, although a large content variety exists, forms have not been accurately perceived, and O% is either low or consists of only O– (odd, rather than intellectually superior O). In these cases, the subjects evidence flightiness of thinking; they are not able to concentrate.

It is obvious that people who are working professionally in a technical field, for instance, or persons with technical interests or talents, will produce "technical" responses. Architects, for example, and individuals who are interested or talented along the lines of architecture see, among other things, architectonic motives and reveal an understanding of perspective, etc.

Both Rorschach and Behn maintain that subjects who present a coarctated experience balance (they include many *small biting and stinging* insects among their responses) are characterized by "petty ambition" and petty greediness in real life. People like these may be quite well-to-do, yet they derive a great deal of pleasure if they succeed in cheating a bus driver out of a dime.

In addition to those produced by gardeners, numerous plant responses are produced by subjects who think of themselves as being bound to nature by some pantheistic feeling of communion. On the other hand, these may be misanthropes with esthetic ideas.

G. SOME FURTHER FACTORS

POPULAR RESPONSES, P AND P%

P expresses "the adaptation of thinking to collective thinking." Twenty to thirty-five per cent is the norm.

If, however, a subject produces more than 25 responses, among them 4–5 P, we are not in a position to say that his thinking is less well adapted to that of his fellow men, even though the P percentage is reduced. Thus, many users of the form-interpretation test prefer to consider the *absolute* P number; they say that, if the number of P in the Zulliger Test equals 3–5, we may deduce that the subject's thinking *can be* adapted to his environment; if the number of P amounts to 6 or more, then his thinking approaches the commonplace; if there is only one P, the subject comes close to being entirely ignorant of the world in his thinking. Through experience, one learns to evaluate these various degrees without any difficulty. Yet one must always keep in mind the relationship of P to the total number of responses. The same significance cannot be attached to 4 P produced by a subject whose total response number is 15, as one attaches to 4 P in a total of 30 responses.

ORIGINAL RESPONSES, O+, O—

Two distinct varieties can be differentiated among O+.

a. Responses in which the *originality of apprehension* of the blot is striking. Subjects with such O+ give their responses

119

quickly and skillfully. They are playfully flexible in their formulations. Frequently, they use *bon mots;* their answers are witty, although showing a tendency toward a somewhat sketchy concept. In Card I, for instance, "A zealous priest with a fat stomach."

Apparently, it is not only in the form-interpretation test that these subjects show wit, display their creative ability, manifest their generosity, and exhibit their inclination for a playful and flexible conception and formulation. Usually, they are of very superior intelligence and theirs is a wide horizon. It is quite certain that they will not "talk shop." Most of them possess artistic abilities.

b. Responses in which our attention is drawn to the *originality of elaboration upon the blot.* Subjects with these O+ are less quick to respond. On the other hand, their concept is less sketchy; they "perceive more keenly" and more soberly. Card III, for example: "A market scene. Two chimney sweeps perform magical tricks with a red kerchief and from the distance some curious children come running."

Frequently, then, these are WM+H P (O+).

In the chapter dealing with intelligence I shall discuss this factor, at greater length.

APPERCEPTIVE TYPES

People with an abstract and theoretical turn of mind and an ability for planning are primarily W types (these subjects attempt to finish the test by presenting 3–5 W). When their W are simultaneously M, then these subjects are imaginative people.

The W—D individual (6 W and 6 D, for instance) thinks more flexibly than the pure W-type individual. He adapts his thinking more easily to a given problem and his judgments are less abstract. He too is more interested in the problem, however, than in the concrete matter itself.

The W—D type of individual (4–5 W and 8–10 D) thinks in the main practically and concretely. He is more interested in the tangibly objective than in abstractions, theories, and problems. He prefers understanding to learning, and is best characterized by what is commonly known as "good common sense."

If all this is combined with ambiequal experience balance, then in most instances the subject possesses the intelligence of a practical artisan. He can be put to work anywhere and will always "prove himself."

The W—D—Dd type individual (3 W, 10 D, 2-3 Dd) is encountered with the greatest frequency. He is the intelligent, dependable worker. The more his Dd increase in number, the smaller is his abstract and combinatory ability. He is usually an extremely good observer; nevertheless, he often remains involved in small, even petty matters. He is likely to be endangered by the fact that he fails to see the forest for the trees. People who deal professionally with small or minute objects often belong in the category of the W—D—Dd type person (1-2 W, 6 D, 6 Dd).

D—Dd type individuals (O W, 6 D, 8 Dd) become involved with unessential matters. They cannot any longer be considered "practical," although they may be industrious. Often these are people with strange hobbies, or eccentrics who believe that they will succeed in manufacturing something "practical" from the most improbable materials. Occasionally, these are also the eternally fault-finding people, especially if they have produced a few DS within their test.

D—Dd—DS type individuals (O W, 5 D, 6 Dd, 4 S) are eccentric, fault-finding, hair-splitting people.

A subject of the W—Dd type is an impractical person, who avoids concrete problems. He has original ideas, yet he is flighty in working them out. Rorschach says of such people that they may be bold in the abstract on occasion, while at other times they may become wildly excited over some oddity or other. They may be tyrants, or then again they may be forever angrily discontented with their own evaluations and judgments.

The W—S type individual (6 W, 1-2 D, 1-2 Dd, 4-6 S) is problem-conscious. To him, his problem is more important than life itself or his fellow men. He creates a problem for the sake of it, and is capable of "stepping over corpses."

When we evaluate the apperceptive type, the average factor relationship may be expressed as 3-4 W, 9-11 D, 2-3 Dd, 1 S tendency.

EXPERIENCE BALANCE

Experience balance denotes the relationship in the distribution of affects as between those that are directed inward (*intro*) and those turned outward (*extra*).

Behn has made some valuable statements regarding experience balance:

"Decidedly *introversive* individuals (3 M:O C, 3 M:1/2 C) are those in whom psychic energy is mainly directed inward. They may be people whose thinking is abstract, or they may be people with imagination; they may be theorists, or inventors. A certain measure of introversion is one of the components of normal intelligence: too little of it implies inner lack of independence in its various modifications; too much signifies unworldliness, awkwardness, improper adaptation in its many different nuances.

"Decidedly extratensive individuals (O M:4 C, 1 M:4–6 C) are those in whom psychic energy is chiefly directed toward the outer world. They are usually governed by their emotions. Their affectivity may be well adapted or adaptable, and altruistic; it may also be unadapted and egocentric. Extratensive people are skillful in their external environment, in their contacts and differences. They are quick-witted, but above all they are people who are driven by affects. Again, a certain amount of extratensiveness is part of any normal intelligence. When there is too little of it, an impoverished inner life is the result. The attitude toward life is intellectual, business-like perhaps, and purely rationalistic. When there is too much of it, emotional instability follows, as well as unrestrained and neglectful behavior, moodiness, and the inability to understand others.

"Introversion and extratensiveness are not opposites, but simply two *different* concepts. Their oppositeness is only apparent. For both these aspects exist in all human beings, although in quite different proportions. The balance according to which introversion and extratensiveness are combined in a human being has a part in regulating a substantial segment of what is commonly called intelligence, as well as essential 'character' components and, in addition, certain aptitudes and other mental potentialities. The relationship between introversive and extratensive elements in a human being, which may be established by the test, is his *experience balance.*"

The most commonly occurring forms of experience balance vary for different age groups, the two sexes, and different races. Transformations and deviations of particular intelligence components, personality varieties, and talents are *eo ipso* related to fluctuations and variations of the experience balance.

Ambiequal human beings (3 M:3 C, 4 M:3 1/2 C, 3 M:3 1/2 C) are those in whom introversive and extratensive elements are either of the same or nearly the same intensity.

Coarctated human beings (O M:O C, O M:1/2 C, 1 M:O C) are those in whom extratensive and introversive elements are exceedingly reduced and curtailed. These people experience mainly with their intellect. Their inner and emotional lives (affectivity) are greatly restricted, even atrophied.

"One-sidedly" coarctated human beings compress either their introversive (O M:6 C) or extratensive (5 M:O C) potential powers.

Dilated human beings are those who produce many M and C in the test. In real life situations they are characterized by many modifications, which can be observed in their emotional reactions. Such multiple modifications lead to erratic behavior or to emotional disintegration.

As to the relationship of M to C, the "golden mean" is most normal here too.

People with many talents and a sanguine temperament are ambiequal, while pedants and people who are suffering from depressions are coarctated.

Two- to three-year-old children are seemingly always ambiequal and tend toward dilatation. It is the task of education to develop coarctated *capabilities,* for conscious creativity, precise thinking, and all of logic are possible only with relative coarctation. The goal of education, however, is not total coarctation or mere intellectual schematization, but a harmonious relationship between coarctative, introversive, and extratensive elements.

Of course, these are nothing else but formal principles. The *substance* that a human being possesses within the boundaries of his introversion, or the question of whether an extratensive individual chooses to exploit his passion for good or for evil, for instance, are problems of content. The test does not reveal in what manner a human being *acts* in a life situation. It only shows how he *experiences*.

The *experience balance* of an individual fluctuates; it changes during his lifetime. At first, young children produce chiefly CF, which are replaced by FC during their later childhood. The original largely egocentric and coarse instinctive impulsivity, and the egocentricity of affective behavior, decrease with the years and become "tamed." Emotional adaptation improves.

Changeability of the experience balance persists and is a symptom of mental health. Adaptability remains flexible and comes to a standstill in some measure only, provided that abnormal stabilizations and fixations do not interfere.

The fact that the experience balance of a human being does not signify a constant mental organization may be experimentally demonstrated by making certain suggestions in *hypnosis* and then performing the test, after ordering amnesia with regard to all experiments carried out before. (This is according to a personal communication by E. Blum, Ph.D. and M.D., Bern, who has conducted such tests with the Ro series.)

Frequently we observe an almost sudden change in a subject's experience balance under the influence of *narcotics,* in even moderate amounts. Fluctuation of experience balance in *alcoholics* is not unequivocal. It can change during various stages of intoxication.

Egocentric individuals (CF types) are not necessarily *selfish*. Similarly, FC types—in other words, emotionally well-adapted people—are not always altruistic. At one time, Rorschach pointed out that a "fortune hunter" or a diplomat, although they are indeed selfish, must both be capable of adapting themselves. On the other hand, egocentric human beings may be good-natured and altruistic merely because they are driven by unsatisfied desires for association with others.

According to my own observations, D—Dd—S type people, who exhibit a *definite egocentric affectivity,* are egoists, while W̲—(D)—S types are *not*. They are extremely egocentric with respect to their concepts, their ideology: they are "wrapped up in themselves," even though they do not have any real creative imagination. They may be dogmatic, never willing to gain insight into somebody else's point of view. They are arrogant, blasé, and often snobbish.

The *capacity for emotional adaptability* may manifest itself in various ways.

FC are indicative of an affectivity that is natural, spontaneous, unreflective, unconscious.

At times it happens that, although CF are predominant in the color series, they are balanced by a considerable number of M, which stabilize affectivity. A person who produces 3 M, 2 FC, and 2 CF may act impulsively (despite his kinesthetic responses), but not egocentrically. He possesses "temperament," which he tries to control and is able to activate with moderation.

If there are 3 M, 2 FC, 1–2 CF, and 1 C, then the subject is "unbalanced." In such a subject, extratensive and introversive periods, phases, and stages often alternate. The extratensive side of his affectivity erupts in the form of emotional outbursts. In cases with pure C, the outbursts become explosions. Where there is S too, then these are usually obstinate people, with quarrelsome traits, especially if $F+\%$ is low.

Several sorts of characterological information may be obtained through the relationship between experience balance and space responses. If several S are produced and the experience balance is:

a. *extratensive,* then we find craftiness in the subject, as well as a tendency toward distrust and criticism. These are often argumentative people; they are aggressively contradictory and obstinate.[2]

b. *introversive,* then S signify opposition against one's own inner self, self-criticism, often extreme self-mistrust, doubtfulness, and lack of determination, inferiority feelings of every

[2] In accordance with the subject's superior intelligence, the content of what is diagnostically expressed by the S may under certain circumstances become sublimated in a profession. For instance, polemic capabilities may be used in the field of law or politics; or, perhaps, by a clergyman who is trying to "defend" his "salvation" dogma ("valid for all") painfully and intolerantly against any other such dogma.

kind, and frequently "a mixture of phlegmatic and ascetic traits" (Rorschach).

c. *ambiequal*, then opposition is directed equally inward and outward. The subject is characterized by conflicts. He is skeptical both with regard to himself and concerning his environment. Self-doubts and an attempt at constraint exist side by side, as well as hesitancy and wavering, pedantic scrupling and compulsive thoroughness, a defensive attitude and vindictive obstinacy, self-surrender and stubborn self-persistence, and finally, often a mania for acquisition and a need for over-all perfection. Ambivalence and ambitendency are typical of such human beings. They are unpredictable in their emotional and mental attitudes.

Extratensive individuals with color shock (chiaroscuro shock) are people who tend to convert their inner conflicts, particularly their fear of life, into physical symptoms. They suffer from all kinds of "aches and pains." They have found a roundabout way of subordinating the world to themselves by "being weak," thus making it serve them while they rule over it. Since they suffer from 365 different diseases during the course of a year, they demand constant consideration from their fellow men and force them to dance to their tune. People of this sort react in a "hysteroid" fashion, which leads us to suspect actual hysteria.

Introversive subjects with color shock behave quite differently. They are often hypochondriacs. They are turned inward, refined and delicate; they cannot "cope" with life, being "gentle" and inefficient. Occasionally, they assume an attitude of pessimistic hopelessness, and are convinced that the world is a "place of misery." They generally remain silent; but when they do talk, they complain about their general lack of competence or about the diseases that they have endured or which they fear.

Much like extratensive subjects with color shock, ambiequal individuals with color shock establish reaction-formations against their conflicts and their anxieties. These manifest themselves less in physical weakness, however, than in panic-like or superstitious reactions. Thus, if the experience balance shows a predominance of M over C, then we find "flight of ideas," obsessive fantasies, sudden "blank spots in the flow of associations," and other such phenomena. All these reactions take place on the intellectual level.

If C predominate over M in the experience balance, we have superstitious or well-determined motor behavior (rituals). A discharge takes place on the motility level which, to the subjects themselves, appears peculiar, unexplainable, "alien." (These are compulsive neurotic reaction types, suspected of compulsion neurosis.)

The three last-mentioned categories of subjects (extratensive, introversive, and ambiequal with color shock) usually do not fall any longer within the range of complete normality, for often these subjects are emotionally not in a state of equilibrium. They are in need of psychotherapeutic help. This is even more necessary for subjects who produce a chiaroscuro shock. It seems that, in these individuals, a disturbance has occurred in some much more deeply situated layers of their inner selves. In my practice, I have gained the impression that Ch shock is not only equivalent to color shock; it is also a danger sign, an indication of a basic inner threat. As a rule, I am more concerned about it than I am about a color shock—which, at the present time, must be regarded an almost "normal" reaction (smaller conversion neurosis). "Nervousness" is more the rule than the exception for our times and our Western hemisphere. We could hardly even exist without certain "inhibitions."

Summary concerning various experience balance types:

Introversive. Example: 3 M : 1/2 C (1 FC).

Energy is turned toward inner experience. Therefore, these are people with inner productivity, who think in the abstract (with many W+, high F+%). They are creative theoreticians, scientists, discoverers; they have imagination. If they produce too many M, then they are mystics. Their adaptive capabilities are more intensive than extensive. They are emotionally stable but less well equipped in motoric and speech skills. They have a feeling for language, but little actual language ability. They are awkward, clumsy, "unworldly." They are not very well adapted to reality, but are "culture-oriented." They have a differentiated intelligence. They are given to introversion, and are composed and quiet by nature. If their M belong in the category of flexor kinesthetic responses—as, for instance, *"sitting men"*—then these subjects are not capable of converting their imagination creatively or into actions. They are content with their "dreams," enjoying them; they are the "day-dreamers."

Introversive without extratension. Example: 3 M : O C.

These subjects are met with less frequently. Usually they are "serious" in mood. They withdraw into themselves, to an extent that is close to complete paralysis.

Extratensive. Example: O M : 3 C (1-2, CF, 2-4 FC).

Energy is directed toward the external world. These subjects are guided by affectivity, rather than by their inner selves. They are impulsive by nature, and have reproductive minds. They are gifted in the language field; they are motile, and better adapted to reality: they are "civilization-oriented." They are easily excitable and have an erratic disposition.

Adaptive extratensive. Example: 1 M : 4 C (namely, 1 CF and 6 FC, FC predominating.

These individuals are better adapted, and are capable of empathy and insight. They make friends easily, and are good companions. They have a conciliatory attitude, and are jolly.

Egocentric extratensive. Example: O–1 M : 4 C (1 C, 2 CF, 1 FC).

These are obstinate people, not because they take pleasure in opposition, but rather because they believe that only their own judgments are correct and should be considered valid. They are moody, self-centered, highly impulsive. Their intellectual ability is usually inferior or poor. If the number of C is larger than 1, then these persons are strongly subject to their own instincts. They have the tendency to act on impulse, with abruptness.

Ambiequal. Examples: 4 M : 4 C; 3 M : 3 1/2 C; 2 M : 1 1/2 C. These are many-gifted people, of "sanguine" temperament. They can "function anywhere."

Coarctated. Example: O M : O C.

These are the pedants, the depressively ill-tempered individuals. They cannot be moved; they are arid, "wooden" human beings.

Coarctative. Examples: 1 M : O C; 1 M : 1/2 C.

These are people with an ability for abstraction and logical discipline. They are depressively ill-tempered, and often emotionally impoverished.

Dilatative, with relatively many M and C.

People of this category are cheerful, capable in many different areas, strong and gay by disposition. They are aware of their creative powers and enjoy them. Frequently they are artists. They possess great vitality (expressed in their easy production of M and C). A variegated mixture of intuitive, combinatory, constructive, and abstract W is produced. There is uninhibited interpreting at the appearance of the first red blot. The conceptions of such individuals are slightly playful. They are, however, just as much removed from being blasé and bored as they are from taking the experiment or even life itself too pedantically seriously. They are imperturbable; in a sense, they are the "Olympians."

Dilated, with very many M and C.

Usually, these are the undisciplined "geniuses," not capable of concentrating for any length of time, although they can "do anything." They are the "intellectual he-men," with short-lived interests. Their productivity is as astounding as it is erratic, uneven, and sporadic. Their mind is scintillating and playful; it appears as if it were not possible for them to take *anything* really seriously. Everything is as superficial as it is "brilliant."

Rejections

True rejections—namely, rejections that have not been caused by the wrong conduct of the examiner—always suggest the existence of stuporlike states, or unusually intensive color or chiaroscuro shocks.

Under certain circumstances, such stuporlike states will also be observed in real life, in subjects with "rejections." Actually, "rejections" are equivalent to "deadlock reactions." Primarily, they imply some kind of *arrest of intellectual functioning, on the basis of emotional causes.* It implies "losing one's head" and reactive paniclike states.

From time to time, "rejections" also occur because quite knowingly a subject does not wish to give himself away or because he finds the test situation unpleasant or embarrassing. This is especially true for children and adolescents.

Since "rejections" are extremely suspicious at all times, one must obtain by inquiry, after having finished the whole test, as much information as possible about the reasons for them. For the most part, this information enables us—even in cases in which the subject himself is not aware of the underlying reasons for the rejection process—to establish deep insights into the subject's psychology. Thus, quite suddenly, "complexes" are discovered that play a basic role in terms of a subject's behavior, his "character," and his personality structure.

THE SEQUENCE

As Rorschach pointed out, a *rigid sequence* occurs almost exclusively among pedants and people guided largely by intellect.

An *orderly sequence* is the one most frequently observed. It is found in people with "common sense," in the favorable meaning of the term; it is the normal pattern. Such people neither particularly emphasize their personal logic, nor are they in any way disturbed because they must discipline their ideas by logic.

A *loose* sequence is primarily found in all artists who are engaged in creative and productive work, as well as in actors and dancers. It is also found in individuals who perceive the world by intuition, rather than by "brain function." In addition, it may be commonly observed in schoolchildren, who either have not yet learned how to discipline their thinking, or who are suffering from disturbed ability to concentrate.

An *irregular* sequence never occurs in healthy and mentally normal subjects. It is always a matter for suspicion. It appears often in schizophrenics and epileptics, as well as in mentally retarded persons with erethic traits (excessive irritability). Individuals with an irregular sequence are "unpredictable" in their reactions. Usually, it is difficult to understand them or to gain insight into them and to have empathy with them.

An *inverse* sequence is displayed by anxiously cautious people. It appears in individuals who do not like to form a judgment directly and easily. They want first to "touch" everything (they are also commonly depressed, to a larger or lesser extent).

As a rule, people whose thinking is inductive exhibit an inverse sequence in the Zulliger Test, while people whose thinking is deductive present an orderly sequence, bordering on a rigid one.

In general, the sequences of the form-interpretation test provide information about a subject's powers of logical functioning.

In order to enter into the psychodiagnostic values of the different factors of the Zulliger Test, it was necessary to enumerate its various points as suggestive of certain traits, behavior patterns, forces, capabilities, tendencies, and talents. However, it would be erroneous—and this should once more be kept in mind—to use these individual factors as a code. *Every single factor must be regarded and examined in its relationship to all other factors, to groups of other factors, and to the entire record.* If one does not proceed in this careful manner, the picture becomes distorted and superficial. It does not quite correspond with reality, or at least loses all resemblance to it.

In discussing some of the individual factors and their psychodiagnostic equivalents, we were frequently forced to consider several different factors simultaneously. This procedure implied the necessity and importance of always keeping the results of the *entire* experiment in mind, when attempting an evaluation. One needs to have a great deal of experience before one succeeds in obtaining a synthesis of this kind and develops fluency in the use of it. Once this has been acquired, however, one ceases to scrutinize separate scoring symbols and single individual factors, and invariably sees the whole instead, as a configuration and interplay of all factors. One instantaneously sizes up the significance of diagnostic data, and the weight that they carry within the framework of the "total" human being, the subject. The beginner must learn to estimate, to compare and to judge, to weigh and to measure the factors. Only gradually, after a great deal of practice and experience, will he become as familiar with the test as is deemed to be desirable.

The form-interpretation test supplies information about psychic qualities. How these qualities are activated and manifest themselves in real life is another problem, having to do with the quantity of existing forces, traits, etc. Again, a great deal of practice is needed, to form a valid opinion about quantitative factors. It is self-evident that examiners with psychological intuition and fine intellectual and emotional insight (both intro- and extra-oriented) are much better equipped to prepare evaluations on the basis of the form-interpretation test that psychologically conform to reality than, for instance, more theoretically gifted psychologists. The latter will always find it much more difficult to master the experiment itself and to understand a subject's fine and finest personality traits, which are often mirrored in the form-interpretation test and deserve to be recognized.

9. Supplementary Ideas on Evaluation

a. A *"position response"* is an interpretation produced by the subject because of a certain position of the blot. For example, Card I, the very dark center area: "This is the heart because it is situated in the center" = DF – anat, position response.

Or Card I, the largest S: "This is the appendix, right in the middle of the abdomen."

Position responses are always suspicious. They are frequently found in epileptics, in the mentally retarded, and in psychotics.

b. *Personal reminiscences* are produced by people who cling to their past. For instance, Card I: "This dog's head reminds me of a doggy I once had."

Personal reminiscences must be differentiated from *"self-references."* "Have these pictures been made especially for me?", asks an epileptic subject thus producing an authentic "self-referring" response. Another example, (Card II, S within the red area): "Is this *my* spinal column?"

c. *Inverse responses* are produced if a subject interprets an inverse picture, as, for instance, in Card III, a-position: "A man smoking a pipe is sitting here" (EDC 4/3). Usually this "man" is not seen unless the card has first been turned into c-position.

Young children may produce responses of this kind. Yet I believe that in their case abnormality should not be diagnosed only because these responses have occurred.

Adults rarely interpret in the manner just described; however, some do. Fritz Salomon (Paris)[1] has found that adults who pro-

---

[1] Personal communication to the author (1952).

133

duce inverse responses are suffering from an organic brain injury or epileptic changes.

d. As a rule, subjects who produce responses that contain *many small animals*—insects, wood-lice, spiders, etc.—do not have a good relationship with their siblings. Therefore, in their responses, these animals are usually "squashed" or "crushed."

e. The responses of subjects with decidedly sadistic and masochistic personality traits contain *"severed"* human or animal body parts and heads. In addition, these body parts are often *"crushed"* or *"torn off."*

f. "Gasoline" and "oil *spots,*" "water *puddles,*" *"downward flowing* water," "small water *pools,*" *"ponds,*" etc., are, as a rule, concealed sexual responses and are related to active or repressed masturbation or masturbation fantasies.

g. Subjects who, after they have already progressed to successive responses, *return to their earlier responses* in order to add to them, to supplement some details, to elaborate upon them, are not exactly "practical" human beings. They are, in fact, somewhat long-winded; they have a need to correct themselves.

h. Subjects whose responses contain *"eyes,"* especially if the latter occur several times in a test, are self-observant. They keep control over themselves. Often they feel that they are being observed by others. If other psychotic symptoms are present as well, then these phenomena indicate paranoid traits, which are part of the illness.

i. *C and Ch impressions* are displayed by subjects with a great deal of sensitivity. They attempt to dilute their emotions by esthetic manifestations, in order not to succumb to them without defense.

j. The *"thievish syndrome."* Subjects who produce DW and perhaps Dd W, and simultaneously exhibit an extratensive experience balance with several CF and perhaps even a C, have, as a rule, a thievish bent. Whether it is overt or latent depends on the number of M and Ch and cannot ordinarily be established without a great deal of difficulty. If, in addition, a relatively large number of S have been combined with the factors mentioned above, then these subjects steal because they are socially resentful. If color shock is added, then stealing is a neurotic symptom.

Kleptomaniacs produce all of these symptoms (including color shock). In my own experience, they do not produce FC, merely CF and C.

Obviously, there are thieves who do *not* exhibit any of the signs mentioned above. These are rather rare cases, however (mainly psychotics).

Therefore, when a test record contains the signs mentioned above, we may safely deduce that thievish tendencies are present.

A thief who has been imprisoned for some time usually does not show a "thievish syndrome" any longer. Imprisonment effects a very special emotional reaction; its extreme implementation is what is generally called "prison psychosis." In this case, M increase. In the majority of cases, they are flexor kinesthesias and reveal autistic traits, which have grown more active during imprisonment, and come to dominate the character image.

One might say that thievery is confabulation at the motility level. One could also say that "a person who steals, also lies" (but not "a person who lies, also steals," for that is ordinarily not the case with a liar). However, thievery can also develop on the basis of strongly autistic tendencies: an autistic individual disregards the property claims of other people. He uses everything as it happens to suit him, in sovereign fashion.

As the most striking illustration of stealing in an introvert, showing that his stealing implied some other psychological motivation than would be the case with extratensive (egocentric) persons, the theft performed by a *catatonic* patient will always remain in my memory. In an attack of relative frankness—ordinarily, this man just sat there with a look turned inward, like a Buddha, without taking notice of anything going on around him—he took a wrist watch from a visitor and, fastening it around his own wrist, said: "I am pleased to accept this from you!" When his attention was drawn to the fact that he had just committed a theft, he answered, uncomprehending in the face of such an accusation: "How is that possible? Does not everything belong to me, since I have created the world?"

The concept of personal property is alien to some *primitive peoples,* just as it is alien to our own *very young children* who must be *taught* to respect the property of others. "Honesty" is a product of education.

Furthermore, we must take into consideration the fact that, under certain circumstances, any adult may find himself in a situation of appropriating something. Suppose I were hungry and had no money and no chance of obtaining bread. If I happened to pass a bakery, under those circumstances, and the odor of freshly baked bread rose into my nostrils and my mouth began to water, an almost inhuman measure of self-control would be necessary to overcome the temptation to steal a loaf of bread.

Sometimes a truthful human being may tell a lie, just as a liar may be telling the truth this one time.

One should not ever think too much in stereotypes, and one should certainly not do so when evaluating projective tests!

k. *Neuroses.* Hermann Rorschach was of the opinion that the *presence of color shock* is quite definitely a sign of neurosis.

In the case of extratensive experience balance, *hysteria-like* symptoms are the predominant features of the neurosis.

In the case of an ambiequal experience balance, we are dealing with *compulsion neurosis.*

If the number of M is slightly larger than the number of C in introversive experience balance, then the subject is suffering from obsessive thoughts, compulsive ideas, compulsive brooding, and other similar compulsions (all these symptoms occur at the intellectual level).

If in a (fairly) ambiequal experience balance colors predominate, then the subject acts compulsively and is compulsively ceremonious in his behavior.

If the experience balance (always assuming that there also occurs color shock) is introversive, then neurosis becomes apparent in the form of either *psychasthenia* or *neurasthenia.*

People with *obstinacy neurosis* show several S, in combination with color shock and ambiequal experience balance.

If a definite color shock (red shock) appears upon presentation of Card II, and the red area is then interpreted as CF ("pieces of meat," for instance; "blood spots," or "blood") the indications are that *anxiety* exists, even though this anxiety may have been transformed in some way. If experience balance is *extratensive,* we are dealing, as a rule, with *anxiety hysteria.* If experience balance is *ambiequal,* the indications are that *anxiety neurosis* is present. If experience balance is *introversive,* then anxiety is *manifest, crippling,* and panic-creating. (Communication by Emil Oberholzer, M.D., at a lecture held at the Psychological Society in Bern, 1933 [?]).

l. Psychoses can hardly be established with one-hundred-percent certainty on the basis of the test. However, if a subject produces contaminated responses, there is reason to suspect a psychotic affliction. From time to time, such an affliction may be quite clearly recognized from the test. (Examples are cited in this book.)

m. Subjects may be *coarctated* either in the extensive or the introversive direction, or in both directions. A completely "dried out" office worker, always conscientious, grown old during many years of faithful service, will produce neither M nor C any longer. However, a normal human being, being "alive," produces both M and C. His "coarctative" and "dilatative" abilities may be evaluated by the alternating interplay of these factors. In order to perform a thinking operation, one must be able to coarctate, and in order to experience at first hand one must be able to dilate. A normal, "live" human being is capable of both.

If a subject does not produce *any M* but gives a few color responses, this does not at all mean that he does not possess any inner life. It does signify, however, that he experiences and "lives" primarily in an extratensive fashion.

If a subject does not produce any FC at all, producing instead one or more CF, it does not mean that he is incapable of emotional adaptation. It does signify, however, that in general his adaptation ability is deficient.

n. *Autism and egocentricity.* The autistic individual avoids color responses. On the other hand, he produces a relatively large number of M, which are principally flexor kinesthesias. He appears to be "sucking at" his own fantasies and at the creations of his imagination. (By contrast, the person with extensor kinesthetic responses feels the need for realizing his fantasy creations, "placing them in the world.") Since he is self-sufficient and, in effect, creates his own world, the autistic individual has no need for the external world. Prototypes are the Buddha and, among mental patients, torpid catatonics.

The *egocentric* human being regards himself as the center of the world surrounding him. He needs the world for self-reflection and self-confirmation. Everything must be at his service for him to be able to feel enhanced. For the most part, he is a narcissist, a human being who is capable only of loving himself. He loves the declarations of love bestowed upon him by the world around him, he is starving for them; but he himself does not "love" the world, all he desires is to derive pleasure from it. The egocentric individual is capable of "transference" to a limited degree only, but he is quite capable of identification, insofar as he considers everybody to be an equal to himself, or conversely, believes himself to be "like the others."

The concepts of autism and egocentricity are often used as synonyms. Basically, they have an entirely different meaning, however, even though frequently the effects of both upon the personality are quite similar. At any rate, the psychologist should know the difference, for occasionally such knowledge is essential to attaining better understanding and arriving at a clearer definition of certain behavior patterns.

o. *Number of responses and reaction time.* Initially, when I began working with the Zulliger Individual Test, I used to obtain an average of 15 responses from my first subjects—children and adults, 10–50 years of age. The reaction time amounted to 7–14 minutes.

As time went on a strange phenomenon took place, which I am unable to explain. The longer I continued working with the test, the larger became the number of responses produced by the subjects, whereas their total testing time diminished.

By that time, Salomon (who was then in Paris) had informed me by letter that, as a rule, he was obtaining many more than 15 responses. I was inclined to believe that this might be due to the national character of his subjects. Both the French and the

Moroccan nationals whom Salomon had been using for his experiments, are more talkative than the "introvert" and usually not very communicative inhabitants of Bern. Then I heard about experiments performed in Freiburg, in Breisgau, Germany. Here the average number of responses was still smaller than that obtained with subjects from Bern. The next 300 subjects whom I tested rarely produced fewer than 18-23 responses. Occasionally the number of responses increased to 30-40 or more.

Independently, the director of the Bieler Institute for Mental Hygiene (Switzerland), which maintains a "Psychological Consultation Center for Adolescents and Adults," reported to me that, in employing the Zulliger Individual Test, he had encountered a peculiar phenomenon: the longer he used the test, the more numerous became the responses. Yet the testing time did not increase significantly, as he would have expected, fluctuating instead around 15 minutes for 25-35 responses. Furthermore, Professor A. Friedemann, M.D., who like myself has examined primarily subjects from the Canton of Bern, has had the same experience, and—like myself—cannot find any explanation for it.

It would be of interest to ask other examiners from different localities and different countries to observe carefully whether they too have had similar experiences. If this is the case, then someone ought to explore the situation, in order to find a psychological explanation for it.

It must be noted emphatically that the instructions given to the subjects tested later did not in any way differ, in terms of their phrasing, from the ones given to the very first subjects. Nothing had been "suggested," which would explain the production of almost double the number of responses by subjects who were tested later.

p. *"Object criticism."* Someone has invented the term "object criticism" and included it in the recording and evaluating of the form-interpretation test.

If, in the Zulliger Individual Test, a subject gives the following response, for instance: "There, in the center, on top, is clearly a human head—oh, no, it is perhaps rather a skull with round sockets and damaged on its right side; it is less perfect there than it is at its left half," then we are dealing with "object criticism." The perceived "object" is criticized because the picture that has been interpreted as a certain object does not fully correspond with that object.

Further samples follow:

Card I, dark area, center: "Here is a butterfly. But one does not see the division of the two wing pairs clearly enough; also, the body and the head are poorly defined and not visible enough."

Card II, c-position, inner darker red area (DCB 5/6): "Two well-mannered little men are sitting here, smoking a pipe or a cigar—but there is also something added, something like a bushy tail (B 5/6). Perhaps they are animals, not men."

Card II, a-position, orange blots: "These could be mole-crickets. The color is generally right for them—but here, the design of the wings (F 3 and 8) is not correct."

The diagnostic significance of such object criticism is varied. In order to determine its significance, other test factors must be taken into consideration. If Do are present, then object criticism may have its origin in a slightly anxiety-tinted pendantry. The subject wants to demonstrate his awareness of the fact that he is not assigning anything but an "approximate interpretation" to a picture blot, that "essentially" this picture blot is not really the image of the (interpreted) object. The subject wishes to communicate that he is aware of the fact that he is giving an interpretation (interpretation awareness), not forgetting for one instant that the pictures that he sees (and interprets) are not real images of certain objects, but merely their approximations. If, in addition, anat or geog (some plant diagrams, perhaps, or geometric responses) are present in the test, then we may deduce that object criticism is based on "fanatic perfectionism" of the schoolboy variety and on a constantly operating trend toward intellectual safety. The subject, being essentially uncertain, does not want to "disgrace" himself. For emotional reasons, he is therefore compelled to demonstrate that he is perceiving accurately, using his critical powers. Quite often, such object criticism is nothing but a device to prevent further loss of associations (association impoverishment after shocks, for instance). In these cases, object criticism is equivalent to a "description" and aims at simulating a forward movement in the flow of the associative series. At the same time, it intellectually dilutes the experienced emotion, thus overcoming the shock.

"Object criticism" must be clearly differentiated from the kind of nagging that is often found in schizophrenics and epileptics, as well as in schizoid or epileptoid "normal" subjects.

Examples:

Card I: "Why is the skull unevenly drawn there on top and in both its halves?"

Card II: "Here one can see clearly a man with a cane" (DEF 3/4/5). "Why is it that one cannot see him on the opposite side?" (DEF 6/7/8). "The picture is poor there!"

These subjects are disturbed by the fact that symmetry has not been painstakingly adhered to in the cards. Or else:

If a subject gives verbal expression to his recognition of symmetrical deficiencies in the manner suggested above, by complaining about them, then we are not dealing with a phenomenon defined earlier as "object criticism," but with a disturbance that conceals very definite, often abnormal fundamental traits.

It would certainly be erroneous for an examiner to declare a subject schizophrenic or epileptic, *merely* because this particular subject has expressed his opinion in the manner indicated, about lack of symmetry in the form-interpretation test. However, if in combination with other schizophrenic or epileptic symptoms, the characteristic "nagging" of the variety described is added, then the suspicion gains support that the subject may be a victim of schizophrenia or epilepsy (a question that an expert should clarify and decide upon with the aid of his *own* measures).

We could also formulate this in the following way: If we are faced with a subject whose test might perhaps lead us to suspect schizophrenia or epilepsy, and if we find that such a subject voices "protests because of deficient picture symmetry," *then* the examiner may come to feel that his previous suspicion has been sustained.

q. *"Infantile abstractions."* I use this term because I cannot think of a better specification. For instance:

Card III: "This is a human head" (points to the blots' contours); "here should be the mouth" (points to inner red area), "but not because of the red color" = DWF – Hd inf.

Card II, c-position: "This is a triangle" = DWF — abstr/geom inf.

Card I, a-position: "This is a cut through an apple" = S → DWF — pl, inf., tendency towards ChF.

Such unifications of the whole blot, in which only the outer contour of the blots is taken into account, and the response occasionally has the appearance of "figure-ground fusion," are presented from time to time by children. When adults produce them, one may suspect that they think in the manner of children: they abstract as children do—which means that, in their development, they may have fallen prey to mental regression.

In the case of children, one may merely deduce, on the basis of such "abstractions," that they are endowed with an ability to form abstractions. This holds a great deal of promise in terms of future mental development, especially if F+% is generally a high one. However, the further the children have advanced into the "age of reality" (beginning with the age of 8-9 years, and reaching the final stage at the onset of puberty, at which time a separation between "realistic" and "rational" thinking should have taken place), the more these "infantile abstractions" become related to developmental mental retardation.

"Infantile reactions" are not equivalent to "infantile responses."

An example of the latter would be the response for Card II, b-position, green area CDE 2/3: "A little deer running into a bush" ("deer" = C 2/3; or for Card III, d-position, DE 4: "People out for a walk. The last one jumps over a ditch."

Often these are miniature animated scenes, revealing elaboration of the "fairytale" variety and "imaginative thinking concerned with small things." Diagnostically this is rudimentary naiveté, a sentimental investigation of small details, using imagination in "cute" ways, lovingly and "nicely," as children would. Thus it is an emotional rather than an intellectual phenomenon.

r. *Repetitions of the same responses. Perseverations.* Occasionally it may happen that a subject presents the same response repeatedly. For instance:

Card I

A *small crab*	WF +	A P
A fog cloud torn apart	WChF	nat
A tree leaf (dark center portion)	DF +	pl
Insect antennae or pincers (top portion) .... Do →	DdF +	Ad
A monkey head (center top portion) .... S →	DF +	Ad
And the whole looks like a *small crab*	WF +	A P

Card II

Here are *two bulls fighting with each other* (orange area)	DFC	A, aggression
A sea fish (green area)	DF +	A
These could also be greenish jelly-fishes	DCF	A
Blood stains that have run (red area)	DCF	blood
This is the spinal column	SF −	anat
And here are *two fighting bulls* (orange area)	DFC	A, aggression

etc.

The responses "small crab" in Card I and "bulls" in Card II are repeated. The subject does not seem to realize that he has already given the responses earlier.

If the subject is a young person, an *organic brain injury* is usually present. If he is an older person, we often find the beginnings of arteriosclerosis. It may even be that arteriosclerosis has already reached an advanced stage.

In addition, I have discovered that numerous repetitions may occur in certain cases of mental retardation.

Repetitions must be differentiated from *perseverations.*

Holding the card in b-position, a schoolboy interpreted the D/9 blot portion as "Italy." From then on, he could no longer detach himself from geographic responses. FG/8 is "India," DEFC/2/3 is the "shore of Norway," the large S in b-position is "Lake Geneva," etc. The subject perseveres in producing geographic responses. Either he is barely capable of detaching himself from thinking processes after having established them, or else he is trying to lessen the strain of thinking—thinking as such. As a rule, a persevering subject is *mentally inferior,* or else suffers from a disease that is detrimental to his mental capabilities. The subject remains stuck to his first method of perceiving and thinking, as if he had put on blinkers.

Whether we are dealing here with some mental weakness, or with an emotional or physical illness that is blocking the subject's mental capacities, must be determined through a consideration of other factors.

10. *Various Remarks*

A. TOWARD STANDARDIZATION

If anyone should attempt to restandardize the Zulliger Test with the Ro or the Bero, he must be advised to take careful note of the fact that his experiments should be performed with healthy and normal subjects.

However, even then he may not expect the evaluation figures of the Zulliger Test to correspond with those of the Ro or Bero in an exact ratio of 1:3 according to the 3:10 cards of these tests.

In general, this ratio (1:3) will be verified. However, it may happen that with the same subject the Zulliger Test will show 1 DW and the Ro and Bero Tests will also show only 1 DW (instead of 3 DW).

It may happen that the Zulliger Test will contain 1 FC and 1 CF, while the Ro and Bero contain 1 FC and 2–3 CF. It means that Ro and Bero too contain *only* 1 FC and 1 CF.

It has happened that 1 ChF is produced in the Zulliger Test, while only one single ChF is produced in Ro and Bero, in addition to 1-3 FCh, and that 2 S responses are produced in the Zulliger Test, while only 1 is produced for each of the Ro and Bero.

Thus, one may perhaps deduce that the Zulliger Test is "poorly" standardized.

I believe I am justified in maintaining that the opposite holds true. The Zulliger Test is extremely sensitive (Zulliger, 1953b). It brings to light facts that (sometimes) are merely "hinted" at in Ro and Bero. It registers finely.

In emotionally unstable subjects, the figures may vary a great deal more, especially if the Zulliger Test is performed first, and the Ro or Bero Tests, or both, later. It may happen, for instance, that in the Zulliger Test an experience balance of 2 M : 1 FC + 3 CF contrasts with a Ro experience balance of O M : 1 FC + 4 or more CF. On the other hand, it may happen that the Zulliger Test's experience balance appears as O M : 1 FC + 3 CF + 1 C, while in the Ro it contains 1 M : 1–2 FC + 5 CF + 1 C. If, for control purposes, I also perform the Bero, its experience balance may appear as 3 M : O FC + 5 CF + 2 C, etc.

What is the meaning of all this? It signifies that this particular subject is emotionally highly unstable.

If I submit a subject of such an unstable personality structure to only the Ro and Bero (omitting the Zulliger Test), or if I administer the Bero only, repeating it within an interval of a few hours or days, I shall again be faced with the "frightening" phenomenon of a largely changing experience balance. From appropriate experiments, I should have seen that, alternately, Ro has shown first a rather introversive, and the second time a rather extratensive experience balance. The same phenomenon becomes apparent in some subjects (for instance, in alcoholics, epileptics, etc.), when Ro and Bero are administered to them. This is all the more astounding insofar as it has been demonstrated (and it is evidenced by these subjects with nearly complete regularity) that the intellectual factors remain almost exactly the same.

On the basis of these "experiences," some people may reach the conclusion that testing with the form-interpretation test is not reliable.

I feel that, in the cases that have been mentioned, nothing has been established but the existence of greater lability within the emotional area. I should again like to point out that it is necessary to perform several tests if one wishes to be certain, and never to depend on only one single test.

Thus, assuming, for instance, that administering the Zulliger Test first would lead me to the discovery that the subject is greatly unstable, I still would never dare to make a statement to that effect, on the strength of nothing but the Zulliger Test. I would certainly perform one more form-interpretation test with the subject, as well as other tests, in order to be in a better position to weigh the facts.

Regardless of whether one is dealing with the Zulliger, Ro, or Bero Tests, form-interpretation testing does not produce "unreliable" results, as one might believe right off, when confronted for the first time with the different experience balances mentioned above. One must just have patience with one's own experiment, learning to decipher its fine points, and not to magnify a small discovery (which is not a discovery at all) into a full-fledged discourse that would have only very limited significance for the future. We would not maintain that the barometer is not a useful invention, because it registers weather changes immediately with great declinations; on the contrary, we might say that, since the weather is "changeable," a barometer is an excellent device, in that it reacts to these changes instantaneously.

We see that the results of the Zulliger Test are confirmed. Instability has been very clearly demonstrated. The subject coarctated chiefly the C side, but permitted herself even more emotional freedom in the Bero than could be observed in the Zulliger Test (Table 1).

After graduating from school, Nelly F. attended a girls' vocational school in a city away from home. There she joined a so-called "existentialist" group. She became a truant from school, using various excuses for her truancy, and spent long nights with "artists" and "philosophers" engaged in discussion and dancing. She "treated" everybody by buying wine, liquor, etc., for them, and paying with her father's money. Since her school reports were poor, her father surmised that things were amiss and took Nelly home. Next he was faced with the problem of his daughter's vocational training. In addition to some other tests, the guidance counselor administered the 3 form-interpretation tests and asked me to inform him about the results.

TABLE 1

Examples of Greatly Different Form-Interpretation Test Results of the Same Subject

Subject: *Nelly Farner, 18 years old*

Time:	7 minutes	19 minutes	16 minutes
Responses:	25/9	39/10	40/11

Zulliger Test—Rorschach Test—Behn-Rorschach Test

	Zulliger	Rorschach	Behn-Rorschach
F+ =	17 (−2, 5)	29 (−4)	23 (−4.5)
M =	2	3	1
MCh =		1	1
Ms =	2	1	1
FC =	1	1	4
C =	2	2	6
C =	2	1	6
FCh =	1		1
ChF =	3		
Ch =		2	
F (C) =			

	Zulliger	Rorschach	Behn-Rorschach
P =	2	5	4
O =	5	5	6
H =	1	3	1
Hd =	1	1	1
anat =		1	
sex =			
blood =			
clothing =		3	2
A =	10	13	18
Ad =	3	7	6
obj =	2	3	6
pl =	2	3	4
nat =	1	2	1
geog =			
shadow, cloud =	3	3	1
fire =	1		
stains =	1		

	Zulliger	Rorschach	Behn-Rorschach
DW =			
SW =			
WS =			
W =	4	8	9
D =	17	21	30
Dd =	2	4	1
Do =	1	2	1
S =	2	4	1

	Zulliger	Rorschach	Behn-Rorschach
F+% =	84	86	80
A% =	52	51	60
P% =	8	13	10
O% =	20	13	15
H% =	8	20	10

	Zulliger	Rorschach	Behn-Rorschach
Sequence:	loose-orderly	loose orderly	loose
Experience balance:	2 M : 5½ C	3 M : 2 C	2 M : 11 C
Apperceptive type:	W — D — Dd/Do—S	same	same
Shocks =	—		

Remarks:	combinatory	same	same
	WMHP III absent	same	WFAP absent
	description	same	—

148

Subject: *Heini Pauli,* 11 years old

Heini is the only child in his family. His parents are business people; they own their business, and are well-to-do. Both parents are occupied with the business, and, as a result, their son has been raised chiefly by servants. The boy has always stolen, but never outside of the house. He stole from the maids and occasionally from his mother. He has a strong need for love, but he is stubborn and easily provoked to fights. He has always been healthy. According to the doctor's certificate, he is at present in good physical condition. He is tall and slightly overweight.

The parents would have liked Heini to attend a secondary school. This was the reason they decided to have Heini psychologically examined, and not at all because of his thefts (see Table 2).

Experience balance changes, even though everything else remains quite constant. If we had based our conclusions only on the Zulliger and Ro Tests, we could not have made the deduction of active stealing. It became apparent in the Bero.

The fact that Heini cannot make a good candidate for secondary school also becomes clear enough (F+% is too low, the sequence is poor, confabulation is present, and A% is too high).

After all three form-interpretation tests (instead of only one) were completed, Heini's *instability* became apparent. It will always color his attitude.

Subject: *Carlo Beutler,* 19 years old

Carlo is the eighth child among 11 children in a small-farm and peddler family. His mother died when Carlo was 5 years old. After her death, an older sister took care of the household. Carlo has always been healthy. After graduating from grammar school, Carlo became a farmhand. He was not able to stay on his jobs for any length of time, but changed jobs constantly. He was cruel to both animals and people. As a result of a brawl at an inn, Carlo was brought before the juvenile court. At the court investigation, it came to light that Carlo has always been dishonest: he had cheated a friend at the inn and this had caused the original argument.

TABLE 2

Scoring of a Zulliger Test ——— Bero ——— Ro
Subject: *Heini Paul*, 11 years old

	5 minutes	30 minutes	33 minutes
Number of responses:	14	30	24

		5 min	30 min	33 min
DW	=	1	2	1
W	=	1	2	1
D	=	8	21	18
Dd	=	1	3	7
S	=	3	2	3

		5 min	30 min	33 min
F	=	11(−3)	24(−5)	20(−5)
M	=	2	—	2
Ms	=	—	1	—
FC	=	1	1	—
CF	=	1	3	2
C	=	—	1	—

		5 min	30 min	33 min
P	=	3	7	5
O	=	—	2	1
H	=	1	1	2
Hd	=	1	1	1
A	=	6	12	10
Ad	=	3	10	6
obj	=	—	1	1
pl	=	1	2	2
geog	=	1	1	—
nat	=	1	2	2
F+%	=	73	79	75
A%	=	64	73	66
P%	=	21	23	24
O%	=	—	7	4
H%	=	22	7	12

	5 min	30 min	33 min
Sequence:	loose	loose	loose
Experience balance:	2 M : 1 C	0 M : 6 C	2 M : 2 C
Apperceptive type:	(D)W – D – Dd – S	same	same

No shocks

Remarks:	conf D	conf D	conf D

150

TABLE 3

Scores of the Ro —— Bero —— Zulliger Test
Subject: *Carlo Beutler*, 19 years old

	10 minutes	8 minutes	3 minutes
Number of responses:	24/6	23/6	12/4
DW =	2	1	2
SW =	1	1	−
W =	8	8	3
D =	12	10	5
Dd =	−	2	−
S =	1	1	2
F+% =	65	84	75
A% =	62	38	58
P% =	8	17	8
O% =	16	9	25±
H% =	33	26	25
F =	17(−6)	19(−3)	8(−2)
M =	3	−	−
FC =	2	1	1
CF =	−	1	2
C =	1	1	1
FCh =	1	1	1
Ch =	−	−	(1)
Shocks	−	−	−
Sequence:	loose	loose	rigid
Exp. bal.:	3 M : 2½ C	0 M : 3 C	0 M : 4 C
Apper. type:	DW—W—D—S	DW—W—D—Dd—S	DW—W—D—S
P =	2	4	1
O =	4	2	3(−1)
H =	3	−	−
Hd =	4	6	2
blood =	1	−	1
A =	8	5	6
Ad =	7	4	1
obj =	1	2	−
pl =	−	3	1
nat =	−	3	1

First the Ro, then the Bero, and finally the Zulliger Individual Tests were administered to Carlo (Table 3).

The test differences are significant in this case. In order not to commit evaluation errors, it has proven valuable to compare the Ro and Bero averages with the Zulliger Test figures (Table 4).

TABLE 4

Average Ro + Bero
Zulliger

| Time: | 9 minutes | 3 minutes |
| Number of responses: | 24/6 : | 12/4 |

						P	= 3 :	1
						O	= 3 :	3 (−1)
DW	= 1.5 : 2	F	= see F+%	H	= 1.5 :	−
SW	= 1 : —	M	= 1.5 : —	Hd	= 5 :	2
W	= 8 : 3	FC	= 1.5 : 1	blood	= 0.5 :	1
D	= 11 : 5	CF	= 0.5 : 2	A	= 6.5 :	6
Dd	= 1 : —	C	= 1 : 1	Ad	= 5.5 :	1
S	= 1 : 2	FCh	= 1 : 1	obj	= 1.5 :	—
F+%	= 75 : 75			pl	= 1.5 :	1
A%	= 50 : 58			nat	= 1.5 :	1

P% = 13 : 8 Sequence: From Ro over Bero to Zulliger Test

O% = 14 : 25±   progressively more orderly

H% = 30 : 25 Experience balance: Introversive-ambiequal
extratensive-extratensive

Now these averages may be compared and balanced with the three records.

Not only does Carlo's experience balance change, but also his intelligence factors. While on the basis of the Ro we would be compelled to deduce that Carlo is mentally almost retarded, the Bero seems to indicate that his average intelligence is rather high (F+% of 84, orderly sequence; A% is too small in the Ro and too large in the Zulliger Test). F+% decreases again in the Zulliger Test; on the other hand, the sequence becomes rigid, although the experience balance is definitely extratensive (in clearly extratensive persons, as a rule, the sequence is rather loose). While, in accordance with the Ro, we must believe that the experience balance is ambiequal, the prominence of extratensive conditions is quite clearly apparent in both the Bero and Zulliger Tests.

On the whole, the three form-interpretation tests and their "average scores" (half of Ro + Bero:Zulliger Test) disclose an individual who is unstable from all points of view, unpredictable, and undependable. Very likely, he cannot be regarded as emotionally sound any longer. He is a brute, a fact illustrated by the DW—W tendency, viewed in terms of its relation with S (including SW) and pure C, or their psychological equivalents. One can see, too, that Carlo steals. If one examines reaction time, and the number of responses, and considers the absence of shocks (neurosis would inhibit the youth's cruel affectivity, would "civilize" him, so to speak), and his entire changeable intellectual and emotional mode of behavior, his dishonesty and instability become distinctly evident.

Without any doubt, a psychiatric examination is indicated in the case of Carlo Beutler.

Subject: Mrs. *Herta L.,* 21 years old

The tests were sent to me because they exemplified a case of discrepancy. Mrs. H. L. is a housewife, about to be divorced because of her heavy drinking (Table 5).

It seems to me that the differences between the Zulliger Test and the Ro are not really very great. H% of 19 is too low for the Zulliger Test. It should amount to about 30. In the Ro, H% equals zero, which is the most conspicuous fact.

In other respects, everything agrees. In both instances, experience balance is dilated in the direction of C. The subject "lets herself go" more completely in the Ro, while in the Zulliger Test her Do indicate some uneasiness, and yet reveal some self-control. Finally, in the Ro, aggression (WS and S : 4C) is more obviously apparent.

For *purposes of comparison,* two Ro of a drunkard were performed on two successive "sober days" (Table 6).

We observe that, even though the experiment is repeated with the same series, differences appear, since the subject is unstable. Moreover, in Karl "pioneering" is revealed with the help of the first test. In the second test reaction time becomes shorter and the number of responses increases.

TABLE 5

Scores of the Zulliger Test —— Ro
Subject: Mrs. *Herta L.*, 21 years old

Time:	6 minutes	16 minutes
Number of responses:	11/3	24/7

	11/3	24/7			11/3	24/7			11/3	24/7
DW =	1	1	F =	4(−2)	9(−3.5)	P =	2	3
WS =	—	1	M =	1	—(1 AM)	O =	—	1
W =	3	9	Ms =	1	—	H =	2	1
D =	5	12	FC =	—	5	Hd =	(1)	—
Dd =	—	1	CF =	1	—	anat =	2	6
Do =	2	—	C =	2	4	A =	2	1
S =	(1)	1	CCh =	2	2	Ad =	1	1
			ChF =	—	2	obj =	1	5
F+% =	50	60	Shocks =	+	++	pl =	—	1
A% =	36	30				cloud =	3	1
P% =	19	12				others =	3	10
O% =	minus	minus				Color naming	+	+
H% =	19	—				Description	+	+
						Criticism	+	+

	11/3	24/7
Sequence:	orderly	orderly
Experience balance:	1 M : 4½ C	O M : C
Apperceptive type:	DW—W—Do (S)	DW—W—D—S

TABLE 6

Scores of two successive Ro

Subject: *Karl B.*, 38 years old, construction worker

	18 minutes	15 minutes
Time:		
Number of responses:	22/8	30/12

DW	=	1	3	F	=	9(−2)	18(5)	
SW	=	2	2	M	=	3	1	
W	=	4	6	FC	=	1	1	
D	=	13	18	CF	=	5	4	
Do	=	—	1	C	=	2	3	
S	=	1	—	FCh	=	1	—	
F+%	=	77	71	ChF	=	—	1	
A%	=	45	30	Ch	=	1	2	
P%	=	18	13	Shock	=	+	—	
O%	=	18±	10∓					

P	=	4	4
O	=	4(−2)	3(−2)
H	=	3	1
Hd	=	4	6
anat	=	1	1
A	=	8	5
Ad	=	2	4
obj	=	3	7
cloud	=	—	1
fog	=	1	2
others	=	—	3

Sequence:	loose	loose
Experience balance:	3 M : 6 C	1 M : 9 C
Apperceptive type:	DW–W–D–S	DW–W–D–S

Whoever wishes to "validate" anew must be advised to employ different methods for testing groups:

first with the Zulliger Test, next with Ro and Bero;
first with Ro, next with the Zulliger Test and Bero;
first with Ro, next with Bero and the Zulliger Test;
first with Bero, next with the Zulliger Test and Ro; and
finally, first with Bero, next with Ro and the Zulliger Test.

This will supply him with an illustration of the fact that the results agree in the case of stable subjects and disagree in the case of unstable ones, and also that, in the latter case, it is completely irrelevant which of the three tests is performed first, second, or last.

I have carried out such comparisons. I could add still more "material" to that already submitted here. It seems to me, however, that this would serve no purpose, for the aim of this book is not to supply statistics and the results of computation, but to provide instruction and a course of study. Still, I did want to point out experiments which would of necessity be imposed upon the examiner, when he encountered differences during the use of more than one form-interpretation test.

B. VARIOUS PHENOMENA ENCOUNTERED WHEN EMPLOYING SEVERAL TESTS WITH ONE SUBJECT

It is quite obvious that, if we use several form-interpretation tests with one and the same subject, the test that is administered first will often have a "pioneering effect" on successive tests.

Thus we may occasionally observe a subject producing a very conspicuous color shock in the first test, whereas this color shock is largely covered up or altogether absent in successive tests (we are here singling out only one phenomenon). In such cases, we are dealing with subjects who are capable of recovering quickly after they have been shocked. They can be "trained," for they possess extensive adaptation capacities.

"Which of the three form-interpretation tests is the best one, then?" somebody may ask. The answer must be: "All three of them are equally good!" Their sum total conveys only one specific aspect with regard to the subject, who has reacted to all the tests in one particular manner and not otherwise.

Continuing with color shock, we observe conversely subjects who produce strong and pronounced color shocks in their performance on each of the three tests. In this case, we are inclined to state that the reaction capability of the individual tests has been confirmed!

Indeed, the subject has reacted in this manner, in addition to his other reactions. The essential fact remains, however, that the subject is highly susceptible to shock, that he does not overcome shocks easily, that he is not easily adaptable and cannot be easily trained, and that he is more neurotic than individuals of the type described above.

The "pioneering effect" may show itself in other ways, too. Occasionally it is seen in curtailed reaction time (the norm for Ro and Bero is one response per minute; for the Zulliger Test, it is one response per 1/3–1/2 minutes).

What is the meaning of this from the psychodiagnostic point of view?

It signifies once again (assuming that F+% has remained equally high) that the subject has a relatively easy aptitude for learning new things. He is a type that can be "trained," whose quantitative production improves after a while, but not until he has made a certain amount of "headway" first.

Other subjects increase the speed with which they produce their responses, when testing is repeated, but their F+% is remarkably reduced.

They tire easily, or else they are individuals who cannot concentrate upon the same thing for any length of time, their interests fluctuate, or they react with "negligence." Their mental discipline is poorer than that of individuals who retain their F+%.

There are subjects who produce relatively few W in their performance on their first form-interpretation test, regardless of which card series is used. The number of their W increases in the second test, and even more so in the third test. The number of W occasionally affects the apperceptive type, which becomes different for the three tests.

When such a phenomenon is observed, it must be investigated in order to determine whether these W constitute accurately perceived (F+) forms at all times, or whether form accuracy has diminished.

If the forms remain accurate with the increased number of W, then we are dealing with subjects whose unconscious qualitative ambition can emerge by degrees only.

Let us assume that the subject is an employee, for instance, whom his employer has sent for testing. We may predict: "This employee will 'surprise favorably.' The more time he has in which to adjust himself to his work, the better will be his performance. He will develop gradually, even though his initial performances are only about average."

On the other hand, if the number of W increase, but become more and more WF—, then we are dealing with a subject who, having adapted himself, becomes "liberal" in the adverse sense of the term. He will grow inattentive, let things slip through his fingers without checking them, and become less and less dependable. He would like to organize and to make arrangements, but he lacks "staying power." In his work, the subject is without constancy and grows to be unmethodical. Although he may be admired at first for his excellent ideas, as time passes, one is disappointed in him: he does not live up to his initial promise.

There are subjects who are constrained, keep themselves under guard; they manage to control themselves well when they take the first and second tests. Initially, they produce only a few responses, while their reaction time is long. At first, one can usually observe a strongly coarctated experience balance in them. Repeated testing with other card series loosens their coarctation, the number of responses increases, and F+% decreases.

These subjects do not expose their *real* selves unless they are somewhat tired. Therefore the last test performed is the most valid one. This does not at all mean that the tests performed earlier are useless for diagnostic purposes, or that they plainly present an "incorrect picture." For we come to realize that the subject is capable of holding himself in, so long as he is not tired to even a slight extent, but that, once he is tired, his performance becomes poorer. We also realize that the subject protects his affectivity as long as he can preserve it in terms of his life pattern, not letting it find expression and become effective. We understand, too, that he does make an attempt at emotional reserve, but finally "lets himself go" even more.

We must note the following with regard to the form-interpretation test. If, within the framework of a more extensive test investigation (using a "battery of tests," in other words), we employ one single series, then it is hardly necessary to repeat the form-interpretation experiment with other series, for the results of the form-interpretation test may be compared and balanced with those for the other tests.

However, if we perform form-interpretation tests with various card series, considering in addition anamnestic information, we are, as a rule, in a good position to work out a very pertinent image of the subject.

In general, the following rule should be applied. When differences appear in the form-interpretation test, as it is performed with the various card series, we are not justified in inferring that the procedure is unreliable. The examiner must ask himself *what it is* that provokes these differences, *why* they have developed and *what psychodiagnostic "value"* is manifested in them.

In more or less stable subjects, scoring figures and factor relationships remain remarkably constant, when several tests are performed with different (or the same) card series.

11. About Inner Sequence

Test specialists have drawn my attention to the fact that frequently one may make extensive deductions about the subject's personality structure or his characteristics, on the basis of the sequence of the responses, since a record shows an *inner sequence*.

Example: 12-year-old boy with enuresis, who produced his responses in 9 minutes.

I.

A witch in rags. She comes along
carrying daggers .... { WMCh H O
      combinatory { DF + weapon, aggression
One can clearly see her black heart
 (dark center area) .... DF − anat, confabulation
A big girl bending protectively over
 her doll (BCD 2/3/4) .... { DM + H
      combinatory { DdF + obj
A boy, seen from above, defending
 himself with a stick (EFG 3/4/5) { DM + H O
      combinatory { DdF + weapon, aggression
A small deer leaps away into (D 2)   DF + A
 water (outer rim of the card) ... S tendency

II.

(Prolonged reaction time, turning
 of the card) .... shock
c A beautiful white magic plant .... SFC pl
         white as color
a This is one, too, it is in a flower pot { SFC pl, perseveration
      combinatory { SF + obj

160

Dwarfs with protective shields, they
are walking with long steps . . . . ⎧ DM + H O
combinatory (green area) ⎩ DdF + obj
Two sheep or some such animals,
attacking each other with their
heads . . . . DF + A, aggression
tendency FC, "or"
The red is smeared blood . . . . DCF blood, tendency CCh
Or, perhaps, these are ham slices? DCF food, "or"

III.

There are a man and a lady in
trousers, arguing violently with
each other . . . . WM + H P (O), aggression
Two boys running *away* . . . . DM + H P
In the center there is a butterfly, a
beautiful red and big one, of a
kind that we do not have . . . . DFC A P
b A wild boar playing with his tongue
(EDCBA 2/3/4) . . . . DF + A, tendency F(C)
Or a duck or a turkey, looking back
and chattering (EDC 1/2/3/4) . . DF + A "or"
c And here are some piggies, they
want to slip into the stovepipe . . ⎧ DF + A
combinatory (small dark figure) ⎩ DdF − obj, confabulation

The boy had been sent to the guidance counseling service
because of his bed-wetting. His Zulliger Test is a real "model
case," indicating the facts of "inner sequence." That is why I
have selected it for purposes of demonstration.

The responses give us a complete case history of the illness.
The very first response reveals the boy's "mother conflict." The
"witch" is the archetype of the "angry mother." She approaches
threateningly, armed with daggers. She has "a black heart" (an
expression for "wicked heart").

A "good" mother is contrasted with the "angry" one: the girl
bending over her doll in a protective manner. Since we have
learned about the 12-year-old boy's relationship with his mother
from preceding responses, we recognize the image of the "good
mother" as wish fantasy.

A "defense fantasy" follows: "A boy . . . defends himself with
a stick." This boy is certainly the subject himself. With the as-

sistance of dream symbolism, we may arrive at the following interpretation: the boy defends himself with his penis. (Relationship to bed-wetting?)

An "escape fantasy" then follows: the deer that leaps "away" into water—could this not again be the subject himself? Could not the water, perhaps, signify his own urine, his bed-wetting? Or could this be a regression into bed-wetting? On the basis of many psychoanalyses, we understand the meaning of bed-wetting. The bed-wetter regresses to the level of infancy. When he is wet, the "loving" mother comes to him, makes him dry, cares for him; she is close to him, and he feels "safe." Regressing into early infancy, the bed-wetter attempts, by way of unconscious fantasies and impulses, to return to the situation in which he had sensed the mother to be a "protective power," who saved him from all his fears.

When the second card was handed to him, our subject initially experienced a definite color shock. Reaction time became extended, and the boy grew embarrassed because an association stupor had overcome him. He turns the card into c-position. The response of the "white magic plant" is produced, white having been perceived as color. This is done by subjects who, being highly sensitive, make an effort to disguise their hypersensitivity for purposes of self-defense. Moreover, S regularly suggest an attitude of antagonism, which may assume the form of active or passive obstinacy, if numerous S appear and CF responses are present. Obstinacy is passive when the number of M is larger than the number of CF—in other words, if it is accompanied by an introversive experience balance. M are predominant in our subject; we may therefore assume that the boy's obstinacy is of the passive kind, and that he will act accordingly in real life.

Next follows the response, "Dwarfs with protective shields, walking with long steps." A "dwarf" is a child's archetype. In other words, by comparison to adults ("giants"), the child's concept of himself is that of a dwarf. The boy experiences himself as a dwarf, but he is armed with a protective object. He does not have to surrender without defense.

The same idea is expressed in the next response, although somewhat less colorfully: "Two sheep or some such animals attacking each other with their heads." Since children are still much closer to totemistic ideas than adults are, they identify easily with animals.

The red spots have irritated the subject. This is the reason for the 12-year-old's escape into S responses. Now he had detached himself from his color shock, he has recovered, and he is finally capable of interpreting the red color blots. They are "smeared blood" to him. Individuals who produce "blood" responses are usually tortured by manifest or hidden fears, or their neurotic equivalents. Among them, those who produce both a color shock and blood responses, and also show an introversive experience balance, have succumbed to an *anxiety neurosis*.

The boy has already provided proof of his uncertain attitude toward his own "self" by his frequent use of "or" in his responses, and he catches himself immediately after the "blood" response. "Or, perhaps, these are ham slices?" he asks. The unpleasant ("blood" = anxiety) is replaced by something pleasant ("ham slices" = food). Food is part of the "mother" complex. Originally, it is the mother who offers *food* to her child. The "oral bond" of the child to the mother is his very first bond. Feeling his ego endangered, our subject escapes regressively into the oral mother relationship. We can conjecture that the emotional disturbances of this 12-year-old, which developed into his bed-wetting symptom, are related to his "oral phase," which originated long ago in his early infancy (perhaps toilet-training was begun at that time).

The first response to Card III is as follows: "There are a man and a lady in trousers, arguing violently with each other." In a certain sense, this response is unusual. Although it must be scored as a "popular response" (with P), it is at the same time an original response, or even an individual one. Ordinarily, the two dark blots in Card III are interpreted as "two men"; a "lady in trousers" means a woman clad in trousers. In our region, this has occurred more and more often as time has passed; but only a very few years ago, it was rare. Women and girls did not wear trousers except for skiing, never in their everyday life. When it was said about a woman that she "wears the trousers," it was implied that she was the authority in the family, and occupied the position that "normally" belonged to her husband. We ask ourselves: "Is the boy describing a real situation in his first response to Card III, as that situation exists in his parents' house? Is it possible that, in his parents' house, it is the mother who 'wears the trousers' instead of the father? Has an actual marital conflict just been described?"

This suspicion is not pure invention. For in the second response, the "boys" do not "approach," as it is usually interpreted, but are "running away." Both these responses seem to be correlated with each other, to supplement each other, describing an experienced situation. The son would like to dodge his parents' quarrels, which make him anxious; he would like to "run away" from them, to escape.

And just as happened at the end of the responses to the second card, where something unpleasant ("smeared blood") was converted into something pleasant ("ham slices"), in Card III too a pleasant response follows immediately, "a butterfly, a beautiful red and big one, of a kind that we do not have." With insight into the total situation, this response must strike us as a diversion from the earlier disagreeable state of affairs. It is as if it were self-comforting, resembling a wish-fantasy: "unfortunately, we do not have such beautiful big butterflies." In the evaluation of Card I we had already been able to establish the boy's tendency to seek comfort in wish-fantasies.

Actually comfort is not achieved, however—at least, not conclusively. For immediately there appear the "bears playing with their tongues" and the "duck or turkey, looking back and chattering." These are less dangerous. Once again the boy's tendency to change threatening situations into less threatening ones is clearly apparent: danger is made to look pleasant.

The last response follows: "And here are some piggies, they want to slip into the stovepipe." Who, then, is the "piggy?" According to our idiomatic usage, a bed-wetting child is often referred to as a "piggy" (= little sow, little pig). Would it be too daring to think of self-description? Our 12-year-old himself is the piggy who wants to slip into the stovepipe.

What is the meaning of "stovepipe"? If we call once again upon dream symbolism for assistance, "stovepipe" signifies the mother's womb, her uterus. The boy describes his unconscious regression wish as far as the uterus. There he is completely out of danger; he is safe, even though he sees himself confronted with all the world's monsters, his unconscious fears, the witch with the black heart threatening him with daggers, his quarreling, disagreeing parents, the bear playing with its tongue (mother symbol), the chattering turkey (father symbol), and the chattering duck (mother symbol).

The total picture shows us that the boy has been seized by a *"complexe d'abandon"* which manifests itself in the *bed-wetting* symptom. Moreover, we may surmise that there exists a marital conflict which has had an intensifying effect upon the boy's affliction.

(A cautiously conducted interview with the mother of the 12-year-old revealed that she had been "forced into marriage" because she had been expecting the birth of the boy, and that she is suffering from frigidity.)

It has been my intention to present nothing but the "inner sequence," as it is exemplified in the case of a 12-year-old boy. If an interpretation of the other test factors were to be added, further facts about the boy would come to light, such as his superior intelligence, the form of his intelligence (highly creative ability!), and other details concerning his personality structure.

There are some people who do not score a form-interpretation test, but evaluate it solely on the basis of its "inner sequence." It seems to me that this procedure is dangerous. It leaves much too much freedom to the imagination of the evaluating examiner. Under certain circumstances it may induce him to "brag"; in a kind of self-satisfaction, he might attempt to prove both to himself and to others how masterful he is. Consequently, self-control and caution must never be neglected.

On the other hand, our example (it could be multiplied) demonstrates that "inner sequence" frequently—quite frequently—discloses certain facts that could *not* have been understood by *merely* scoring the test factors. These latter facts are significant for a subject's psychology, however, and greatly supplement all other facts obtained by "scoring."

In order to be able to recognize and evaluate an "inner sequence," it is not sufficient to be familiar with test psychology alone; it is also necessary to have a knowledge of general, and especially of depth, psychology. It seems to me that all test psychologists should be versed in general psychology, as well as in depth psychology, in order to be able to evaluate tests, regardless of which ones they employ. In addition, they should also be familiar with the fundamentals of psychopathology.

12. Forms and Levels of Intelligence
in the Zulliger Test

It is not possible to calculate a subect's IQ with the Zulliger Test. The test merely shows *innate* intellectual *ability,* in other words, the *potential* and *form* of intelligence.

It is impossible to calculate with any of the form-interpretation series to what extent any given intelligence can be realized, and to express that by a single figure—namely, an intelligence quotient.

On the other hand, form-interpretation tests enable us to recognize the presence of emotional factors that are able to inhibit, delay, and prevent the development of a good innate intelligence.

It seems to me that we know much more about a subject's intelligence if we have identified its structure, potential and form, and if we have become acquainted with the inhibitions that impede the exercise of his intelligence, than if all we have at our disposal is his intelligence quotient. This does not mean that obtaining a subject's IQ should be downgraded in its significance in practical school procedures—for instance, when a decision must be made as to whether a student should be admitted to a special school. I merely wish to point out what the various procedures can accomplish with regard to intelligence testing.

To begin with, I should like to differentiate between two categories of *"intelligent"* human beings:

a. those who are rather *reproductive,* receptive and imitative in their thinking; and

b. those who are *productive,* independent, creative and original in their thinking.

The first-mentioned type excels in schools and is generally well liked by teachers. Students in this category are able to grasp and concentrate easily. Actually, they are observant and skillful "collectors," endowed with an excellent memory. Also, they are usually quite capable of prompt association and combination. Their knowledge is always at their disposal, and they know how to utilize it in every situation. That is why they excel in school.

In the Zulliger Test, their reaction time amounts to 1/3 minute per response. The number of their responses is considerable, often more than 30. One realizes that their engrams are readily available, and that the subjects are willing to make (conscious or unconscious) painstaking efforts. Such efforts are also demonstrated by the fact that these subjects produce approximately the same number of responses for all three cards. In many cases, the number of responses increases with each successive card. The majority of the responses are accurately perceived abstract form-interpretations (F+%=85–95). The apperceptive type is of the W—D—(S) type: for instance, 6 W, 20 D, 3 Dd, and 1 S may be produced; sequence is orderly to rigid; A% is average, P% is rather increased, more A than Ad are produced. Often there are also 1–2 anat indicating that general intellectual ambition is present. Specifically scholastic ambition is corroborated by one to three geographic interpretations that do not have the form of perseverations; however, M are scarce, and usually only MP are present. At times, they are replaced by Ms, indicating, if this is the case, proficiency in embellishing thoughts with colorful ideas in a seemingly "decorative" manner. H% is usually high, providing evidence of the fact that a human interrelationship is implied in the subject's diligent effort. He wishes to please his teacher or his parents, for he seeks their love. Affectivity is well adapted; yet, as a symptom of impulsive drive, corresponding with a forceful readiness for associations, a CF is added. Experience balance is slightly coarctated, ambiequal. As a rule, however, it is somewhat more extended towards the M side. Especially in adolescence, a slight color shock appears, occasionally closely connected with an attraction to red. The subjects recover from shock immediately, and then produce even more responses for Card II than for Card I and III. In Card III, they begin with WMHP.

As a rule, the second intelligence type is less liked—at times even disliked—by teachers during their school years when it is reproductive thinking that is chiefly expected. For these students "disrupt" lessons by "anticipating developments," by unsuitable questions and remarks, by original ideas—all of which may hinder the teaching process and prevent the completion of the curriculum. Not until they have reached the final highschool grades, where autonomous thinking is a more desirable requirement than reproductive thinking, do these students stimulate the class in a positive manner and become appreciated by their teachers.

The Zulliger Test of these students shows a great deal of similarity with that of students belonging to the first-mentioned category. There is, however, stronger M predominance (the M side of experience balance is not coarctated), O% is high, increased, while P% is correspondingly reduced. Experience balance is rather introversive, yet usually a CF is present in addition to 2–3 FC. The number of responses is slightly smaller, fluctuating between 23 and 28. Once again, orderly-to-rigid sequence and relatively slight content distribution are indicative of ability to concentrate.

At this point, we shall limit ourselves to discussing *symptoms of intelligence disturbances in normal individuals.* We shall describe a case of a child (or adult) who, while possessing excellent intellectual capabilities, is prevented from developing these fully because of certain emotional circumstances.

a. The basic mood-disposition of the subject is *anxiously depressive.*

This is evidenced by one or several Do, inverse sequence, strongly coarctated experience balance, and one or several chiaroscuro responses. The subject is timid in his thinking, especially if he interprets the same location of the blot several times, hesitantly separating the responses with an "or." Usually he reduces his W but retains D. A number of S in relation to M make it clear that self-distrust is present.

169

b. The subject takes pains to think within a *frame of reference alien to him.* He is naturally endowed with a capacity for productive thinking. He clings, however, to an acquired reproductive manner of thinking.

The indications are: the usual M become F, an obvious "M repression" takes place; in other words, original and creative thoughts are suppressed while they are still being formed, and receptive thinking takes their place.

c. *Mentally,* the subject *tires* too quickly. He lacks the ability to persevere at the same level in his thinking, and to think uniformly with accuracy.

The number of responses decreases with each card, and form-accurate perception also decreases.

This kind of intelligence disturbance may be easily determined by administering the Ro or the Bero or even both, following the administration of the Zulliger Test. Thereupon the sequence often grows looser—the subject becomes more "absent-minded"—in proportion to testing time.

d. The subject suffers from *neurotic affections.* This uses up his energies, acting upon him like a suction pump and curtailing the energy at his disposal for intellectual activities.

The test indications are: distinct color shock in Card II, inverse sequence in Card III, perhaps lack of P in Card III.

e. A subject older than 8 years who *has not yet reached the stage of realistic and rational thinking;* he is mentally a "late developer."

In his observations, he does not as yet differentiate clearly between fantasy and reality.

The test factors are DW and DdD.

Also, confabulatory traits and admixtures manifest themselves as infantile wishful thinking, "dreams," and fairytales; his thinking is still vague, imprecise.

We are dealing here with an impairment of development such as may often be observed in rapidly growing children, who have an advanced physical development in relation to their age.

f. Intellectual productivity is too *strongly dependent upon interhuman relationships.* (H% is too high, several FC and two or more S are present.) Such subjects are capable of higher mental achievement if they (assuming that they are students) have a friendly, "positive" emotional relationship with their teacher. If they feel indifferent toward the teacher, mistrust him, or hate him, then their ability to function intellectually becomes restricted, despite their basically rather rich endowment.

These are, then, the six major varieties of mental inhibition in normal individuals. Not infrequently, several of them are found simultaneously in the same subject.

Let us turn now to the various *intelligence categories*. We shall speak first about *individuals of average intelligence* dividing them into three groups:

a. *"Low average."* An individual of this group is not interested in anything intellectual. He is most suited for an occupation that is stereotyped, consistent, standardized, and manual. At the low point of the curve, he borders on slight mental retardation; at the high point, on "medium average" intelligence.

In the Zulliger Test he produces but a few W, chiefly D and Dd. His reaction time is somewhat prolonged; the number of his responses is average-to-scanty, depending on how industrious the subject is; F+% is 68–78, the sequence is loose, A% is high, P% is high, O% is low and contains O—; there are no anat, except in subjects who possess hypochondriacal traits. Only popular M occur and the experience balance is coarctated. However, there may occur 1–2 CF. Often more Ad than A are produced; not infrequently, tendencies toward perseveration are apparent.

We are dealing here with intelligence that is of a typical "elementary-school" variety. The requirements of a "junior high school" (secondary school or an academic school of some kind) would be too demanding for subjects in this group.

Not infrequently, some better elementary-school pupils present an F+% of 78–82. If they succeed in passing the entrance examination to a junior high school, they range there in the last third of their class; later, they almost always have to repeat a grade. Sometimes they may be helped by additional (private) tutoring in keeping just above water.

b. *"Medium average."* All candidates for the lower secondary school belong in this group. They are capable of following the curriculum of such a school without being too much pressured by its demands. They are able to graduate or to obtain a high-school diploma.

In the Zulliger Test, they most probably represent the W—D type and show an F+% fluctuating between 83 and 90. Their maximum A% should be 33–45, the P% about 25; their sequence should be orderly-to-rigid, and in addition to the two MP in Card III, at least one MO should be produced. Reaction time should not be longer than $3/4$ of a minute per response; the number of responses should be average to large.

c. *Individuals with "superior intelligence."* The test demonstrates (experience also confirms this) that there exist *completely different kinds* of highly intelligent individuals, many of whom do not belong in the category of people with "school intelligence." Our schools are organized in such a manner as to do justice chiefly to one category of highly intelligent students: those capable of *theoretical abstraction*. From the scholastic point of view, those highly intelligent students who possess *technical capabilities* display certain "deficiencies" and a "one-sided" orientation (not sufficient language ability, for instance; no interest in Latin and Greek, as well as no ability for any living foreign languages, etc.) Students who do still less well in school are often those with *superior artistic ability*. As a rule, they are even more one-sidedly endowed than students with technical ability (discoverers, architects, engineers, etc.). Frequently school repels them, because it interferes with their far-reaching flights of thought and imagination, drawing them away from their absorption in personal problems ("Do not disturb my circles"). They submit most unwillingly to ways of thinking imposed on them in order to fit into a program, agreeing but reluctantly to use their memory, etc., for things that "do not concern" them.

Simplifying roughly, and intentionally leaving all the finer nuances outside the scope of our attention, we may differentiate three categories of highly intelligent individuals. As thinking types, they demonstrate great dissimilarity, yet one cannot say that one type surpasses the other: a. Gift for *abstractive, theoretical, programmatic, scientific* thinking; b. Gift for *technical* thinking; c. Gift for *artistic* thinking.

a. The subject with an *abstractive-theoretical* gift presents in his test, above all, a larger number of W+ that are in part apprehended with originality. In combination with a high F+% of 90 or more, he presents a rather rigid sequence. In addition, some factors that indicate a rich inner life are usually present (several accurately perceived M). O% is relatively high (15–20%); P% is for the most part somewhat too small (merely 12–18%). The variability of thinking is not impaired (30–40% of A). According to the kind of M (MP or MO), we can evaluate whether we are dealing merely with a reproductive or a creative theoretician. Experience balance is rather slightly co-arctated; usually it is ambiequal.

Occasionally, sequence is rigid but inverse. In such cases, we are dealing with cautious individuals. They are mainly human beings who proceed "analytically" from detail, not arriving at comprehensive judgments, combinations, and large-scale conceptions until later.

Where several Dd (usually just as many as D or, perhaps, a larger number of Dd than D) are found in a markedly W-type subject, then this subject is greatly impractical. He is "nothing but a theoretician," who is unfavorably conspicuous in real life situations because he alternates between reacting in either a dashingly generous, or a tyrannical or nagging fashion. When there are more than one or two S among about 23 responses, then the subject is a human being who "rejects the good together with the bad," and believes in finding the proverbial "hair in the soup" at every turn.

b. The *technically gifted* individual displays a much wider scope in producing W. At the expense of abstract WF+, combinatory and primarily constructive WF+ are found in his test. Ordinarily he presents (in addition to a large number of W and D, very accurately and originally perceived F (C) with architectonic perspective contents, and a few M+ with DM predominating over WM. Frequently his attention is drawn to the symmetry of the pictures, and he is capable of combining the separate blots in Card II into a W. His F+% is just as high as that of the abstractive theoretician. Sequence too is quite rigid. Originality of apprehension is greater than elaboration;

173

the latter, however, is always relatively high. Adaptation of thinking to collective thinking is slightly reduced (P% is decreased); A% amounts to 25–40; and many more A than Ad interpretations are presented. Experience balance is ambiequal, for the most part with a tendency toward coarctation. There are a few Dd, yet they are not seen sharply.

c. Finally, an artistically gifted individual is characterized in the test by a large number of WM and DM, which are original in their apprehension as well as in their elaboration. F+% is high, and the sequence is "poorer" than in the two other categories of individuals with superior intellectual gifts, for it is loose-to-orderly-loose, yet it is not confused. Experience balance is rich and according to the individual's artistic area, CF (painters) or M (playwrights) are more markedly represented. For the most part, experience balance is quite ambiequal, with a tendency toward the dilatative. O% is very high; correspondingly, P% is small, as is A%. Frequently Ms appear, or the contents contain a great deal of "scenery." All emotional factors have a very broad scope. Impressionability, enthusiasm, and similar qualities come to light in the C series, as clearly (several CF in addition to FC; frequently one but not several pure C) as does, often, the potentiality for keeping an esthetic distance and retreating from the world of external affectivity into one of inner contemplation (so-called "impression interpretations," "color shock" in Card III, F (C), and some isolated DS).

Midway between individuals with superior gifts and mental retardation are people with good "common sense." This implies average concrete intelligence of the kind found in the good practical craftsman.

In the test, it is indicated by a strikingly large number of well perceived D interpretations. There are but a few W, which are mostly P, in addition to the usual combinatory M and abstract WP. The more or less numerous Dd (as a rule, 3–4 of them appear in 25 responses) imply that the subject is interested in small and smallest things. Usually precision toolmakers and general precision workers produce a larger number of Dd. In people with many abilities, experience balance is ambiequal. It is rather extratensive in those who are reproductive, and in workers whose occupation is of a quantitative character. Quick, agile, energetic (extratensive) human beings contrast with slow, circumspect, introversive ones (it does not follow, however, that the latter are "awkward").

Not all the finer differences can be described at this point. The test supplies information about many of them, in accordance with all the deviations from the averages mentioned above.

The following example may demonstrate the wealth of information that can be crystallized by close scrutiny of one of the factor relationships.

At the presentation of Cards I and III, a subject first interprets a WP. Then he turns to peripherally situated D and (perhaps some) Dd, and next to the centrally located ones; finally he produces another W which, this time, is either a combinatory or a constructive one.

This means that, facing a new and unfamiliar situation, the subject will attempt to cope with it soberly and calmly, without constraint and without frenzy. He orients himself with a single sure glance, as any healthy and clever human being would, observing keenly and with concentration. Later, the subject penetrates deeper into the situation. He does not remain at all satisfied with a superficial evaluation. He wants to come to grips with the "essence of a problem," and he proceeds to do so by approaching it from the periphery. The subject works himself up, as though lifting one veil of obscurity after another, until he reaches the focal point of things. In the course of this procedure, a great many new aspects, partial viewpoints, new "reverse sides" are analyzed and comprehended with intellectual depth. The subject takes his time penetrating deeply into a problem. In doing so, he enters into both the most essential particulars and important secondary conclusions freely and easily—without uneasiness and without spending himself on trifles (small number of Dd, no Do, no S—or, perhaps, just one).

Finally, the total situation, the whole problem is once more conceived in its entirety. An act of synthesis takes place. This implies that all the newly acquired comprehensive judgments and orientations are now arrived at by a different method from the one that was used at first. Combinatory or constructive and original WF or WM are now produced. Thus, after the subject has first given free rein to the collective's way of comprehending, he now arrives at judgments by a method that is inherently his own, personal one. His creative qualities become activated. In the end, the subject gives expression to the results of his "inner perception." He advances by deduction—by means of objectivity and rationality, which lead to induction, to a subjective, constructive arrangement.

As a rule, subjects who proceed from D and arrive at W interpretation are:

constructive in intelligence,
builders,
inductive,
artistic,
subjective,
synthesizers,
leaning toward irrationality,

while subjects who start with a W and proceed to D interpretations possess an intelligence that is rather

abstract,
analytical,
deductive,
objectifying
rationalizing,
scientifically oriented or
more opportunistic.

Subjects who at the very beginning perceive the conspicuous lateral D are practical opportunists who, in a real life situation, will similarly adhere to the readily tangible. They may be characterized by their grasp of everything that is concrete; they are skillful and know assuredly when to lend a helping hand; they are technically oriented, and are never "sicklied o'er with the pale cast of thought."

Subjects who, proceeding from the center line of the cards, make an effort to comprehend the centrally located parts first, have a need for systematic goals; they pursue their goals. They too are aggressive, and try to grasp the most important facts first. But they are more inclined to "worrying" than are the "purely practical people." They are less opportunistic in their behavior, less quick in their actions, less self-assured and "self-evident." Frequently a search for support based upon a feeling of inner instability, a "fear of becoming lost," corresponds with the need to hold on to the central locations, especially if these attempts bear the mark of slight tenseness. Then their desire for concentration contains an element of exaggeration and rigidity.

W types are characterized by an unconscious desire to establish a record. From the psychoanalytic point of view, they exhibit "oral" traits. D types are people with a genital character. Dd types are marked by "anal" personality traits; S types by aggression.

IMAGINATION

Among other factors, good intelligence is strongly dependent upon the individual's imaginative activity.

In connection with the form-interpretation test, the concept of "imagination" has a narrower meaning than is usually attached to it.

"We do not refer to 'fantasies' but to productive imagination, autistic productivity, implying an awareness of its own autism, however. One aspect of its presence is co-determined by the existence and strength of introversive elements. This, then, is highly subjective imagination. In its extreme it is implicit in the creative imagination of the artist, the poet. Its opposite would be on the one hand confabulation, pure autism, and on the other, factual, concrete, reality-determined thinking. Also, imagination (as we understand it) may be purely receptive, indicating pleasure derived from the products of imagination. It is, however, a talent too and its pure autistic confabulation is the opposite of pleasure.

"Confabulation is a conscious or unconscious deceit; imagination is 'fiction,' a conscious product of introversion."[1]

[1] Hans Behn-Eschenburg, M.D., *Schueleruntersuchengen* [Tests performed on students], Bern, 1923.

The term "fantasy" as we use it in our daily language, when we apply it to the activity of a person, may be related to completely different qualities and abilities:

a. The individual who confabulates and the pathological liar fantasize, consciously and unconsciously, things that do not correspond to reality. DW and DdW are the experiment's characteristic signs for them. Frequently confabulation becomes apparent in D also (which could be termed DdD; in other words, a Dd has been accurately perceived and combined by confabulation with a larger part of the blots). Often both confabulation and combination are clearly present in one response. In such a case, the subject has unconsciously succumbed to a misinterpretation of reality as well as to self-deceit leading to "illusions." Or, as in the experiment, he adorns everything in life too by exaggerating and being consciously deceitful. Under certain circumstances, people with confabulatory tendencies of this kind may be *thieves*.

b. If a subject produces several DW, a few M, an average to small F+%, and many O—, then his is the imagination of an eccentric. He is an unworldly human being, bungling in his thinking or in his profession. Usually he overrates himself, thinking that he is a "genius," believing that his way of thinking is by far superior to that of his fellow men; or else he considers himself to be an "inventor." He usually makes an impression on others of being peculiar or even ridiculous.

c. The "imagination of an esthete" is reflected in the test by descriptive sensory impressions. He may find, for instance, that the colors in Card II are "summery," and in Cards I and III "chaotic" or "dirty," etc. Without stating what the forms of the blots remind him of and what he perceives, he refers merely to the impressions that the colors make upon him.

d. The essentially *creative imagination* of individuals with superior intelligence—inventors, artists, poets—is expressed in the test by a significant number of WM+. All or the majority of them must be evaluated as O+.

In a true "poet," for instance, such imaginative ability corresponds to an " inward look" in search of one's own primary

178

images, to an unconscious, specific, self-regulating pensive and comprehensive faculty of perception.

The *writer's* imagination is of a different character. The poet's images force themselves upon him while he *finds* the words in order to portray something; the writer *seeks* his words and images. This may occur to such an extent that his works will be called "mannered." Conscious effort rules over the observation of external occurrences and phenomena, and governs their expression in word representations. It is an original and imaginative way of presenting things easily; often it is accompanied by a sensation of playful pleasure.

ORIGINALITY

In order to differentiate between *creative* and *re-creative* imaginative activity in the test, O+ must be examined closely, in addition to M. In the re-creative individual, the *originality* of M is more strongly apparent in the *formulation* of his responses, while in the creative individual originality is expressed through the apprehension itself. (Originality of interpretation vs. originality of apprehension.)

For instance, the re-creative individual presents the usual WM+ H P in an original manner. Thus, in Card III he interprets, for example: *"Two boys are cold and they are warming themselves in front of a small fire."* The creative individual responds to Card III by saying: *"Two explorers have caught a strange, butterfly-like animal and two boys come running in order to see it."* Both in combination and in imagination, this surpasses the first interpretation.

The creative individual interprets mainly MO, while the re-creative individual is more likely to interpret only the usual MP.

The division into creative and re-creative individuals is rather theoretical, inasmuch as all productive people must possess reproductive capabilities as well. Whether in a life situation a person proves to be "creative" or "re-creative" is a question of his capabilities and their "libidinization" (utilization). Still, there exists an original re-creative type, described earlier as a "writer." He may be, for instance, an excellent "reporter."

In evaluating test results, it is worthwhile always to investigate all well-defined, well-perceived, and creative *original responses* more carefully, in order to establish precisely the specific manner of their production and to determine their nature.

One should scrutinize, for example, all original F interpretations, in order to ascertain whether they concur with W, as well as which special category of W is involved, or whether O responses have been given mainly in D, Dd, S, etc.

A subject who produces original WF+ of an abstract kind is a person who is capable of utilizing his theories, his theoretical dispositions, and his intellectual planning for original achievements.

Combinatory and constructive original WF+ are produced by subjects who use their own specific methods in combining and constructing. They are original in their concrete thinking.

Original DF+ are produced by people whose "practical" thinking is characterized by a great many astonishingly excellent ideas.

Original DdF+ are found in people who have original ideas mainly when they are confronted with the manipulation of minute things. For instance, they make a discovery, within the boundaries of their work, that may be practically useful in some small area of it; they succeed in producing something useful out of some unimportant thing, which somebody else might not even notice. These are the people who manufacture a fish hook from a small nail or perhaps some "button" for suspenders. Their discoveries bring them close to the "eccentric"; while practical, their ideas nevertheless seem more or less funny.

Original S+ occur in individuals whose thoughts and work are original only when they are in some way able to use their predilection for contradiction. If their experience balance is extratensive, their originality becomes apparent in criticism and polemics; if their experience balance is introversive, their originality is expressed in self-criticism. Extratensive individuals are often quick-witted and ingenious debaters. In some "brilliant" lawyers, with coarctative-ambiequal experience balance, as well as in many politicians, we find a mixture of original W and S.

An O% of 10–15, P% of 25, A% of 40–50, and F+% of 80–90 in a subject indicate his excellent adaptability to the thinking of his fellow men and, with regard to his thinking and intelligence, a capacity for so-called "empathy."

A good mixture of original abstract and combinatory constructive WM and DM is characteristic of all artistically gifted people.

Among them, individuals with extensor kinesthetic responses are mostly people with productive talents, while those with flexor kinesthetic responses are rather reproductive, or else belong in the category of people who, because of their autism, never bring any of their work to an end or finish it.

13. The Symptoms of Mental Retardation

F+% below 60.

Presence of DW and DdW.

Few or no M, or secondary M—in other words, M constructed by degrees from D, Do, and Dd.

Presence of Do (although they may often be missing). Do indicates fearful embarrassment. In the retarded, they are also indicative of an inability to comprehend larger picture parts.

Color naming because of association impoverishment and embarrassment.

W— rather than W+ interpretations.

Inability to point out the locations that have been interpreted.

The number of Ad is larger than the number of A (often number of Hd is also larger than number of H. This may occur in normal individuals, too, if they have an anxious hypochondriacal disposition, or if they have suffered from a disappointment trauma).

O% minus-plus or minus.

P% is rather low; occasionally it may be extravagantly high, however.

Usually, the number of responses is above average; in rare cases, below average.

Obsessions, perseverations.

Attachment to one perception type—as, for instance, W—, Dd, Do, DW, DdW.

Attachment to one stereotyped content, such as anat.

Absence of color and chiaroscuro shocks.

Sequence is orderly, loose; frequently it cannot be determined
at all, since only one single response is produced for each card.
Some position interpretations.

Enumerating of colors, enumerating of the number of blots.

Absence of "interpretation awareness." The retarded subject
believes that the card actually presents the picture of whatever he interprets.

Pfister (1925) pointed out that in the Rorschach Test oligophrenic Dd may be differentiated from schizophrenic Dd.

"Oligophrenic Dd differ from schizophrenic Dd in being
analogous among themselves as to picture size, their conspicuous position within the picture, and their form. Schizophrenics,
on the other hand, produce among some more usual Dd, bizarre
picture parts interpretations. Normal people have difficulty in
finding their locations for they are not at all conspicuous." The
same phenomenon holds true for the Zulliger Test.

It is obvious that retardation must not be conclusively accepted as being present if only one of the enumerated factors appears in a record. Contrariwise it does not follow that all the
enumerated signs are found in every retarded person. However,
if several signs are present, then the conclusion may be drawn
with almost complete certainty that retardation exists—especially if F+% is low.

Pseudo retarded persons produce records that are similar to
those of normal individuals. F+% is higher than 60; usually
it is close to 80. In addition, shocks become apparent. Later it
turns out that the apparent retardation is a symptom of a neurotic illness.

The greater the accumulation of signs in the test and the
lower F+%, *the higher is the degree of retardation.*

14. Anxiety as It Is Reflected in the
Zulliger Test

Anxiety is an emotion that is associated with physical manifestations. It must be termed a psychosomatic phenomenon.

It has been established that, in a state of anxiety, inner secretion does not function in the same manner as it does under ordinary circumstances. Adrenal gland secretion is increased; thyroid secretion is higher; blood pressure is augmented; the sympathetic nervous system is agitated, etc. Many people perspire when they are in a state of anxiety; they may also become cold and begin to tremble. They stutter and turn pale, or else their face is covered with red blotches. They feel as if a lump had come into their throat. If anxiety reaches a high enough level, urination and bowel movement may occur. Palpitation of the heart, shortness of breath, oppression, anguish may also come into play. In a state of anxiety, a person may sometimes vomit.

Emotionally the effects of anxiety are associated with intense displeasure and a reaction to anticipated danger. This danger may come from one's external surroundings, from one's environment, in which case we speak of *reality anxiety* or *fear* (Freud). On the other hand, it may originate from within, and then we are dealing with *neurotic anxiety*, which is anxiety of the danger that instinctual drives may cause, a superego fear, anxiety about anxiety itself, etc.

A human being (an animal, too) responds to fear with various counterreactions. The most essential are:

a. Aggression,
b. Escape,
c. Paralysis.

Some other neurotic counterractions are:

d. Anxiety may be made non-existent with the assistance of neurotic mechanisms, such as amnesia, compulsive neurotic ceremonial behavior or hysteria, binding anxiety to a certain animal, place, etc. (phobias) or to certain foods. Thus, the individual succeeds in evading anxiety by escape or rituals. In this sense anxiety is a signal for *anticipated external or internal danger;* it may appear in many specific forms (phobia, castration anxiety [= fear of physical injury], guilt feelings, fear of being alone, fear of losing love, "fearfulness" in general, etc.).

Freud has stated that three varieties of anxiety are inherent in the young child:

1. Anxiety about losing the mother (mother substitute),
2. Anxiety with regard to darkness,
3. Anxiety with regard to strangers.

These three anxieties may be reduced to one formula: anxiety about losing the mother. Under certain circumstances, a *"complexe d'abandon"* may develop on the basis of the latter.

From the psychological point of view, *"fear of nothingness,"* postulated by *existential philosophy* as a primordial phenomenon, could mean fear of losing the mother.

Since a human being, in the throes of anxiety, experiences the same sensations as in the process of birth, Freud regards the latter as the primordial, original anxiety experience. Every later anxiety would then be a repetition of the birth trauma.

It should be added that many modern writers deny that there exists any relationship between anxiety and birth trauma. This is one of the repudiations commonly leveled against psychoanalytic theories. We should like to mention that some of the theories that have been opposed by scientists of a certain era were later accepted by science. A great many findings in the field of medical science, for instance, are now recognized as correct and have been supplied with new evidence, while our old

185

"folk medicine" has had this very knowledge for a long time, during which period it had been repudiated as unscientific or was even tabooed.

It seems to me that we should acknowledge the psychoanalytic theory of anxiety until somebody postulates a better one. Only then will we be justified in reproaching Freud for not searching deeply enough, and in considering his postulation obsolete.

Having summarized the most recent scientific research concerning the *theory of anxiety,* we shall now attempt to set forth the indications that an anxious or fear-ridden individual may present in the Zulliger test. The results are valid for the two other card series (Ro and Bero) as well.[1]

Anxiety is most clearly manifested in subjects who suffer from ideas of persecution, e.g. paranoid schizophrenics and paranoiacs. In the following, I shall present a record that originated with a subject who has been clinically diagnosed as a paranoiac.

Emil A., 21 years old, locksmith

| *Zulliger Test* | Time: 13 minutes |

I.

(After very long contemplation, turning the cards repeatedly)	initial shock
This is a jet-flame; devil's death (the "jet-flame" is the S in the center of the picture)	SW MCh H contamination O—
He threatens me with sabers	DF + obj aggr., ego reference, sado-masochism

Nothing more!

II.

| A blood bath .... | DW CF blood, O— sado-masochism |

[1] The work at hand is an extension and addition to an essay, "Die Angst im Formdeutversuch nach Dr. Rorschach" ["Anxiety in the form-interpretation test as indicated by Dr. Rorschach"] which I published in the Oktober-Dezember Heft [October-December issue] 1935 of *Zeitschrift fuer psychoanalytische Paedagogik* (Wien) ["Journal for Psychoanalytic Pedagogics" (Vienna)]. At that time, I was not familiar with the work of Binder about chiaroscuro responses, since it had not yet been published.

Would you like to do this to me? ..... ego-reference
(Keeps silent. Requests to continue
  with the interpretations are disregarded)

III.
Rejection

We make the following observation: after an initial shock,
which here means much more than mistrust toward an unusual
task (interpreting picture blots), for it also implies open mistrust toward the examiner, a long time passes until finally the
first response is produced. It is a contamination and has a confabulatory flavor. The "jet-flame" is related to the subject's profession; the "devil's death" by "sabers" is associated with the
subject's persecution ideas and his expectations—his *death anxiety*. The response given to Card II brings out the subject's fear
of death even more clearly. The examiner turns into a menace
and is identified with the "devil's death." Some kind of paralysis
then follows, perhaps defiance (observe the S that has been incorporated into the response for Card I). Therefore, being unable or unwilling to continue interpreting, the subject persists
in keeping silent. No further response is produced for Card III
(rejection).

Rorschach says that "rejections of cards almost never occur in
normal subjects." A number of writers have disputed his statement. I am of the opinion that Rorschach did not formulate this
sentence about rejections thoughtlessly. If rejections occur in
normal subjects, especially in children, it may mean that the
test has taken them by surprise or that, without being aware of
it and without having intended to, the examiner has frightened
them by his appearance. Or it may also come to pass that some
sexual object has already been seen in Card I, even more likely
in Card II (red areas and S), which the subjects do not wish
to mention to the examiner. The tendency to reject is invariably
related to anxiety, but may be equally applied to the retarded
individual with hysteria. Rorschach is referring to the latter
when he says that, because of a very sensitive intelligence complex these subjects are *"anxiously"* careful not to "present inter-

pretations that seem stupid to them." That is why rejections occur in these subjects, why they limit themselves to interpreting unusual Dd, minute S, and Do. They do not dare to produce whole interpretations, and their anxiety becomes apparent in the manner in which they search the card, gazing all the while fearfully and with mistrust at the examiner.

Practical experience with both the group and the individual Zulliger Tests has convincingly shown that all the subjects that produce MCh, regardless of whether these are WMCh or DMCh, suffer from anxiety. Usually these subjects suffer from more or less severe delusions of persecution, even though they may be otherwise "normal." In any event, they are inclined to experience great anxiety. (MCh must be differentiated from MC. I believe that, when a subject interprets the dark figures in Card III as "chimney sweeps," he has produced an MC and not an MCh. In Card I an MCh would be, for instance, "a man in a dust cloud," "a ghost with veils," etc.).

We are touching here upon the meaning of Ch with regard to anxiety. I have gained the impression that whenever Ch is produced, anxiety, the readiness to experience anxiety, or, in any event, defense against anxiety is always present to a greater or lesser degree.

If only one single FCh occurs, one must not ascribe too much importance to it. On the basis of FCh, Binder infers the presence of "controlled" or controllable "sophropsychic" impulses. Although in addition to FCh, a subject may also produce some CF, he still has a tendency towards "serious" moods; his impulsivity has been checked from inside. Frequently educational influences, and often a conscious and deliberate tendency toward adaptation, find their expression in FCh. In any event, subjects who produce FCh do not give themselves fully, with spontaneity and without constraint. Anxiety lurks in the background, although perhaps to a small degree. Anxiety is more intense, if ChF and pure Ch or Ch impressions appear (barring the case in which the subjects are photographers or are working in the field of graphic arts. In these individuals, all Ch responses may correspond to "shop-talk interpretations" or *déformation professionelle*).

Some FCh, as well as a few ChF, usually bring us to the conclusion that the subject is trying to adapt himself in a shrewd and cautious way. This is especially the case when some CF are present, too. For the subject is afraid that he might give offense to his surroundings, if he were to "give" himself without any reservations.

For the most part, the subject is not consciously aware of his anxiety, as it is expressed in his Ch interpretations. Frequently, one is dealing, in cases such as these, with people who have long ago contrived all sorts of avoiding or evading rituals, in order to escape their manifest anxiety. This is especially true of adults. Children, on the other hand, solder their anxiety (expressed by Ch responses in the form-interpretation test) onto phobic animals or phobia-invested places and situations. The more that children produce such interpretations as "dead rabbits" (Card II, orange area), "knocked-off head" (Card I, top portion), "a crushed human leg" (Do in Card III, smaller dark blots), etc., the more is readiness for aggression (or for masochism, if it has been repressed) present, as a more or less intense defense mechanism against anxiety.

Insofar as they are not produced by retarded individuals (retardation may be established on the basis of other test factors), all Do indicate anxiety. Inverse sequence points in the same direction. If it does not appear until Card III is presented —in other words, if it occurs in the course of the experiment, and not at its onset—the greater is the readiness to experience anxiety. On the other hand, if an "inverse" sequence appears at the very beginning (instead of W—D—Dd, Dd and D are produced, finally being united into a W), the subject hardly experiences manifest anxiety any longer, since he has become "cautious" and so manages to protect himself against his anxiety. He escapes anxiety by some ritual that evolves at the mental level. In any given situation, he first searches for details in order thereby to orient himself. He proceeds from the periphery, examining it first and then gradually moving forward until he has reached the core of things; only then does he permit himself to form an over-all judgment (W). In this way he seeks to protect himself from all those events that are still unknown to him and which he should really fear. Yet he searches out these new, unknown, and adventurous incidents, for often anxiety becomes soldered to pleasure as "anxiety-pleasure," as we see in kleptomaniacs, for instance.

All shocks are symptoms of anxiety.

This statement is nothing but a simplified synopsis, however. One must not, as a rule, diagnose anxiety, anxiety equivalents, or anxiety elaboration on the basis of only one single factor of the form-interpretation test. One is also not permitted to assume positively that one or the other neurotic disturbance exists, if a color shock is produced in combination with the corresponding experience balance. The *total* diagnosis (record and scores) must always and in all instances be kept in mind. The test can never be "read" as if it were a code message.

If several anxiety indicators are found in a test, and if the subject has produced flexor kinesthesias, then one may assume that the subject has a tendency to withdrawal from a menacing anxiety situation into the isolation of his own self, thus renouncing the world. Such a human being is passive, paralyzed.

If, however, extensor kinesthesias are present, as well as some other symptoms of aggression, then one is dealing with subjects who are fighting their anxiety by aggression. People such as these are active human beings. If other, *direct* aggressive signs are absent, then one is dealing with human beings who are always inclined to seek ways to escape.

Both shyness toward other people, and disturbed human relationships growing out of anxiety, are expressed in the test by the fact that more Hd than H are produced. Children who are still at the "totemistic" stage usually also produce a larger number of Ad than A. (If older children or adults produce more Ad than A, that is a sign of low intelligence. While young children are still at the "totemistic" stage, they often replace humans with animals, or experience animals as if they were humans— as if they were their brothers—especially rabbits, kittens, puppies, bear cubs, kids, lambs, etc.) In cases of explicit shyness towards other people, H and Hd are altogether absent. Instead, the number of plant or object responses increases. In retarded people with hysteria, the number of anatomic and O— responses becomes larger, while H% falls below 15.

Anxious individuals who use their aggression as defense show several S in addition to CF. If they produce a color or chiaroscuro shock as well, then their aggression is usually turned inside, toward their own selves. Such subjects display masochistic personality traits, and the manifestations of their intelligence are often partially or completely impeded ("pseudo retardation") despite the fact that their intelligence potential is good. If a pseudo retarded individual then submits to psychotherapeutic treatment and it becomes possible to "release" his aggression (in other words, if one succeeds in making him dare to turn his aggression toward the outer world, to discharge it into the outer world), then, correspondingly, the manifestation of his intelligence will also become possible. Subsequently, the aim of the treatment will be to channel and tame this liberated aggression, making the individual capable of controlling it consciously along the lines of accepted manifestations (desire for activity, delight in work, etc.), and using it for healthy sublimation.

In the following, we shall enumerate *anxiety indicators* that occur in the *Zulliger Test*.

The reader is asked (and this must be stressed once again) not to interpret this list in such a way as to deduce that anxiety exists (although the presence of shocks and MCh would make that permissible) if he encounters *one* of the anxiety symptoms in the test. As a rule, *several* signs must be present before a diagnosis can be made with any degree of certainty.

The following enumeration does not pretend to be absolutely complete.

1. Slackening of associative activity, leading to prolongation of test time in proportion to the number of responses;

2. Decrease in the number of W to the advantage of Dd, Do, and S;

3. Reduction of interpretations, of the number of responses in general;

4. Increase of F+%, because of coarctation of experience balance;

5. Increase of A%, in an attempt to be safe and to think rather in a reproductive-receptive than in a creative manner. Using an old army expression, I might say that one thinks "according to army regulations," in order not to make a mistake. This is why P% is frequently increased;

6. Decrease of O+%, occasionally increase of O−% in people with low mental ability;

7. Reduction of H%;

8. A larger number of Hd than H. Intelligent children frequently produce a larger number of Ad than A;

9. Increase of obj%, plant interpretations, and anat% in people with an intelligence complex;

10. Kinesthesias and color responses decrease, while experience balance becomes coarctated;

11. S, Do, CF are rather on the increase;

12. Sequence changes during the course of the experiment; it either turns into a rigid one, or becomes loose to disorderly, if the individual becomes bewildered;

13. Shocks appear. Among them, chiaroscuro shock points to conscious feelings of anxiety;

14. MCh responses are produced;

15. Ch interpretations of all kinds increase;

16. Rejections occur;

17. Escape into descriptions or idle talk; avoidance of the real task at hand—namely, the *interpretation* of the pictures;

18. Stress on symmetry; irritation because of lack of symmetry.

PART II

The Test Evaluation

15. The Psychogram

A. GENERAL REMARKS

A test evaluation contains everything that may be observed solely by way of the test. It is *by no means, however, a complete diagnosis.*

In a practical situation, it may happen that somebody wishes to obtain nothing but a test evaluation. For instance, a physician sends me a record of a Zulliger Test, asking me to find out what it shows. I do not have any other information about the subject than what may be deduced on the basis of the record and its scores. I do not have any data pertaining to the subject's anamnesis; I do not know the subject's name, what he does, what his profession is, why he went to the doctor, whether he is ill or healthy, whether his illness is psychogenic or purely physical, etc. It is my task to supply the physician with data, since he would like to compare them with his own observations. The test evaluation never reaches his patient; it is meant for the physician alone, and he will integrate it into his own findings concerning the subject.

For *purposes of exercise,* students in training would do well to prepare a number of test evaluations *for their own benefit* (not for that of their subjects).

In working out a test evaluation, one may use various methods. At this point, drawing upon my experiences with people whom I have taught, I should like to suggest a course of action.

Thus, one may begin in the following manner:

Looking over the scores and comparing them with the averages given in the Zulliger Test, one then proceeds to establish which of the scores do not correspond with the averages and are therefore "conspicuous."

For the sake of exercise while studying the test, it has proven advantageous to write down all factor scores on the left side of a sheet of paper, and the psychological meaning that one attaches to them on the right side. After this has been done, the different results must be compared with one another, in order to enable us to determine the degree of intensity that these factors assume within the total picture.

Next we must try to classify these results, and finally, a test evaluation may be worked out.

B. SAMPLES OF TEST EVALUATIONS

Luise Roth will serve as an example.

Let us assume that I proceed in the manner described above under (A). My attention may be drawn to the fact, perhaps, that the number of W is much too small as compared with that for the 6 M. The subject's intelligence must be impaired, I tell myself. Although she possesses excellent productive and creative qualities (many M), she lacks the ability to achieve unification, to comprehend complicated relationships quickly, to orient herself with relative ease within a partly complicated aggregate situation. She manages to organize and to plan, but not without difficulty; she is not capable of correct abstract thinking, and for the most part sticks closely to practical details.

Scrutinizing the M (in the record) more closely, we discover that most of them are flexor kinesthesias. Thus we should expect the subject to be strongly introverted, fond of "dreaming," and not very active. Against this hypothesis stands the fact that the subject produced 23 responses in 12 minutes. We must admit that Luise is not lacking in eagerness for expression, or in the ability for quick formulation. Also, her ability to observe must be noteworthy, for F+ amounts to 91%.

Why, then, does she not produce a larger number of W?

We may arrive at an evaluation by considering that she has produced 6 Dd (and one S). The girl is extremely conscientious (her object criticism points in the same direction). Although Luise has a strong and well-grounded tendency toward combination, she is governed by intense criticism—that is, by self-criticism—for, with an introversive experience balance, S are by necessity directed inward, toward the productive sphere.

As matters stand, Luise recognizes, more or less consciously, the danger that threatens her because of her strong introversive tendencies. She senses that they may induce her to "dream" and lead her to "nursing her own fantasies." Luise escapes from this danger by maintaining strict control over herself. Her self-control does not permit her to be generous in her thinking. It is somewhat tensely that Luise thinks in terms of reality—along the lines of what is obvious and practical, instead of building theories, achieving unification, and using her combinatory capabilities, without always remaining dependent on facts.

The risk of her getting "lost" in her fantasies is also suggested by Luise's slightly loose sequence. Since the girl is still of school age, she must have had a schoolgirl's unpleasant experience—in arithmetic, perhaps—which put her on her guard. As a result, Luise intensified her control. In her behavior, this finds expression in the form of a certain insecurity, as shown in the test by her using "or," which is associated with a tendency to consider different judgments or arguments, and not to commit herself too soon to one specific point of view.

Could this tendency be neurotic? Since no shocks have appeared, we are disinclined to draw such a conclusion. (Strictly speaking, however, we should have expected that a girl at puberty would produce shocks.)

Since there are no shocks and, furthermore, since affectivity seems to be quite well adapted and adaptable (2 FC and 1 CCh), we may conclude that, although Luise controls the expression of her emotions well, she is a warm and gay human being.

H% is quite high and we see, indeed, that Luise stereotypes with H instead of with A. The girl must therefore be strongly dependent upon human relationships. She is concerned, sympathetic, and, since she has produced an Ms, we may assume her to be a "little mother," especially well suited to deal with small children. (This characteristic could be important for her choice of a profession.)

Despite the fact that A% is low, Luise is capable of concentration. The content series supports this finding. It is not too broad in scope and therefore it must definitely be made possible for the girl to "stick" to whatever she may be doing.

In addition to a large number of H responses, the number of object interpretations (21%) is relatively high, as is often seen in children. Luise's comparatively high obj% may indicate that she still manifests strongly infantile traits, such as artless trustfulness (considering H and FC), despite her rather high intelligence level, as well as a clearly apparent school ambition (the test's geographic responses also testify to this). On the other hand, Luise's thinking is completely free from infantile confabulation (absence of DW and DdD).

If, after we have submitted to Luise's father all that we have brought together for a "test evaluation," the surprised father informs us that it is absolutely correct and describes his daughter as if we had known and observed her for a long time, instead of only for the 30-odd minutes that she spent with us while she was being tested, then we have the right to assert that the test is reliable. And if later the girl's teacher also expresses the opinion that confirms everything we have established concerning Luise's intelligence formation, her attitudes, and her deficiencies (Luise is just fair in arithmetic), then we are more than ever convinced that although a "test evaluation" is by no means a "diagnosis" (we shall discuss the differences between a test evaluation and a diagnosis below), it is valuable in itself.

With the assistance of depth psychology, and supported by our knowledge of the symbolism of the unconscious mind, we may amplify the information obtained from the record and the scores.

"Evil eyes" (Card I, second response) indicates a human being who believes that he (or she) is being followed by "evil eyes." Whether this notion is entirely the subject's own paranoid idea, or she is actually being kept under strict control by somebody who makes her uncomfortable, can usually be established with hardly any doubt, on the basis of all the other test factors.

Since Luise is an accurate observer and since, as we have seen, her thinking is fully realistic and not confabulatory, we may assume with a high degree of certainty that whatever is hidden behind these "evil eyes" is real. Somebody is closely guarding Luise and curtailing her freedom. As a result, Luise should manifest intensified self-control, a suggestion already established on the basis of other test factors. It is as if Luise were constantly asking herself: "Am I saying the right thing? am I behaving correctly?", etc.

Is it really only by chance that, after having given the interpretation of the "evil eyes," Luise sees the dark blot situated under the "human head" not as a "butterfly," an "ivy leaf," etc., but as a "pansy"? [In Germany a pansy is called *Stiefmuetterchen,* which means "little stepmother"].

Indeed it is not by chance, for this corresponds with the "inner sequence" (Biaesch). The *Stiefmuetterchen* [pansy] concept gives us information about Luise's "guardian." It is the girl's mother.

We are in the position to support this explanation by some of the other findings. Luise is now 15 years old, and we may assume that she has reached puberty. Among other things, this means that the child is beginning to detach herself from the circle of her closest blood-relations. In the natural course of events, the child must give up old ties in order to be free to establish new ones. It is faced with the task of finding a love object outside its family, and it must be emotionally free, sufficiently to accomplish this task. As a rule, when a girl detaches herself from her fixation to her parents, especially to her mother, she experiences feelings of guilt. According to the strong fixation that the test has shown (H%, FC), Luise projects her guilt feelings onto her mother. Consciously, Luise feels that her mother is accusing her because the child is alienating herself from her, preparing to select another love object. In addition, we must consider still another principle—that, after their daughters have reached puberty, mothers often guard them even more strictly than before. One could say that mothers, too, have become aware of something unspecified. They are conscious of the fact that some change is about to take place or is taking place in their daughters, and they sense or know what it means. They want to protect their daughters, to watch over them, being unwilling to surrender them to strangers (in the sense of a love object). Not infrequently, an element of unconscious jealousy is added. The daughters are begrudged the pleasures of newly blossoming heterosexual love.

On the basis of a multiplicity of emotions, certain tendencies make themselves felt in the mothers, causing them to supervise and control their daughters with more or less mistrust. Precautionary impulses are also in effect, but usually these are conscious.

Employing psychoanalytical terminology we may say that, during a girl's puberty, her female Oedipus complex undergoes a new and final transformation. Correspondingly, the female Cronus complex becomes effective in the mother.

Let us examine the other responses given by Luise to Card I: in line with the "evil eyes" and "pansy" interpretations, the girl expresses her inner insecurity by "or." Then she "escapes into nature" and an "ivy leaf" is interpreted. However, the emotional complex that has been aroused in Luise produces an after-effect. Luise returns to her early childhood; she sees "a little girl with a feather in her head, speaking to her doll while holding it on her lap." An experienced infant-mother situation has been revived, which gives the girl pleasure and makes her laugh, as she offers this response. In a "progressive" sense, this interpretation reveals Luise's wish: motherhood. At the same time, as though calling upon the father to protect her against the fulfillment of her wish, she continues with the following interpretation: "There is a man; he looks up and waves with his cane." Again, this interpretation has a dual meaning: it is concerned with the protecting father, but it also refers to the dreamed-about future husband.

We thus arrive at the following formulation: In her responses to Card I, Luise reveals all the romantic characteristics of her development. After having produced at the very start the commonplace response "crab," in all her succeeding interpretations, she relates to us her basic psychic situation.

Now there appears the colored Card II. The effects of the complexes that were stirred up within her are fading away. There are still the "sisters kissing each other goodnight." This illustrates a persistence of family ties.

The two "curious little boys" in Card III are most revealing to us. They would like to watch the "men" who are carrying a "large butterfly of a strange kind." Here Luise is describing her own curiosity and possibly also her former little-girl wish to be a boy.

The explanations offered above may seem strange to readers who know nothing of depth psychology, not having been able to gather experience in this field. One might say that the examiner has imposed his own fantasies upon the subject, and assert that his statements are mere intellectual constructs.

There is, of course, a great danger that the examiner may have attributed some of his own fantasies to his subject. In order to establish to what extent this has or has not occurred, prevailing conditions should be examined, after the test evaluation has been completed, by a carefully conducted inquiry and by questioning both the subject and the members of his family. Such a procedure should result in establishing whether the examiner has merely imagined things or whether his observations were correct. However, that sort of problem has to do with diagnostic practice, and at this point we wish merely to discuss the work involved in the "test evaluation." On the other hand, since Luise Roth's record and scores are highly interesting and informative, I wanted at this point to indicate to the student the far-reaching perspectives that may be anticipated by using such a simple device as the three-picture Zulliger Test.

It happens, relatively often, that "complex interpretations" and "individual interpretations" are delivered by a subject as soon as Card I is presented to him, and that he thus exposes (to somebody who is capable of comprehending it) everything that fundamentally occupies and affects him.

At this point, something else should be stated emphatically: if we examiners do succeed in uncovering some unconscious processes in the subject, we should not, in a rush of joy over our discovery, inform the subject about it.

In the following (see Tables 1-11 at the end of this chapter), I shall show how a student may carry out and evaluate the scoring by another method, mentioned in the first part of this chapter. Perhaps this is the easier method.

Subject: *Martin Balz,* 12 years old (see Table 1).
Evaluation:

Testing time and number of responses	average.
Number of responses	eagerness for expression; pleasure in expression; unconscious diligence; unconscious quantity ambition.
DW	confabulation.
W and W tendency	tries to unify; has a need for combining.
Confabulation and need for combination	*would like* to combine, but is incapable of doing so; need for completion.
F+% of 60	poor accuracy of observation; most likely low intelligence, close to retardation.
14 D	a rather "practical" individual, who possesses quality ambition, however (DW and W). Lacking nevertheless in intellectual "substance."
Dd, Do	not petty, but easily made anxious.
Do : DW and W	strange mixture of self-consciousness and a tendency to be "generous"; indifferent, confabulatory thinking. Infantile in his thinking; still partially at the fairy-tale age.
S	opposition tendency.
SW	utilizes small details that irritate him, by building them up, in the sense of "making a mountain out of a molehill."
S and F+%	since F+% is low, the S factor cannot be considered indicative of accurate thinking.

S and CF and C	more likely, this is an obstinacy symptom that must become activated (C).
Above factors and intelligence . .	since the boy is not intelligent, his stubbornness may become converted into aggression; C indicates impulsive aggressive outbursts.
M content	indicates aggressive tendencies.
FC, CF, C : M	affectivity is regulated from within, but to a small extent only; extratensive, possibly moody; egocentric attitude; sensible and sensitive, easily hurt, but reacting in a rather coarse manner to the outside world (predominance of CF and C). Easily irritated.
ChF	tendency towards depressive reactions, which are not easily controlled.
Colors and ChF	alternating between being agitatedly gay and morosely ill-humored, uneven in attitude.
FC and H% (too low)	affectivity is partially adaptable; yet, strictly speaking, there are no strong relationships to fellow men; instances of "good fellowship" are established with relative ease, to be sure, but they cannot lead to profound and longlasting friendships; changes companions according to his moods.
A% is of low average	has some difficulty in concentrating.
A%, number of responses and F+%	likes to "chat" about anything and everything; lively "talker."
Sequence	lack of logical discipline in thought processes; deficient in concentration ability.
Apperception type	too broad. Since intelligence is limited, it is not very effective in promoting broad interests and frankness. On the contrary, it is a disturbing factor; thinking is disconnected and confused; here again there is an indication of poor concentration ability.

Perseveration .... lazy; cannot free himself from certain thought contents; although otherwise quite desultory, subject may suddenly become fixated to one idea.

Does not see symmetry .... is complete in himself, does not have a "feeling of inner conflict"; in his egocentricity, the subject is "secure."

Absence of shocks .... no neurotic inhibition at all, no neurosis.

Total general summary .... subject borders on retardation and, since he is an egocentric with too many S and one C, he is probably "erratic; C indicates affect "explosions" (sudden and impulsive acts).

CONCLUSIONS:

Martin's intelligence potential is of such a nature as to barely permit him to follow the lessons in an elementary school. He will be at the bottom of his age group; it is possible that at one time or another he will have to repeat a grade. Although he is industrious—he can be industrious (if he *wants* to be)—intellectually he cannot perform any more satisfactorily than has been described above. It would be fruitless to torment him with homework, etc. On the other hand, Martin is "practical." This is where his capabilities are to be found, and his training should begin with it: model-building, with a view toward later vocational choice. Martin is easily irritated, and his feelings are easily hurt. He alternates between being gay and carefree and depressively ill-humored, stubborn, and morose. His obstinacy may become converted into aggression. Martin finds "pals" easily, but he also gives them up just as easily. His emotional life is intense, yet his emotions are not very deeply felt. If provoked, Martin may become rude. In general, however, he tends to be jolly, in a slightly superficial manner—especially if his friends obey him, if he can boss them, make them do what he wants them to do, and order them about (DW-W tendency!).

Subject: *Hanni Steinmann,* 21 years old (see Table 2).

Evaluation:

Testing time, number of responses	slow-thinking; a slow worker.
W	hardly "generous"; poor in organizing, combining, managing.
D	practical ability.
Dd and S	accurate, conscientious; may be pedantic.
High F+%	thinking well developed; possesses a rather high intelligence; some disturbance must have occurred, preventing the subject from producing a larger number of W! For the same reason, she produces only a few M.
A% of 31	slightly impaired concentration ability.
P% too small	thinking insufficiently adapted; has difficulty thinking with sympathetic understanding. "Dull-witted"; impaired comprehension ability.
High H%, in addition to 3 FC ..	great need for dependency; succeeds in doing excellent work only when she is not frightened by her superiors, when she likes them and feels that she is respected and loved by them. She does not work "objectively," but rather like a child who tries to bring home good report cards, in order to win his parents' love.
Anat	hypochondriacal ideas, apparently based upon susceptibility to illness; "intelligence complex"; believes herself not to be in the right position, from the point of view of her intelligence ability; on the other hand, suffers from feelings of insufficiency.
M (clearly "repressed")	mistrust toward her own inner life; doubts productive, "creative" thinking; subject thinks as if she is forced to, in a reproductive manner.
FC	emotionally relatively well adapted and adaptable, but

C .... occasionally violent and completely inadequate affect-outbursts will occur. Considering ChF, these may, perhaps, take the form of crying spells.

C and S .... extremely violent outbursts of anger are also possible. They are the more surprising, in that otherwise the subject is emotionally restrained (FC).

White seen as color .... the subject does not manifest her hypersensitivity, but disguises it. Her feelings are easily hurt, she is extremely sensitive.

S and C .... tendency toward aggression; may suddenly become aggressive.

"or" .... insecurity.

FCh and ChF .... slight inclination to depressive, dysphoric moods.

Initial shock followed by anat and S .... lets herself be tricked and, when she is tricked, her reasoning stops functioning for some length of time; after conquering her panic attack, she tries to show off her intelligence, becoming defiant at the same time.

Descriptions .... the subject attempts to dilute her emotions or rather their "violence," by trying to merely contemplate, observe, record, instead of experiencing by empathy.

Sequence .... one might infer that a certain insufficiency of logical thinking is present; however, since F+% is as high as 86, this is hardly possible; more probably, the logical function is slightly disturbed by some other symptom.

Experience balance .... extratensive, rather ambiequal, considering the repressed M. Consequently, the subject is gifted in many areas, yet somehow "inhibited," for emotional reasons.

Apperceptive type	broad in scope; the subject's self-critical tendency (S : M) may be too intense; it prevents her from producing more W and M; self-criticism destroys all her intellectual courage; she is much too conscientious and thus unable to be "outspoken" in her test interpretations; in real life, she is much too pedantic to be capable of broad abstractions.
Shocks	neurotic repressions.
Shocks and ambiequal experience balance tending to be extratensive	presumably, compulsion neurosis; in the foreground, however, hysteroid symptoms; compulsive thinking, fussiness, self-doubts, nagging; at the same time, possible headache attacks, or some such conversion symptoms.
Religion	the subject tries to find comfort in religion; she still sees herself, however, as a "small fir tree hanging over a precipice" (individual response), and is afraid for herself.
Absence of WM H P in Card III	loses her head under the influence of emotional excitement; in such circumstances, she is incapable, for a while, of observing the very obvious; paniclike reactions.

CONCLUSIONS:

The subject is a highly gifted girl with many talents; undoubtedly, however, she is prevented from developing fully her intellectual and creative potential, for neurotic reasons. Her religious orientation cannot counteract her insecurity. Her moral sense may become sharpened to scrupulosity—which, among other difficulties, would hold back her progress and slacken the tempo of her work. Because of the young woman's strongly dependent relationship to her fellow men, her ability to perform both quantitatively and qualitatively is highly affected by the attitude of others toward her, as well as by her attitude toward them; this causes conflicts which, under certain circumstances, produce physical symptoms—such as, among others, headaches. Psychotherapeutic treatment must be recommended. Assuming that it is successful, then the young girl should make a professional change, securing a position in which her work would be more than just subordinate. Ultimately, she should change her profession altogether, and find employment at a job in which her work would bring her into contact with other people.

Subject: *Hans Stockar,* 15 years old (see Table 3).

I.

Crab	WF + A P
A tree leaf, a plane-tree leaf (dark inner area)	DF + pl
Rocky peninsula (right outer area, DE/2/3)	DdF + geog

II.

Two moles. "But they should be darker in color" (orange area) ..	DFC A object criticism
Shrubs (green area)	DFC pl
The green also resembles cuttle-fishes	DF— A
"the white in it would be the eyes"	SF ± Ad
Two women's heads (red top area)	DoF + Hd
c Two small monkeys are sitting there (darker red area)	DM + A O

III.

Two Indians, dancing (outer red area)	DM + H P
Tails of little pigs (adjoining the small dark figure, left upper portion)	DoF + Ad
c Fish head (portion in the small dark figure, dark center portion)	DdF + Ad
c A small whole pig (small dark figure, right top portion)	DF + A
c Butterfly (red center area)	DF + A P
Two men talking gaily to each other and swinging [their arms] .	WM + H P

208

Evaluation:

Testing time and number of responses	average performance ability.
Apperceptive type and W	manifold interests, candid; average in abstract thinking and combination ability (possibly below average).
Do, inverse sequence	anxious, careful, self-conscious, shy.
Dd and S	accurate, exact, reliable.
F+%, entire percentage series ..	average, adequate intelligence.
D—Dd type	more of a "practical" nature, technically skillful; M point in the same direction.
M	not without creativity for small things; rather introverted.
Experience balance	controlled by internal guidelines, yet not depressive (absence of F); gay but not subdued temperament; good-natured, not aggressive.
S and experience balance	easily prone to self-doubts.
S, intelligence, and object criticism	thinks quite accurately; slightly critical trait; strong observational powers.
Colors (FC only)	affectivity adaptable and adapted.
P%, O%, and F+% averages ...	adequate intellectual grasp.
H%	average ability to sympathize with others, to feel their pleasure or grief.
O response	friendly mockery; childish pleasure in animals.
Shock	beginning of puberty, no doubt. With regard to all other test factors, "neurosis" can hardly be diagnosed; however, since Hans produces in a rigid sequence only 3 responses to Card I, then 6 and finally 5 interpretations for Card II and III respectively, and a Do for Card II, loosening and inverting the sequence in Card III, one may assume that inner uneasiness is a possibility, and surmise that it is associated with his age.

CONCLUSIONS:

The subject possesses adequate elementary-school intelligence. His interests are practical rather than theoretical. He is manually skillful, probably a builder of models. He is candid and, emotionally speaking, friendly. He is not moody (absence of CF) and is controlled from within. He is jolly, without "going overboard"; observes well, but not without criticism, which he applies also to himself. He is amiable, a good companion; he loves animals. Generally speaking, the subject is a lively boy. He has a sense of humor and, although he easily becomes shy and self-conscious, he occasionally delights in teasing others, but never in a wicked, malicious manner.

It seems that at present Hans is laboring under certain conflicts—puberty conflicts—yet he can hardly be called neurotic.

Subject: *Heini Zumbrunn,* 16 years old (see Table 4).
(Blind diagnosis for foster father. Recorded by family doctor.)

I.

(Turns the cards back and forth,
  b-c-a-d-a) .... initial shock
Animal with *horns* or two animals
  with horns; hornets, which are
  against each other — .... DWF ± A "or"
It could also resemble a butterfly.. WF + A
Head of a cat seen from behind
  (B 4 and 7) .... DF ± Ad

II.

Blood stains on the ground. Here
  is grass .... ⎧ DW CF nat, C tendency
                combinatory ⎨ DCF earth
                             ⎩ DFC pl
This could also be a piece of bark,
  torn off from a fir tree. It is
  reddish and *eaten up* by beetles ⎧ DCF pl
                combinatory ⎨ SF + Ad/pl O
Halloween mask (red area with S) S → DF ± mask
Cut off roots (orange area)[1] ...... DFC pl

---

[1] In response to *inquiry:* "Cut-off roots do have such a color!"

210

Mountains on a map (within
   orange area) .... DdCCh geog
Lake and (S within green area) .. $\Big($ SF ± lake
            combinatory $\Big\{$
Grass around it (green area) .. $\Big)$ DFC pl
c A cloud that has been torn apart
   (red area) .... S → DCF cloud

III.

c A man sitting in a tree (large dark   DM + H O, flexor kinesthesias
   blot, top towards center) ......   "tree" = confabulation
b Face of a *wicked* animal (large
   dark blot on top, a portion of it) DdF ± Ad
a "As if one has spilled water; then
   there are such spots" (total dark
   area) .... ChF → WF ± water O—
d Dragon, a *wicked* animal (large
   dark blot on top) .... Ch → DF + A

Evaluation:

Testing time and number of
   responses ....

since H. Z. displays a prolonged reaction time but produces 18 responses in spite of it, the conclusion
may be drawn that his thinking is
sluggish and regulated by quantity
ambition.

DW and confabulation ....

infantile "wishful thinking." Fantasies and observed contexts are
woven together; thinking is inaccurate, not "neat," and the reliability of his statements is questionable; deceives himself and others.

D type and 1 MO ....

practical-minded by inclination;
should be skillful in the area of
manual work.

Dd and S ....

nagging characteristics.

S and CF ....

stubbornness; aggressive tendencies.

S and M and "or" ....

uncertain of himself, cautious;
taking Ch into consideration, probably also adaptation by conscious
shrewdness.

H% and FC ....

poor relationship to others; H. Z. is
quite indifferent to other people.

"Mask" .... | suggests a masklike attitude; he does not reveal himself as he really is; tendency toward concealment.

Flexor kinesthesias .... | "nurses" his fantasies autistically; autistic introversion.

Absence of WM H P in Card III . | represses his inner life; escapes in the direction of extratensive experience.

Low F+% .... | inferior intelligence; lower than average for an elementary-school student.

P% and initial shock .... | when confronted with a new situation, does not orient himself at first; has difficulty "imagining himself" within a given situation; his intellectual grasp is rather poor.

A5 and sequence .... | his power of concentration is easily thrown off balance; does not think "logically."

DW and experience balance and S .... | could be a thief; it is possible that he steals because of resentment, a desire to harm others, and autism.

"Against each other," "eaten up," "cut off," "torn apart," "wicked" .... | sadomasochistic characteristics; there is an element of morbidity in him, a fact that is also indicated by his tendency to produce pure color responses. Taking this into account, we may suspect an *active tendency to steal.*

"Horns," "wicked" .... | probably feels himself under attack; feels that he "comes last"; possibly *social* resentment.

28% pl .... | escapes from people into nature; lives more "vegetatively" than "humanly."

Geog .... | the schoolboy's attitude is not alien to H. Z.; this attitude could be his "mask."

CF and sadomasochistic characteristics and S CCh .... | this is *not harmless;* he is endangered; *delinquent* tendencies; he would

212

	like to control his impulsive emotions but, because of his inferior mentality, he can hardly succeed.
DW CF in Card II	poor combinatory power; it may very well be that he is brutal (in view of his sadism).
O+ and O—	has original ideas, alternating between being true to reality and being strange.
"Water spots"	masturbation.

CONCLUSIONS:

The subject is intellectually poorly endowed. He probably has delinquent tendencies and tends to steal because of social resentment, with the aim of harming and destroying. Doubtless his hereditary characteristics are deficient. Since H. Z. conceals himself behind masked behavior, it may be assumed that he has a brittle, unpredictable personality.

He could be a candidate for a "special training home," where he might be disciplined by habit formation. (At any rate, H. Z. is endangered.) Perhaps he could be subdued and restrained in a trade school that would meet his own demands ("professional training"), and where he would be trained for a trade (cabinet maker, gardener [C!], house painter). The prognosis for his development is rather poor.

The *family doctor's report* by telephone after the conclusions had been forwarded: H. Z. has committed a number of thefts and has destroyed some bicycles in a "devilish" manner. The physician suspects him to be a *psychopath;* he believes that referral to a special training school is indicated.

The subject is an illegitimate son of a slightly retarded farm girl; his father is a vagrant. H. Z. has always been a "difficult" child. His foster parents are "proper" people, and their patience is to be admired; now, however, it is exhausted. H. Z. was employed as a farmhand; he was cruel to the farm animals, withdrawn, "peculiar" with other people. One never knows where one stands with H. Z.; he can be "nice" if he wants to, and if it suits his interests.

Subject: *Peter Stoll,* 12 years old (see Table 5).

I.

This resembles a leaf (dark inner
   area) .... DF + pl
Head of a crab .... DoF + Ad (P)
Prongs of an earwig (the "sickles"
   on top) .... DF + Ad

II.

Fishes (orange area) .... DF— A
Or beetles attacking each other ... DFC A, aggression, "or"
Fish bone (S within red area) .... SF ± Ad/anat
Thigh of a slaughtered animal, at
   a butcher shop (red area) ...... D CF food O

III.

Two little men with long noses
   (large dark blots) .... DF + H Ms tendency
Butterfly (red area) .... DF + A P
Two gnomes (small dark blots) ... DF + H Ms tendency
c And here is a wild boar (portion
   of the small dark blot) .... DF + A

The test is meager; yet the Bero, Ro, Wartegg, and Matrix
tests, which were performed with Peter in order to check the
results of the Zulliger Test, did not produce additional or different results. We shall reply to the foster parents' question:
"What about the boy's intelligence—is he retarded?"

Evaluation:

Testing time and number of
   responses: average, only 11
   responses .... not especially happy or eager to ex-
                               press himself; rather somewhat with-
                               drawn and anxious; observes keen-
                               ly, however.
Absence of DW .... distinguishes very well between
                               reality and fantasy; is reliable in his
                               thinking.
Absence of W .... incapable of grasping large com-
                               plexes, of combining and thinking
                               abstractly. He is also unable to
                               organize. Among other children, he
                               is certainly not the "leader type." He
                               is rather modest.

S and CF	outbreaks of suppressed opposition are possible ("suppressed" because P. S. does not like to talk).
A%	somewhat easy-going, "lazy."
H% and FC	his interest in other people is not strong.
Ms tendency	likes to play by himself, slightly lonely, without being troubled by it.
S and aggressive response (although absence of M)	he may become aggressive, if he is not too lazy to exert himself; his capabilities are of a reproductive nature.
Sequence and other intelligence factors	he hardly likes to think, has no interest in it.
anat tendency	does not want to be taken for a "stupid" person, however.
Experience balance	lack of inner experiences; "takes life as it comes to him," takes experiences as they offer themselves to him.
Considering everything observed so far	short-sighted realism; lives "from hand to mouth."
Content series	"vegetative existence" rather than "experiencing" and "living."
Food	not many interests; scanty, non-spiritual; oriented primarily toward the physical needs of life.
Color series	sensitive; in general, no strong emotions, however. Somewhat dull in his emotional reactions; slack.
Apperceptive type	according to his predisposition, he is a "practical type." His manual skills should be promoted; he could perform in this field more efficiently than in school.
No shocks	no sign of neurosis, no "repressions."
Answer to the question pertaining to retardation	the subject is not retarded, yet he is uninterested; he has no ambition to succeed in school.
Absence of M	lacking in inner qualities and creative abilities.

CONCLUSIONS:

There is no doubt that the boy is not retarded. However, he is not interested in school work, but rather in playing and model-building. He is capable of engaging in these activities by himself, although he needs to be supervised, for otherwise he daydreams. Since boys of Peter's age are usually not as "lazy," it may be assumed that, physically, he is not entirely fit. It would be therefore advisable to give Peter a thorough physical examination, including analyses of blood and hormone secretions.

Subject: Miss *L.B.*, 18 years old (see Table 6).

I.

	This is a human being who has been cut open; one can see that	ChF → DWF ± H O—
	the head, ...	DF + Hd
	the eye sockets, and	SF + Hd
	here the lungs	DF— anat
c-b-a	This could be a water lily, here is the stem (bottom left)	DdDF— pl, confabulation

II.

	A woman's abdomen (red area), (smiles)	S → DCF sex
	It could also be the stomach	DCF anat
	Here is a beet root (orange area) .	DCF pl
	White flower with green	SCF pl
	leaves	DCF pl
	Plant in a flower pot (S within the red area and S adjoining the lower portion of the red area) .	SF + pl
	A lion's head (orange confluent area)	DdF— Ad
c	The stomach of a cow with its various parts (orange area)	DCCh Ad/anat O—
c	Dandelion leaves (orange area, upper periphery as card is held in c-position)	DdF ± pl
a	A lady's fur piece with animal heads (entire orange area)	DCF fashion, clothing
	A pair of lovers (red area) (laughs sweetly)	DM + H
		individual interpretation, sex

216

III.

A mask (large dark blot, outer upper portion)	Do → DF + mask
A whole human figure	WM + H P
Two little monkeys from a picture book (outer red area)	DF + H (P)
A rat (entire small dark blot) ...	DdDF— A
This too is a human head (lowest portion of the small dark blot)	DdF ± Hd
Bridge, viewed from above (center line of the inner red area)	DdF— obj O—
A little church (small blob situated on the "head" of the "men")	DdF— obj
Mountain (at the left dark blot, left upper portion on the "head" of the "men")	DdF + nat

Evaluation:

Number of responses F+%	considerable eagerness for expression, yet brings forth mostly just "empty talk"; inferior intelligence.
DW and DdD	taking confabulation into account, there is suspicion of mental retardation.
DW, DdD, and CF	stealing tendencies which are most probably active (CF and S are too numerous).
Apperceptive type is too broad, while A% is too small	cannot control herself by self-discipline, cannot "pull herself together." Apperceptive type is too confused, and ability for stereotypy is too inadequate; lets herself go, lets herself be carried away by the instancy of the immediate situation.
Lacking in W	cannot generalize, deceives herself in this respect; "near-sighted."
DW + confabulation tendency S and experience balance	obstinate to aggressive
Sex, S, and CF	sexually aggressive; her interest in others is chiefly sexual, it is physically determined.

anat . . . . in part, they are disguised sexual interpretations, although they are otherwise displayed in an unrestrained fashion; in other words, the subject is even more influenced by sex than is directly expressed by the two sexual interpretations in the test; since there are so many CF, her sexuality may be slightly cruel. The subject's instinctive drives and instinctive needs must be intense.

Mask . . . . these instinctive drives and needs are disguised, however, with full awareness. The subject has acquired a masklike attitude; she "plays herself up."

Clothes . . . . she "plays herself up" with clothes too. On the basis of her intelligence, one would expect L. B. to be the type who would wear fake costume jewelry, etc.

No shocks . . . . nothing is repressed, no neurosis.

Number of responses, intelligence factors and CF . . . . busy, active, lively, "something" must be "going on" all the time.

CF type . . . . prone to moods; but is gay, carefree.

Absence of Ch . . . . by no means depressive; she is thoughtless and inconsiderate with words and most certainly with deeds as well.

nat . . . . possesses infantile characteristics.

anat . . . . believes herself to be intelligent; believes that she is not sufficiently appreciated in her environment with regard to her intelligence ("intelligence complex").

P% and O% . . . . inadequate intellectual grasp; finds it difficult to understand the ideas of other people.

H% . . . . strong need for people. However, since CF predominate, this need is egocentric: the subject would like to see her own reflection in others; she regards them as her servants. In view of her sex responses, her interest in others is mainly sexual.

CONCLUSIONS:

L. B. is endangered from two directions: she could steal (if she does not do so already), and she is predisposed to prostitution. Her extremely strong sexual needs, her undisciplined conduct, her stupidity, and her desire for fashionable clothes constitute an intense drive to which she *submits*. The picture of a prostitute presents itself; she could become a prostitute who steals.

Additional statement: The girl could not endure employment as a housemaid anywhere, or for any length of time. She has changed her jobs continuously, taking along some of her "madam's" clothes and jewelry (mostly quite valueless). When she was leaving one of her jobs, L. B. stole a valuable gold ring from the woman for whom she worked; the latter reported her to the police, to whom she confessed to a long list of other thefts. On this occasion, it was also revealed that she had been going out nights, attaching herself to a soldier or some other man who bought her drinks and with whom she then had sexual intercourse in some park, etc. She did not know the names of her "lovers," and never visited them in their homes. Nor did she ever directly ask them for compensation. (From the files of the youth agency.)

Subject: *Nelly Farner,* 18 years old (see Table 7).

I.

This is a faded ink blot which has been folded together	ChF → WF ± blot, description
Bat	WF + A
Cloud	ChF → WF ± cloud
Animal paw (B4 and 7)	DF + Ad
A dog's face (top center)	S → DF + Ad
A plant leaf (center, dark area) ...	DF + pl
Sole of a shoe (left gray portion) ..	DdF ± obj clothing
This is a monkey, sitting there (left bottom portion)	DM + A O

II.

Roots of a plant (orange area); they are kind of reddish	DCF pl
But also some animal from the earth	DCF A
Two bears are smelling each other (red area)	DM + A

219

b Infant in diapers (S within upper
   green blot) ....   SMs H O

d Lion or tiger, sitting (upper green
   area) ....   DF + A "or"

a A sea monster with many feet
   (green area) ....   DF ± A

b Face of a monkey with a long nose
   (orange portion in upper blot) ..   DdF + Ad

a Fighting buffaloes (orange area) ..   DF + A aggression

  Also, the earth that they have
   kicked up (orange area) ....   DC earth

III.

  Butterfly (red center area) ....   DF + A P

  Or also a lion jumping through
   fire (red center area, the ani- {   DdMs A O "or"
   mal figure is the center line) {   DC fire   combinatory

  Shadow of a wash line (dark blots)   ChF → WF ± shadow O

  Face of a dwarf (large dark blot,
   upper left outer portion) ......   DoF + Hd (F)

c Thumbtack remover (small dark
   blot) ....   DF + obj

  Mouse running away (part of small
   dark blot) ....   DF + A

  Cloud (small dark blot) ....   ChF → DF ± cloud
                           Duration: 7 minutes

Evaluation:

Relative reaction time and num-
  ber of responses ....   strong need for communication; de-
                                light in talking; ability for very easy
                                productivity.

Since F+% is high ....   keen power of observation; strong
                                sense of reality.

Since absence of DW ....   no confabulation.

O% is high, P% is too low .....   has a gift for thinking originally,
                                rather than adjusting her thinking
                                to that of others.

"A lion jumping through fire"
  (III/2 and 3), "shadow of a
  wash line" (III/4), "earth
  kicked up by buffaloes" (II/9),
  and other such responses.....   the subject's "own" thinking may
                                be occasionally somewhat bizarre;
                                this also holds true with regard to

Loose-orderly sequence ....

her affectivity, which displays a tendency toward exaltation.
the subject's logical function is inconsiderable; her thinking is slightly undisciplined.

Broad apperceptive type, versatile content column ....

many-sided interests, but insufficient power of concentration; flighty ideas, supported by affectivity; her interests constantly turn toward new things.

Few M : C ....

more energetic activity than intellectual depth.

Rather extratensive experience balance ....

not persistent in her interests; changeable, fluttering everywhere like a butterfly.

Experience balance = 2 M : 1 FC, 2 CF, 2 C ....

unstable, moody, highly egocentric (C), explosive; given to enthusiasm, typically "sanguine" temperament.
"shooting to the skies" with delight, then utterly miserable; emotionally exuberant and uneven; strong and extensive vitality, strong instinctive drives alternating in between.

ChF ....

C, egocentricity ....
Flexor kinesthesias ....

emotional outbursts and autistic daydreaming.

Low H%, few FC, "bears" are interpreted instead of H in II/3, they are "smelling each other" (sex) ....

would like to adjust her affectivity, yet it is not adjusted; needs other people for her own confirmation; she does not actually "love" them, however, for she loves only herself; narcissism, most probably egoism as well.

M and C, MO and absence of MP ....

instability must be considerable; subject may well change from extratensive to introversive orientation. She is emotionally unstable, unpredictable, unreliable.

Ch and descriptions .... subject tries to master her affectivity by making every possible effort to do so, instead of permitting herself to experience spontaneously. Whenever the subject consciously holds back her emotions, she becomes depressed.

C .... tendency toward impulsive outbursts, emotional behavior.

S .... tends also toward violent defiance, which evaporates quickly, however.

S and aggression .... violence may change to aggression.

CF and Ms .... egocentric need for adornment and elaborate attire; infantile vanity, self-reflection. Yet also real pleasure in beauty (Ms O), as well as in fairytale and decorative settings.

Most responses to Card II, no Ch in Card III, ending with C .... does not feel comfortable until affectivity is stimulated and can be given free rein; otherwise, lets herself go and under certain circumstances even "sinks."

Interpretation II/3 is a disguised sexual interpretation .... sexuality is repressed, probably rejected, because it is "animallike" to her.

Number of responses, reaction time, F+%, P%, O%, affectivity .... the subject approaches everything with too much freedom from constraint; her personality is interwoven with a somewhat playful and effervescent attitude.

No shock, yet absence of WMH P in Card III. Do appears in Card III following a C and ChF and then immediately F+ again .. although there is no real neurosis, because the subject is emotionally too outspoken, passing neurotic behavior patterns are not unknown to the subject; however, she "catches herself" immediately, and overcomes inner inhibitions with relative speed and ease.

CONCLUSIONS:

Our attention is drawn primarily to N. F.'s instability. It causes the subject to be unpredictable, unreliable, and moody, and it induces her to change her interests often and abruptly. She can hardly stick to any job. Although N. F. has a better than average intelligence (high average) and considerable creative ability, her work performance is only poor-to-inferior, because she is superficial and scintillating. At times she attracts one's attention by an occasional brilliant performance, but she does not live up to what one would expect on the basis of such promise. She is "shouting with joy" at one moment and "utterly miserable" at another, alternating between depression and gaiety, enthusiasm, exalted emotional loftiness. At the same time, she is egocentric and in flight (probably from herself). Somehow N. F. is endangered, although hardly from the sexual point of view. Stealing impulses are absent in the subject, but she tends to let herself go, to become generally demoralized although not delinquent. Roaming about, her interests are always shallow and change rapidly. She is capable of only passing enthusiasm; she is highly egocentric and her egocentricity alternates with autism. N. F. has a sense for beauty, for adornment, she has artistic impulses; but she is not stable enough to accomplish anything either creatively or reproductively in the artistic field. Most probably, the subject could apply herself to dancing. With time she could, perhaps, become productive in this field, although her endeavors might not be of a permanent nature; yet change is inherent in dancing. There is some danger here too, however. Already the subject's attitude shows certain "star mannerisms." Emotional discipline is completely absent. N. F. is not endangered sexually because she is much too narcissistic.

The total picture resembles that of a spoiled "only" child who reacts with depression if her changing desires and impulses are not gratified without delay. She is emotionally "without a master," regarding herself as the center of the universe and, if the world does not comply with her wishes, turns away from it, wrapped in autism.[2]

---

[2] See also the results of other form-interpretation tests performed with N. F. in the section on "Post-Standardization."

Subject: *Arnold Gamper,* salesman of farm machines, very successful in his profession, yet discontented; 27 years old. Asks whether he should change his profession and become a teacher (see Table 8).

I.

Crab	WF + A P
A dog's face (top center portion) .	S → DF + Ad
b,d Two mice facing each other. The fat round body and the tail are very distinct, the head less so ...	WF + A object criticism
Marble stone sculpture, depicting mother and child (upper left outer periphery)	FCh → DF (C) scene
c Here there is a lovely woman's face looking out (c-position, bottom left dark area in gray area)	DdF + Hd
c Strawberry leaf (dark inner area) or ivy	DF + pl "or"
c Cross (around the round S, center surrounding it)	DdF + obj
c Monkey hanging with its head down and doing physical exercises (in c-position, upper right dark portions)	DM + A (O)

II.

Beetles or ants, red ones (orange area)	DFC A, "or"
The whole is something from plant anatomy; parts of a flower have been taken apart; blossoming flower (red area) with green, wilted, dry leaves	WCF pl O
This red color: whether I want to or not, a sexual image forces itself upon me—a female organ	S → DCF sex
Red and green are not compatible, they are too harsh in their relationship to each other	description, criticism, color shock
c It represents a map with islands and fjords (orange area)	D CCh geog
a Exotic plant in a flower pot (S within red area)	SF + pl

224

III.

Carousel figures dancing around something	⎧ WM + H P (O)
Or two old maids bowing to each other and presenting each other with bouquets of flowers (red center area)	⎨ WM + H O (P) combinatory "or"
	⎩ DCF pl
Butterfly (red center area)	DF + A P
Little dancing bears (red outer area)	DM + A (P)
Men wearing pointed helmets, lifting their legs, stalking in step (upper inner portion of the large dark blot)	DM + H O
Mice (portions of the small dark blot)	DF + A
Some saurian, looking back, threatening, with a long neck (in d-position, portion of the upper large dark blot, portion adjacent to the right part)	FCh → DdF + A

Duration: 11 minutes

Evaluation:

5 W, F% equals 100, 21 interpretations with an average reaction time of 30 seconds, combinatory tendency, orderly sequence, broad apperceptive type, 4 M, one of them in Card II ....

ability to produce and to work; superior intelligence; quality and quantity ambition; planning and organizing ability; good practical ideas.

Ambiequal experience balance ..

gifted in many areas: "manifold abilities."

4 M extensor kinesthesias .....
Preponderance of extensor kinesthesias ....

introversive qualities, which persistently press toward realization.
subject is not a person who is satisfied with "dreams" alone.

M repression, H repression ...

has somehow experienced disappointment in other people.

Object criticism and S : intelligence ....

critical attitude; keen ideas; keen thinking.

M : C ....   affects controlled by inner forces; self-restraint, temperate affectivity, spirited, controlled impulsive behavior (CF : M).

P%, A%, O% ....   has worthwhile ideas of his own (high F+%), yet his thinking is well adapted to that of others, ability to comprehend with empathy, better than average and effortless intellectual grasp.

Reaction time, experience balance, F (C), FCh, and apperceptive type ....   capacity for empathy; ability for both extratensive and introversive contacts; wide horizons in both the emotional and intellectual areas, "maturity" in both; serious-joyful mood.

H% ....   supports the evidence of a better-than-average capability for human contact.

A% and content column ......   capable of concentration.

Shock[3], experience balance, and S ....   self-doubts, self-criticism, neurotic compulsion to be exact.

F+% (too high) ....   compulsive precision, tendency to "over-conscientiousness."

Counseling: Subject should continue in his profession, yet should work in another of its branches, where he could be more independent. He has the capabilities for becoming an independent business executive, for he is generous and yet exact. He will never be happy in a subordinate position, but will always be dissatisfied. He should have the possibility of "developing," of building himself up. He is well suited for the position of a plant director, for in such a position he could be competitive. He is a "leader" type.

He would not be happy as a teacher, because a teacher's position is too subordinate. Dealing with students is not quite appropriate for A. G. (too few Dd, absence of Ms) because he needs to compete with adults and not with children, among

---

[3] Also shown by the fact that among 21 responses only 5 were produced for Card II!

whom he would be too much of a superior. He needs opposition, in order to overcome it; opposition rouses him to action. It does not inhibit him; on the contrary, its effect is stimulating to him.

Therefore, the advice to the subject is not a change of profession, but a change of the department within it.

His "hobbies" should be model-building (M, F (C) and **CF**, the latter as an expression of motor activity), not too strenuous athletic exercises, some sports, gymnastics.

Remark: If it is possible to carry out a detailed anamnestic investigation beforehand, a sufficient amount of insight for advice may be supplied in cases like A. G.'s, on the basis of a Zulliger Test alone.

Encouraged by the Zulliger Test and counseling, A. G. applied for a position in a fine-art printing firm. He was employed, obtained power of attorney very soon thereafter, and is today (has been for the last three years) the happy director of the firm, which is prospering progressively under his leadership.

Subject: *Margarethe Schenker,* 23 years old, student of philosophy. Asks whether she should change to the study of medicine or enter a nunnery (see Tables 9 and 10).

I.

Like a mask that is transparent .. ChF → WF ± mask O perspective
Also something like a dry leaf .. FCh → WF + pl
Dwarf blowing his nose, ABC 3/4 DM + H O

II.

Two brown insects (orange area) DFC A P
a-b-d In the foreground two buffalos
    facing each other; "seen from
    the back, this is not correct"
    (red area) .... DF ± A, object criticism
The white has a nice form ...... SF + form criticism;
                      tendency toward description

Dove above the cross, on top (in
    response to inquiry: "The
    dove is white") .... SFC religion
                      SF + obj, religion
                      white as color
                      DdSF + religion

God's face, trinity (dark red area
behind dove, and, in part,
portion of S situated under it
are included) .... combination, intuition, O;
guilt feelings.

c On top there is again a dove
(situated between red and
orange areas) .... SF + A
Somebody raising himself up,
stabs the insect behind the
mask; it is humanlike, but it
is an animal (green area) ..... DM + H/A O Ms tendency
aggression, H repression

III.

Two chaps with a butterfly in
the middle .... $\left\{ \begin{array}{l} \text{WM} + \text{H P} \\ \text{DF} + \text{A P} \end{array} \right.$ combinatory

Little fire devils are jumping out
of the chaps (red outer area) .. DMC H P O
c A little devil is falling now, and
he pricks one of the chaps in
the nose; another one is sit-
ting upon the back of his neck DM + H O combinatory
And on top of him a gnome is
sitting as well; it is not easy
for him (small dark blot) ..... DF + H
b Something like fire is escaping
from the chimney; it is like
an explosion .... D CCh explosion O
This is a chap like a caricature .. DM + H
with legs (small upper blot,
when the card is held by the
b-corner in a slanted position) DF + H ➔ M repression
Duration: 16 minutes

Evaluation:

S, number of responses, reaction
time and F+% ....

the subject's keenly critical mind
holds her productivity back.

High F+%, large number of M
Extensor kinesthesias and FC/C
Flexor kinesthesias ....

markedly "creative" mind.
drive to give form to imagination.
(less strong) drive for autistic enjoyment of imagination.

228

Combination, MC, intuition, dramatization, perspective ...	pronounced dramatic ability; also ability for plastic formations. The subject has a feeling for languages, rather than a gift for mastering them (although such a gift is not to be ruled out).
Small A%, orderly-loose sequence with high F+%	marked "artistic" intelligence.
Stereotypy with H	strong human ties; power of concentration is not reduced, although A are few.
Broad experience balance	broad outlook; many interests, wide horizon.
FCh, ChF, Ch	tendency towards dysphoric, elegiac moods, etc.
C, aggression, S	these moods are driven away by way of aggression; aggression is for the most part expressed in the form of sharp criticism.
White as color	hypersensitivity, which the subject tries to cover up.
H%, H repression and DdS.... (this occurs as an attempt to incorporate S into the larger context, analogous to WS)	has been disappointed by people who were close to her.
Religion	strong religious feelings and fantasies.
W tendency (see apperceptive type)	the subject is longing for generosity in a positive sense (high F+%); ability for combining and organizing; desire for freedom with regard to artistic potential, desire for free formative expression.
H%, FC, guilt feelings	tendency to subordination, because of guilt feelings; the discrepancy between the desire for freedom and the tendency to subordination creates tension, which may be the explanation for Ch tendency, indicating depressive moods. Intense feeling of discouragement.
Ch : ChF : FCh : M, C and S	the subject raises herself out of depression, like the Phoenix rising

from his ashes. Her vitality is strong, it is more intensive (M) than extensive.

Shock, description, and experience balance .... traces of psychasthenic characteristics, such as self-doubts, feelings of insufficiency; seen from this point of view: escape into religion, religious devotion.

Counseling: The subject should neither enter a nunnery nor study medicine. If she should decide on studying medicine nonetheless, then she should take up pediatrics. At the same time she should write, occupy herself with dramatics and formative arts (become a sculptress, for example). Whenever possible, she should have systematic artistic training, with a specific artistic goal for the future. Ultimately she may enter the field of commercial art or ceramics, in order to make a living and to become acquainted with the technical side of this field.

Why would it be erroneous for the subject to enter a nunnery? This idea of hers is only partially derived from an authentic religious desire. In part it is determined by a need for escape: it is a "means of getting away from people." In the nunnery (of the "mother"), God (the loving "father": see the corresponding response for Card II) is sought as a protector; guilt feelings too are at work here, promoting the subject's wish to become a member of a nunnery. In view of her *strong* desire for freedom, however, the subject could not be happy in a nunnery in the long run, not even if she were permitted to devote herself as far as possible to art. Furthermore, from the religious point of view, the subject, being a "faithful servant," is bound by duty to apply the "talents" which were given to her by the "Lord" in such a manner as to "draw interest"—in other words, to make something of them.

Comparison of the results of the Zulliger, Rorschach, and Behn-Rorschach Tests of Margarethe Schenker (Table 10): After the factors have been evaluated, the results of the Ro and Bero are to a great extent in agreement with those of the Zulliger Test, and confirm them. They do not contain anything that could not have been clearly seen on the basis of the Zulliger Test alone.

Through practical experience, one gradually acquires such familiarity with the meanings of the factors that, when one is evaluating, one does not consider the individual factors of the test but "sees" the entire test, its total scores as well as the record.

Consequently, one will hardly use the method demonstrated in the last ten samples, but will rather begin arbitrarily at some point, delve into the test, and then add all the remaining factors.

The next example will illustrate this procedure (see Table 11).

Subject: *Celine Kohler,* 19 years old, a domestic

I.

Dry, faded tree leaf	ChC → WF + pl
A sea crab	DF + A P
Pansies (center dark area)	DF + pl
b It could also be a country with mountains and small lakes—it is so blurred	ChF → DWS F ± geog
And here now is the boot of Italy (D 9)	DdF ± geog

II.

Caterpillars; only there aren't such brown ones, they should be green (orange area)	DF + A P object criticism
(After long hesitation) Sex organ (red area including S)	DSCF sex O—
Map with mountains (portion of orange area, F 3)	DdCCh map, geog
c Seafish (green area)	DF + A
c Flower (D 5/6)	SF + pl
Peasant painting, there are such strange plants there (S)	SW? WSCF ornament O tendency to C

III.

Two she-devils	WM + H P
Fire (center red area)	DC fire
Or a butterfly	DF + A P
c Head of a wild animal (CD 1/2) ..	DF ± Ad

231

c Mouse (E 3) .... DF + A
a Dwarfs running about (red outer
    area) .... DM + H P
b A rabbit's foot (C 4) .... DdF + Ad
c Trunk of an elephant (B 3/4) .... DdF + Ad (sex)
    Spilled black and red water colors   WC water colors
                                         Duration: 15 minutes

CONCLUSIONS:

The fact that a female subject, while being examined by a male examiner, produces sex interpretations indicates frankness. These are not any less suspicious, however, and suggest that such a subject is harboring a great many sexual ideas and fantasies. After a color shock, Celine produces a sexual SCF interpretation and another one that does not become conscious. It appears in the symbol of a "trunk" (a vulgar term for "penis"). This indirect expression shows (as does her hesitancy in response II/2) that Celine fights her fantasies, trying to ward them off; she does not succeed, however. Undoubtedly sexual repressions take place nevertheless and exert their influence. The question must be raised of how this influence is effected, and what substitute formations have occurred.

Combining all CF and S, as well as considering Celine's tendency to confabulation, as expressed by DW (Card I) and WSCF (Card II, the latter score is more likely an SW), we come upon a "thieving syndrome." As happens quite frequently, unconsciously Celine may have chosen stealing as a neurotic sexual substitute (Zulliger, 1953e). It seems, however, that the girl is capable of overcoming such an impulse, because she produces M and is highly intelligent (high F+%, A%, and P% suggest better than average adaptability; inverse sequence indicates caution). Are these inhibitions sufficient to control her impulses to steal? H% is low and FC are absent. On the other hand, there is a CCh, which indicates that self-controlling tendencies are effective in Celine.

We shall now weigh the facts. Since H% is low, since the subject produced two S and one WS, and since FC are absent, the impulse to steal should not become active except when Celine takes on an attitude of defiance (2–3 S!). Since (strangely enough) the dark configurations in Card III are interpreted as "she-devils," one may be permitted to assume that the girl would steal from women who intimidate her or whom she hates ("negative mother complex"). Celine is a maid, although on the basis of her intelligence she could be something else; when her employers treat her as a "stupid nobody," feelings of resentment, possibly social resentment, must spring up in her. The girl may steal out of revenge, with the intent of harming others. In that case, we could advance the following hypothesis: "Under the influence of tendencies for vengeance, latent impulses to steal become activated in Celine. They may be connected with unconscious (frustrated) love wishes. In situations in which Celine is able to love and to accept love, she does not need to steal."

We do not want, however, to expose ourselves to arbitrary speculations and we shall therefore keep to the record and to the scores. There we see that Celine's affectivity is quite unadapted. Although her affectivity is inclined to adaptation, it is not capable of it, as is shown in CF and the amount of explosion-prone affectivity expressed by the 2–3 C. Impulsive and impetuous actions, as well as hasty thinking (M and C), may be a possibility. Considering C and CF and, on the other hand, FCh and ChC, we may surmise that it is possible for Celine to succumb to morose moods, which are strengthened by defiance (CF and S), and may lead to violence and motoric abreaction (S and C). Since Celine, being a servant, cannot abreact her impulses in a straightforward, open fight with the "she-devils" (she is too cautious for it—inverse sequence—and too shrewd (caution and intellectual adaptation, FCh)), she must act differently. Her tendency to harm others is the most obvious reaction.

When we ask ourselves further what vocation Celine should pursue that would be more in keeping with her capabilities than that of a maid, we must consider the W tendency, D—Dd type, and F +%. W tendency suggests a drive toward free enactive and self-controlling powers; D type signifies technical skill; the relatively numerous Dd (including S and sequence inversion) indicate an ability to handle difficult work tasks. Celine could become a seamstress, or work as a milliner (her delight in colors is expressed by her numerous color interpretations), or as a flower girl. Preferably, she should choose millinery, with a view toward future independent self-employment. By becoming a member of the working force in a "superior" vocation and sharing in its collective "professional pride," Celine would gain the strength to resist her impulses to steal. If she gets married at some not too remote future time, marriage will enable her to abreact her sexual desires in a normal and permissible fashion, and Celine will be saved. WS tendency testifies to the fact that at present Celine is deeply unhappy and dissatisfied.

Follow-up report from the files of a youth agency: Celine had stolen some linen articles from her mistresses, and had been "fresh" to them. The youth agency had secured millinery training for her. The girl was delighted. She is doing fine, and is happy because her present mistress appreciates her and lets her know so. During the last two years (since training began), no further delinquent acts of stealing have occurred.

TABLE 1

Scoring Sheet

Subject: *Martin Balz,* 12 years old; son of Anton, businessman.

Date: February 14, 1950

Time: 11 minutes
Number of responses: 21/7

Cd.	DW	SW	W	D	Dd	Do	S	F+	F—	F±	M	FC	CF	C	ChF	P	O
I	1	1	1	2	1		1	4	2	1					1		
II				5			2	1	1	1		2	1	1		4	
III			+	7		+		3	2	1	1						
	1	1	1	14	1	(+)	3	8	5	3	1	2	1	1	1	4	—

F+% = 60
A% = 38
P% = 20
O% = —
H% = 10

H = 2
Hd = 1

A = 8
Ad = 1

pl = 5
cloud = 2
geog = 1
holes = 1

shocks = —

Sequence: loose—confused
Experience balance: 1 M : 3½ C
Apperceptive type: DW — W — D — Dd/Do — S

Remarks: tendency toward perseveration, confabulatory responses, disregard for symmetry.

TABLE 2

Scoring Sheet

Subject: *Hanni Steinmann*, 21 years old, office worker

Date: October 16, 1950   Time: 15 minutes

Number of responses: 16/5

Cd.	W	D	Dd	S	F+	F−	F±	M	FC	CF	C	FCh	ChF	P	O
I	1	3	2	1	6							1			
II		3		2		1	1		3		1		1		1
III		3	1		3		1	1	3	−		1	1	2	1
	1	9	3	3	9	1	1	1	3	−	1	1	1	2	1

F+%	= 86		H	= 1
A%	= 31		Hd	= 2
P%	= 12		anat	= 3
O%	= 6		blood	= 1
H%	= 50		rel	= 1
anat%	= about 20			

A = 2 (3 with "dove," "Holy Ghost")
Ad = 1
obj = 1
pl = 3

Sequence: loose

Experience balance: 1 M : 3 C

Apperceptive type: (W) — D — Dd — S

Remarks: initial shock

    "or"

    white seen as color

Shocks = +

description
aggression
WM HP absent in Card III
aftereffect of shock
M repression

TABLE 3

Scoring
Subject: *Hans Stockar,* 15 years old

Time: 7 minutes
Number of responses: 15/6

Cd	W	D	Dd	Do	S	F+	F−	F±	M	FC	P	O
I	1	1	1			2		1	1		1	
II		4		1	1	1	1	1	2	2		1
III	1	3	1	1		4					3	
	2	8	2	2	1	7	1	2	3	2	4	1

H = 2   A = 6   pl = 2
Hd = 1   Ad = 3   geog = 1

Strictly speaking, there is 1 H more and 1 A less because the "small monkeys" are conceived as an H.

F+% = 80
A% = 55–60
P% = 27
O% = 6
H% = 27

Shocks: indicated by inversion of sequence and its becoming loose.

Sequence: first rigid, then orderly-to-loose; tendency to inversion.
Experience balance: 3 M : 1 C
Apperceptive type: W — D — Dd — Do/S

Remarks: object criticism

237

TABLE 4

Scoring
Subject: *Heini Zumbrunn*

Time: 22 minutes
Number of responses: 18/11

Cd.	DW	W	D	Dd	S	F+	F−	F±	M	FC	CF	C	CCh	FCh	ChF	Ch	P	O
I	1	1	1			1		2										1
II	1		7	1	3	1		2		3	3	tend.	1		1	(1)		2 (−1)
III		1	2	1		1		2	1	3	3	tend.			1	(1)	−	3 (−1)
	2	2	10	2	3	3		6	1	3	3	tend.	1		1	(1)		3 (−1)

F+% = 66
A% = 33
P% = 0
O% = 16±
H% = 11

H = 1   A = 1   = 3   = 3   obj = −   sea = 1
mask = 1   Ad = 1   pl = 4 (5)   cloud = 1
nat = 1   water = 1
geog = 1   earth = 1

Sequence: orderly—loose
Experience balance: 1 M : 5½ C
Apperceptive type: DW — W — D — Dd — S

Initial shock

Remarks: "or"
flexor kinesthesias   confabulation   mask
WMHP absent in Card III   water and earth

TABLE 5

Scoring
Subject: *Peter Stoll*

Time: 5 minutes
Number of responses: 11/4

Cd.	W	D	Do	S	F+	F−	·F±	M	Ms	FC	CF	P	O
I		2	1		3							1	1
II		3		1	4							1	
III		4				1	1		tend.	1	1		
		9	1	1	7	1	1		tend.	1	1	2	1

F+% = 85
A% = 63
P% = 22
O% = 10
H% = 27

H = 2
food = 1
A = 4
Ad = 3

pl = 1

Sequence: orderly-loose
Experience balance: 0 M : 1½ C
Apperceptive type: D — (Do) — S

Shocks = −

Remarks: aggression; "or"; tendency toward anat; tendency toward Ms; absence of M in Card III.

TABLE 6

Scoring
Subject: Miss *L.B.*

Time: 10 minutes
Number of responses: 24/11

Cd.	DW	W	D	DdD	Dd	Do	S	F+	F−	F±	M	FC	CF	CCh	P	O
I	1		2	1			1	2	1	1	1	1				1—
II		1	7		2		3	1	1	1	1		5	1		1—
III			2	1	4	(1)		2	3	2					2	1—
	1	1	11	2	6	(1)	4	5	5	4	2	1	5	1	2	3—

H	= 4			A	= 1	
Hd	= 3			Ad	= 2	
anat	= 3 (2)			pl	= 6	
sex	= 1–2			obj	= 2	
clothing	= 1			nat	= 1	
mask	= 1					

F+% = 50
A% = 12
P% = 8
O% = 12−
H% = 54
anat% = 12
sex% = 10

Sequence: loose-orderly
Experience balance: 2 M : 6½ C (1 FC : 5 CF : 1 CCh)
Apperceptive type: DW — D — DdD — Dd — (Do) — S

shocks = —

Remarks: confabulation; 1 individual interpretation; 1 DdF— obj O— (Card III/6) indicating psychopathy; tendency toward ChF.

TABLE 7

Scoring
Subject: *Nelly Farner*

Time: 7 minutes
Number of responses: 25/9

Cd.	W	D	Dd	Do	S	F+	F—	F±	M	Ms	FC	CF	C	FCh	ChF	P	O
I	3	4	1		1	4		3	1		1				1		1
II	—	7	1		1	3		1	1	1	1	2	1			2	2
III	1	5	1	1		4		2		1			1		2	2	2
	4	16	3	1	2	11		6	2	2	1	2	2		3	2	5

F+% = 82
A% = 52
P% = 8
O% = 20
H% = 8

H = 1
Hd = 1
S = 1

A. = 10
Ad = 3

obj = 2
pl = 2
cloud = 2
fire = 1
shadow = 1
earth = 1
blot = 1

shocks = —

Sequence: loose-orderly
Experience balance: 2 M : 5½ C (1 FC-2 CF-2 C)
Apperceptive type: W — D — Dd/Do — S

Remarks: combines; WMHP III is absent; first attempts to elude by way of descriptions (1/1).

241

TABLE 8

Scoring:
Subject: *Arnold Gamper*

Time: 11 minutes
Number of responses: 21/5

Cd.	W	D	Dd	S	F+	F–	F±	M	FC	CF	CCh	FCh	F(C)	P	O
I	2	4	2	(1)	6			1	1			(1)	1	1	1
II	1	3	1	1(2)	1					1	1				1
III	2	5		1(3)	5			3	1	1		(1)		4	3
	5	12	3	1(3)	12			4		2	1	(2)	1	5	5

H = 3   A = 8   obj = 1
Hd = 1   Ad = 1   pl = 4
sex = 1   geog = 1
scene = 1

shock = +

F+% = 100
A% = 43
P% = 23
O% = 23
H% = 30

Sequence: orderly
Experience balance: 4 M : 3 C (2 FC – 2 CF)
Apperceptive type: W – D – Dd – S

Remarks: object criticism
description, C impression
"or"; combinatory tendency

M repression (I/4)
H repression (I/8)

242

TABLE 9

Scoring
Subject: *Margarethe Schenker*

Time: 16 minutes
Number of responses: 19/8

Cd.	W	D	Dd	S	F+	F—	F±	M	Ms	FC	CF	C	CCh	Ch	ChF	Ch	P	O
I	2	1	—	—	1	—	1	1	—	—	—	—	—	1	1	—	—	2
II		3	1	5	4	—	1	1	(tend.)	2	—	—	—	—	—	—	1	2
III	1	7	—	—	3	—	—	4	—	—	—	1	(1)	—	—	1	2	3
	3	11	1	5	8		2	6	(tend.)	2	—	1	(tend.)	1	1	1	3	7

F+% = 90, rather more   H = 9 (8)
A% = 26   Hd = —
P% = 16   rel = 3
O% = 36   mask = 1
H% = 68

A = 4 (5)   pl = 1
Ad = —   expl = 1

shocks = +

Sequence: orderly-loose
Experience balance: 6 M : 2.5 C (2 FC, 1 C)
Apperceptive type: W — D — (Dd) — S

Remarks: Perspective, criticism, combination, intuition, MC, M repression, guilt feelings, flexor kinesthesias, extensor kinesthesias, white as color, dramatizing combination, aggression, tendency to description.

TABLE 10

Subject: *Margarethe Schenker*

Zulliger Test → Ro → Bero

Reaction time:	16 minutes	22 minutes	20 minutes
Number of responses:	19/8	46/13	40/15
WS =	—	1	
W =	3, tend.	8, tend.	6, tend.
D =	11	31	28
Dd =	1	3	3
S =	5	4	4
F+% =	90	94	97
A% =	26	30	37
P% =	16	11	17
O% =	36	20	20
H% =	68	56	42
Shocks:	II	VI and X	VII and VIII

F =	10 (−1)	27 (−1.5)	20 (−0.5)
M =	5	13	12
MC =	1	several of them	several
Ms =	tend.	1	2
FC =	2	3	1
CF =	—	1	1
C =	1	—	1
CCh =	tend.	—	1 (2)
FCh =	1	(2)	1
ChF =	1	1 (2)	1
Ch =	1	(2)	—
F(C) =	—	1	—
P =	3	5	7
O =	7	9	8

Sequence:	orderly-loose	orderly-loose, in VI inverted	orderly-loose
Experience balance:	6 M : 2.5 C	13 M : 2.5 C	12 M : 4 C
Apperceptive type:	W D — (Dd) — S	same	same

Remarks:

perspective
criticism
combination
intuition, MC
M repression
guilt feelings
flexor-extensor kinesthesias
white as color

same

C impression

TABLE 11

Scoring

Subject: *Celine Kohler*, 19 years old, a domestic

Time: 15 minutes
Number of responses: 20/6

Cd.	DW	WS	W	D	Dd	S	F+	F−	F±	M	FC	CF	C	CCh	FCh	ChF	P	O
I	1	(1)	1	2	1		3		2				(1)				1	
II		1		3	1	2	3					2	(1)	1	1	1	1	2(−)
III			2	5	2		3		2	2			2				3	
	1	1(2)	3	10	4	2	9		4	2		2	2(4)	1	1	1	5	2(−)

F+% = 84
A% = 40
P% = 25
O% = 10±
H% = 15–20

H = 2
sex = 1(2)

A = 5
Ad = 3

pl = 3
geog = 3
fire = 1
water colors = 1
ornament = 1

shocks = +

"or"
object criticism
"she-devils"

Sequence: orderly-loose, tendency towards inversion
Experience balance: 2 M : 6 to 7½ C
Apperceptive type: $\underline{(DW - WS)\ W - D - Dd - S}$

245

16. Five Examples Pertaining
to Vocational Guidance

1. *Meyer, Max,* 18 years old, high-school student.

Oldest son; has a sister 2 years his junior. The parents would like him to have a professional career—if possible, to become a lawyer.

He has already had to repeat a grade in junior high school. In all probability, he will not be promoted to the next grade (notation on his December report card reads: "Promotion doubtful!"). He has had tutoring in Latin and Greek; nevertheless, his promotion is "dubious" (the teacher's statement).

He has taken a dislike to school; suddenly sulks (previously he has always been a well-behaved, obedient child); wants to drop out of school; plays truant part of the time in order to go fishing.

He has fights at home and the parents ask themselves whether Max may be mentally ill (see Table 1).

Counseling: The subject should leave high school. He should have some practical training: gardening, mechanics, and later engineering school; druggist or some technical trade where exactness, perseverance, and diligence are important. Quantity ambition is more essential in this case than quality ambition.

Reasons: Max Meyer is not a studious type; his capabilities are rather of a *practical* nature (D, Dd). He thinks in a reproductive rather than productive manner; he is not capable of organizing and planning well; he lacks the ability for abstract thinking (W).

246

TABLE 1

Meyer, Max, 18 years old, son of Max, office manager

Zulliger Test → Rorschach → Behn-Rorschach

	Zulliger (12 min.)	Rorschach (31 min.)	Behn-Rorschach (35 min.)
Time:	12 min.	31 min.	35 min.
Number of responses:	24/8	33/12	42/14
F =	19(—3)	26(—7)	31(—8)
M =		1	1
Ms =	1	1	
FC =	3	4	6
CF =	1	1	1
C =			
FCh =	(1)	1	2
ChF =			
Ch =			
F(C) =			
DW =			
SW =			
WS =			
W =	2	3	4
D =	10	20	27
Dd =	2	9	10
Do =			
S =	(1)		1
DdS =			
F+% =	84	76	80
A% =	50	54	57
P% =	25	24	
O% =	5	3	
obj% =			
H% =	37		40
P =	6	8	8
O =	1	1	2
H =	1	1	1
Hd =	6	8	7
anat =	2	3	2
sex =			
scene =			
blood =	1	1	—
A =	9	15	21
Ad =	3	3	3
obj =			1
pl =	2	2	6
nat =			1
arch =			
others =			
Sequence:	orderly-loose	orderly-loose	same
Experience balance:	1 M : 2½ C	1 : 3	1 : 4
Apperceptive type:	W — D — Dd/S	same	same
Red shock:	+	+	+
Color shock:	—	+	+
Chiaroscuro shock:	—	—	—

Remarks:

Zulliger Test, Card II. "I can't do anything with the red. Perhaps these are blood stains!"

Ro, Card III. WM and HP are absent; M does not appear until Card VI (effect of shock).

Card II. "Again just blood stains!" (First response after prolonged reaction time.)

Bero, Card II. Only one interpretation: "dogs," after turning the card back and forth for a long time.

Card III. WM + HP is the only response to this card.

Card IV. Ms HP is the only response to this card.

Intelligence: Average (F+% about 80; D type; A% is almost too high; O% is low; sequence is slightly loose); industrious (the number of responses increases at the end in Bero); tenacious, persistent. Has a rather *practical mind;* many D + DP; exact.

He is a somewhat anxious type, relying on others for support. He is subordinate and dependent.

Report: Max Meyer became a druggist, then changed his profession and became a laboratory technician. At present (1953), he is employed in a chemical plant. He is very happy there and has the reputation of being an extremely industrious and therefore respected worker.

His parents have reconciled themselves to Max's not becoming a lawyer.

2. *Keller, Hans,* 16 years old, high-school student (see Table 2).

The subject is the only son of a civil service official, the only child of his parents. His mother would like him to enter a teachers' college. His teachers, however, doubt that he will be able to pass the entrance examination.

His father could help him to obtain a job in a garage (motor mechanic). Yet the son would prefer not to take it, for he is afraid that the work might be too hard for him and tax his physical strength too much.

Counseling: When I proposed to Hans Keller that he go into training for office work, he was delighted. Subsequently, he finished this training and is today employed in a community near his home village. He is happy in his work. "I am following in the footsteps of my father," he says proudly. He anticipates being employed in his own home village: as soon as the holder of the head position, who is an old man, retires, all the other employees will move ahead, and there will be a job open for Hans Keller.

It is indeed true that Hans Keller would not be strong enough to endure the rigors of training as a motor mechanic. In addition, people who produce no W but Do lack the ability to think comprehensively. In the transport industry, they might run the risk of losing their head sometimes while driving.

For the teaching profession, the subject's intelligence is hardly sufficient. One wonders how Hans Keller could have attended high school without repeating some grades, and even

248

TABLE 2

Keller, Hans, 16 years old, 1932, son of Jacob, civil service official

Zulliger Test → Rorschach → Behn-Rorschach

	Zulliger Test	Rorschach	Behn-Rorschach
Time:	8 min.	26 min.	24 min.
Number of responses:	9/3	24/9	22/8
DW =	—	—	—
SW =	—	—	—
WS =	—	—	—
W =	1	—	1
D =	5	16	14
Dd =	1	5	4
Do =	1	2	2
S =	1	1	1
DdS =	—	—	—
F+% =	70	76	70
A% =	55	83(1)	64(1)
P% =	30	33	36
O% =	—	5	4
obj% =	—	—	—
H% =	44	12	13
F =	6(—2)	21(—5)	17(—5)
M =	1	1	1
Ms =	—	—	—
FC =	1	1	1
CF =	1	—	1
C =	—	—	—
FCh =	(1)	(1)	—
ChF =	—	—	—
Ch =	—	—	—
F(C) =	—	—	—
P =	3	8	8
O =	—	1	1
H =	1	1	1
Hd =	—	1	—
anat =	2	(1)3	(1)2
sex =	—	—	—
scene =	—	—	—
blood =	1	—	—
A =	4	13	8
Ad =	1	7	6
obj =	—	—	1
pl =	—	—	1
nat =	—	1	3
		tendency to perseveration	
Sequence:	orderly, tendency to reversion	same	same
Experience balance:	1 M : 1½ C	1 : 1½	1 : 2
Apperceptive type:	W—D—Dd/Do/S	same	same
Red shock:	—	same	—
Color shock:	—	—	(+?)
Chiaroscuro shock:	—	same	—

Remarks:

Ro VIII: turns the card immediately and interprets first the red-and-orange area as "crystal rock" (DCF).

Intelligence: Low average; reproductive (F+% only about 70, Dd/Do/S). The subject is timid (Do); cautious (tendency towards inverse sequence); does not have a sufficiently large number of W; is easily tired (small and decreasing number of responses), and slow. (Responses : reaction time). Lazy (A%). Not completely without "ambition" (anat). All his M are MP!

how he succeeded in passing the entrance examination. He has the intelligence of an elementary-school pupil, sufficient, however, for performing stereotyped work-tasks. In addition, the test shows that Hans Keller is capable of working with exactness and conscientious effort, and that he is well suited for technical as well as precision work. One thinks immediately of a man at a typewriter. In office work, which is relatively easy and physically not very strenuous, and can be performed quite mechanically, the fact that the subject quickly grows tired does not have too great an inhibiting effect. Quantitative output is much more important here than "creative" quality work.

These were my considerations when I gave my advice in counseling Hans Keller.

3. *Barth, Aline,* 17 years old, trainee in dressmaking (see Table 3).

She was sent to me by her physician because she dislikes dressmaking.

She is the only child of her parents, and has had a stepmother since she was 10 years old. Formerly, she had been over-indulged; later, she was treated with strictness. Sickly.

Counseling: first of all, the subject is in need of psychotherapeutic treatment. Pronounced obstinacy neurosis. Most likely, she should change her environment. Tendency towards sexual depravity and stealing. The subject is instinctively oriented. Inclination to dishonesty. Could have a talent for photography, for making flower patterns, or for millinery.

Report of the physician, secured later: Aline Barth is a "difficult child," who sulks at home and at work, never returns home at night, spends her time badly with a group of so-called "existentialists," dancing and drinking. Up to the present, nothing is known about sexual escapades; she has stolen her instructor's scarf, but there is no evidence that she has stolen money. Flighty, cannot be taught.

Report: was placed at a florist's nursery in another town. Submitted to psychotherapeutic treatment. Pursues photography (color photography) as a hobby; would like to become a flower arranger.

TABLE 3

Barth, Aline, 17 years old.

Zulliger Test → Rorschach → Behn-Rorschach

	Zulliger Test	Rorschach	Behn-Rorschach
Time:	3 min.	8 min.	4 min.
Number of responses:	15/6	17/6	14/5
DW =	4	2	1
SW =	1	2	2
WS =			
W =	4	7	8
D =	2	2	1
Dd =			
Do =			
S =	4	4	2
DdS =			
F =	8(—4)	9(—3)	5(—2)
M =			
Ms =			
FC =	4	3	
CF =	2	1	
C =	1	1	
FCh =	2	3	
ChF =			
Ch =			
F (C) =			
P =	3	4	3
O =	4(—2)	5(—3)	3(—1)
H =			
Hd =	—	4	1
anat =	1	3	1
sex =	1	1	1
scene =			
blood =	1	1	—
A =	6 pers.	4	6 pers.
Ad =	2	5	1
obj =	1	—	1
pl =	2	—	1
nat =	1	—	2
arch =			
others =			
F+% =	50	66	60
A% =	53	53	50
P% =	20	23	28
O% =	26±	30∓	21±
obj% =			
H% =	—	24	7
Sequence:	loose	same	same
Experience balance:	0 M : 5½ C	0 : 4	0 : 6½
Apperceptive type:	DW — W — (D) — S	same	same
Red shock:	—	—	+
Color shock:	+	+	+
Chiaroscuro shock:	—	—	—
Remarks:	Infantile interpretation	Infantile interpretation	Infantile interpretation

Intelligence: poor to average. Strong inclination to pseudo logical thinking. May be a thief. The girl is strongly governed by instincts. Obstinancy neurosis.

Body build: Big, well-developed; round face with rosy cheeks.

Psychotherapeutic treatment proceeds with relative success after the doctor put his foot down when Aline Barth spent the night with a young man. Does not steal any more.

I do not believe, despite the doctor's approving report, that the prognosis is very favorable. Perhaps Aline Barth will be able to keep her head above water because of her Ch tendency. She should marry early, and should have children. Otherwise, there is danger that she may drift along and continue stealing.

4. *Mueller, Traugott,* 19½ years old, high-school senior.

The parents would like Traugott to become a lawyer, but the son is opposed to the idea. He would like to become a high-school teacher but this, too, only half-heartedly. Because of arguments at home, which Traugott carries on with passion, he is slightly depressed (see Table 4).

Counseling: Should study theology. Reasons: The subject is student material; likes problems. These take precedence over everything else; but he is also capable of great sympathy. He is generous, too generous for a lawyer: not obdurate enough for a "successful" lawyer; too "soft" (M) for a lawyer, despite W/S apperceptive type. "Hovering angel" in Card X Ro may suggest religious interests. He is delighted at the thought of studying for the ministry, but at the same time fears that he does not have "what it takes" for it. I must influence him by suggestion in order that he may accept the proposal.

Report: Although the parents did not care for religion so much as to wish that their second son, Traugott, should become a minister, they were ultimately persuaded. After obtaining his secondary-school diploma, Traugott entered the theological seminary in the fall of 19–. In the spring of 19– he graduated, became a curate and then, in the fall of 19–, a permanently appointed Protestant minister in a small town, with a mixed Reformed and Catholic population.

He is very contented, is respected, and has the reputation of being a good pulpit preacher. He is on friendly terms with his Catholic colleagues in town. He takes excellent care of his communicants, especially of teenagers, and is therefore well liked.

TABLE 4

Mueller, Traugott, 1923, 19½ years old, son of Alfred, teacher

Zulliger Test → Rorschach → Behn-Rorschach

	7 min.	26 min.	24 min.
Time:			
Number of responses:	15/5	26/9	29/10
DW =			
SW =			
WS =	—	1	1
W =	8	10	9
D =	3	8	10
Dd =	1	2	4
Do =			
S =	3	5	5
DdS =			
F+% =	90	82	88
A% =	40	46	55
P% =	27	22	24
O% =	13	19	14
obj% =			
H% =	40	34	34
F =	10(−1)	17(−3)	18(−2)
M =	3	4	5
Ms =			
FC =	2	2	3
CF =	(1)	1	1
C =			
FCh =	1	2	2
ChF =			
Ch =			
F(C) =			
P =	4	6	7
O =	2	5	4
H =	3	5	6
Hd =	3	3	3
anat =	1	1	1
sex =			
scene =			
blood =			
A =	5	9	12
Ad =	1	3	5
obj =	1	3	1
pl =	1	1	—
nat =			
arch =			
others =	1	2	—
Red shock:	—	+	—
Color shock:	+	+	+
Chiaroscuro shock:	—	—	—
Sequence:	orderly-rigid	same	same
Experience balance:	3 M : 1 C	4 : 2	5 : 2½
Apperceptive type:	W — D — Do — S / — —	same	same

Remarks:

Ro X. "hovering angel" DMFC H O (inner yellow area).

High intelligence (W type, F+% is larger than 80, orderly-rigid sequence. Both A% and P% are average; apperceptive type: W—S).

Problematic person (apperceptive type), capable of great empathy (FC + high H%).

Asthenic, tall, slender, angular face, long limbs and hands. Antagonistic toward the father.

253

He is happily married, and has one child. The parents are reconciled, and proud of their son.

5. The question was raised whether *Martin Kunz,* 16 years old, junior-high-school student with good-to-very-good report cards, who was about to graduate from school, should continue his schooling at a high school, or else begin some kind of trade training. He would like to enter a high school (see Table 5).

Zulliger Test

I.

	Bat	WF + A
	Monkey head (B 5/6)	S → DF + Ad
	Butterfly (CD 4/7)	DF + A
b	Porcupine (EF 3/4)	DF + A
c	The face of a farmer with a peaked cap (GF 3)	DdF + Hd
a	Map (DEF 2/3/4/5)	ChC → DF − geog
c	Clown with a stick (FE 4) waving	DM + H O
	A woman's head with a feather (AB 4/5)	Do → DF + Hd
	Sitting monkey (CD 6/7)	DM + A O
	Doll (BCD 4)	DF + obj/H

II.

(Turns the card immediately into c-position)

b	Head of a monkey (F 5)	Do → DF + Ad
	Lungs (red area) and	DCF anat
	Spine (S within red area)	SF − anat
	A snake's head (tiny Dd in E 4)	DdF + Ad
b	The head of a man wearing a beret (C 3)	DdF + Hd
	Bisons (orange area)	DFC A P
d	Bust of a man (EF 4/5)	DF + obj/Hd
a	Bed rug made of fur, bear skin	DFC Ad

III.

	Butterfly	DF + A P
	Clowns (red outer area)	DM + H P
c	Wild boar (EF 3)	DF + A
a	A pistol (C 4)	DdF + obj
	A devil's head (A 4)	DdF + Hd
		Duration: 10 minutes

254

TABLE 5

Martin Kunz, 16 years old

Scores of the Zulliger Individual Test — Ro — Bero

Time:	10 min.	16 min.	20 min.
Number of responses:	23/8	53/15	48/20

	10 min.	16 min.	20 min.
W =	1	2	3
D =	15	32	22
Dd =	6	17	20
Do =	(2)	1	2
S =	1(2)	1	1
F =	17(—2)	41(—6.5)	48(—7)
M =	3	4	2
FC =	2	5	2
CF =	1	1	1
C =	1	1	—
FCh =	—	1	—
ChF =	—	1	—
ChC =	1	—	—
F+% =	88	85	84
A% =	48	50	50
P% =	13	19	16
O% =	9	4	6
H% =	43	28	34
P =	3	10	8
O =	2	2	3
H =	2(3)	1	6
Hd =	4(5)	13	7
anat =	2	1	1
A =	7	17(18)	14
Ad =	4	9	10
obj =	3	6	4
pl =	—	4	4
geog =	1	2	2
Color shock:		+	+

Sequence:	orderly-loose	same	
Experience balance:	3 M : 3 C	4 M : 3½	same
Apperceptive type:	(W) — D — Do — (Do) — S	same	same

255

Counseling: The subject does not meet the requirements of a secondary school, in that his capacity for abstract thinking is poor (too few W), while his thinking is too reproductive and receptive (D and Dd, too few W and O). His ability for abstract summation and unification is inadequate (too few W, absence of WM). His is rather an intelligence of a practical and technical variety, with a tendency to schematization (P% is too low for it to be anything but "practical"). He is very industrious (reaction time and number of responses) and still has a schoolboy's attitude (geog). He has an intelligence complex (anat and shocks) and therefore would like to make a "scholar" of himself (he would be unhappy in a secondary school, however; his achievements would be based only on diligence and "cramming"). As a human being, he is friendly (H%), possesses sympathy and empathy. On the other hand, he is strongly dependent on other people in regard to his work performance; he wants to please them (H% and a schoolboy's attitude).

The subject should neither attend a secondary school nor go directly into vocational training. His zeal (diligence and anat) must be sufficiently satisfied. I recommend that Martin attend a *technical school,* perhaps taking an *electrotechnical* course. Later he should be exposed to practical work and finally enroll in a technical institute (electrical engineer). He must have the awareness of possibilities for further development, otherwise a trade, like a profession, would not inspire him.

Electrotechnical training should be recommended, because Martin has interpreted many Dd. This means that he is able to handle small things with exactness, as a watchmaker does. To become a watchmaker would not be "enough" for him. (Besides, this occupation is too specialized and standardized, and such work would be too automated for Martin).

Since he is not onesidedly gifted (ambiequal experience balance), he could also study chemistry (*laboratory research*) or perhaps attend a business school (he could become a bookkeeper, since he is exact and conscientious—Dd, S, and Do).

Martin must decide himself, choosing within the framework of the possibilities mentioned.

(Martin has passed the entrance examination into technical school as a chemistry major. He is happy and well-liked by both his teachers and fellow students.)

17. Toward Diagnostic Practice

A. THE DIFFERENCE BETWEEN A SHORT EVALUATION AND A DIAGNOSIS

A diagnosis is differentiated from a short evaluation by the fact that in a diagnosis both the test and its results are placed within the proper framework. It must be stressed time and again that the test is only *one* of the supporting devices that we have at our disposal for the study of mental and emotional phenomena. As we interpret some "short evaluations" on the basis of test results, or place the test in a central position in a book, the impression may easily be gained that nothing else but the test is of importance in a psychological examination.

In the realities of practical application, the test is no more significant than some of the other methods of investigation. Thus, it plays a much more modest part than may be judged from the fact that the author has been compelled to write a monograph about it. Above all, it should be understood that the test is not "everything."

On the other hand, neither should one underestimate the test, for then one may make the mistake, as has been shown in experience, of using it superficially or even in a slovenly manner, without examining the results profoundly, or inquiring into its fine points, and utilizing it only for coarse summaries, thereby preventing the recognition of its full value. This error is made by those who believe that the science of testing is nothing else but a purely mathematical and statistical task, and think they can understand a fellow human being by fitting him into a statistical formula. It is perhaps ridiculous to have to discuss this point, yet it occurs again and again: there are some people who do expect to be able to capture and delineate human souls with the aid of averages, curves, and other such mechanical contrivances. They act like the botanist who classifies flowers according to the "flora" and the Linnaean system. When people who work in this manner realize that all their labors are to no avail, they then condemn the test, saying that it is worthless and "unscientific"—because it does not correspond with their view of "science."

Once one has become intimately familiar with the Zulliger Test, one does not need to enter into polemics with these "exact scientists," who are able to prove everything with numbers, by performing tricks that are undoubtedly admirable, even though they do not have much semblance to real life, possibly none at all. One should ask such individuals to enter into a joint contest in the handling of a case of vocational guidance or educational counseling, etc., on the basis of diagnostic investigation and by using a test. It would then become quite apparent who is capable of employing a test as an auxiliary device and who is not.

"Short evaluations" as such have shown us what the test may achieve. The fact that it sometimes produces meager results, thus necessitating the use of other tests as well, has already been dealt with.

B. DIAGNOSTIC CASES

1. The director of an educational institution for girls would like to know whether he can discharge 19-year-old *Vroni Blaser* from his institution in good faith, or rather whether he may submit an application for her discharge to the proper authorities. Since Vroni has conducted herself well during the 1½ years at the institution, her "guardians" would like to release her: they have found a job for Vroni as a domestic worker with a grocer.

Vroni had been admitted to the home when she was 17½ years old, because she could not hold a job for any length of

time, because she had committed a number of thefts of clothing
and money, and because it had come to light that she had been
having sexual intercourse ever since she was 15 years old, searching it out herself. She never knew who her partners were: she
would meet them at a market place, or in the vicinity of some
barracks. Fortunately, her sexual intercourse has never resulted
in pregnancy.

Vroni is the oldest child in a quite "complicated" family. Her
mother was divorced when Vroni (the second child, following
a girl three years her senior) was two years old. After another
two years, her mother married a divorced man with three children of his own: a boy of 7, a girl of 5, and a girl of 4.

Vroni's mother had divorced her father because he was peri-
odically drunk.

Three more children were born to the newly married couple.
The father is a small "traveling salesman" (actually, a peddler).
The family's financial situation is not bad, for the father's earn-
ings are ample; but he is "never at home," and it has been the
mother's duty to raise, or rather not to raise, the three groups
of children, eight in all.

Allegedly, Vroni was never sick. Her birth was normal; she
was breast-fed for ¾ of a year; weaning and toilet-training
were effected without any resistance on her part.

In school, the girl had to repeat one grade. After graduation,
she herself chose to train as a domestic worker, and was given
the opportunity by a kindly old couple who lived in a small
town. The man was an official of some sort. Vroni was happy at
this job, but quarreled with the tenants who lived in her employer's house and had to change positions. At this point, it was
revealed for the first time that Vroni stole. Upon leaving her
job, she took some clothes and a small painting; she returned
everything upon request, however. She had graduated from
school when she was approximately 15 years and 3 months old.
No sooner had she arrived at the small town than she at once
proceeded to indulge in sexual intercourse indiscriminately.
However, this fact did not become known until later, when she
was already living in the institution. During the first week at a
new job with a butcher, she again committed acts of dishonesty;

she stole small sums of money, with which she bought cheap costume jewelry in department stores, such as rings, earrings, armbands, bracelets, pins—all of which she hung upon herself. Adorned in this manner, she would go out looking for men. A widow for whom she was working reported her to the police, because she was missing a fifty-franc bill. The police found it in Vroni's closet, hidden behind a pile of old underclothing. They also found other items that she had stolen, such as blouses, stockings, and a scarf.

At the investigation it was revealed that Vroni had lied to the widow. When the young housemaid had said that she had to go home, that had been just another excuse to get a day off. She utilized the time loitering and picking up men. Vroni went with the men to the movies and bars, and then followed them to their rooms; or else sexual intercourse took place in some wooded area or public park. Returning home to her employers at night, she had tales to tell about her own home, and they believed her.

She took all her jewelry along to the institution, where she was permitted to keep it, but not to wear it. She showed off the jewelry to all her numerous girl friends.

For the testing, Vroni appears fully ornamented with her cheap jewelry. Later it was learned that she had taken it along secretly, and had put it on while on the way.

At the girls' home, Vroni has behaved flawlessly. She has been industrious and applied herself to her work.

Vroni looks fully mature. She has a trim and well-rounded figure and is quite tall. She behaves subserviently and at the same time "absorbingly," flinging her hair back in a flirtatious gesture, and stretching as if her sweater were too small for her. She has a pretty, rosy-cheeked face, but her chin is too coarsely shaped.

In addition to the Zulliger Individual Test, the Tree Test, the Wartegg, and the Color-Pyramid Test were administered to Vroni. Since time was limited, further tests could not be performed with the girl. The results of all three tests are in agreement. The diagnosis may be worked out on the basis of the Zulliger Test (see Table 1).

Zulliger Test

I.

Owl because of the face and the angry eyes	S → DWF ± A
Or a "mountain gnome" (Alps) in a dust cloud	WMCh H O "or"
Or a thunderstorm sky	Ch → WF — nat "or"

II.

These could also be the lungs (red area) because of the color and because it is right in the middle ...	DCF anat/position
or— (looks furtively at the examiner, smiles sweetly, bites her lips)	
(Examiner: "Or?—What else did you want to say?")	
Subject: "Well, you know!" (smiles)	masked sex interpretation
Rabbits because of the color and the shape (orange area)	DCF A
Something like a coat of arms (lower portion of S within the red area)	SF — heraldry O—
b Sunset reflected in a lake (red area)	DC nat O—
a Water plant (green area)	DFC pl
c Ploughed-up clay earth (orange area) with	DC earth
furrows in it (within orange area)	DdCCh nat
a The whole is a garden	DWCF nat

III.

These are just masked figures	WM + H P/mask
Bears (red outer area)	DF + A (M?)
Butterfly (red inner area)	DF + A P
c A piggy (within the small dark figure)	DF + A
These could also be simply blood stains (red area)	DCF blood
Or fire	DC fire "or"
The whole could also be clouds ...	ChF → WF ± clouds
Or else a zoo	DWF — A O— "or"
	Duration: 6 minutes

TABLE 1

Scoring
Subject: *Vroni Blaser*, 19 years old

Time: 6 minutes
Number of responses: 19/8

Cd.	DW	W	D	Dd	S	F+	F—	F±	M	FC	CF	C	CCh	FCh	ChF	Ch	P	O
I	1	2			1		1	1	1	1							1	
II	1	2	5	1	2	3	1	1	1	1	3	2	1			2		2(—2)
III	1	2	4				1	1	1	1	1	1			1		2	1(—1)
	3	4	9	1	3	3	3	2	2	1	4	3	1		1	2	3	·4(—3)

F+% = 50   H = 2   pl = 1   A = 6   "Or" 1 position interpretation
A% = 31   Hd = —   earth = 1   Shocks = ?
P% = 10   anat = 1 nat = 4   Sequence: loose, tendency to reversion
O% = 21∓   blood = 1 fire = 1   Experience balance: 2 M : 9 C
H% = 21   mask = (1) cloud = 1   Apperceptive type: DW—W—D—S
            sex = (1) heraldry = 1

EVALUATION:

The far too many C and the MCh indicate a basically morbid disposition. Extreme impulsiveness alternates with deeply depressive ill-humor, to which the subject reacts with obstinacy (S together with inferior intelligence) and aggression (S and C). The latter could also turn inside (MCh). Suicide is a risk; the threat of it almost always exists when pure C and pure Ch occur together in a test. The subject is shifty, and enjoys her emotions and her instincts. She is capable of pretenses (ChF and inverse sequence); her adaptation is cautious and consciously willing. She is stupidly shrewd, and possesses quality ambition (W tendency), without having the necessary inner substance for it. She also has quantity ambition (number of responses, reaction time).

The "thieving syndrome" is markedly pronounced—confabulation, instinctive drive. In addition, she has a tendency toward obstinacy. The sexual interpretations—in all probability, the "blood" response belongs in this category, too—lead us to suspect intense sex fantasies and sex needs, especially if we consider her general impulsiveness and vitality.

In addition to the too numerous pure C, the position interpretation (II/1) is also greatly suspicious. Such interpretations are found in psychopaths and among those with similar general psychopathological conditions.

Since it would be hardly permissible to infer the presence of color shock in the test, neurotic repressions or psychoneurosis are not a likely possibility.

One is surprised to hear (from the home's director) that the girl is satisfactorily obedient and that she has found many friends. One would have expected her to have many fights with her fellow-students. Still, the test indicates that Vroni is wearing a mask. Also, we have determined that her adaptation is by cunning. As a result of these traits, the girl is probably able to hold her own among the other girls; perhaps she makes herself interesting and "worthy" by showing off her jewelry and, possibly, by relating her sexual adventures to them.

When Vroni was confronted with Card II, we noticed that she produced many more responses to it than to Card I, which is dark. Her pleasure in interpreting continued into Card III. It appears at first sight that Vroni is one of those individuals who "swim" in their emotions, enjoying them at the same time; they feel happy only in such situations.

We may state that Vroni's stay at the home did not result in inner progress, in terms of better adaptation and "improvement." The girl remained as she always was, and it is hardly likely that anything about her can ever be changed, because her morbid basic disposition (probably inherited) cannot be altered. One should not accuse the director of not making a strong enough educational effort in Vroni's case. Neither educational influence nor intimidating punishment would be of any avail, since these cannot change the fundamentals.

BRIEF EVALUATION:

All indications suggest that Vroni Blaser is not a completely "normal" human being. Vroni's deviations, which are expressed in a strong impulsivity, along with sexual needs and a tendency to stealing, are based upon hereditary factors and have probably been transmitted to the girl in her infancy by way of heredity. Since her father was a drunkard, it is possible that Vroni has inherited his lack of restraint. At any rate, her strong impulsivity and her inclination to commit delinquent acts by stealing are very clearly registered in the tests. Whether, under such circumstances, anything can be accomplished by education is questionable. It would also hardly be of any use to attempt to tame Vroni by intimidating punishment. One would only succeed in depressing her and, under the influence of depression, she might become a suicide risk.

Since the girl is unintelligent, she cannot restrain herself through mental effort. Vroni is defenseless against her own impulsive and instinctive outbursts.

If Vroni were to be "set free," she would again run around with men and would probably continue to steal.

Since she behaved well while she was detained in a home, it would probably be best for her to remain there. In order to give her the illusion of some "freedom," she might be employed as a kitchen maid and paid wages. Perhaps she could be sent to another girls' educational institution for this purpose. I believe it would be permissible to disguise her institutionalization by employment. It may be that a "promotion" would provide some stability for her and, by long-lasting habit formation, she might perhaps finally succeed in restraining her impulsive behavior to some extent. She should expend her energy to the fullest, by working constantly, without ever "catching her breath."

In the light of the test investigation, the prognosis for Vroni's further development is not exactly favorable. Since it is not very promising, it is difficult to give advice.

Would it be sensible to have Vroni examined by a psychiatrist, too? He might perhaps discover that psychopathology or schizophrenia is present in her case but he would hardly be in any position to help.

On the other hand, it would indeed be indicated to consult an internist, in order to establish whether it might not be possible to channel the strong sexual needs of this 19-year-old girl, with the help of medication. It would hardly be desirable if, one of these days, Vroni were to become pregnant, burdening society with illegitimate offspring. Also, the physician might perhaps establish whether Vroni is incapable of conceiving (since it has not happened yet). If this were the case, one could afford to be less concerned if the girl again embarked upon a sexual adventure. It is highly probable that this might happen again (we are not entirely certain that, during the course of the 1½ years of the girl's stay at the home, sexual escapades did not occur; we have seen [from the files] how easily Vroni succeeds in establishing relations and in having sexual intercourse, quickly and almost "incidentally." Even if a girl is kept in a home, she occasionally escapes "outside the prison walls" and may use a short sojourn in the free world to satisfy her desires). Considering Vroni's overwhelming, quite strong and coarse sexual needs, it is improbable that she would be able on short notice to abstain entirely from "habitual" sexual intercourse.

It would be much easier to arrange that Vroni did not have the opportunity to steal. Her sexual difficulties are of much greater consequence, and one should be in a position to deal with them in some way.

2. The father, Mr. Gurtner, a well-to-do businessman, brings his 12-year-old son, *Jorg*, for examination because the boy has been failing in school.

The boy has two brothers: one is two years older, the other two years younger than he. The family lives in a house with a big garden. Jorg's education has never been a problem. The father would like Jorg to pass the entrance examination for Junior High School (as his older brother did).

Upon the suggestion of the counselor (who made the diagnosis), Jorg was given a thorough examination by a physician. The latter reported that Jorg is in perfect health, and that one does not have to worry about adverse hereditary factors. If there is anything amiss with Jorg, psychogenic causes must be held responsible.

Mr. Gurtner asked the examiner:

1. What are the facts with regard to the boy's intelligence? Is Jorg retarded in his development?

2. What should be done with Jorg (educational measures)?

The Zulliger as well as the Bero Tests were performed with this 12-year-old, and the Matrix Test was used as a control test. The latter showed an impairment of intelligence, which is also clearly evident in the form-interpretation tests; moreover, these latter tests substantiate the finding.

The diagnosis was discussed in person, with the support of the form-interpretation tests. The scoring is interesting, because it is clear that the Zulliger and Bero Tests are congruous (as is always the case with rather stable subjects).

Subject: *Jorg Gurtner*	*Comparison of Zulliger and Bero Tests*	
	Zulliger Test	*Bero*
Reaction time	shortened	shortened
Responses to the dark and to the colored cards	(19)/7	(46)/16
Confabulation DW	1 (tendency)	1 (tendency)
WS as indicator of the tendency to mask and inhibit obstinacy, and of the inclination to criticism	3	2
Total number of W	7 in 3 cards	20 in 10 cards

D	10 in 3 cards	22 in 10 cards
Dd	—	1
Do	1 (tendency!)	1 (tendency)
S	1	2
F	16 (—4)	33 (—6)
M	1 (M repression clearly seen in Card III)	2 (M repression in Card III)
Ms	1 (tendency)	1 (tendency)
FC	1	2
CF	1	3
FCh and ChF	1	4 (2 and 2)
Ratio of P : O	3 : 3	8 : 7
H, Hd	6	6
A	7 in 3 cards	20 in 10 cards (consequently, corresponding)
Obj	4 = 21%	11 = 24%
F+%	80	82
A%	40	43
P%	16	17
O%	16	15
Obj%	21	24
H%	30	13
Sequence	loose	loose
Experience balance	1 M : 1½ C	2 M : 5½ C
Apperceptive type	W — D — (Do) — <u>S</u>	W — D — (Dd/Do) — <u>S</u>
Red shock	+ (II)	+ (II) (III)
Color shock	+ (II)	+ (inversion of sequence; IX whistle, pause)
Ch shock	("Oh!")	VI ("Oh—this is difficult!")
Remarks	perseveration tendency	same
	M repression (III)	same (III)
	figure ground fusion; "or"	same
	strong WS tendency	same

Intelligence factors (innate intelligence)

Reaction time, number of responses with an adequate F+% — enjoys verbal expression; eager to express himself; keen observation ability; therefore, he is not a chatterer.

F+% is close to 80 .... possibly average intelligence, assuming that it has not been impaired by some factor.

Large number of W .... rather above average, considering the relatively high F+%.

Abstract and combinatory W ... the subject is capable of abstract as well as combinatory thinking.

W : M, *too few* M .... impairment, inhibition of intelligence.

DW tendency .... admixture of confabulatory elements; inaccurate differentiation between reality and fantasy; evasion from reality into the world of wishful thinking; infantile thinking confirmed by high obj% and nat (in the Bero).

Ratio of W : D
(7 : 10; 20 : 22) .... tendency toward bold unifying thinking; tendency toward organization and planning, taking into account the extratensive experience balance (1 C in the Bero!) and

(Experience balance)
(WS and S) considering WS and S as indicators of impulses toward opposition and obstinacy; tendency toward somehow wanting to have his way.

WS .... "impeded" pig-headed obstinacy, disguised stubbornness, repressed opposition, perhaps "impeded" aggression; makes an effort to adapt himself, to be obedient, but hides criticism and mistrust. He does not succeed fully, however, for pure S are present too.

A% .... the ability to form and to resolve stereotyped thought processes exists to an optimal degree.

P% .... the adaptation of thinking to that of other people is partially reduced; in other words, intellectual grasp

268

is partially impaired. One does not notice it too much, because ideas follow each other rapidly (test time ÷ number of responses), and because observation is keen. Moreover, the subject amazes one by his tendency toward unification (W) and originality (high O%). In effect, subject "bribes" by these qualities; as a result, one does not notice the elements of impairment that are present.

O% .... too high as compared to the few M (intelligence impairment!)

M repression .... the subject mistrusts independent thinking, and makes an effort to think reproductively.

Sequence .... reduction in logical thinking; thinking is somewhat sporadic, as will become manifest in a lack of permanent or occasional concentration power.

W : D .... the subject is more of a thinker than a doer; his practical endowment is not too great. At any rate, he is not actually a "manually skillful" type. According to his potential, he is rather an "intellectual" than a manual worker. However, since numerous D and a tendency to M are present, neither is he altogether "impractical."

Apperceptive type
  W and S are well marked .... inclined by nature to thinking in terms of "problems"; attempts even now (at 11½) to find "problems"; there is a chance that he might become a "brooder."

Do and tendency to inverse
  sequence .... anxiously cautious in his thinking. At times, anxiety is so great that courage deteriorates. Occasionally the subject appears "dull-witted," and succumbs to the limitations in the scope of his horizon.

269

"Or" .... insecurity: does not wish to commit himself; certain amount of intellectual conciliation: "strives" for adaptation.

FCh tendency .... some shrewdness (mixture of consciously sought adaptation and the will to succeed).

Why is there an impairment of intellectual development?

Shocks .... red shock indicates anxiety, as do Ch shocks. Color shock suggests a rather neurotic conversion of anxiety, while Ch shock indicates fear of own aggression. All shocks indicate that neurotic processes are effective and repressions are present.

Relationship of experience balance to shocks .... hysteria symptoms.

Since M repression is added ... probably also compulsive neurotic symptoms.

Since Ch interpretations are added .... "crushed" will-power; educational errors have been made, and forced good behavior is compensated for by neurotic mechanisms; aggression is dammed and impeded.

Aggregate evaluation: The boy has a high average innate intelligence, and may even be highly gifted intellectually. However, the development of his inherent intellectual capacities has been inhibited by neurotic, or rather emotional, forces; therefore, his manifest intelligence corresponds only in part with his potential ability. The partial "impediment" of his intelligence (a certain lack of intellectual courage; occasional dullness; reproductive instead of creative thinking; regressive perseveration of infantile thinking [wishful thinking]; a certain way of thinking nervously, sporadically, and illogically, etc.) is neurotic in origin and corresponds with neurotic symptoms at the intellectual level.

Since shocks appear in such large numbers, I doubt whether the boy could overcome his inhibitions (which must certainly

also be instrumental within his affectivity and personality structure, producing corresponding symptoms that very likely are
even more pronounced than those produced at the intellectual
level), if he had to do so by himself, without outside help.

Psychotherapeutic treatment is indicated, especially since
ChF suggest that the boy may succumb to depressive moods,
which he himself is not capable of mastering and controlling.

Follow-up report: Jorg was sent to a child psychotherapist.
With three sessions weekly, the treatment lasted for about one
year. Afterwards Jorg was capable of passing the entrance examination into Junior High School, although he was one year
behind. As of the present, he has been attending the same school
for the last three years, in other words, he is now a sophomore
in High School. His school performance is fully satisfactory. He
is in the upper third of his class, and his marks are good-to-very-
good. Especially his mathematical ability proved to be much
higher than had been estimated before the treatment. Evidently
it had been prevented from manifesting itself, because Jorg had
repressed M.

3. *Walter Roth,* a child of divorced parents, is 15½ years old
and in 7 months will have completed his schooling. He is the
eldest son, and has two younger brothers, one of whom is 10 and
the other 8 years old (see Table 2).

The father is a college graduate and occupies a very good position; the mother has inherited a small fortune. All the children
have been assigned to the mother; nevertheless, the father must
provide for the professional education of his three sons. As matters stand, he pays a substantial alimony for their support.

Walter's birth was normal; he was breast-fed for 9 months,
and toilet-training proceeded without difficulty. He has not had
any unusual diseases, accidents, or operations. He is in good
health. Supposedly, he has no adverse hereditary traits. Prior to
his parents' divorce, he utilized his position in the family to play
one parent against the other to his own advantage. In general,
and especially lately, he sides with the mother against the father, because he is afraid that, after he leaves school, the latter
might insist on his parting from his mother.

With the mother, he plays the part of a master. In the past, he had changed schools very often. When he was in his 11th year, he changed from the elementary school to High School, changed again to a private school, and finally, after spending a year there, changed once more to an academic High School. He then transferred to a public academic High School, and again to another secondary school. There, too, he has certain difficulties, because he does not like school.

In order to obtain a satisfactory diploma, he will try to make an effort during the course of the last school term. Then he wants to begin commercial training (practical work).

His father is of the opinion that he is quite capable of finishing secondary school and of studying.

Question: What should be done with W. R. after he graduates from school? Should he enter an educational home in the country? Should he go into practical training? Should he or should he not leave his mother?

Zulliger Test   Time: 6 minutes

I.

A grapevine leaf .... DF + pl
A potato beetle .... WF + A P

II.

"Ts—ts!" (turns the card around,
    raises his eyebrows, shakes his
    head. Prolonged reaction time)   shock!
A face (mask) with cut-out nose
    and mouth, made from a red
    scarf; the eyes look through slits S → DCF — mask

III.

Butterfly .... DF + A P
A clown running around .... DM + H P/mask
The face of a ghost ...... ChF → DoF + Hd (P)
Mouse (within the small dark blot) DF + A
 c A *sitting* butterfly (tiny Dd at the
    "leg" to the left, at the "ear" of
    the "small pig") .... DdF + A

272

Rorschach Test   Time: 19 minutes

I.

A human being *without any head,*
  or, perhaps, he has bent it down
  so that one cannot see it (center
  portion) .... DM + H/flexor kinesthesias "or"
c Acorn (a part of the center
  portion) .... DdF + pl

II.

"Ts—ts!" (Prolonged reaction
  time. Turns the card) .... shock
A small fir tree (confluence in the
  center) .... DF + pl
Young acorn, the cap is still big ... SF + pl *perseveration*
Head of a human being (red upper
  area) .... DoF + Hd

III.

c A ball of red wool (red inner area) DFC obj O
c Face *with eyes covered* (the
  "baskets"—"face"=entire center
  portion) .... S → DF − HdO−

IV.

(Turns the card around)
Leg and *house slippers* (lateral) .. DF(C) obj
A masked face (mask) (center por-
  tion) .... DF ± *mask*
c Collar and sleeves of a man's jacket
  (top portion) .... Do → DF + *clothing*

V.

b Face with a beard (right periphery) DF + Hd
Butterfly .... WF + A P

VI.

Moth (large portion) .... DF ± A
Or a grapevine leaf .... DF − pl "or"

VII.

Head of a lion (2) .... DF + Ad P
The Melide Dam with the lake on⎰DF ± geog
  both sides (confluence and S) ...⎱SF− geog

273

VIII.

(Turns the card around for a long
time, shakes his head) .... shock
Well, it is an animal, almost a cat
(red area) .... DF + A P
A jacket *without sleeves;* in the
middle the shirt has come out, it
has a Schiller collar .... DdF (C) clothing
b Ornamental fish (gray area) ...... DF + A
c Or a flying bird .... DF + A "or"

IX.

A violin .... SF + obj
Head of a bird of prey (within the
grey area)
(the "crocodile's head") .... DF − Ad
Bone (center purple area) .... DdF + obj

X.

"Oh boy!" .... shock!
c Head of a god's statue in the
Amazon (center dark area) .... DF + Hd
                               demonstration of intelligence
a Sea-horse (green center area) ..... DF + A
b A mountain range (red area. In
answer to a question about it:
"Only because of the form") .... DF + nat

Bero Test   Time: 14 minutes

I.

A dog .... DF + A P
c Pitcher with handle (center portion) .... DF + obj

II.

"Oh well!"
c A mummy (confluence) .... DFCh H
A miniature terrier .... DF + A P
Two dancing dwarfs (red area) ... DM + H P

III.

"Oh well, oh well!" (turns the card
around for a long time) .... shock!
b A snail or a snail's shell (upper red
center area) .... DdF + A *"or"*

274

IV.

Butterfly .... WF + A P

V.

Almost the same. Flying fish ...... WF + A
Or a bird .... WF + A *"or"*
Face (center portion) .... DF ± Hd

VI.

(Turns the card absent-mindedly,
   sitting in a sloppy position)
A rocket's shell chamber and a   ⌈DF ± obj combinatory
  rocket (center dark portion) ....⌊SF + obj aggression

VII.

The roof of a chapel and its upper
   part .... SF + architecture
A sitting figure .... SM + H O
                        flexor kinesthesias

VIII.

c A bird, a partridge (orange area) .. DFC A P
a A mountaineer fastening himself
   with a rope to a rock (red area) DM + H O confabulation
  Small fishes (blue area) .... DF ± A infantile
  Stones (grey area) .... DCF obj

IX.

An angel with wings (blue area) .. DF ± H O− confabulation
A lady's red blouse with wide
   sleeves (orange area) .... DFC clothing
(Sighs; "This is difficult!") .... shock!
c This is shaped like wings (blue
   area) .... Do → DF + Ad

X.

c Antlers (orange c) .... DdF + Ad
b Mouse (inner blue area) .... DF + A infantile
  An *eye* (within brown area) *look-*
   ing at one .... DdF ± Hd

The intelligence factors:

Testing time and number of
   responses .... ideas appear quickly; eagerness for
                             expression is higher than average.
High F+% .... good ability for observing and
                             formulating.

Few W .... poor ability for unifying, arranging, organizing, planning; manifest intelligence is lower than one would expect it to be, on the basis of the high F+%.

All W are P .... confirms the lack of combinatory and abstractive ability.

Number of D is large. In addition, Do, Dd, and S are present .... intelligence is more "practical" than theoretical; thinking may easily become anxious and cautious, brooding and tending toward opposition.

Inverse sequence .... confirms caution; mistrust is accentuated by anxiety.

M is larger than C (experience balance), inverse sequence and S .... self mistrust, self-doubts at the intellectual level; does not want to disgrace himself; he proceeds in his thinking from a detail to the whole, orienting himself through details; has difficulty in forming ideas.

Do .... his thinking is inhibited; occasionally he "does not see the forest for the trees."

Low A% .... it is difficult for him to retain stereotyped thought processes, or to reproduce them; he may have difficulty in concentrating; his thinking is somewhat confused, flighty, scattered.

High P% .... the subject's thinking adheres to the commonplace; with regard to the factors mentioned above, we are dealing with an individual whose thinking is realistic; he is, however, a shortsighted opportunist.

M repression (WM is absent in Card III) .... typical puberty phenomenon: flight from inner life despite the fact that he is an introversive type. His thinking clings to the objective world, to reality, to everything that is reproductive; he mistrusts productivity. Independent thinking is inhibited;

	the scope of thinking is rather narrow, coarctated.
Low O%	confirms the facts mentioned above.
Flexor kinesthesias, H%, taking into account the above factors, in addition, "sitting" contents	strongly autistic thinking.
Clothing	confirms opportunistic and autistic attitudes; the subject strives to appear in a favorable light.
Geography, demonstration of intellectual ability	the subject would like to present himself as more intelligent and "educated" than he really is; he has a strong need to show off his intellectual resources; he has a schoolboy's "intelligence complex."
Large number of S, easily flowing productive output (number of responses ÷ reaction time), sloppy conduct	a visible attitude of knowing everything better than anybody else, together with self-doubts; the subject compensates for his feelings of insufficiency by intellectual presumption; his intellectual self-esteem is inflated.
Some single FCh, "mask"	the subject believes himself to be "shrewd"—and he *is* shrewd.
Tiny Dd	inclined to be pedantic.
S added to them	disputatious.
Tendency toward perseveration .	inclined to be lazy in his thinking.

Since he is endowed with the kind of intelligence described above, it is to be expected that the subject will not feel comfortable in school, insofar as he believes himself to be superior. Because the discipline of thinking processes, as required by the school, is opposed to the subject's autistic thinking, the subject must feel uncomfortable. He is averse to everything truly "intellectual," in that it disturbs him in his autistic indolence and in his opportunism. School seems "stupid" to him; it pays attention to things that—seen from the viewpoint of the subject's "lack of foresight"—are "valueless" to him. He believes himself to be "above" school.

PERSONALITY FACTORS:

In discussing the subject's intelligence factors some personality characteristics have already been delineated.

Thus, it has been established that autistic, rejecting, and mistrusting traits are present.

Coarctated-introversive experience balance and, in addition,
S ....
withdrawal from the outside world; in general, the subject's affectivity is rather shallow.

CF ....
affectivity tends to erupt; sensitivity.

M and CF ....
emotional restraint; but irritability, followed by outbreaks of violence.

S and CF.....................
obstinacy and tendency toward aggression.

CF ....
subject tends to submit to moods. If sensitivity is provoked, outbursts ensue; vitality is extensive rather than intensive; rather noisy and loud; enthusiasm is short-lived rather than lasting.

Anxious caution, "mask," and autism ....
despite his attitude of opposition and mistrust, in his dealings with the outside world the subject wears a "mask" of cautious shrewdness and even sneakiness, whenever such an attitude seems to be advantageous to him.

CF are added ....
then again his attitude becomes that of "fighting for elbow-room"; he is beset by outbreaks of inconsiderateness toward others; he alternates between self-restraint and "letting himself go." In its extreme form, this implies fluctuating between furtive and rude behavior.

Shocks ....
neurotic traits.

experience balance added ....
compulsive and hysteria symptoms, such as brooding; autistic anxieties, which are most likely concerned with the health of the subject.

Autistic M .... ("sitting"—"house slippers")	physically awkward, he is not the "sportsman" type; he is too lazy, and has the nature of a "pasha."
"Or"	considering his traits of sneakiness, uncertainty; he does not want to take any chances; he has a tendency toward concealment.
"Eyes," "faces"	feelings of guilt; he fears to be observed; also, self-observation and vigilance.
"without head," "without arms," etc.; "lady's blouse" ...	castration complex, probably masturbation, and therefore guilt feelings and hypochondriacal traits.

It is clear that such an immature youngster should have further schooling and education. However, since he does not like school, he would just "sulk" if he were moved to another school.

Would it be advisable to provide trade training for him?

He might be suited for it. It must be anticipated, however, that he might quit as soon as the demands made upon him became too severe (affective outbreak).

He might be suited for some other professions, however—for instance, those in which mental activity is not the only requirement, but where he would be able to use his hands as well (he is a "practical" type, a D type with several M). He might be intelligent enough to undertake studying in a technical school, for instance, in order to prepare for the profession of laboratory worker. Or he could train more directly, in a drug store or in a laboratory that manufactured perfumes. Perfume manufacture might be a fitting occupation for him, because "proper appearance" ("clothing" interpretations) is quite important to him. To be "nothing but" a salesman of clothing would not be in accordance with his tendency to act as a pasha and to overrate his own intellectual powers; he would think it a degradation.

It would be best, indeed, if one could try to win time. The youth should have the opportunity to mature; first of all, he should be guided away from the pasha position with regard to his mother.

TABLE 2

Subject: *Walter Roth*, 15½ years old

	1. Zulliger Test	2. Rorschach	3. Behn
Time:	6 minutes	19 minutes	14 minutes
Number of responses:	8/1	28/10	24/10
DW	1		
SW	3		
WS			
W	1	1	3
D	3	20	16
Dd	1	2	2
Do	1(2)	(1)	
S	1	4	3
DdS			
F	6(−1)	25(−4.5)	19(−4.5)
M	1	3	1
MS			
FC	1	2	1
CF	1	1	1
C		1	
FCh		1	
ChF		1	
F+%	83	82	87
A%	50	28	46
P%	50	11	21
O%	8±	8	
obj%			
H%	25	20	33
P	4	3	5
O	−	2(−1)	2
H	1	1	5
Hd	1	3	2
masks		1(2)	1
anat			
clothing		3	1
sex			
scenes			
blood			
A	4	5	8
Ad		3	3
obj		5	4
pl		1	4
nat		1	
geog		2	
arch			
others			1
red shock:	+	+	+
color shock:	+	+	+
chiaroscuro shock:			
Sequence:	inverse	same	same
Experience balance:	1 : 1	1 : 1	3 : 1.5
Apperceptive type:	W – D – Dd/Do/S	same	same

Remarks: WM III absent | WM III absent — people with faces | WM III absent

280

SUGGESTION:

W. R. should go to the Welschland (the French part of Switzerland) for a year; only afterward will the problem concerning his vocational training be solved. Since he does not like to exert himself physically and since, being fixated to the mother, he is probably quite interested in food, he could become an errand boy in a bakery or a butcher store. He should not be allowed to work for a farmer. It would be best to find a place for him in a drug store, in some larger village that is far enough from the city, however. In a village, there are fewer opportunities to yield to temptations: there are no movies, etc. Being removed from the mother will promote his liberation from her. It will force the youth to make progress toward self-reliance; in other words, it will further his independence.

After a year, W. R. should be re-examined. Some changes may have taken place during this period. Perhaps he may be willing to continue his schooling then.

If he should still insist on trade training, and wish to go through some "practical" training, I would suggest pharmacy apprenticeship for him. It might well be possible that once he was working in a pharmacy, he will feel the need for further schooling, which would later enable him to work in a laboratory.

It is conceivable that, as soon as he has been confronted with real life, W. R. will collide with it—to such an extent as to find his neurosis greatly intensified. This will provide him with the occasion for some "insight into his illness"; then it will become possible to treat him. It cannot be done at present, for he feels completely "well."

Currently, W. R.'s problem is not one of vocational choice. It is much more the problem of getting him to surrender his pasha position with regard to his mother. It seems that this situation is also desired by the mother; son and mother have a relationship of unconscious agreement. The mother's attention must be drawn to the fact that she must relinquish her demands, for the benefit of her son.

It would not be sufficient simply to take W. R. away from his mother and give him to his father. The son could still see the mother daily, and complain to her about the father. For he

281

would be antagonistic to the father and construct situations with which the father would be unable to cope. While the son created the opportunities for complaining about the father, the divorced mother would welcome his tales in order to pity her son. Thus, he would simply re-create the situation of his early childhood, when he always had somehow to be "in the right."

Despite the fact that until now nothing has occurred to reveal the untenable conditions prevailing in W. R.'s life, the situation is nevertheless extremely critical for him. He runs the risk of becoming unsuited for life, since he will always continue to want to be pampered, as he was during his childhood. His parents have indulged him, and he had derived pleasure from it.

He must be pried loose from this situation without using force, for the youth would react to force with extreme opposition. Therefore, his being "transplanted" from his mother's house should be made as easy as possible for him. He should be bribed into it, so to speak; it is necessary for the mother herself to insist on it. It would be best if the father kept himself in the background, while the mother arranged the transfer. W. R. must meet with and experience a "disappointment in love"; he must be thrown out of the mother's "nest" by the mother herself. This will either stimulate him into acting "normally," or else deepen his neurosis (which should then be treated, without fail).

On this basis, it must be stated that this case is a very precarious one, almost without a present solution. The boy has taken a course that will definitely lead to social behavior, if it is left unchecked.

4. *Heini Frick,* 14½ years old, a young thief (see Table 3).

Mr. Frick brings his 14½-year-old son, Heini, for a psychological diagnosis, because Heini has committed a number of thefts. The worried father, who is a businessman and owns his own business in a small town, asks whether Heini is a delinquent or suffers from schizophrenia.

There is no history of psychosis in the family. The subject's paternal grandparents were a vicar and his wife; his maternal grandparents were respected farm people. Nothing is known of alcoholism or of any other suspicious traits in the family. A physical examination has revealed that Heini is in perfect health. The boy is well developed for his age. He is as tall as a fully grown man, and his voice has already changed.

In terms of work performance, Heini has never had any difficulties in school. Yet he has always avoided other children of his own age and has found companions among those who are older, who have already graduated from school. One could meet him at gatherings where smoking went on. Once he participated in a beer party, running the risk thereby of being thrown out of the little town's secondary school. To prevent his being expelled, Mr. Frick enrolled his son in a boarding school. There Heini stole from his fellow students: he would empty out their lockers and buy smoking articles with the stolen money; then he would generously distribute them among the boarding-house students, including those whose money he had appropriated. In this manner, he attracted attention to himself. The director of the home suspected that Heini might be the thief who stole the money that was reported missing, because the youngster had so much money to spend. Heini was questioned and, although at first he tried to deny everything, he then confessed to it, although seemingly unmoved and without remorse. Thus, the impression was gained that he might be schizophrenic. The change to a boarding school had not been made merely because of the expectation that he might be expelled from school. At home, Heini refused to obey. Although his parents did not permit him to associate with the young members of the sports club, Heini simply disregarded their wishes. Violent altercations ensued, but no agreement could be reached. That is why everybody was glad when the decision was made for Heini to attend a boarding school. Heini himself agreed to the change of environment. Later, however, he said that he had imagined life in a home to be completely different. After his thefts were discovered, the boarding school refused to keep him.

The Frick family, both father and mother, did not know what to do next. Following the advice of their family physician, who had given Heini a physical examination, they brought Heini for a psychological diagnosis, expecting to obtain some counseling as to what to do with the youngster.

Heini has a brother who is six years his junior, and a little sister nine years his junior. As far as one can remember, he has always been indifferent toward his brother, but he has a friendly attitude toward his little sister. Occasionally he plays with her, and at times he gives her candy, or some small toy that he has either bought or made himself, for he is skillful at making things. He never obeys his mother at once: almost invariably, he first teases her for a while, irritating her by his opposition and making her lose her temper. But after such overtures, he does listen to her and fulfills her wishes. On the other hand, he opposes his father altogether or else he avoids him.

First the Zulliger Test, then the Ro, and finally the Bero test were administered to Heini. As a control test, the Duess Test was also performed on him.

Zulliger Test

Time: 7 minutes.   July 1950
23 responses, 7 of which
were produced for the
colored Card II.
The subject maintains a
somewhat stiff, "manly"
attitude.

I.

A beetle	WF + A P
In the center there is a tie	DF + clothing
It could also be a crab	WF + A P
"There is such a lot there but one can not exactly say everything!" "What is this?" Points to S underneath the dark center blot	(SF — sex)
c The whole is an animal's head. One must disregard the holes; the head might be that of a dog, here is his snout (FG 3 and 7/8)	DWF — Ad
a A human head (top center)	S → DF + Hd
(laughs) it is rather a monkey head with round eyes	S → DF + Ad
c Here it looks like the footprints of a cat, especially on the right side (FG 3)	ChC → DF + Ad O

284

II.

(Turns the card immediately into
c-position!)

Antlers—belonging to some Iceland animals (he means elks);
also, because of the color, yes, because of the color .... DCF Ad

Sea plants (green area) .... DCF pl

Two bears holding their paws together, standing up (dark red
area)[1] .... DM + A

Their shadows are on the outside
                        FCh → DF + shadow

A skeleton's spine .... SF − anat
(He drops his cigarette!)

Pieces of tree bark with tree rings
(brown area) .... F (C) → DCF pl

Thistles (green area) .... DFC pl

III.

A human Halloween head .... DoF + Hd (P) mask

b Caterpillar (leg) .... DF ± A

a Jumping boys (outer red area) .... DM + H P

Butterfly (red inner area) .... DF + A P

Hand .... DoF + Hd
and arm (adjoining the large
dark blot) .... DoF + Hd

Pistol (inner center portion, adjoining the large dark blot) .... DdF + obj

c Head of a dragon (large blot at the
leg) .... DdF + Ad

Rorschach Test   Time: 19 minutes
                                Number of responses: 43/13

I.

c Something almost like a pyramid . DWF − geometry

a Small forked deer antlers (center
top area) .... DF + Ad

Puppet heads (upper S) .... SF + Hd

II.

Head of a rhinoceros; the nose is
in the middle; there is the horn
on top of it .... DWSF − Ad O

[1] Upon inquiry, after completion of the test: "The bears have raised themselves
up on their hind legs and are bowing to each other."

285

Butterfly (red lower portion) ..... DF + A

Torso of a dog, head and paw
(dark area) .... DF + Ad

b This is a four-legged animal; it
has turned its head away; the
ears look out .... DF + A

III.

A human torso, head, chest, and
arm .... DoF + Hd (P)

They have a bag in their hand ... DF + obj
M repression

Fish (small dark blot) .... DF + A

Butterfly (center red area) .... DF + A P

It could also be a little red tie .... DFC clothing

b A child's rocking horse (outer red
area) .... DF + A/obj O

c The head of a mouse (part of the
large dark blot, at the outer rim) DdF + Ad

IV.

The head of an animal (center
portion) .... DF + Ad

Boots (outer lower portion) ...... DF + obj

Snakes (outer upper portion) .... DF + A

V.

Butterfly .... WF + A P

c Bat .... WF + A P

b Open beak of a crow (right center
portion) .... DF + Ad

a Head of a crocodile with open
mouth (outer rim) .... DdF + Ad

Head of a hare (center top portion) DF + Ad

VI.

c A scarecrow .... WF + obj

a Head of a tapeworm (top center
portion) .... DF + Ad

Human head with a horizontal
beard and a peaked cap (large
dark portion) .... DF + Hd

c Claws of a bird of prey (uppermost
portion) .... DdF + Ad

286

VII.

c Two women with bushy hair;
   dancers, perhaps .... WM + H O
a Women's heads. (3. part) .... DF + Hd P
c Clouds (confluent portions) ...... DChF clouds
a A painted mouth (confluence) ... DdF + Hd

VIII.

c A lady's or a child's jacket (red-
   orange area) .... DFC clothing ⎫
   Slacks to go with it (blue area) .... DFC clothing ⎬ combinatory
                                                  ⎭
a Sea plant (gray area) .... DCF pl
c Well, this is the head of a stag
   (gray area) .... DF + Ad
b An animal—from foreign regions
   (red area) .... DF + A P

IX.

b The head of a stag (orange area) .. DF + Ad
   Owl with wings spread out—except
   that owls are never red .... DF + A obj crit

X.

   "I cannot seem to get anything
   any more!"
   A pair of glasses, old-fashioned
   ones (center orange area) ...... DdF ± obj
   The head of a hare (inner green
   area) .... DF + Ad
b A sheep lying down (outer orange
   area) .... DF + A
   Two small animals (inner gray
   area), like mice .... DF + A P
   Sea plants; some are bluish (outer
   blue area) .... DCF pl
   Peninsula on a map (green outer
   area) .... DF − geog

Bero Test   Time: 17 minutes
                                     Number of responses: 39/13

I.

   Two dogs pull .... WM + A P
   —on a tree root .... DF + pl
c A moth without a head (center
   portion) .... DF + Ad

II.

Two dog heads .... DoF + Ad (P)
Sea plants (inner red area) ...... DF ± pl
c A human head with a helmet that
    comes to a point .... DF + Hd
A human being with his arms cut
    off (center portion toward the
    red area); he stands at attention DM + H complex interpretation
b A hand with a pointer (left upper
    portion) .... DF + Hd
The head of a monkey (large dark
    lower portion situated at con-
    fluence) .... DdF + Ad

III.

A human torso .... DoF + Hd (P)
                           M repression
Legs .... DoF + Hd

IV.

A tree leaf .... WF + pl
c Butterfly .... WF + A P
A person .... DdF + H (P)
The whole also resembles some old
    tree bark .... DWChF pl O−

V.

A wide butterfly .... WF + A
c It could be rather a bird .... WF + A P
A seal (center portion) .... DF + A

VI.

A fir tree covered with snow ..... FCh → WF + pl P
c An animal's head (upper third
    portion) .... DF + Ad

VII.

Insignia of a pilot (bottom S) .... SF + obj
A bull's head "because of the
    horns" (upper portion) .... DF − Ad confabulation
c A many-legged animal; a wood
    louse (upper portion) .... DF ± A
b Cloud (large dark blot) .... DChF cloud

a Cheese container (bottom S) ..... SF + obj
A rubber stamp (the "bridge" in
   the center) .... DF − obj
VIII.

c Mountain rocks (gray portion) ... DCF obj O
a Flamingoes (gray area) .... DdDF − A
c Partridges (orange area) .... DFC A P
Crocodiles (red area) .... DF + A P
The tail of a lizard (a portion of
   the blue area) .... DdF + Ad

IX.

c A butterfly (purple area) .... DF + Ad
a Africa (one half of the orange area) DF − geog
c Bird (blue area) .... DF + A P
b A sparrow flying upward .... DFC A

X.

A piece of a tree with its branches
   cut off (brown area) .... DCF pl
b A chicken (pink area) .... DF + A
Cloud (outer blue area), a winter
   cloud .... DCF cloud
d A human head (inner blue area,
   below) .... DF + Hd infantile

When one compares the scoring tables, one is tempted to agree with the Yugoslav physician, Dr. Schwezensky, who has stated that the Zulliger Test frequently yields better results than the two other form-interpretation tests, if only because all perceivable factors appear in it in a much more concentrated form.[2]

In Heini Frick's Zulliger Test we may indeed discover everything that is also found in the Ro and Bero tests. Above and beyond these findings, however, Heini's attitude towards sexual impulses—in other words, the adolescent's inner sexual perception—are revealed as well.

To begin with, the ease with which the boy produces his responses is extremely striking. It shows that he must possess a considerable need for communication. If form accuracy were not as high as it is—namely, between 80 and 88%—one could assume

[2] Personal communication

289

TABLE 3

Heini Frick, 14½ years old

Zulliger Test → Rorschach Test → Bero Test

	7 minutes	19 minutes	17 minutes
Time:			
Number of responses:	23/7	43/13	39/13
DW =	1 } 3	2 } 6	1 } 7
W =	2	4	6
D =	19	30	25
Dd =	2	5	2
Do =	3	1	3
S =	2(4)	2	2
F+% =	80	88	83
A% =	44	58	50
P% =	17	16	25
O% =	4	7±	5±
H% =	35	21	20
anat% =	8	—	—

	7 minutes	19 minutes	17 minutes
F =	17(—3.5)	36(—4)	30(—5)
M =	2	1	2
FC =	1	3	2
CF =	3	2	3
FCh =	(1)		(1)
ChC =	1		
ChF =		1	
F(C) =	(1)		
shocks =	+	+	+

	7 minutes	19 minutes	17 minutes
P =	4	7	10
O =	1	3(—1)	2(—1)
H =	1	1	1
Hd =	4	5	2
anat =	1		5
sex =	1		
clothing =	1	3	—
A =	5	12	13
Ad =	5	13	6
obj =	1	4	4
pl =	3	2	6
geog =	1	1	1
cloud =	1	1	2
geom., shadow =	1	1	—

	7 minutes	19 minutes	17 minutes
Sequence:	orderly, irritated, and color shock	same	same
Experience balance:	2 M : 3½ C	1 : 3½	2 : 4
Apperceptive type:	(DW)W — D — Dd/Do — S	same	same
Remarks:	M repression mask	M repression combinatory tendency	M repression complex interpretation confabulation infantile

that he is a chatterer or perhaps a cheat. Heini cannot be either. It is more likely that we are dealing here with a rather gifted boy who has at his disposal precise engrams and a lively associative mechanism.

Although some very pronounced indicators appear of anxiety-determined caution—such as Do and reversed sequence—the flow of associations is not inhibited. The disturbance, which has been experienced as anxiety, makes itself felt in the quality rather than the quantity of thinking. Heini wants to set limits to his uncertainty by making a pedantic effort to observe and to formulate with accuracy. This does not prevent him, however, from confabulating occasionally. Not only the fact that he produces DW bears this out, but also his D interpretations, which have a confabulatory construction. Moreover, his thinking is still partially infantile despite the form accuracy referred to. In other words, it is permeated with wish fantasies, which he experiences as "real."

During a period of some two decades, I have been able to observe the following facts: if an adolescent produces DW, and if, in addition, his experience balance is highly extratensive; if there occur S, and if the number of CF predominates and even pure C are present—then a latent or manifest impulse toward thieving is effective in him. If, in addition to C, the subject's M are entirely or partially flexor kinesthesias, this means that the impulse is a strong one and the probability is high that it has become manifest. It still remains to be clarified whether autistic M types *also* steal and how the "thieving syndrome" appears in the form-interpretation test in such cases.

One must ask whether, in general, adolescents produce DW. No, normally they do not produce DW; they produce M and predominantly FC (instead of CF).

On the basis of the Zulliger Test as well as of Heini's other form-interpretation tests, we would suspect, if we did not already know it, that he may be a thief. Considering his intelligence, however, we see that Heini could not steal out of sheer "stupidity." Also, his stealing is not compulsive, for in true kleptomaniacs—at least, I believe that I have established this fact through many examples—FC are as a rule completely absent, and experience balance is for the most part rather ambiequal. In addition, S and a color shock are found. What, then, is the reason for Heini's stealing?

In the area of affectivity, infantile wishful thinking corresponds with regression or an inhibition of development. It makes itself felt spontaneously; it "overcomes" the subject, so to speak. If the subject then becomes stimulated by a measure of unadapted affectivity, which is immediately converted into motility, and if he is not capable of discharging his affects by creative imagination, because of his insufficient inner life (extensor kinesthesias), then he will fail to resist his wishes for possessions. He will steal like a small child who takes some candy from a candy jar, if he has the chance.

If, as with Heini, a considerable degree of obstinacy is added —a fact supported by the S:CF combination—then a tendency to harm others results, which may find release in thefts. Heini's stealing may be explained by his infantile impulses, which are the result either of regression or of an inhibition of development. They are probably strengthened by impulses of obstinacy.

Let us test the insights that we have gained by comparing them with Heini's real life situation. He was put into a home by his father because he opposed his father and disregarded the commands and orders of his village teachers. At the home, he was expected to adapt himself to the conditions of his new environment. He wanted to impress his companions, to win their favor; he believed that he would succeed in achieving this by giving them something—"smokes," for instance. But his allowance was not large enough to permit him to buy substantial cigarette supplies and he therefore obtained additional funds by stealing. His attitude toward his companions is ambivalent: he would like to win them over to his side, and yet he is angry with them because he has to *do something* in order to gain their approval, because they do not simply offer themselves to him and do not treat him from the first as if they had been waiting for him.

If one thinks about the mistrust with which newcomers are generally received by adolescents, and especially by those in boarding homes, if one tries to visualize the quarreling over rank that ensues until the "newcomer" has finally found his place, one can well imagine Heini's position. By understanding Heini's simultaneous feelings of longing (high H%) *and* defiance with regard to his fellow-men, one is able to gain insight into him.

We have before us a relatively gifted boy. At any rate, his capabilities are above average. The development of his intelligence has been more or less inhibited by certain infantile residues, as well as by his tendency to be obstinate. His thinking is tinted by confabulation, and is therefore not really "neat," not completely reliable. In addition, Heini is endowed with an easy intellectual grasp and is capable of observing keenly (see the "scoring sheet's" percentage column, sequence, and apperceptive type). Heini must be aware of the fact that he is unable to think really "neatly," for he produces Do and, if he is affectively irritated, reverses the sequence (after having, for example, experienced a red or color shock). This means that, because of a certain anxiety, he makes an effort to be cautious. He does not wish to disgrace himself, for he undoubtedly possesses a strong quality ambition; this results in a drive for whole perceptions, supported by some specific intellectual ambition. In the Zulliger Test, this may be established by the occurrence of an anatomy interpretation and, in the two other tests, by the map and geography interpretations (Ro).

Despite his clearly pronounced W tendency, Heini's intelligence would not be suited for purely theoretical activities, because D predominate. It has been found that D types can be either "practical" or "schematizing" people. Since Heini has produced several M, one may deduce that he tends to be practical rather than schematizing. On the other hand, Do and S lead us to suspect him of being inclined to nagging, of becoming lost in pettiness, of brooding. He is distrustful as well as self-distrusting, for he clearly "represses" M—which means that he avoids "dreams" because he distrusts them. Considering the disguised sexual interpretations in the Zulliger Test, we can well understand why Heini "represses" his inner self, why he avoids it. We are confronted here with the typical picture presented by many young people at puberty. They do not know what to do with their newly awakening forces; they are not capable of integrating them, and therefore they attempt to find a way out, by escaping in the direction of extraversion, external activity, motility, etc. The present-day enthusiasm for sports among adolescents offers welcome relief.

Finally, if we take a look at the contents of the interpretations, our attention is attracted by the following:

In Card I (Zulliger Test), the interpretation of a tie is produced. As experience has taught us, people who produce clothing or jewelry responses are not without a certain superficial vanity. We may assume that this has its effect in Heini. Narcissism, as well as a tendency to narcissistic injury, should be quite pronounced in him.

The fact that Heini is inclined to sex repression is shown by his remark regarding the lower S in Card I of the Zulliger Test.

His last response to Card I of the Zulliger Test is interesting too: "Here it looks like the footprints of a cat." Hunters frequently produce "footprint" responses. In their case, this is some kind of "shop talk." In non-hunters—and Heini is a non-hunter —footprint interpretations often have their origin in a certain romantic, Indian-like, boyish curiosity. At the same time, they indicate anxiety: the youth is afraid that his "footprints" might be discovered. Although he is still completely "normal," a slightly paranoid character trait comes to light, suggesting guilt feelings that are hidden within the personality, and result in the tendency to give oneself away. We see the effects of this in the way Heini gives away the items that he has stolen. He must be found out, and he actually is found out by the home's director.

It is also interesting that, after having produced the "skeleton spine" response (Card II, Zulliger Test), Heini drops his cigarette. We may surmise the nature of the shock that the youth has experienced here. Keeping in mind the discoveries made by psychoanalysis, are we entirely wrong in suspecting the existence of a strong castration complex? This would provide the basis for the sexual repression that we have already established and which, as a rule, originates in sexual fears. It would also confirm the guilt feelings.

The strong evidence of shock experienced in Card II becomes evident in Card III, for which Heini is incapable of producing the usual WM + H P. In his "human Hallowe'en head" response

294

he interprets a Do instead. Here his intelligence inhibition becomes clearly apparent. Thus the arrest of intelligence is the result of affective elements.

As Kuhn has indicated, people who produce mask responses are, as a rule, not frank and do not show themselves as they really are. They have acquired a certain mask-like way of acting, in order to protect themselves.

In Heini's case, this corresponds with the somewhat rigid pose which he assumed during the testing, displaying a "manly," "composed" attitude. His remaining unmoved, when he was questioned after his thefts had been discovered, was most likely the expression of an attempt to appear "heroic" before his investigators and judges, not to betray what really motivated him.

By surveying all that has become understandable to us with respect to Heini, we are in a position to compose the following *short diagnosis,* which we offer to his father.

There is no doubt that Heini is not a schizophrenic. Nevertheless, there is still a great deal of infantilism about him, despite his age, his physical maturity, and his development. Furthermore he is childishly obstinate, and therefore behaves compulsively in a "manly" fashion.

His stealing impulses correspond with these personality traits. Heini steals as a small child does, not being able to offer enough resistance to his desires and being supported by defiant impulses of resentment: he wants to harm others to avenge himself.

He is endowed with a good intellectual potential. Sometimes Heini does not use his intelligence properly, because it is inhibited by his inner conflicts, which absorb his energy to such an extent that—partially—he is unable to use it for intellectual achievements.

In addition, he is at present going through a "difficult developmental stage" of the maturation process. Heini does not know how to handle his newly aroused forces properly—mainly, his sexual impulses. He is unable to assimilate them, and he "runs away" from them. He tries to expend them in sports and is afraid of the sexual fantasies that may beset him. More instinctively than consciously, he feels that he can best escape these fantasies by plunging himself into some outside activity (sports). By developing an interest in sports, for instance, he withdraws his attention from other matters that may be secretly troubling him.

One phenomenon of puberty is characterized by the fact that the subject is faced with the task of liberating himself from his parents. In other words, in keeping with his own development, he must make an effort to find a new relationship to his parents. Heini does not reject his female blood relatives; on the contrary, he tries to attract his mother's attention by irritating her. He is antagonistic towards his father and pays no attention at all to his brother.

To the extent that this situation does not become fixated, these are absolutely normal, although somewhat affectively intensified, development determined phenomena, which may and will disappear, as soon as the youth passes puberty. In the meantime, patience is indicated and the father is advised to avoid situations that would give rise to his oldest son's defiant impulses.

I think that the abnormal traits of Heini's personality are the outcome of a so-called "puberty neurosis." Its characteristics of defiance are noteworthy.

The advice that Heini should undergo psychotherapeutic treatment suggests itself. It seems to me, however, that something else should be tried first. It is much more necessary now for the young man to be guided than to be analyzed.

Therefore I suggest:

1. Heini should return to his family, and both father and mother should treat him with the most possible equanimity. If the father finally succeeds in persuading his son to perform certain small tasks in his business and expresses his appreciation, a "reconciliation" will follow. Thus Heini's readjustment will be made easier.

2. Heini should attend a private school in Bern, commuting from his small home town. The trip to and from school will shorten his free time to a considerable extent, which will have a favorable effect on him, for he will have less time to spend loitering with his older companions.

3. At the same time, Heini must be given an older friend and leader, who is aware of his task regarding the boy and will treat him correspondingly, devoting himself to Heini. He should be

able to interest Heini in "superior things" and to stimulate his productive powers.

This leader could be a Boy Scout, perhaps, intelligent enough to understand his responsibility toward Heini and to carry it out. From time to time, it is possible to find such a Boy Scout leader. The prerequisite must be that Heini should be able to recognize his own ideal image in his leader, and at the same time to love, respect, and admire him.

Perhaps it would be even safer to entrust this task to a grown-up man with special psychological capabilities. In this case, Heini could be treated. Yet treatment should not consist of the "classic" psychoanalytic method; instead, a psychoanalytically-oriented approach should be employed. (As a rule, young people at puberty should not be submitted to psychoanalytic treatment—at least, not just then—because at that age everything is still too changeable, and because at puberty most adolescents suffer from the fact that their ego has not as yet been sufficiently integrated.)

FOLLOW-UP REPORT:

Heini has been treated by the method indicated above. The treatment was carried out by a man toward whom Heini developed a positive transference from the start. The "technique" of this treatment took the form of discussions during long walks. Gradually Heini became "attached" to his "leader" and, in order to please him, tried more and more to pull himself together. They met twice a week; the walks lasted two hours or longer. In bad weather, Heini and his leader visited exhibitions, museums, etc. The "treatment" lasted for a year and a half. Then the close attachment was gradually loosened, by progressively spacing the meetings farther and farther apart in time and shortening them, as well as by guiding Heini's interests towards other goals. During this period, Heini had entered the academic division of the private school, where he developed a strong interest in chemistry. His father supported this interest, furnishing a small laboratory for his son at home and in his spare time helping him with his experiments.

This is how matters stand at present. Everything seems to be well in hand. One is under the impression that actual psychotherapeutic treatment is unnecessary. Heini has not ever stolen again. Today his Zulliger Test appears as follows:

Heini Frick, 16 years old   December 1952
                                   Time: 8 minutes
                                   Number of responses: 20/6

I.

An enlarged insect	FCh → WF + A P
There is a maple leaf in the center	DF + pl
A human head is above it	S → DF + Hd
A girl is sitting there playing with a doll (BC 4/5)	DM + H
And there is somebody seen from above, he looks up and waves with his cane (DEF 3-4)	DM + H O

II.

(laughs at once): There are two young ladies talking eagerly to each other (red area)	DM + H
On the outside there are dwarfs; they carry shields and take long strides	DM + H O
One could also say that these are shrubs	DFC pl perhaps CF
Below there are some animals—as one looks at them, they become foxes tucking their heads under themselves	DFC A
but they are rather moles (orange area)	DFC A
b Inside (within the red area) there is an animal with a bushy tail ...	DF + A

III.

Here are two men—are they chimney sweeps? .... MC →	WM + H P
Children are dancing around them	DM + H P
Butterfly	DF + A P
A small beet ("leg")	DF ± pl
c At the left side there is a human head (red area, c)	DF + Hd
At the right side it is rather an animal head	DF + Ad

O, combinatory

298

And this here looks like a rusty can
opener ("leg") .... FCh ➔ F + obj
b This is a dog with a hump (lower
red area) .... DF + A
d And here is a suckling pig (within
the "leg") .... DdF + A
One could see a great many more
things in the cards, but they
would be just details!

Scoring:

Time: 8 minutes
Number of responses: 20/6

Cd.	W	D	Dd	S	F+	±	M	FC	CF	FCh	P	O
I	1	4		(1)	3		2			(1)	1	1
II		6			1		2	3	(1)			3
III	1	8			6	1	2			1	3	1
Total	2	18		(1)	10	1	6	3	(1)	2	4	5

F+% = 95	H = 6	Experience balance:	6 M : 1–2 C	
A% = 40	Hd = 2	Apperception type:	W — D — (Do/S)	
P% = 20	A = 7	Sequence:	orderly	
O% = 15	Ad = 1	Shocks:	—	
H% = 40	obj = 1	Combination:	+	
anat% = —	pl = 3			

When we compare this test with the preceding one, we see
that affectivity has become more adapted (predominance of FC)
and better controlled (increase of M). Confabulatory elements
have disappeared (there are no DW any more). Inner factors
have become stronger (M). There is considerable progress and
one can not be wrong in believing that the "case of Heini" is
prognostically favorable.

The Zulliger Test performed in 1952 brings out a few facts
quite clearly; we may have known them for a long time, but we
now find them confirmed.

1. After successful treatment, or as the result of development
that could be the consequence of education, unadapted although
adaptable affectivity changes into adapted affectivity. The case of
Heini is a paradigm case: the earlier CF have become FC.

2. Although in evaluating the first test we had to assert that
"M were repressed," the second test shows that this repression

has been resolved. This corresponds with the normal, quite common development of young people. When they enter the period of puberty, they are troubled by sexual fantasies and frequently by corresponding physical drives. These frighten the youngster, and he often reacts by escaping from introversion into extraversion. In all probability, this is a quite natural process. In order not to have to think about himself, and in order to avoid the hated sexual fantasies, he turns to outside activities. He is inclined to discharge his libido in muscle eroticism and sublimated exhibitionism. Thus the youth turns to some sports activity, of which we then say that it serves to "divert" or expend his energy. Frequently we call such energy "expendable"; but this is rather energy that has not yet been adjusted and that cannot as yet be adjusted. At the same time, the young person expresses a desire to exhibit his physical prowess publicly—as, for instance, in some sports event. Or he might want to be photographed by the sports photographer and to appear in sports and daily newspapers as a "star in sports," which is consistent with his sublimated exhibitionism. In order to be "on top of it," however, the youngster must definitely abstain from all such physical satisfactions as smoking and the intake of alcohol. This means that he must also forego all sexual activity, something that every adolescent knows well. To a great extent, sports serve the purpose of gaining self-control and attaining a postponement of the fulfillment of instinctive drives.

Later, when the storms of puberty have subsided a little—and this is frequently achieved with the passing of time—a reverse process takes place, which leads from extraversion to introversion. The young person becomes more thoughtful, more turned toward himself; his imagination becomes more activated, but now it is not fixed mainly upon sexual issues, but rather upon a profession, which too is normally libido motivated.

3. In the course of development, a change of experience balance may take place. This occurs not only in young people. The experience balance of a human being is not constant. On the other hand, it seems that innate intelligence is constant.

Often we may indeed make the observation that the development of potential intelligence is "obstructed," handicapped by such circumstances as, for instance, certain neurotic conditions.

As a result, we are faced with partial or even complete "pseudo retardation" (which is frequently not recognized, yet can, as a rule, be established with absolute certainty by the form-interpretation test). In examining the form-interpretation tests of such people, one is often able to recognize not only the presence of pseudo retardation, but also its origin. For pseudo retardation may be caused, for instance, by a retardation in development, by a fixation to infantile stages (as in the case of Heini), by neurotic anxiety, etc.

4. One may very often observe that, at the onset of puberty, youngsters succumb to a neurosis. Hans Behn-Eschenburg speaks specifically of a "physiological compulsion neurosis" as being typical of this period of development.

Where a neurosis of this kind exists, and we find it in the test, it is usually difficult to decide whether the young person should be referred for psychotherapeutic treatment, or we should put our trust in the natural process of development and the self-healing capacity inherent in every individual and look to them to rectify the situation.

I myself have been very often in a position to observe that "puberty neuroses" disappear by themselves—in other words, without psychotherapeutic interference.

In my opinion, it is very difficult to establish whether or not treatment is indicated. I should like to offer the following suggestion. If the symptoms are not too grave, and do not hinder the subject too greatly from adjusting to the group and to the work process, I would be in favor of patient waiting. On the other hand, if the neurosis causes serious disturbances, then I would recommend treatment—especially if, as an expert, I have gained the discomforting impression that the neurosis has begun to become fixated, and is threatening to develop into a permanent one.

It is impossible to explain how such an impression is formed. From the point of view of the specialist, a judgment of this kind is based on a great deal of experience. It is possible that, after we have gathered much more experience, we will be in a position to establish increasingly accurate indices with which to diagnose the more serious puberty neuroses.

In general, the poet's words are especially appropriate for the adolescent at puberty: while following his unconscious drive, a human being is nevertheless well aware of the correct course that he must take. For the observer, however, it sometimes takes a little too long before the right course has been found; as educators, we are sometimes too impatient, too dubious; we become disappointed too easily.

BLIND DIAGNOSIS OF A 15½-YEAR-OLD BOY

5. A guidance counselor sent me a Zulliger Test record with a short note:

"Dear Mr. Zulliger: Can you do anything with the enclosed test of a 15½-year-old boy? I am deliberately not adding any further explanations.

With best regards, yours, XY."

December 27, 1952
Zulliger Test   Beginning: 3:10 P.M.

I.

	10′ 30″	A head, a dog's head	DF + Ad
		with angry eyes	SF + Ad eyes
	55″	It could really be a human head too, a skull	DF + Hd anat
	11′ 10″	The whole is actually a dog	DWF − A
c	40″	A pansy or a tree leaf (center area)	DF + pl "or"
	12′ 10″	And here is a boy, a handsome one, he	DM + H O aggression
		defends himself with a stick against	DdF + obj
		a large animal	DdF + A

combinatory (bracketing DM + H O aggression, DdF + obj, DdF + A)

b	50″	The Walen Lake	SF ± geog

II.

	13′ 50″	"This is harder!" (turns the card around)	shock
	14′ 10″	Something like a potted plant	SF + pl
		A white butterfly hovers above it	SF ± A
		Or a hawk-moth	combination; white as C "or"
	15′ 20″	Perhaps a white handkerchief with grass, dirt,	

302

and blood stains ...... SWCF obj O—
combination-confabulation
white as color

III.

16'   A head—one does not
know whether the face
is in front or in the back DoF + Hd (P) O!
16' 50" A mouse .... DF + A ⎱
devouring a snail ...... DdF + A ⎰ combinatory
(small dark blot on the
right side, the dark
portions within it)
c 17' 10" A weather-vane (red
center area) .... DF − obj
c 17' 50" Most likely a butterfly
(red center area) ...... DF + A P
a 18' 40" I don't know—perhaps
a wall-paper pattern
in two colors .... DWCF ornament O—

End: 3:19 P.M.

Scoring
Zulliger Individual Test   Time: **9 minutes**
Name: a 15½-year-old boy   Number of responses: 18/3

DW	≐	2	F+	= 7	P	= 2	O = 2
SW	=	1	—	= 2	H	= 1	
WS	=		M	= 1	Hd	= 2	
W	=		MCh	=	anat	=	
D	=	7	Ms	=	sex	=	
Dd	=	3	FC	=	blood	=	
Do	=	1	CF	= 2	A	= 6	
S	=	4	C	=	Ad	= 2	
F+%	= 80		FCh	=	obj	= 3	
A%	= 44		ChF	=	pl	= 2	
P%	= 11		Ch	=	nat	=	
O%	= 22±		F(C)	=	geog	= 1	
H%	= 17		CCh	=	cloud	=	
anat%	=				ornament	= 1	

Sequence: orderly-loose, tendency towards inversion   shocks = +
Experience balance: 1 M : 2 C
Apperceptive type: DW — D̲ — Do/Do — S

Remarks: "eyes," "or," combination, confabulation, white as color.
M are absent in Card III

SHORT DIAGNOSIS:

The subject is a strange mixture of a keen observer and a confabulator. His innate intelligence is good, but it is impaired by confabulation whenever he tries to combine details into a whole response; he is unable to grasp large concepts accurately. On the other hand, his "practical thinking" is well developed: he possesses a "sense for the practical"; he could well be a builder of models. He is not lacking in diligence and school ambition. He is cautious, anxious, distrustful—even against himself. He has an attitude of defense (I/5), mistrusts his own instinctual drives, escapes from introversion into extraversion. He makes plans that are built upon fantasy and that can not be realized practically. Yet he is quite capable of handling practical situations.

He is rigidly balanced (in evaluating, it must be especially kept in mind that M is an MO and an extensor kinesthesia at the same time); his adjustment is forced and poor. Probably violent affect manifestations break through (perhaps we should note and score the "grass, dirt, and blood stains" in Card II/3 separately). In all probability, abrupt acts occur, which are aggressive defense acts. The subject has an attitude of strong defiance, with which he disguises his hypersensitivity. He may be a rowdy and a fighter, although these tendencies are partly controlled by his good intelligence; he is probably a thief. His thieving impulses are the result of an "obstinacy neurosis," which manifests itself in compulsive kleptomania. In addition, the subject probably suffers considerably from guilt feelings ("angry eyes").

Telephone report given to me by the test examiner: the boy, a student in a secondary school, has stolen money during the swimming period in school. According to his own statement, he does not know why he did it. He bought cigarettes and candies with the stolen money, and distributed them among his companions in such quantities as to arouse suspicion. He confessed right away. Since he has always been a good student, and until now has hardly given any reason for complaint—except once when, before the end of the term, he beat up a fellow student and made him bleed, because the latter had teased him about a poor showing in mathematics—the boy was not immediately thrown out of school. It was decided to obtain advice by arranging for a psychological evaluation of the boy.

He is a skillful model builder with original ideas. He is a discoverer, although sometimes his ideas and plans are somewhat fantastic. The subject is the only child in a family of craftsmen, who are respected people. He suffers from strong feelings of guilt because of masturbation, which he is unable to suppress without a great deal of effort. He believes that one can recognize his "dirty thoughts" from his appearance.

The consultant recommended treatment and advised that the boy be kept in school, with the proviso that the treatment will be carried out.

6. *Bertha M.,* 17 years old, traumatic mental retardation (see Table 4).

Bertha M. attends a trade school, in which she is in a class for the mentally retarded. The girl's passivity is striking. She does not have any confidence in herself; she is lonely and fearful. Bertha's achievements in practical work are considerable, and her memory is quite good. However, she generally fails in all her academic classes. She is physically awkward, and constantly afraid of being laughed at.

She has a brother, who is six years her junior. Her father is a peddler; her mother, a housewife. The family runs a small farm.

When Bertha was three years old, she fell on her head. Perhaps she suffered a brain concussion that went unnoticed, and has since become feebleminded because of it.

The doctor's report: Bertha developed late, physically; she is healthy but retarded. Bertha M. is small and stockily built; she is still underdeveloped. She gives the impression of being confidently obliging and shyly cautious at the same time.

Bertha's teachers differ in their opinion as to whether Bertha should or should not be kept in school.

Questions: 1. What is the extent of the retardation? What is its level?

2. Is there a possibility that the girl may still develop?

3. Ought she to be kept in school, or should she learn some trade?

4. What educational measures should be taken?

First the Zulliger Test, then (since Bertha is retarded and the Bero is better suited for children than the Ro) the Bero, and finally the Ro were administered to Bertha. In order to give Bertha the opportunity to rest a little, the examiner chatted with her after each test. As a control test, the tree test (Koch) was performed with her between the Bero and Ro tests.

THE TESTS

1. *Zulliger Test.* (6 minutes). The subject smiles continuously in an embarrassed, plaintive, and forced manner. She is amiable.

I.

A beetle	WF + A P
A dog's head (upper center area) ..	DF + Ad
with round eyes and a mouth ..	SF + Ad
A rag that has faded and is torn ...	
it has holes here (center S) like a	
wound (she pets her lap unin-	
tentionally with her right hand	
while holding the card with her	
left hand)	Ch → WSF— obj O—
	probably sex

II.

Two brown caterpillars	DFC A
Two eyes with white stars in them	
(green area and S within it)	DF — Hd O—/Ad
Blind people sometimes have such	
white stars in their eyes—also	
crows	SCF Hd /Ad
"I do not know what this is!" (red	
area)	color shock
Perhaps—a wound	SDCF sex O—
Or smeared blood, the red only ...	DCF blood, "or"

III.

Two men without legs point at	
each other	Do → DM + Hd (P)
Or two women bending down	WM + H P O "or"
and carrying a bloody paper bag or	
a piece of clothing	DCF blood

Here, little men or girls are run-
ning away (outer red area) .... DM + H P (O) "or"
c Hands and arms (the legs of the
W) .... Dd → DF + Hd

2. *Bero* (24 minutes)

I.
Skull .... WSF — anat
Butterfly (center portion) .... DF + A

II. Prolonged reaction time
Blood spots (upper red area) ..... DCF blood
"I don't find anything further!"
   ("Try just once more!")
Dogs .... DF + A P

III.
Again some rags torn to shreds, by
   animals, perhaps .... WChF Ad O—
(Turns the card back and forth for
   a long time)
Women bending down (upper dark
   portion) .... (Do) DM + H (P)
b A little bird (outer red area) ..... DF + A

IV.
A dog's coat .... FCh → WF + A P
c Almost a butterfly .... WF + A P

V.
Fish (center portion) .... DF + A
A little swallow (W) .... WF + A P

VI.
Shadow .... WCh shadow O
Faces looking at a foaming water-
   fall .... combinatory { DdF + Hd / SCF nat
("faces"=grey area next to the dark
   inner area; waterfall=S) .... white as color

VII.
Gorge and a bridge .... WSF + nat
Two people bending towards each
   other (larger dark blots) ...... DM + H

307

VIII.

c Two horses (orange area, not be-
    cause of C) .... DF ± A
  Small water animals (blue area) .. DF + A
  Again a wound (grey area) .... DF — sex O—
  Once more two small water animals
    (yellow area) .... DF + A
  Perhaps mice (red area) .... DF + A P
                                    shock

IX.

  A strange butterfly . . . from foreign
    lands (blue, purple, and brown
    areas; yet not because of the
    colors!) .... DF ± A O—
  A bird (blue area) .... DF + A P
  A spear (center line) .... DF + obj

X.

  Chickens (orange area, center por-
    tion of the picture, not because
    of C) .... DF — A
  Greenish shells; "once my brother
    brought such shells home" ..... DFC obj
  Two young ladies bending down
    (pink area) .... DM + H O
  Butterfly (green inner area) ..... DF — A infantile
  Cut-off hands (orange area, center
    portion of the picture) .... DF + Hd
  A "birdie" (upper orange area) ... DF + A P

3. *Ro* (21 minutes)

  I.

  A bat with wings full of holes .... WSF + A P
  A girl raising her hands, her head
    has been cut off .... DM + H P (O)
  b The head of a bear (right bottom
    outer area) .... (Do) DF + Ad

  II.

  A hole (S) .... SF + hole   infantile
  Blood spots (upper red area) ..... DCF blood
  Wound (red bottom area and S) .. S → DdCF sex O—

III.

Two men bending down .... WM + H P
c Cut-off arms (the "legs") .... (Do) DF + Hd
Blood stains from them (red outer
    area) .... DCF blood combinatory

IV.

Monster, an evil, bent man ...... WM + H O
Snakes (outer area) .... DF + A

V.

Butterfly .... WF + A P

VI.

Bat (small figure) .... DF − A
c Shingles (upper large portion) ... DF − obj O−
"This is hard!" .... shock!

VII.

Shreds of fog .... WChF fog
A swan (upper third portion) .... DF − A
c Butterfly (confluent third portion) DF + A
Faces (center third portion) ..... DF + Hd P

VIII.

(Prolonged reaction time)   shock
Chest and ribs .... SF + anat
Fir tree (grey area) .... DF + pl
Mouse (red area) .... DF + A P

IX.

Blood stains, fresh and old ones
    (orange and red areas) .... DCF blood perseveration
(Turns the card back and forth for
    a long time)
Mouse (orange area) .... DF + A perseveration

X.

Spiders (outer blue area) .... DF + A
Weasel (green center area) .... DF − A
Or rather earth worms .... DFC A P "or"
Crabs (outer grey area) .... DF − A

TABLE 4

Scoring
Subject: *Bertha M.*

Z - Test → Bero → Ro

	6 minutes	24 minutes	21 minutes
Time:			
Number of responses:	14/5	30/14	27/9

Location scores

DW =	1		
SW =			
WS =	1	2	
W =	2	5	
D =	9	21	
Dd =	(1)	1	
Do =	(1)	(1)	(2)
S =	2(3)	1	2(3)
	14	30	27

F+% =	66	75	70
A% =	42	56	48
P% =	28	23	26
O% =	28±	16±	15±
obj% =			
H% =	71	26	37

Sequence: geo, tend. to inv.
Experience balance: 3 M : 4½ C

Apperceptive type: W — D — S / +/—

Red shock: +
Color shock: +
Chiaroscuro shock: +

Determinants

	6 minutes	24 minutes	21 minutes
F+ =	6(—2)		
F— =			
F± =		22(—5.5)	18(—5)
M =	3	3	3
Ms =			
FC =	1	1	1
CF =	2	4	2
C =		4	
FCh =	(1)		
ChF =	1	1	1
Ch =	1	1	
F(C) =			

Sequence: geo, tend. to inv.
Experience balance: 3 : 2½

Apperceptive type: W — D — S / +/—

Red shock +
Color shock +
Chiaroscuro shock +

Contents

	6 minutes	24 minutes	21 minutes
P =	4	7	7
O =	3±	5	4
H =	2	3	3
Hd =	2(4)	2	2
anat =	1	1	1
sex =	1	1	1
scene =			
blood =	2	1	3
A =	3	16	12
Ad =	3(1)	1	1
obj =	1	2	1
pl =			
nat =			2
arch =			
others =		1	2

Sequence: geo, tend. to inv.
Experience balance: 3 : 4½

Apperceptive type: W — D — S / +/—

Red shock +
Color shock +
Chiaroscuro shock +

Remarks: Plaintive smile; infantilism; perseveration; O—; combines well, need for combination; flexor kinesthesias; "cut off"; "or"; white as color.

310

EVALUATION OF THE TESTS:

Since F+% amounts to about 70, A% as well as P% approximate an average rate, and sequence remains orderly, retardation cannot actually be present. On the other hand, Bertha M. is not especially gifted, either. However, according to her intellectual potential she should range within the lowest third of the student body, or perhaps at the bottom of the second third.

Yet, as measured by her performance, she cannot even follow the lessons in a class for the mentally retarded.

Therefore some forces exist in Bertha M. that prevent the girl from achieving intellectually whatever she ought to be capable of achieving.

Certain differences among the results on the form-interpretation tests attract our attention. We shall consider them first.

Experience balance is rather extratensive in the Zulliger Test and in the Ro; in the Bero it is rather introversive (experience balance is fairly ambiequal in all three tests). The majority of the color responses are CF. Bertha produces responses of "blood spots"; she perseveres with "blood spots." Therefore, we must not overestimate CF in relationship to M within the experience balance. When we evaluate, we should avoid considering the bare figures alone. It would be better to keep in mind that Bertha is most probably introverted; this is borne out by the fact that almost all M are flexor kinesthesias.

It is characteristic of people with flexor kinesthesias that they "roll themselves inside themselves" for their own protection, as do some animals when they feel themselves threatened by danger (a porcupine, for instance).

In the light of the CF connected with blood interpretations, it becomes unimportant whether there are one or two more of them in the different tests; the change of experience balance (from the numerical point of view) does not have any special meaning. Once more it becomes clear to us, as interpreters of the form-interpretation test, that we must beware of paying attention to scoring, to the exclusion of everything else. Such a procedure would not be satisfactory; it would not permit us to gain insight into the subject. We must weigh each single factor in its relationship to all our findings.

When we consider the numerous (persevering) blood responses, and see that Bertha has produced many shocks, we feel justified in assuming that the girl is neurotic, and that anxiety must play a substantial role in her case. As a rule, this set of circumstances prevails when a CF interpretation follows a shock, especially a red shock. After a very pronounced red shock, Bertha produces a disguised sexual interpretation (wound=S ➔DCF sex O—) in Card II of the Zulliger Test. The "wound" reappears in the two other tests.

Are we deceiving ourselves in assuming that Bertha's fears are mainly sexual fears?

May it not be that the girl is frightened by her own instincts, which endanger her? And that she is repressing some or all of her "sexuality"?

We do not know; at least, not yet.

However, we have been able to observe clearly in the tests that Bertha is also avoiding an escape into her inner self—which is extremely strange. For she tends strongly towards introversion, as indicated by the M. Her introversive tendencies are autistic rather than creative and externally formative. This is evidenced by her producing many flexor kinesthesias. At the same time, the girl "represses" her kinesthesias, as may be seen from the fact that, more than once, she initially produces an M that corresponds to a Do. She also produces it as soon as Card III of the Zulliger Test is presented to her. The girl does not perceive the whole configuration that is usually interpreted as an M. She first perceives only a portion of it and arrives only later at the usual M interpretation.

Let us consider the confusion that must prevail in Bertha, when the girl escapes from the outer world into her inner self, only to shy away from her "inwardness" at the same time and thus evade it as well. Her "disorientation" must be considerable. When the first card of the Ro is presented to her, Bertha sees a girl whose head has been cut off, raising her hands. This picture interpretation could well describe her own condition: a panic-like, "headless" state; an extreme uncertainty; a "fear of life," of an intensity that one does not often observe.

Thus we have indeed got to the root of Bertha's basic frame of mind. She tries to dissimulate it by a smile; but it is a smile that is forced, embarrassed, plaintive, helpless. She also makes an attempt to disguise her hypersensitivity and vulnerability (as indicated by her interpreting white as a color in Card VI of the Bero).

We can now make the following statement: the girl is hypersensitive and easily hurt; she therefore escapes from the external world into her own inner self, into the world of autistic "dreams." At the same time, she is frightened by this internal world.

How can she free herself from such a conflict? She can best do it by way of a "deadlock reaction": "I do not know anything!" —words that give expression to her emotional condition. Thus we have found an explanation for Bertha's "mental retardation."

Bertha's conflict leaves no other door open for her but to pretend that she "does not know anything"—in other words, that she is stupid. This is not a consciously deliberate function, but a neurotic repression mechanism. People who are really retarded are not neurotic, and do not produce shocks in the form-interpretation tests.

Bertha's retardation must therefore be evaluated as a neurotic symptom. It is the result of a maladaptive elaboration of anxiety. As we have seen, or have been able to surmise, her anxiety is related to sex.

Proceeding from the symbolism of the unconscious mind, and taking into account such interpretations as "cut-off hands" (Bero X/5), "rags torn to shreds" (Bero III/1, Zulliger Test I/4), "a cut-off head" (Ro I/2), "cut-off arms" (Ro III/2), as well as numerous blood responses, we may assume that a strong castration complex exists in Bertha. Also, the nightmarish figure that Bertha sees when Card IV of the Ro is presented to her indicates anxiety. This figure could have been taken from a dream indicating phobic anxiety.

It is hardly surprising, indeed, that a human being who is so greatly tormented by anxiety should be not only "stupid" but depressed as well. Therefore, it was to be expected that we would

313

find ChF and pure Ch in Bertha's record, indicating depressive moods that she is incapable of controlling any longer. It is possible that these betray Bertha's "inner danger"—namely, that the girl is afraid of depression if ever she surrenders to her inner self, to her introversive drives.

Now, then, we must ask ourselves: how could it have happened that such vast anxiety has taken hold of the girl? For anxiety to such a degree is unusual. By analogy we may assume that a trauma occurred in Bertha's early childhood. She must have had a terrible experience during her early life, which she could not mentally absorb; perhaps she experienced a direct sexual assault. We have no immediate clue for such a conjecture; yet the over-all record is of such a nature as to force it upon us.

THE TREE TEST:

Could the girl's "headless" state be expressed more clearly than by this tree?

Its thickened trunk and its dense branches (see right side of the picture) suggest the utmost *rigidity* and neurotic traits.

The branches, with their falling—or, as one might say, "dropping"—fruit (see upper right side), have been drawn in the shape of penises, revealing the trauma that the girl who drew them must have experienced.

Still other facts may be diagnosed on the basis of the tree test. The expert will be able to do so without difficulty. But the statements made about Bertha's tree will indeed be understood, even by somebody who is not familiar with the tree test.

This example proves how well the tree test often amplifies, confirms or verifies the results of form-interpretation tests.

COUNSELING:

The teachers should be advised to have patience with Bertha and to keep her in school, for the girl certainly has potentialities for developing. Encouragement, appreciation, and kindness would help Bertha. Reprimands and criticism should be avoided as much as possible, because they would reduce the girl's self-respect to an even greater extent.

Therapeutic treatment should be made available to her.

Bertha's teachers should be informed about the fact that Bertha's retardation is a pseudo retardation rather than a real retardation, even though the girl's actual capabilities are no greater than those of an elementary-school student.

I received the following information about Bertha's case history:

Bertha's mother reported that, when Bertha was 4 years old, she had been assaulted and raped by a feeble-minded farm worker. To the mother's surprise, the child was able to "forget" this incident completely—"as one forgets a bad dream!", said Mrs. M with a sigh.

Thus, our assumption that Bertha had suffered a sexual trauma was confirmed, and in this girl's case we can speak of a *"traumatic pseudo retardation."*

FOLLOW-UP REPORT:

It was possible to begin treatment, which turned out to be successful. Bertha has become a seamstress and is able to make her own living. She owns a workshop in the village where she lives, and is capable of doing all the necessary bookkeeping herself. Her timidity toward other people has disappeared, and her intellectual ability is quite sufficient to permit her to practice her trade.

7. *Madelon M.,* 13 years old; a "problem child" (see Table 5).

The Court of Guardians of a large village in Bern Canton refers a 13-year-old girl for educational counseling. The girl comes from a poor background. Father M. is a skilled worker, but a periodic drunkard; the mother is a "woman of easy morals." She is not a proper housekeeper and spends her money mainly on candies. The M. family is on relief. There are 8 children, of whom Madelon is the fourth. It was decided to take Madelon away from home because she:

1. does not do any work in school; all her report cards state that "her performance could be better if she would apply herself!"

2. spends all the money that she can get hold of for sweets, sharing them with her mother. Although Madelon has never stolen money outright, she finds ways and means of acquiring money by cheating or begging. The immediate cause for Madelon's transfer from home was based on the following incident: supplied with a folio sheet, Madelon went to a suburb of the city and collected money "for the Red Cross"; after obtaining a sum of about 20 francs, she bought chocolates, candies, and cake and brought them home. The story got out because one of the contributors became suspicious and, after having secured the collector's name, went to the authorities to inquire whether Madelon had been entrusted with the collection. The father made up the money that had been spent on sweets and it was given back to the Red Cross.

The father gave his consent to a change of environment, stating that he has lost all authority over the child, who had been utterly spoiled by his wife.

The court asks the following questions:

a. Should Madelon live in a private household? If the answer is yes, what kind of environment would be most beneficial for the girl's further education?

b. On the basis of the results of the examination, might it perhaps be better to put Madelon into a girls' home? In case this is desirable, what kind of home should it be? a detention home, or some other institution that permits more freedom to its inmates? Should preference be given to a larger institution, or to one that is run like a big family and has fewer children?

Madelon is introduced to the counselor. She is a child of medium height, relatively underdeveloped (as compared with other children of her age). Although she wears clean clothes, she is nevertheless sloppily dressed. A few buttons are unbuttoned in the back of her blouse, and her shoes look as if they had not been polished for the longest time. She has a healthy appearance. She is blonde and has pale blue eyes, with which she looks around the room in a slightly shrewd and cautiously inspecting manner.

Experience has shown that, when one sets out to perform form-interpretation tests with children, one should avoid overwhelming them at the start. Children feel more or less strange in an alien environment, and therefore cannot conduct themselves freely and uninhibitedly in such a situation, even though they may pretend to be unperturbed. Frequently, their pretense of being unperturbed is nothing but a defensive measure, like that of a soldier at war who becomes courageous and aggressive simply because he is incapable of enduring the tension any longer.

When a conversation is begun with her, Madelon, too, behaves at first somewhat rigidly. She dissimulates her discomfort by replying with a great flow of words. When she arrived to see the counselor, the latter noticed the girl's interest in watching his wife, who was in the garden planting peas.

This supplies a topic for conversation. "Have you already planted peas at home, too?" asks the counselor. The girl replies that they have not yet done so, for the peas would freeze, her mother had said. Then Madelon proceeds to explain why it is better not to plant peas until the end of April, and tells of experiences that neighbors had had. Gradually, her talking becomes more relaxed, and within 15 minutes the girl has calmed down. She has become somewhat better accustomed to the new environment, as well as to the counselor; presently, the latter can begin testing.

A small test battery was carried out with Madelon. From among all the other tests, the Zulliger test was chosen to be presented here, because it offers ample data for answering all the questions asked by the authorities. All other test results confirm the results obtained with the Zulliger Test.

The record and the scores follow.

Card I

This is the picture of a human being with an evil heart	WF + H
(Subject points to the whole blot, then to the dark center blot) ...	DF — Hd/position O— symbolism
He wears dirty clothes	ChF → WF± clothing
And he has round eyes and a tufted mouth (indicates the S)	SF + Hd
He is beautiful outwardly and ugly inwardly	symbolism

317

Well, perhaps it is a girl
(Examiner: "Why a girl, why do
you think so?")—One can not
mention it! (subject indicates
the S underneath the dark center
blot) .... SF — sex

Card II

(Immediately): He has black spots
in his heart .... DCF Hd
(On inquiry, after completion of   DdCF spots
the test: the "heart" is the whole
red blot, the "black spots" are
the bluish color tonality underneath the uppermost S within
the red area) .... symbolism, perseveration
The whole is again the interior of
a human being .... WCF anat/symbolism
Here one can see the spine ...... SF ± anat
And all around—and on the out-
side, he looks pretty, and on the
inside, he is so—(searches for
words) .... confabulation
This here (orange area) is the color
of truth.
But it is at the very bottom and
above it are the sins as red as   DC symbolism O—
blood .... DC blood
The green is honesty, there isn't
much of it .... DC and symbolism O—
A person can be clean, even if he is
not pretty on the outside; he
can be pretty on the outside,
and still have an evil heart .... idle talk, disguised shock

Card III

Here are two people quarreling
with each other .... WM + H P (O)
They draw their hands back in
order to hit each other .... DF + Hd
In the center a fire is burning .... DCF fire
Here are pictures of two dwarfs
laughing and dancing with joy
because the big people are
fighting (outer red area) .. M ➔ DMs H P (O)

318

b Small animals, moles, because of
     their pincers (smaller dark blot) . DdDF ± A
c Deformed red beets (carrots)
     (outer red areas) .... DFC pl
c A road sign (red inner area) ..... DF ± obj O
c A tree with roots (dark D, larger
     dark blot) .... DdDF − pl

Duration: 20 minutes

Taking the test into account, we shall first re-examine the two reasons for the court's decision to take Madelon away from her family.

The first is that Madelon does not perform well enough in school. According to the statements made by her teachers in all her school reports, she should do much better work.

What is the extent of Madelon's intelligence?

F+% indicates a basic intelligence potential that places Madelon at the low average borderline of an elementary school student. The number of W is relatively high, yet one half of the W is inaccurately perceived and, in part, these W have a confabulatory flavor. Incidentally, this is also the case with some of the D, especially with the DdD in Card III ("moles, because of the pincers"), which has been produced in exactly the same manner as a DW. The subject has perceived a Dd sharply and then, on the basis of this Dd, has arrived by confabulation at the interpretation of the smaller dark blot, unconcerned with its form. Thus, we may assume that Madelon's thinking is inaccurate. The girl does not differentiate between the things that she observes and fantasy-falsifying reality, according to her desires. Her thinking is infantile; the too numerous C and CF indicate that she is guided primarily by her emotions, and not by logic and objectivity. The loose sequence also points in the same direction. The extremely low P%, the even lower A%, and the high but devious O% (half of the O are O−) suggest a range of ideas alien to the customary thinking of 13-year-old girls. Madelon's world of ideas is a strange one; she lacks empathic understanding of the thinking of others. Her intellectual grasp is defective. Once she has started a thought process, Madelon is unable to detach herself from it. On the presentation of Card I, she

319

TABLE 5

Scoring:
Subject: *Madelon M.*

Time: 20 minutes
Number of responses: 20, of which 7 were given to the colored Card II

Cd.	W	D	Dd	S	F+	±	—	M	Ms	FC	CF	C	ChF	P	O
I	2	1		2	2	1	2						1		1—
II	1	4	1	1		1					3	3			2—
III	1	6	1		1	2	1	1	1	1	1			2	3+
Total	4	11	2	3	3	4	3	1	1	1	4	3	1	2	6(—3)

H = 3	F+% = 50	Sequence: loose
Hd = 8	A% = 5	Experience balance: 1 M : 9 C
anat = 1	P% = 10	Apperceptive type: W — D — Dd — S
blood = 1	O% = 30∓	Shock = in Card II, probably already in Card I.
sex = 1	H% = 65	Colors perceived as human traits.
clothing = 1	anat/sex = 10	
A = 1	position responses	
obj = 1	symbolism	
pl = 2	perseveration	
fire = 1	confabulation	

320

initially saw a "human being" (yet not so much the image of a human being in his outer appearance, as the representation of his qualities—such as, "ugly inwardly and beautiful outwardly," etc.). She believes that Card II also represents human qualities of truthfulness, wickedness, etc. As one often observes in epileptics, Madelon clings with perseveration to a train of thought, once she has embarked upon it. Heedless of reality, she works out a scheme and, by falsification, forces everything that she observes or experiences into this scheme. Nevertheless, Madelon does not lack certain practical skills, as she indicated in the test by her numerous D, and primarily by her first few interpretations to Card III, where both of her P appear.

In the name of justice it should be added that her school reports read: "She has a better aptitude for practical work than for theoretical thinking."

The scores of the content series, the lack of A and Ad, and the loose sequence suggest insufficient ability for concentration. However, this seems to be contradicted by her "clinging" to certain thought processes. The reason why Madelon is unable to concentrate objectively on anything is to be found in the fact that her range of ideas is bounded by very definite contexts. As indicated by the very high M%, these contexts refer to people. Three-quarters of the total response number are responses concerned with human affairs, with matters related to morals and sex.

The morals that have taken hold of Madelon seem like a foreign body; somehow one gains the impression that they have been drilled into her by training. A child of 13 does not normally think about the outer appearance of people and their inner morality, about "black spots in the heart," etc. And when we consider that the appearance of even a single FCh or ChF in the form-interpretation test often suggests pseudo adaptation affected by education, we may surmise that Madelon's moralistic thinking may, perhaps, correspond to an active wish-fantasy. In accordance with it, the girl would like to be, or to appear to be, more virtuous than her strong instinctual drives (C and CF) permit her to. Outwardly, this trait should take the form of hypocrisy. It would then correspond with a strong inner distress, and we have to be careful not to look upon Madelon's "deceit" from a moralistic point of view. As psychologists, our task does not consist of judging a human being morally, but of understanding him, and possibly of helping him if he is in distress. Since Madelon produced a sexual interpretation in the test, I believe it possible that, being on the verge of pre-puberty, she is tormented by sexual thoughts. This is usually the case with 13-year-old girls. Children who produce sexual responses in form-interpretation tests are usually more troubled by sexual thoughts than one finds to be true in average cases. The corresponding part of Madelon's test record shows that the girl consciously repulses her sexual thoughts and fantasies. This does not prevent such thoughts from besetting Madelon, however, and creating a problem and an inner conflict for her.

The fact that inner conflicts exist is proven, indeed, by the shocks. Individuals who experience a color shock upon the presentation of Card II, and immediately produce a CF response to the red color, are usually affected by direct (now converted) anxiety. And "Anxiety makes one stupid!" (Meng). We may assume that Madelon's stupidity is partially the result of emotional disturbances, which produce an intellectual inhibition in the form of a pseudo retardation (this is in addition to an inadequate innate intelligence, as we have already mentioned).

If Madelon's teachers maintain that "she could do better work if she only wanted to!", they are right insofar as the girl's mental capacity is not fully developed and therefore cannot manifest itself. But they are wrong in believing that the realization of the girl's intellectual capacities could be improved merely by the exercise of her own free will. Madelon is not capable of better achievement, because she is incapable of making the mental effort. In order for her to become capable of wanting better achievement, she must be liberated from her anxieties; she must be inwardly at peace. In the test the girl expresses her inner restlessness, partly by producing CF and C (which indicates an affectivity that is pressing toward an explosive drive discharge), and partly by the presence of shocks, which suggest mechanisms of repression. Thus, on the basis of the test, it becomes easy to understand the girl's intensive inner tensions and conflicts.

As is often the case, we see that in Madelon, too, intelligence factors are greatly influenced by emotional ones, and that we cannot make a conclusive statement about intellectual functioning unless we include this relationship in our evaluation and give it our consideration.

If we succeed in calming Madelon and, above all, in liberating her from her anxieties, the road to better intellectual development will be paved for her. Of course, even at that, the girl will never be very bright; she will not even become a "good" elementary school student for, as we have seen, she lacks intellectual substance.

Her fraud was the second reason for wishing to put Madelon into a home for re-education: she collected money under false pretenses, and spent it on herself. Being 13, she should have had the good sense to realize that such conduct is not permitted. On the other hand, the schoolchildren in our country are so frequently used for collecting money (sometimes as often as almost once a week), that one may easily understand a child choosing such a method—which can be carried out with so little effort—of securing money for himself. It is not our intention to excuse or belittle Madelon's misdeed, but the means that Madelon employed in order to obtain money must not be regarded as particularly cunning; it was a rather clumsy and stupid act of apery.

The authorities are mainly troubled by Madelon's undesirable traits, which led her to such an apish action. They consider the girl "endangered," and they are definitely justified in making such an assumption.

In terms of her character structure, Madelon *is* endangered. Yet the poor environment of her parents' home cannot be made solely responsible. It is merely that the activation of certain innate traits has not been controlled or prevented, as might have taken place under different environmental and educational influences.

The test offers indubitable evidence that Madelon is inwardly threatened with becoming delinquent. We encounter three pure C, which suggest a strongly egocentric, impulsive, and drive-oriented personality structure, such as cannot be kept in check either by introversive factors (only one single M) or by intelligence.

Madelon is incapable of resisting her instinctual desires; she surrenders to them. Moreover, she is not able to empathize with other people, and therefore cannot act according to the maxim: "Whatever you do not want others to do unto you, do not do unto others!" She does not have a sufficient degree of adaptable affectivity (only one single FC) at her disposal. At the intellectual level, this becomes apparent in a certain chattiness which the girl uses to make herself important, and to pretend that she is intelligent, although actually such intelligence is absent here. Undoubtedly, this trait is correlated not only to a need for recognition, but to anxiety as well. Talking for the sake of talking— as we observed in Madelon, during the test, at the end of her responses to Card III—serves to ward off anxiety. As one can also see in other people, Madelon attempts to deceive herself about her own terrifying emptiness by means of "clever talk." By "talking her head off," Madelon also tries to deceive her environment. Once again, her trait of hypocrisy—which we observed previously—becomes confirmed.

In this connection, we shall examine in greater detail her response to Card II. It is as follows: "The whole is again the interior of a human being, here one can see the spine, and all around —and on the outside he looks pretty and on the inside he is so—. This here is the color of truth. But it is at the very bottom and, above it, are the sins as red as blood. The green is honesty, there isn't much of it. A person can be clean even if he is not pretty on the outside; he can be pretty on the outside and still have an evil heart." Actually Madelon proceeds in this interpretation by starting from the intermediate form. We have scored the individual parts of the long interpretation separately, in order to understand its complexity in all its implications; however, we might have scored: SWCF H O—. The SW corresponds with a confabulated whole interpretation. In its structure, it suggests another of Madelon's character traits. If something irritates her into opposition, she projects her emotions onto the whole situation. She confabulates that the entire situation is hostile to her, and she opposes it. Considering her chattiness, one may assume

324

that this opposition, observed above, is swelled by confabulatory tendencies and then expressed in slander. The environment is regarded with mistrust and interpreted accordingly; since the girl likes to talk and does not hide her opinions, she gives voice to suspicions and slander. "There is not much honesty—a person may be pretty on the outside and yet have an evil heart." This statement gives away Madelon's entire mental state, as well as her way of behaving and reacting to her environment. Essentially, the girl has a hostile, aggressive attitude toward her environment; she therefore confabulates projectively that the world is hostile toward her. Since she is a talkative girl, she speaks about it. The *contents* of her conversation express suspicion; observed outwardly, this suspicion creates the impression of slander.

In any event, Madelon's attitude toward other people is greatly disturbed and falsified.

One might expect that a subject who produced an H% of 65 in the form-interpretation test would produce mostly FC, thereby indicating a considerable degree of adapted and adaptable affectivity. This would imply a great and well-developed capacity for empathy, and a well-formed sense for everything "human": compassion, pity, sharing in the pleasures of others, lovingly agreeing with others, etc. But Madelon's test record shows a predominance of CF and C. In addition to three CF and three pure C, she produces only one FC. Thus, her high H% does not indicate an interest in concrete, real people. It is more an interest in theoretical and abstract questions involving people. The underlying basis for her high H% is not a capacity for devotion, a need for empathy, a sense for everything that is human, but confabulatory fantasies that the girl creates about her fellow human beings—for instance, about their morality.

Since Madelon produces such an overly high H%, she certainly needs other people. But Madelon's preoccupation with others is determined less by her need for giving love to them than by her inclination to criticize them, and to use them for the verification of all the theories that she has formed about the human environment. Madelon needs her fellow human beings for her own confirmation. This corresponds with the girl's intense egocentricity, which the test's pure C reveal.

Madelon longs for love, for being loved. But she does not strive for the manifold interplay of loving and being loved. She wants to be loved only for the sake of her own confirmation. If this were not the case, FC would predominate within the color series, and there would be many more M, indicating a wealth of inner life; instead, Madelon produces one single M. It is the usual M in Card III: its content is a scene describing a fight, and it could have its origin in an engram that the girl has experienced in her own family, in which the parents do not get along with each other. "Here are pictures of two dwarfs laughing and dancing with joy because the big people are fighting." Since this is an individual interpretation, it may indicate one of Madelon's own characteristic personality traits: the delight of a bystander when two people fight with each other. Who are these two? They are the "big people." The "dwarfs," on the other hand, are laughing and dancing for joy. When children talk about "big people," they usually mean their parents, while "dwarfs" are children to them, as has been proven by dream symbolism. It is possible that in Madelon's family all the children are happy to see their parents fighting. Frequently children make use of their parents' disunity, taking the side of the one of them and thus securing some special declaration of love from that one. In Madelon's case, we have heard that her mother gives her sweets and that the girl, too, shares her own sweets with the mother. In all probability, the girl identifies herself with her immoral mother and accepts sweets as a proof and declaration of her mother's love.

Inasmuch as Madelon identifies herself with her mother, whose moral sense is wanting, she is endangered to an even greater extent. There is a chance that, in time, the child too will become a "woman of easy morals."

Subjects who do not produce any M or only one single M in the form-interpretation test, but who do produce colors (mainly CF and C) are usually unstable; they are in need of a strong leading hand. This does not mean merely that strict rules should be applied. On the contrary, these people must be treated with loving consideration, for otherwise they wrap themselves in defiance. The three S in Madelon's test indicate that the girl could become hardened by stubbornness. By correlating C with them, we see that her stubbornness could turn into willfulness. Madelon should be surrounded by adults who would treat her with love, patience, understanding and gentleness. But they should also be able to stimulate Madelon's conscience by setting her a good example. For a child not only loves and respects the person who serves him as a model; he also embodies in his inner self the moral qualities, ideals, and requirements of a loved and respected human being.

In changing Madelon's environment, such a process should be initiated. It is high time that this were done, for Madelon is on the verge of maturity, a period during which everything that has been changeable and adaptable becomes stabilized.

We shall consider our answers carefully, before giving them to the court in reply to its questions.

With regard to the first question, we shall supply a personality diagnosis based upon our psychological examination. In accordance with it, we have proven that Madelon must be pitied rather than condemned. She is what she is because she *cannot* be any different; her conscious intentions are not bad. If proper treatment is carried out, the prognosis is not a negative but rather a positive one.

With regard to the second question, as to whether education in a foster home or a re-education home would be more desirable for the girl: If a child with such a poor background is placed in a foster home with private people, the latter usually meet their task with ambivalent feelings. They believe that they personally are being put to a test. If they succeed in achieving progress with the child, then their educational narcissism becomes inflated. If the child has some insurmountable difficulties—or rather, seemingly insurmountable difficulties—which the foster parents are not able to handle, then they are narcissistically hurt; they are indignant about the child and refuse to keep it any longer in their care. As a result, the child wanders in and out of a succession of foster homes without taking firm roots anywhere and becomes completely demoralized.

A child with as poor a hereditary endowment as Madelon's needs teachers with therapeutic training. It would hardly be possible to find private foster parents who could meet this requirement.

Above all, the risk should be avoided of Madelon having to leave her foster home after some six months, because her foster parents have despaired over her. Madelon must "grow roots"; she must be able to feel at "home" in her foster home. She should be guided by the same people for a few years, and become accustomed to them, in order to have enough time to find new ideals for herself, by shaping them after her new models. She must have sufficient time to integrate her personality, as much as that is still possible for her. It is not improvement in school work that is essential for her future success in life, but change and improvement of her character.

We must therefore come to the conclusion that it is better for Madelon to live in a home. Since, in addition to adverse heredity, her problem is her family, the home selected for Madelon should not be a large institution, such as might be suitable for some other child with different personality traits. It should be a home run more like a "family." It would be best if it were an institution with one dozen or at most two dozen girls (in the latter case, it would be organized as two "families").

With the corroboration of the diagnostic findings, the director of the home should be informed about Madelon's individual personality traits, as well as about the dangerous factors that may threaten her, in the hope that such an orientation will facilitate his understanding and supply him with some cues. The institution need not be a detention home, for Madelon should not feel that the change of environment is a punishment, an "imprisonment." Since it seems that she is well suited for manual work, she should be told that, with the help of the home, she could become a weaver, a polisher, or a seamstress, or find occupation in some similar trade in order to become independent later and make her own living. The move into an institution should be made as acceptable as possible for her.

It would be in Madelon's interests if one were able to find an institution as far removed as possible from her parents' home. It could only be a disadvantage for the girl if her mother were able to visit her too frequently. It would probably be advisable to leave visiting privileges to the discretion of the director, who would limit visits as far as possible, especially during the initial period. And it would be desirable if not only the mother but both her parents came to visit Madelon. For the child should not be allowed to feel that it is "loved" by the mother alone.

Madelon should become more and more detached from her natural parents and grow attached to her new "parents." If this is achieved, she will be saved from depravity, and a relapse into such a state will be averted for the future.

In order to verify the validity of the Zulliger Test results, further inquiries were made, by asking Madelon's teacher and her guardian for information. We were supplied with the following report:

"Madelon's work is especially poor in mathematics. As far as science subjects are concerned, she shows some interest in natural history. Her essays are poor; she does not keep to the point, exactly as she does in her conversation. Her reading is good, but she is incapable of repeating satisfactorily whatever she has read. She reads mechanically, rather than with understanding. On the other hand, her needlework is very good. Her work in the school garden is also excellent. Her worst characteristic is that she does not get along with her fellow-students. She is a troublemaker and, when she believes herself to be unobserved, she chatters endlessly. She does not take truthfulness very seriously; often one has the impression that she believes her own lies."

The above was the teacher's statement. The guardian informed us:

"Among the children of her family, Madelon seems to be the most endangered one. Two years ago an attempt was already made to take Madelon away from home; yet the father refused to give his consent, maintaining that he was quite capable of handling his daughter. According to him the mother is responsible for the difficulties, because she continuously 'covers up' for her daughter and keeps her mischievous deeds a secret from the father. Usually, the father resorts to unrestrained beatings, for which the mother tries to make up with sweets. Yet the father loves Madelon and the girl shrewdly utilizes her parents' disputes to her own advantage. The deceptions that Madelon has currently perpetrated have finally provided the authorities with a 'handle' with which to convince the father that a change of environment is necessary."

Thus, both statements confirm the results of the Zulliger Test.

A psychiatrist would probably have diagnosed "psychopathy" in this case.

For us and for the authorities, however, it serves no purpose to put Madelon's deviation down on record as some specific, psychiatrically expressed modification. We are interested in solving the problem of what steps should be undertaken in order to prevent the girl's complete demoralization, in which case she would eventually have to be supported permanently by public funds. The problem is one of psychology and pedagogics.

We believe that the Zulliger Test has contributed a great deal toward the clarification and solution of this problem.

In using the Zulliger Test for the purpose of examining an individual human being, it is less important merely to establish arithmetic averages and statistical norms than it is to penetrate into all its fine points, and to evaluate and understand them in their relationship to all the results. In fact, this is a postulate that is valid for every individual test.

Madelon's case proves particularly well how much may be deduced on the basis of one test that has been studied thoroughly and carefully.

8. *Meinard,* a cheat (see Table 6).

We shall call this youth Meinard. When he was about 17 years old, a juvenile court sent him for a psychological examination.

Meinard L., who is pyknic in his physical appearance, is the illegitimate son of a farm girl, and grew up in a farm environment. Nobody, not even he himself, knows very much about his early life. The farmer has always been strict with him. Although Meinard has never had the reputation of being bright in school, and although every spring he has had some difficulty being promoted into the next grade, his foster father has not been willing to think that he is stupid. When he was still very young, the boy was already a skillful trader. To begin with, he showed skill when he bought and sold rabbits among his friends. Later the farmer consulted him every time he traded pigs, calves, and goats. In general, the farmer was well satisfied with his foster son. Although he was undoubtedly inclined to be lazy, under supervision Meinard accomplished almost as much work as a grown-up farm hand.

His teachers in school were of the opinion that he is one of those students who could do better work if he made an effort, and that all he needed was a stronger will and more endurance.

After Meinard graduated from school, his guardian found him a place with a baker, Meinard himself had wanted to learn the bakery trade; yet now he did not like to get up so early. His master complained that the boy was more interested in playing cards than in working at his trade and, after a few weeks had passed, he threw Meinard out.

The youth did not take his predicament too seriously. On the very same day, he found another job in town as an assistant waiter, and his guardian agreed to the change.

Meinard liked his new profession very much. He felt, however, that his wages were too small and that he did not get a large enough share of the tips. Nevertheless, he seemed to behave well, and his employer praised him as an eager, skillful, and gay young man.

Then it came to light that Meinard had committed a burglary by breaking into a ship with an older fellow-worker. The two young men stole a good many cigarettes, and some sausages and money, by smashing the glass in showcases and picking the lock of the cash-register. After the crime was committed, they tasted all the brandy and liqueurs and became dead drunk. Consequently, in escaping they did not get further than the wharf, where they were found by the police, sleeping under a tree. The stolen money, as well as everything else that the two delinquents had not eaten or drunk, was recovered intact.

During the court hearing, Meinard managed to present a picture of himself as a seduced fellow-traveler; he was believed. Since the older burglar was over 20 years old, he was brought before the ordinary court; Meinard appeared before the judge of the juvenile court.

Meinard's guardian too believed that his ward had been seduced, and he urged that clemency rather than justice should prevail. In the meantime Meinard had applied for another job, at one of the foremost Swiss resorts. He had been promised higher wages and the boy also hoped to collect better tips. "If I had been making more money," he said, "it would never have occurred to me to take part in a burglary."

The juvenile court attorney noted that Meinard displayed an indifferent, cold manner, that he did not show any signs of remorse. The boy had tried to clear himself by "stupid" yet shrewd talk, putting all the blame upon his accomplice. The attorney therefore thought that matters were more serious with Meinard than his guardian would admit. The latter finally gave his consent to Meinard's psychological examination although, as he often stated, he did not have too much faith in it.

First the Rorschach and then the Behn Test were administered to Meinard. In order to change the pace, he was next given the Wartegg Test, and finally the Zulliger Test.

The following presentation is based upon the results of the three form-interpretation tests. The Wartegg Test showed Meinard's interest in card-playing and showcases, as well as in games of chance (horseshoe); it also showed his laziness, as well as his detachment from his fellow men (no H).

Rorschach Test

Duration: 7 minutes
Number of responses: 15, (5 of which are produced for the last three colored cards).

I.

An oil spot on the street, in rainy
   weather .... WChCF spot O—
Vermin .... WF + A (P)
Island in the sea, only the white
   spots do not fit in—but there
   are such shores (points to the
   periphery and the ramifications) DWF ± geog

II.

A fire-spitting volcano that has
   emptied itself; but from down
   below more fire is advancing ... SWCF volcano, combinatory

332

III.

A very simply drawn landscape—
rootstocks, etc. .... DWF ± nat O—

IV.

A weeping willow .... DWF — pl

V.

Lake Geneva .... DWF — geog, infantile

VI.

c A cherry tree .... WF ± pl
a A swamp with a canal in its center . WChF — nat

VII.

c A stuffed chair; down below are
its legs; in the middle it has
tapis .... DWSF — obj O—

VIII.

Two Polar bears (outer red area) . DF + A P

IX.

A tree on a wooded island .... DWCF nat (pl)

X.

All kinds of little animals (W)
and .... WCF A O±
water (points to the entire blue
area) with inflowing water ...... DC water
(a blob at the outer blue area) .. DCF nat

| *Bero Test* | Duration: | 5 minutes |
| | Number of responses: | 16/5 |

I.

A candle holder with a candle (S) . WSF ± obj

II.

A water-fountain .... DWF ± obj
in front there is a pond .... DSF — obj confabulation
with animals in it .... D F + A

III.

A scabby, rotten apple .... WCF pl infantile O—

IV.

Switzerland, here is the Pruntrut
    Pick .... DWF — geog

V.

A moth .... ChC → WF + A P

VI.

Treetop .... WF ± pl

VII.

A ravine .... WSF + nat
The entrance to a garden; ...... WF + nat   }
    below is a river bed .... SF + nat   } combinatory

VIII.

Lizards (red area) .... DF + A P
These are all animals .... WF + A

IX.

Flower path with garden beds in
  a row because the colors follow
  each other in a row and because
  the left and the right sides are
  the same .... DWCF pl O—

X.

A Mickey Mouse film (not seen
  as movement!)[3] .... WCF obj/A O
Dirt, earth (brown and orange
  areas) .... DC dirt

Zulliger Test

        Duration: 3 minutes
        Number of responses: 10, 3 of
            which were produced for
            the colored Card II.

I.

A puddle .... ChC → WF ± puddle O—
(Laughs offensively). Four, two of
  which are erected and two of the
  others are partly erected ...... DF ± sex O—

---

[3] After all the tests were completed, the interpretations were once more discussed individually with the subject.

334

II.

Female sex organ with a well-marked slit (red area and inner white space)	DCF sex
	SF ± sex
Dirt (orange area)	DC dirt

III.

Again, just puddles ...... ChC →	WF — puddle, perseveration
(Grinning) An image of a young girl, all dressed up, a little whore (between the torso and the leg of the W, holding the card by its right lower edge)	SF + (H) sex/image O
c A landmap of foreign regions	DWF ± geog
with red clouds	DCF clouds
down below is the sea seen from an airplane	SF — nat, confabulation (a landscape is created from a "map" by confabulation)

EVALUATION:

First, it is remarkable how fast Meinard finished with the tests: both the total and the relative reaction times are low. Instead of producing one response per minute, as is true of an average case, he produces two to three responses. Thus, Meinard does not lack ideas. Either he is an individual who brings things to a speedy conclusion, who "disposes" of everything rapidly and demands our respect for being a good organizer as well as a person who is capable of planning quickly, or—and now we must consider *what* it is that he produces. In addition to Meinard's low F+%, our attention is primarily attracted by his many DW, which prove his tendency toward confabulation. Although his thinking is "generous," it is not accurate, does not correspond to reality. For Meinard, illusions are reality. An individual who thinks as he does and as fast as he does, thinks inaccurately and "indifferently." He has a "need for grandeur," but he lacks substance; this prevents him from being generous and grandiose in the positive sense of the terms. His is rather like the generosity of a jester, who makes arrangements and scatters judgments "out of the blue."

TABLE 6

Scoring
Subject: Meinard

Ro → Bero → Z - Test

Time: 16/5 · 15/5 · 10/3 — (7 minutes · 5 minutes · 3 minutes)
Number of responses:

Scoring			
DW	= 6	3	1
SW	= 1	—	—
WS	= —	2	—
W	= 4	6	2
D	= 3	3	4
S	= 1	2	3
F+%	= 50	70	57
A%	= 20	25	—
P%	= 6	12	—
O%	= 26∓	20∓	30∓
H%	= —	—	—
sex%	= —	—	40

	7 minutes (16/5)	5 minutes (15/5)	3 minutes (10/3)		Content	7 minutes (16/5)	5 minutes (15/5)	3 minutes (10/3)
F+	3	3	—		H	3	7	1
F−	3	2	—		Hd	3	2	2
F±	2	3	—		sex	2	3	4(1)
M	—	—	—		A	3	3	4
FC	—	—	—		obj	—	1	4
CF	4	3	2		pl	4	2	3
C	1	1	1		nat	1	4	3
ChF	1	—	—		geog	1	2	1
ChC	1	2	2		spot	1	1	—
shocks	—	—	—		puddle	—	—	2
					dirt	—	1	1
					volcano	—	1	—
					water	—	1	—
					clouds	—	—	1
					P	1	1	2
					O	4(−3)	4(−3)	3(−2)

	Ro	Bero	Z
Sequence:	orderly	orderly, tendency to inversion	orderly
Experience balance:	O M : 5½ C	O : 4½	O : 2½
Apperceptive type:	DW — W — D — S	same	same
Remarks: confabulates	same	infantile abstraction	same —
combines	same	perseveration	— +

Since his experience balance is decidedly extratensive, we shall find in Meinard not only self-doubts, but an inclination toward deceit as well, which is also indicated by the ChF that occur here and there. People who are stupid—and Meinard is stupid (see intelligence factors!)—and who, in addition, are inclined to deceit, are "foolishly cunning"; they possess the "craftiness of a peasant." Since Meinard has hardly any feelings for his fellow-men (absence of H, Hd, anat, scenes), he must have these characteristics to a large degree. Only in the Zulliger Test does he produce one single H; it is a very special one, for it is related to sex.

An inaccurate, indifferent thinker such as Meinard is not interested in people except in a sex relationship—in other words, from the point of view of his own sexual needs. He does not *love* other people (absence of H, etc.), and he does not feel the need of becoming attached and adjusted to them (absence of FC) as he would if he were influenced by emotional motives. He is egocentric (CF and C). By adding everything that we were able to establish thus far, and observing the deficient adaptation of Meinard's thinking (both A% and P% are low), we arrive at the picture of a *cheat*. Because he lacks the necessary intelligence, he is merely a cheat and not a swindler. A person who is inclined to confabulation at the intellectual level to such an excessive degree as Meinard, has no inner life (absence of M). Since his affectivity is unadapted and partially incapable of becoming adapted (CF and C), and since he possesses a strong motor "drive" (uncontrolled CF and C, absence of M), he tends to steal other people's property. For, as Sganzini once put it, confabulation at the intellectual level corresponds with stealing at the motility level.

The picture we obtain on the basis of the form-interpretation tests is that of a thief. Even if we did not know anything about the subject's earlier life, the presence of pure C would bring us to the conclusion that he is now an active thief. Such a conclusion must be drawn all the more readily because numerous S (in part, WS and SW) have been produced. In their relationship to other factors, they cannot be characterized in this case as indicators of critical and self-critical impulses, but must rather be seen as

obstinate and aggressive drives, which support the subject's inclination toward deceit (as a desire to trick other people). Although some Rorschach researchers have found that S is an intelligence factor, sustaining the "accuracy" of thinking, this cannot hold true for the intellectually inferior, and not at all for the mentally retarded. It is only conditionally applicable—and Meinard is not an intelligent individual.

The short testing time now appears in a different light. Meinard wants to get everything done "fast," essentially because, in spite of his too low A%, he is indolent, lazy. He wants to "get over with" things rapidly, and avoids becoming more deeply absorbed in his work; in fact, he tries to avoid work altogether, and his work is inaccurate (DW, speedy reactions, absence of Dd). Viewed externally, his speedy reactions give the impression of bustling activity. Since Meinard has such strong motile needs, something must always be "going on." He is restless and impulsive, governed by moods.

The probability of poor hereditary factors is suggested not only by the pure C (Rorschach: "Even one single C is suspicious"), but also by certain contents. Such interpretations as "vermin," "swamp," "scabby, rotten apple" are not merely original interpretations, they are individual and symbolic responses as well. They are probably self-descriptions, projections of Meinard's morbidity.

Meinard's direct and indirect sexual interpretations are also suspicious. They appear in the Zulliger Test, but they are also found in the "oil spot on the street" (Ro I), the "fire-spitting volcano that has emptied itself" (Ro II), the "swamp with a canal in its center" (Ro VI), "water-fountain; in front there is a pond with animals in it" (Bero II), the "puddles" (Zulliger Test I and III), "dirt" (Bero X and Zulliger Test II). They indicate uncontrolled impulsivity, from both the heterosexual and the homosexual point of view (see also Bero I "candle holder with handle").

The anal-urethral interpretations ("dirt—earth—puddle—swamp—water-fountain—volcano emptying itself") confirm Meinard's thieving tendency, his desire for possessions, his greed, his "insatiability" with regard to property. One finds it difficult to decide whether Meinard is more inclined to sexual delinquency or to stealing. On the basis of his uninhibited aggressiveness (S and pure C!), one may imagine that he is, indeed, capable of both. At any rate, he is not only an endangered individual, but also a dangerous one. Although his burglary accomplice has been regarded as the instigator of the crime, one may assert without any hesitation that Meinard too could have been the "leader."

The youth agency was advised to place Meinard—who is endangered, endangering, and dangerous—into an institution for a long period of time, possibly for years. Under the strictest supervision and habit-forming training he could, perhaps, learn a trade while there. Meinard's hereditary factors are poor; if habit-formation is unsuccessful in disciplining him, and making him capable of becoming halfway decent member of society, he will become a "perpetual candidate" for public institutions. Only because of indolence has he abstained from committing more serious crimes than stealing. Under certain circumstances, however, Meinard might become aggressive and attempt a murder. Under no conditions should one take the chance of letting him live in freedom.

I heard later that Meinard, after being told that he was being given "another chance," was permitted to move to the resort and to accept the job of a waiter. He used his chance—to make gambling debts and to steal. Thereupon he was placed in an institution, where he had the opportunity to learn a trade.

After his dismissal, he again accepted employment as a waiter. Hardly six months had passed before he knocked down an old man, in order to steal his briefcase. He was then put into a hospital for the mentally ill, for observation and diagnosis.

I do not know what has happened to Meinard since then.

At any rate, the unfavorable prognosis that could be made by way of the form-interpretation tests had been confirmed. I therefore thought it wise to publish the tests, for perhaps they might be able to teach us something. It seems to me that the publication of studies concerned with the individual is just as important as the collection and compilation of statistical data, the value of which is undisputed.

Studying individual "cases," one learns to recognize "nuances," and to find them in the tests; these are often lost in statistical studies.

If, on the basis of form-interpretation tests, one is forced to admit that there do exist unfortunate conditions or unfavorable prognoses, one is usually tormented by the thought that perhaps one may have done injustice to the subject. It seems almost impossible to form a valid judgment about a person whom one has not seen for more than 2-3 hours. Thus one becomes too hesitant and too conditional, and attempts to draw an indefinite personality and character picture, stressing one's "suspicions" too much and desperately clinging to the concept of *in dubio pro reo*.

On the other hand, in a case like Meinard's, one feels an obligation to express a definite warning.

Nevertheless, in such a case, it may seem to somebody who is not familiar with the form-interpretation test that matters have been exaggerated and the picture painted too dark.

Undoubtedly one's responsibility in giving advice is extremely grave, in a case like Meinard's. Yet this is just as true for cases that are less serious, as, for example, those in which simple educational or vocational guidance is called for. It is evident that the problem of one's conscience must be resolved anew each time. The fact that the "object" is a live human being, and not an inanimate thing, constitutes the heaviest burden for the profession when it deals with diagnostic evaluations.

The fact that Meinard has burglarized a ship should be of special significance.

It seems that neither delinquent intended to steal money; they did not even expect to find any. They were under the impression that the cash register was emptied every night when the ship's personnel went home. The intention of both was to obtain smoking and drinking items, which they hoped to find on board. Upon discovering the cash register, they spontaneously decided to "crack" it too, because earlier the breaking of showcases had given them a great deal of pleasure.

All this was brought to light when Meinard was questioned in greater detail during the psychological examination. The inquiry was conducted with the aim in mind of perhaps finding an explanation for Meinard's lack of remorse.

Meinard related how they found it especially interesting to break into a ship. He said that it all went back to a dream that he had once had, in which he had gone aboard a ship, where he enjoyed royal treatment without any cost, as if he were the ship's owner.

It was discovered that, while the idea of committing a burglary had originated with Meinard's partner in crime, the proposal to break into a ship had been made by Meinard.

In all probability, burglarizing a ship had some special emotional significance for Meinard. This was borne out by the fact that, while he was describing the burglary, his eyes took on a dreamy expression and his voice began to sound sugary. If we were to use analogies based on dream psychology, we would say that, symbolically, the ship signifies for Meinard the mother from whom he would like to extort oral pleasures, while the burglary is related to his infantile wishes regarding possession of his mother.

All this does not tell us anything about the remorseless behavior shown by Meinard. Because of his egocentricity, and because he is caught in the net of his instinctive-narcissistic personality, the boy is not even capable of feeling remorse. He *knew* indeed that he had committed a criminal offense for which he could be punished, but his affectivity did not have any part in this knowledge. Being imprisoned by his egocentricity, narcissism, and impulsivity, Meinard's conscience remained unmoved. *Whatever suited him was "right" for him.*

And yet some small twinge of conscience must have been unconsciously effective in Meinard. For otherwise, being as cunning as he is, he would not have betrayed himself. He would not have permitted himself to stay under a tree, knowing that he would thus draw the policemen's attention to himself.

The objection may easily be made that it happened because he had drunk himself into a stupor. We should say to this: the fact that Meinard was drunk facilitated the breaking through of his unconscious impulse regarding moral judgment (the tendency to give himself away).

Meinard's poor personality structure, acquired by heredity, and his immoral, abnormal disposition, which foreshadows a criminal career for him, touch even more deeply than the unconscious "complex-like" motives that led him to carry out a criminal act.

Occasionally people with Meinard's disposition may be changed, with the help of habit-formation and training, into fairly decent social human beings. In Meinard's case, such an attempt apparently did not meet with success.

9. *Theodor J.*, 15 years old.

T. J. will be graduated from school next spring, and is undecided what to do next. The problem is whether to enter a secondary school, take a teacher's course, or learn a trade. The father would like his son, an only child, to become a teacher.

The son is lefthanded. He has never had any special illnesses (except the usual children's diseases), and has not had any operations. At the age of 10 he was frequently sick; the family doctor recommended that his tonsils be removed. Since the boy recovered, however, this recommendation was never carried out.

There are no adverse hereditary traits. He is the son of a schoolteacher. Both his parental and maternal grandparents held elevated positions in a trade. T. J. is a Boy Scout and likes model building. His school report cards are "very good" to "good."

He is pyknic in body build, and presents all the typical signs of it. He is of medium height. His speaking voice is deliberately amiable, well-behaved, and submissive. It is not completely free from restraint; one senses that it is being kept under control.

Zulliger Test	Time: 13 minutes

I.

Blossom of a flower from a foreign
country, an orchid .... ChC → WF + pl O
A butterfly (center dark area) .... DF + A
b Head and claws of a crab (top
center area) .... DoF + Ad (P)
A small snow-covered fir tree
weighed down by snow (D 3/4) . ChF → DdF ± pl
Mask (top center) .... S → DF + mask
Two bones lie next to it .... DdF + obj/anat/Ad
c A hand reaching (EF 3/4/5) ..... M → DF + Hd O

II.

Two cockchafers (orange area) ...	DFC A
Two green eyes with a white star (green area and S)	DSCF eyes, white as color
Or the dense root structure of a plant (orange and green areas) ..	DCF pl combinatory "or"
c The lungs (dark red area)	DCF anat
Two skinned hams at the butcher's (whole red area)	DCF food
An enlarged head of a fly (red area and S)	S → DF ± Ad

III.

Two figures	WM + H P
A tree branch (EFG 3/4)	DF − pl
A butterfly, once again	DF + A P
b,d Young chicks picking up something (red outer area)	DF + A
c A "piggy" (EF 3 and 8)	DF + A
c Something like an "English key" (EFG 3/4)	DF + obj/technical
d Rootstock, as for instance that of a little cowslip (EFG 3/4)	FCh → DF + pl
Or scarecrows .... FCh →	WF + obj with M repression (P) "or"

EVALUATION: based on the Zulliger Test; to be compared with the Ro and Bero (see Tables 7 and 8).

The 3 W, the average reaction time, the high F+%, sequence, and apperceptive type indicate a relatively high intelligence. The intellectual potential belongs to at least a high-average category.

An impairment of the ability to concentrate may be observed. The A% is too low, although not substantially so, and the content distribution is somewhat too large, suggesting a tendency toward distraction and fragmentation of interests. On the other hand, testing time and number of responses suggest quantity ambition and a tenacious desire for persistence, while the 3 W and the high F+% are indicative of quality ambition. Thus, we may assume that T. J. is capable of maintaining a certain attention span and of directing his attention. Therefore, the content distribution is correlated to openness and to a multitude of

TABLE 7

Scoring
Subject: *Theodor J.*

Time: 13 minutes
Number of responses: 21/6

Cd.	W	D	Dd	Do	S	F+	F—	F±	M	FC	CF	FCh	ChF	ChC	P	O
I	1	3	2	1	1	6		1	(1)			1		1	1	2
II		6			1			1		1	4		1			
III	2	6				6	1		1				1		3	
	3	15	2	1	2	12	1	2	2	1	4	1	1	1	4	2

H	= 1(2)	A	= 5	combinatory
Hd	= 1	Ad	= 2(3)	M repression
anat	= 2	shocks	= —	"or"
eyes	= 1	obj	= 3	
mask	= 1	pl	= 4	
food	= 1	tech	= (1)	

F+% = 90
A% = 38
P% = 19
O% = 10
H% = 38

Sequence: orderly (-loose), tendency to inversion
Experience balance: 2 M : 3½ C
Apperceptive type: W — D — Dd/Do — S

TABLE 8

Subject: *Theodor J.*
Comparisons with Ro and Bero

Z-Test → Ro → Bero

	Z-Test 13 minutes 21/6	**Ro** 47 minutes 46/16	**Bero** 28 minutes 42/16
Number of responses:			
WS =	—	1	2
W =	3	5	10
D =	13	33	26
Dd =	3	3	3
Do =	1	1	1(2)
S =	2	3	1
F =	15(−2)	32(−6)	30(−4)
M =	2	3	4
FC =	1	5	2
CF =	4	6	5
FCh =	1	2	2
ChF =	1	—	1
ChC =	1		
Sequence:	orderly-loose, tendency to inversion	same	same
Experience balance:	2 M : 3½ C	3 : 10½	4 : 6
Apperceptive type:	W—D—Dd/Do—S	same	same
combinatory	same	same	
M repression	same	same	
"or"	infantile abstraction		
F% =	90	81	87
A% =	38	22	24
P% =	19	9	24
O% =	10	4	12
H% =	38	14	16
P =	3	4	10
O =	2	2	5
H =	2	1	3
Hd =	1	2	2
anat =	2	—	—
eyes =	1	—	1
mask =	1	1	1
food =	1	2	—
A =	5	4	9
Ad =	1	6	1
obj =	3	15	11
pl =	4	9	8
tech =	1	3	2
nat =	—	2	2
others =	—	1	1

345

interests, to an infantile "hunger for experiences." Furthermore, the high F+% indicates a sharply observing mind and a "visual" type. Since this is a D type with original M, we may presume that artistic abilities exist. And since we find in the subject's apperceptive type a tendency to produce W and at the same time a tendency to produce S, this leads us to believe that intellectual adaptation is problem-oriented and that, in addition to sketching from nature (plants, animals, objects, etc.), "technical drawing" is well-liked too.

S, partly combined with D, indicates combinatory abilities (which are also apparent in the W); by relating S to the colors, one recognizes a "critical eye" for the external world. From the fact that M repression appears as well, we can deduce that criticism is also directed toward the self. We encounter suggestions of self-criticism and self-control in by the "eye" interpretation (II/2).

The WS, replaced in the Zulliger Test by DS, indicate that T. J. does not often express his criticism outwardly. The "mask" interpretation points in the same direction. Considering the FCh and ChF, we may assume that adaptation is in part a product of conscious effort, and has been acquired by education—in other words, that there exists a conscious desire for adaptation. Inverse sequence bears out the same fact. At the same time, the latter indicates a certain attitude of anxiety, as does Do. This explains why all statements are formulated cautiously. Considering the CF, which are the indicators of sensitivity, and the high H%, we may conclude that T. J. cannot bear to be exposed to "ridicule," but tries to avoid it; he fears to lose love and respect.

On the other hand, anatomic interpretations suggest intellectual ambition and some specific interpretations (such as Card I/1, Do in I/3, II/6, III/6) indicate specific school ambitions.

The M repression indicates that T. J. mistrusts his inner self and has no faith in his own original "creative" ideas, preferring to cling to a learned scheme and to think in a receptive and reproductive manner.

Subjects with a high H% and a preponderance of CF have a strong unconscious or conscious mother fixation. Under certain circumstances, such a fixation may manifest itself in the fact that the mother is tormented by the child, who constantly seeks her attention. This could hardly be applied to T. J., however, for, although his infantilism is still unresolved, the boy has no neurotic traits. Still, he is rather naïve. The importance that "food" has for T. J. also points up his mother fixation.

Interpretations related to technical matters indicate technical interests, while the D type, the M, the "reaching" hand (Card I/7) suggest technical skill (and perhaps masturbation). Also, the "mask" could indicate that something is being hidden. At any rate, it may be assumed that T. J. lives under a certain tension, for he does not behave as impulsively as he would if he were following his natural disposition. Assuming that introversive factors are producing a strong retarding effect upon his impulsivity, T. J. might still be quite impulsive, were it not for the influence of Ch and his intense self-control. They have a leveling effect upon his personality. Since the M remain repressed, we may deduce with some certainty that T. J. is an ambiequal and not introversive type (as he may seem to be, from the purely numerical point of view). CF suggest strong vitality, rather than indicating emotional and impulsive outbreaks.

Taking all these character factors into account, we reach the conclusion that the subject has a dependable (Dd!), conscientious, reliable personality structure. It is "soft" in its basic quality (M!). From the intellectual point of view the subject's personality still displays partly infantile traits while, on the other hand, it shows a "drive for freedom" (W tendency; tendency toward planning and organizing; S).

DIAGNOSIS AND COUNSELING (as offered to the father):

T. J.'s innate intellectual ability is undoubtedly superior; it is high average. A slight impairment of the ability to concentrate is counteracted by conscious diligence and quality ambition. This impairment has been the result of slow mental development. Although T. J. has reached the age of puberty, he is still relatively quite childish—a trait that can almost always be observed in an only child. He is impressionable and interested in many areas. Since he is hungry for new experiences, and since his adaptability is considerable, he wants to give himself to every phenomenon that meets his senses (mainly his vision)—in a still somewhat playfully infantile fashion. He is a visual type, and therefore possesses some talent for drawing. Only by conscious effort and self-control does he succeed in avoiding aimless rambling, even though he tends toward it. His thinking is not pure theorizing, but rather concrete and "practical," although T. J. is not lacking in the ability to comprehend complex relationships. His method is combinatory rather than abstract—yet not completely so. He is capable of observing accurately. With the aid of his conscientiousness, he observes mainly "practical" details. A slight anxiety underlies his conscientiousness, the result of his desire not to "disgrace" himself by his formulations. Since T. J. is highly sensitive and sensible, as well as being in general soft rather than tough, his inner self is easily hurt. Furthermore, in the light of his obvious school and intellectual ambitions, it becomes readily apparent why T. J. can not tolerate disgrace. Thus, he is cautious, employs self-control, has a somewhat distrustful attitude toward himself, and restrains himself in his conduct, his thinking, and his verbal expression. In addition, he has little faith in authority, although he seeks to dissimulate that fact. Being as versatile as he is, he tries to adapt himself to the demands made upon him by conscious effort; under these circumstances, this amounts to a kind of "self-denial." In other words, he ignores his impulsivity; he observes himself and feels himself observed. Possessing at the same time a marked (partially infantile) need for love, and being strongly dependent upon his fellow men (intense mother fixation), he wants to "do everything well," to behave in such a manner as to win the approval of his environment. A somewhat "forced" over-all attitude results, as well as a certain inner tension. It is still not strong enough to effect repressions, and the boy is not "neurotic"—at least not yet.

At the intellectual level, the effects of the somewhat too intense self-control become apparent in the fact that T. J. is incapable of performing at his best unlesss—strange as this may be —he is slightly tired, and his self-control has decreased a little. It is only then that he becomes freer, creates more naturally, mistrusts himself less, and produces with greater ease. It is evident, therefore, that T. J. is a "training type." He needs some time for a takeoff; he needs practicing before he can produce his best achievements. It is only then that he succeeds in fully incorporating his innate imaginative and creative capabilities into his thought processes (earlier, his thinking is so strongly influenced by self-doubts that it is reproductive rather than productive).

Thus we observe the strong dependence of T. J.'s intellectual processes upon mental factors, upon affectivity, and upon emotional factors. In this respect the boy is still a child. He wants to please the loved ones in his environment, for he is afraid of losing their love. He cannot stand being met with coldness. He studies and takes pains with his work, not so much because he has found an objective relationship to his studies, but because he seeks love or does not want to lose the love that he has already won. This, then, is the meaning of T. J.'s "immaturity" and childlike behavior. He is not yet free (as indicated by the slowness of his mental development, which we have mentioned above).

Examining the area of his interests, our attention is drawn to his technical interests. In view of the fact that T. J. is skillful with his hands, we reach the conclusion that he has technical talent. And taking into account his ability to perform abstract and combinatory tasks—an ability that is supplemented by his conscientiousness, his inclination to accuracy ("exactness"), and his intensified self-control—we may further infer that he tends toward schematic speculation.

From the point of view of his personality structure, T. J. is quite well balanced (I am speaking here of those personality traits that have not been discussed earlier). His personality is anchored in a strong vitality, which is intensive rather than extensive. Impulsivity is directed and checked from three points: from within, by self-control, and by educational influences. The resulting personality appears to be tamed and gay, yet it is serious in its structure. It is already quite stable and will probably develop further in the same direction, while the infantile traits will gradually lose their significance. At any rate, we may take it upon ourselves to make a favorable diagnosis.

Why, then, should T. J. not enter a *secondary school*?

It would be regrettable if his "practical" capabilities were not developed. An academic career would hardly satisfy his inner needs and make him happy. Besides, intellectual endowment of a different quality, and a much more pronounced "theoretical" ability, would be more in keeping with the requirements of a secondary school.

This does not mean, however, that from the intellectual point of view T. J. could not meet the requirements of a secondary school. But they would constantly come into conflict with his natural ability and, on the basis of such a conflict, neurotic developments could result. I would not therefore recommend that T. J. be transferred into a secondary school.

T. J. could certainly become a *teacher*. If, in addition to pursuing his profession, he were also to engage in building models, he could bring his capabilities to full realization and attain happiness. But as a teacher he might occupy a subordinate position, and then his work would "get on his nerves" as time passed. He would be unable to plan for himself; he would have to submit his independent planning and organizing to the relatively narrow limitations imposed upon him by the academic rules. One would like to assure him of a greater amount of freedom than the teaching profession could afford him.

Should he learn a *trade*? A technical one? This might seem to be appropriate, in view of T. J.'s technical interests and talents. However, should T. J. choose to embark upon some simple vocational training in technology, his inclination for problematic and systematic thinking would remain unsatisfied. Yet this inclination too should become an integral part of his future profession.

Considering T. J.'s over-all intelligence and personality traits, one reaches the conclusion that the following proposals ought to be made to the boy:

1. He should attend a *technical school,* and then a *polytechnic institute,* where he would obtain a degree in *engineering.* Afterwards, he should try to find an executive position with some firm, in which he would be permitted to work out his own plans and to organize his work according to his own discretion. Such a place would be appropriate for T. J.

2. Or else he should be apprenticed to a *surveyor,* and then resume studying at a *polytechnic institute,* with the aim of becoming a surveyor himself. Among his other talents, his gift for drawing (the special kind of drawing that is without "artistic qualities," for otherwise one would have to advise the study of architecture for him) would serve him well in this field. As a surveyor, T. J. could work quite independently too. (Because the problem of independence, or rather dependence, is such an important one in T. J.'s case, one would not advise him to study *topography.*)

I believe that I have given a fairly accurate outline of T. J.'s talents and potentials. I also believe that the proposals with regard to his further education are in consonance with T. J.'s special abilities, which should be the basis for his choice of a profession. Nevertheless, the final *decision* must be left to him. That should not be taken away from him; it would never do even to want to. By challenging him to make his own decisions, one would force him to make mental progress. He needs it, in order to prepare the way for ridding himself of the "infantile" traits that he still possesses. He must be made to *carry the responsibility himself.* This would make him more *"manly,"* more independent, more self-reliant. Also, it would promote his *detachment from his parents.* He cannot escape detaching himself from them—not if he wishes to become a mature "man," in other words, if he wants to use all the possibilities at his disposal in order to complete his development. Of course, one should not *talk* to him about all this; one should merely *act* with that in mind in educating him.

10. *Caesar Maier,* 14 years old (see Table 9).

Mr. Maier wishes counseling for his 14-year-old son, Caesar. The adolescent boy, who until now has been a good secondary school[4] student, has suddenly taken to failing in all his school subjects, and his promotion to the next grade is in doubt.

Mr. Maier manages his own business. Mrs. Maier was once

[4] In the Canton of Bern, a secondary school is a lower intermediate school, at which two modern languages are taught.

a nurse; she and her husband met at a hospital where Mr. Maier was undergoing an appendectomy. The wife is considerably older than her husband. Two children were born to the couple: first, a son, and then, three years later, a daughter. Both children developed well; they did not have any unusual illnesses, and there is no sign of adverse heredity.

Currently Caesar has been subject to a growth spurt and has grown very tall. He is already taller than either of his parents.

To begin with, the father had been advised to submit Caesar to a complete physical check-up, for it could be that Caesar's intellectual deterioration is caused by physical factors. The check-up ought to include a urine analysis in order to establish whether the urine contains albumen, and whether it is albumen loss—which occasionally occurs in rapidly growing adolescents during puberty—that may be causing the increased mental fatigue and exhaustion that would explain why Caesar's intellectual achievements seem to have deteriorated so suddenly.

The physician's report states that Caesar is in perfect physical health and quite capable of working. No albumen was found in his urine.

We may therefore assume that his intellectual deterioration is the result of emotional causes.

The parents bring Caesar to the counselor in a car. The mother looks very motherly; her hair is completely gray. The father seems to be in the "prime of life"; one would almost think that he is the oldest son of his wife. Their son, Caesar, looks like a young giant. He is slightly ungainly in his body build, and somewhat awkward in his movements.

He maintains that lately he has been "accidentally" harassed by bad luck at school whenever the teachers have given tests or demanded papers. At such time he has been unduly nervous, because of his confusion, he sometimes does not quite understand the questions. Besides, he has not been on friendly terms with his mathematics teacher, because the latter had once found a "copy note," on which Caesar had written some geometric formulae.

First the Zulliger Test is administered to Caesar (see also Table 9).

Test record

I.

This looks like it had rained and
there is a sooty oil spot from a
car in a puddle .... ChF → DWF ± nat O complex
interpretation

(subject points to the darker center
blot)
It could also be a monster with
raised fists .... WM + H O
they are tremendous and knives are
in them .... DF + obj aggression
The eyes are evil .... SF + Hd
and the feet are cut off, it has only
wooden legs .... DF + H castration idea
Looking at it properly, the whole
could also be a bed bug or something like it .... WF + A P "or"

II.

Hey! (Examiner: "why?") .... shock!
Torn flesh (points to the red area);
perhaps a hare's .... DCF Ad, meat
And here is a potted plant (S) .... SF + pl
Above there is a dove or a pilot's
insignia (S) .... SF + A "or"
                                SF + obj
The brown here is crushed clay ... DCF nat
And on top of it are tufts of grass . DFC pl
Or also two foxes drinking water
(brown area, heads seen toward
the outside) .... DFC A "or"
And in there are faces with long
noses, perhaps Halloween masks
(within the brown area) .... DdF + Hd/mask

III.

(Prolonged reaction time) .... aftereffect of shock
Something rotten with worms
crawling out of it ...... ChF → DWF ± nat O
complex interpretation
Or snakes .... DF + A "or"
Or men cut in two, without legs,
with guns .... DF + Hd "or"

353

Some wormlike configurations
  (smaller dark blots) .... DF + A (perseveration)
Butterfly (within the red area) ... DF + A P
Little running devils (red outer
  area) .... DMs H P

End   2:46 P.M.

EVALUATION:

Since F+% is over 90, the sequence is orderly, A%, P and O percentages are average, and interpretation content shows a relatively low variability, we may assume that the subject's innate intelligence as well as his concentration ability are high (otherwise A% would be lower and the variability of contents would be greater). However, this subject's intelligence is of the kind that is usually described as "practical" rather than "theoretical." (Preponderance of D.)

It is threatened in its manifestation from two directions. In the first place, Caesar submits to illusions, mistaking them for reality—a fact indicated by DW. He does not differentiate clearly between the creations of his imagination or confabulation and actually observed phenomena. This is a typically infantile trait. When it appears in adolescents or in older people, it almost always indicates regressive tendencies, especially if shocks are produced as well (as is true in Caesar's case). Caesar's thinking has remained partly infantile, a fact that is corroborated by his nature interpretations. Secondly, Caesar becomes emotionally irritated to a relatively great extent. This observation is confirmed by the very numerous S he produces. If we correlate them to the three CF indicating affectivity—which, although not yet adapted, may be adapted—"defiant" irritability appears. For S always signify a tendency to opposition, which may become apparent in being directed either toward the self or toward the outer world. To begin with, since Caesar's experience balance is extratensive, we must assume that his opposition is directed toward the outside world. However, his approach to Card III, after Card II, shows us very clearly that his "opposition" is also directed toward his inner self. The shock experienced in Card II produces an aftereffect. Caesar is incapable of conceiving the dark configurations in Card III as a whole. He separates the parts

TABLE 9

Scoring:
Subject: *Caesar Maier*

Time: 16 minutes
Number of responses: 20, of which
8 were produced for Card II

Cd.	DW	W	D	Dd	S	F+	F±	F−	M	Ms	FC	CF	ChF	P	O	responses
I	1	2	2	—	1	4	1	—	1	—	—	—	1	1	2	6
II	—	—	4	1	3	4	—	—	—	—	2	2	—	—	—	8
III	1	—	5	—	—	4	1	—	—	1	—	—	1	2	1	6
Total:	2	2	11	1	4	12	2	—	1	1	2	2	2	3	3	20

F+% = 90 approximately
A% = 35
P% = 15
O% = 15
H% = 30

Sequence: orderly
Experience balance: 1 M : 3 C
Apperceptive type: DW — W — D̲ — Dd/S

Shocks = II and III

H = 2
Hd = 4 (mask)
A = 6
Ad = 1
obj = 2
pl = 2
nat = 3

Complex interpretation
Castration idea
"or"; tendency toward perseveration

355

that are usually interpreted as the "legs of men," and does not produce the popular interpretations until the very end (P), when he has recovered from all the shocks. In other words, only then is he capable of "thinking" again as others do. Essentially, Card III is prepared in such a way that an M should be produced in the first response. Under the influence of his irritability, Caesar does not succeed in producing an M. This means that, when he is emotionally excited or irritated, the scope of his creativeness is "impeded" and his thinking becomes impaired.

Strictly speaking, we already see the effects of such impairment in Card I. An almost peculiar or seemingly devious interpretation is produced here; the popular response is not given until the end, just before the card is surrendered.

Thus we may assume that Caesar experienced a shock when the first card was presented to him, and recovered but gradually.

The test indicates that Caesar's intellectual impairment is the result of his own hostility directed against himself. If we ask ourselves how it is activated, we should reply along the following lines. As has been mentioned previously, Caesar's sphere of productivity has been affected. This must be supplemented by still another detail—namely, that two tendencies overlap one another in Caesar. One is a definite trend toward generosity expressed by the W and by DW as a W tendency; the other is a "complaining" trait, which finds its expression in the S. This complaining trait is contradictory to the generosity of Caesar's thinking and comprehension. At the same time, it implies that Caesar doubts himself. He makes life difficult for himself (creating "problems" even when there aren't any), and he insists on considering the "other side" of things. He doubts that his judgements, opinions, etc., are correct, and he broods about everything. Nevertheless, he is still capable of quantitatively adequate intellectual functioning within a defined time-span (his average reaction time is equal to one response per minute). In addition, qualities of brooding and self-doubt are expressed in the test by the usage of "or," to which Caesar reverts more than once. He is never quite certain, being inclined to admit that something other than what he said earlier may also be a a possibility. Diplomatically, he likes to "leave a door open";

he eludes, disguising his eluding by conciliation. He avoids taking chances, and proves his uncertainty by insisting on supplying documentary evidence.

As Hermann Rorschach established earlier, color and chiaroscuro shocks suggest repression and the existence of neurotic mechanisms. By correlating shocks with experience balance, one may go even further and determine the choice of neurosis on the basis of form-interpretation tests. Earlier, when we discussed the development of Caesar's intelligence and the inhibitions of his intelligence, the fact that he reacts neurotically was made quite clear.

We shall now concern ourselves with Caesar's experience balance—which, from the purely statistical point of view, seems to be extratensive. However, we see very clearly, especially when Card III is presented to him, that Caesar "represses" his kinesthesias. Within the experience balance, the M side is larger than the figure 1 (as compared to 3 C) would indicate. The preponderance of colors merely shows us how and by what measures Caesar eludes his inner self, which makes him suspicious and forces him to have doubts. He "escapes into" the external world, seeking out "activity" as a means of forgetting himself. Perhaps he engages in sports; perhaps he plunges himself into discussions with his friends, which enable him to manifest and project his own uncertainty. Most likely he does both!

Furthermore, the mask interpretation found in the test reveals that some slightly compulsive force is effective in Caesar and that his attitude is somewhat rigid and stiff.

Therefore, considering that Caesar's experience balance is probably close to being an ambiequal one, we should expect to discover compulsive rather than hysteroid symptoms in him. We have established at least one of them: his inclination to brooding.

Since brooding is related to self-doubts, it is but a short distance from there to understand another of Caesar's character traits: his self-observation, which is most likely compulsive in nature.

Self-observation is evidenced in the fourth interpretation to Card I, "the eyes are evil." I have found through experience that children and adolescents who produce "eye" interpretations observe themselves painstakingly and in an almost paranoid manner, believing that others are observing them too. This phenomenon is also true of adult subjects, and it is quite certain that guilt feelings are fundamentally responsible for this personality trait.

"But everybody has guilt feelings!" Someone will interject. I agree. However, in children and adolescents who produce "eye" and "evil eye" responses in the form-interpretation test, guilt feelings have reached *overextensive* proportions. They usually have such force that they set in motion tendencies to atonement. These do not necessarily have to be conscious; their influence may find expression in unconscious reactions.

The question may be raised whether individuals with a true paranoid condition will be recognized in the form-interpretation test by their frequent use of "eye" and "evil eye" responses. I am told that this is to be expected. I would like to maintain, however, that this "logical" conclusion may be erroneous. For the material that supports my claims originated with normal children and adolescents—in other words, with non-psychotic subjects.

Let us again turn our attention to Caesar. It seems that his intellectual achievements depend mainly upon four emotional factors:

1. He demonstrates a clearly apparent inclination to anxiety. When Card II is presented to him, Caesar reveals this inclination for the first time by an exclamation. He reacts with a "hey!"; by producing a CF, "torn flesh," immediately afterwards, he indicates clearly that he has experienced a shock. Oberholzer[5] once gave a lecture in Bern during the thirties about the relationship between color shock and experience balance, in which he stated that, if a subject produces a CF or a pure C immediately following a color shock, he is inclined to manifest anxiety symptoms. Caesar belongs in this category.

2. Caesar has produced 2 ChF but no FCh. ChF are indicative of depressive ill-humor, which cannot be controlled by intellec-

---

[5] Hermann Rorschach's friend and collaborator.

tual measures. This means that, whenever Caesar is depressively distressed, his state of mind impedes his intellectual achievements. He is no longer open to reasoning, because his "ill humor" distracts him, consuming all his energies.

Correlated with the relatively too many S, ChF indicate that Caesar surrenders to morose moods, that he takes on a gloomy outlook. And by reminding ourselves of the presence of 2 CF, we see clearly that Caesar is easily irritated, easily hurt, and reacts with dejection to real or imaginary hurts.

3. Caesar succumbs to moods. In the test, CF are indicators for it, suggesting a mainly egocentric affectivity.

Moods too may impair intellectual achievement. Caesar reasons *according to his moods of the moment*. He is not *objective*, but lets himself be deceived by his moods. Guided by them, he thinks in an infantile manner and creates confabulations.

4. As we have indicated earlier, CF correspond with an affectivity that, although it is adaptable, is not adapted. Caesar needs his fellow men, his friends and companions for his own confirmation but he is unable to adapt himself sufficiently to them. Projectively, he feels "disappointed" in them. Caesar's relatively high H% indicates his longing for friendship and love. S show, however, that he has no faith in others. Some of the contents in Caesar's interpretations also disclose this attitude, as, for instance, in Card I/3: "It could also be a monster with raised fists. They are tremendous and knives are in them—the eyes are evil. . . ." Here projection becomes apparent, indicating a trait of distrustfulness.

Distrust creates reserved and cautious, hesitant behavior in Caesar. Such behavior is indicated by the fact that Caesar does not produce popular responses until the end of the first and third cards, thus reversing the sequence. Furthermore, we have observed that he sometimes produces two interpretations for the same blot portion, combining them with an "or."

Finally we should like to point out that Caesar may commit thefts. He possesses a "stealing tendency," for we find the "thieving syndrome" in the test. It is impossible to establish whether the stealing tendency is manifest or latent. In Caesar's interest, by adhering to the *"in dubio pro re"* principle, we assume that he does not steal. We shall take into consideration that he may be able to abreact his impulses by fantasy and that such impulses do not therefore have to become converted into actions. Caesar's inner attitude, expressed by kinesthesias, effects a constant control over his impulsive drives. His inner attitudes are more intensive than would seem, on the basis of the test's one M. For as we observed earlier, Caesar "represses" M. Moreover, Caesar is intelligent enough to realize the consequences he would have to face if he did steal and thus his intelligence too will fight against possible tendencies to steal.

When a subject perseveres in the form-interpretation test with some of the interpretations, the assumption may be made that he is not capable of detaching himself from certain thought processes after he has conceived them. As a rule, perseverations are hardly ever observed in people with normal intelligence. It surprises us to find that Caesar produces perseverations; we suspect that they are caused by a complex.

If we expect the form-interpretation test to provide us with clues about complexes—namely, pathogenic complexes—we are forced to lean upon experiences and analogies. Caution must be exercised, however, for findings have only probable validity. We are dealing here with nothing more than assumptions based on depth-psychological understanding; their reality value must be proven by other means. Nevertheless, such understanding may frequently furnish us with sudden insights into the subject's innermost behavior patterns and make it possible for us to characterize them.

Our assumptions are based upon our ability to recognize symbols and upon our knowledge of dream and daydream symbolism. But they are also founded upon the experience that we have been in a position to gather during very long practice with the test. Occasionally, we find that "individual interpretations" —in other words, such interpretations as are both original and of a kind that could not have been produced by any other than this particular subject—are correlated with certain wish-fulfillments, reaction formations against instinctive desires, and unconscious self-revelations. All these facts had already been recognized by Rorschach. In his *Psychodiagnostic,* he did not attach too much importance to the contents of interpretations. However, after his book had been published, he spoke of "complex responses"; he attempted to elucidate their meaning in later, for the most part unpublished diagnoses.

We shall apply this method to Caesar's test record.

One pertinent point has already been mentioned. Caesar's self-observation, a paranoid trait that causes him to feel as if other people are suspicious of him. We have also mentioned the guilt feelings in which this trait originates.

Now we are faced with a further problem. We must find out whether it will be possible to establish some of the underlying causes for these guilt feelings, or to discover how the subject rationalizes them. For if we had this knowledge, we could perhaps counteract such guilt feelings, insofar as they usually prevent the subject from fully developing his capacity for work.

When Card III is presented to him, Caesar stares at the dark blot. Some time passes (prolonged reaction time as an after-effect of shock) until the first response is produced. And this response contains something completely unexpected, unusual: "Something rotten with worms crawling out of it—or snakes." Later, perseverating, he once more interprets "worm-like configurations." And just as after the "monster" interpretation in Card I, there immediately follow the responses "men cut in two" and "without legs" (in Card I: ". . . and the feet have been cut off; it has only wooden legs").

Dream psychology has taught us that such sadomasochistic fantasies are the derivatives of infantile castration fantasies, which may be either passive or active. We have an inkling that the "something rotten with worms crawling out of it—or snakes" has its origin in sexual contexts, and may actually signify something that Caesar believes to be "rotten," and which he rejects; or else something that seems sinister and "gruesome" to him, such as worms and snakes.

Another complex or individual interpretation can now be added, the first response to Card I: "This looks like it had rained and there is a sooty oil spot from a car in the puddle."

Practical experience has proven that adolescents who produce responses that contain puddles, dirt, rot, waterpools, and running water usually masturbate quite excessively. Does Caesar belong to this category, too, and will his case confirm our previous experience?

Let us assume that we have guessed correctly.

Then Caesar must be suffering from guilt feelings that stem from masturbation, and from the fear that he may be injuring himself by his secret manipulations (castration anxieties) at the intellectual level. We chance here upon a belief than can be frequently encountered in individuals who do masturbate excessively: they believe that they may be destroying their mental capacities. Such auto-suggestion actually does lead to a reduction of intellectual performance. This is conceived as a "punishment," an atonement and an expiation. Thus, Caesar's deteriorating school performance could be traced back to guilt feelings resulting from masturbation.

If we wish to reverse Caesar's intellectual slowdown, we ought not to recommend tutoring or any such measures for him, but we must help him to fight energetically against his masturbatory activities.

However, at this point we are not yet certain whether our assumptions are valid and correspond with reality.

During an interview with the parents, something unexpected occurs. The mother verifies that she has recently found stains on Caesar's underclothing. As a former nurse, the woman is convinced that her son masturbates. Embarrassed, she did not want to talk about it with me, but is glad that I brought the subject up myself. The father states that, in the past, he too masturbated quite frequently and for a long time. Not until he was married did he succeed in controlling himself. It is his opinion that Caesar should be told that masturbation is not as dangerous as the boy probably thinks it is. He, the father, once reproached himself bitterly too, "nearly to the brink of suicide," believing that he would become stupid. Nevertheless, he later understood his error; despite his masturbation, he has managed to have his own business and to make it prosper. "It is going to be a rather ticklish business reassuring Caesar, yet I think it best if I talk to the youth," I say.

"*I* am going to do it!" asserts the father. It is the *parents'* duty, he says, and not the duty of third persons to inform their children about sex; this strengthens the confidence of children in their parents. Furthermore, the son should not feel that his parents do not have enough courage to speak to him about the subject.

The father's arguments seem sound. Thus it was decided that:

1. The father will enlighten Caesar about the relatively harmless nature of masturbation. The really dangerous aspects of it are remorse and the pangs of one's own conscience. Yet these serve no purpose.

2. The father will ask Caesar to control himself just once during a certain period of time—a week, perhaps—no matter how much the desire to masturbate may torment him. Caesar should be made to realize how happy he will be if he has once succeeded in denying himself the gratification of his desire. After a few weeks, Caesar could be induced to increase the requirements of weaning. Instead of abstaining once a week or once in two weeks (depending upon the frequency of previous occurrences), he should exercise control twice during that span of time.

3. In the name of "will-power training," the father will require that Caesar perform some task that is very much against his liking, every week. Such a task should not consist of something connected with school; it should rather be some chore around the house, something that Caesar dislikes doing.

The purpose of such activity is not "will-power training," but should supply Caesar with an opportunity to abreact his guilt feelings in a manner other than "becoming stupid." Thus atonement will be achieved by quite different means—by useful work, for instance. Of course, Caesar should not be told of this; otherwise the effectiveness of this measure would evaporate into thin air ("One grasps the purpose—and becomes upset!").

4. In order to strengthen Caesar's ego, one must not talk about his poor school work at all. If Caesar himself reports it, one would do well to simply acknowledge it without comment. On the other hand, no matter how insignificant, any other achievement of the boy that is not connected with school should

be valued. Appreciation should be shown by some remark, perhaps even by some small reward.

Two weeks later, the father reports that he has enlightened the boy. "And I did it in great detail!", boasts the father, "and with complete frankness!". *The father has informed his son that he too once masturbated quite excessively.* Nevertheless, as the son may see for himself, this fact did not prevent him from becoming successful and rising in economic status. In order to progress to such an advanced position, great mental effort was required; he, the father, had been quite capable of this, despite his masturbation.

Caesar promised his father to abstain from masturbation activities for *three weeks. As a reward he was promised some money as a gift.* Thereupon the father questioned his son closely every night as to whether Caesar had managed to resist masturbating during that particular day. Looking straight into his father's face, Caesar *assured him every single time that he had been successful.*

"The matter seems to be well in hand!", says the father. *"But now Caesar has begun to steal!"*

Caesar had stolen money from his mother in order to buy an electric locomotive, and he had stolen an automobile tire from his uncle, having found it in the latter's garage. Asked what kind of work Caesar has been doing that is supposed to "train his will-power," the father reports that he has completely forgotten to assign work tasks to his son.

Thus we see that Caesar's father was totally unsuccessful in "enlightening" his son about masturbation.

He had approached the boy as a *frère et cochon* [a "brother in filth"], by confessing to him that he too had masturbated excessively. Also, he has *damaged the son's ego* by *"debasing"* himself in the boy's eyes. Formerly, Caesar had an "ideal" image of his father—a man who did not masturbate like himself. Now this living ideal image has been destroyed for the son. Furthermore, the father has demanded *too much* of the son, for nobody who is accustomed to frequent masturbation can suddenly cease completely for three weeks. Weaning must proceed slowly. It should be effected wisely, in small doses, and one must anticipate that nothing at all may be accomplished at first. Ultimately, the goal will be reached by repeated encouragement and patience on the part of educators.

Moreover, the father did not give Caesar an *opportunity to make amends,* which would have made it possible for him to reduce the unconscious part of his guilt feelings at regular intervals.

It is quite obvious that Caesar has brazenly *lied* to his father, in making him believe that he succeeded in suppressing the gratification of his desires for two weeks. That would have required superhuman efforts on his part.

In lying to his father, Caesar has further burdened his conscience. Most likely he began stealing because of his conscience's misguided reaction. The stealing tendencies that the Zulliger Test has uncovered in him have broken loose. It is interesting to note how Caesar has stolen.

He stole from his mother who, as he had learned from his father, was the one who had cured the latter of his masturbation. It is clear that, like the father, Caesar too would like to receive his mother's love in such amounts as to enable him to give up masturbation. In Caesar's unconscious mind, money equals love; since he does not obtain love voluntarily, he takes its symbol— money—and uses it to buy a toy locomotive. The father has model railroad trains. If no trips are embarked on, the trains are taken out on Sundays and put into motion. Now Caesar wants to have a locomotive like his father. Does this not mean that he identifies himself with his father? Indeed, the father himself has been instrumental in bringing about such an identification, by telling Caesar that he (the father) had once masturbated, just as the son does now! And what about the automobile tire that Caesar has taken from his uncle (an uncle is usually a father-image for the unconscious mind, a father substitute)? Like the locomotive, could not the tire too represent a male symbol for Caesar, a symbol of virility at the phallic level? In all probability, after having been submitted to a passive experience of his father's degradation, Caesar now brings the degradation unconsciously and actively to its completion: he takes a virility symbol away from his father (or from the father's substitute, his uncle), "castrating" the father. In many dreams, it has been established, a tire—which can become larger, increase in size, be inflated—may have the meaning of a phallic symbol.

At any rate, it is hardly fortuitous and a matter of indifference what and from whom the boy steals.

It is a well-known fact that very often stealing is essentially a substitute for masturbation. A similar (or the same) *anxiety-pleasure* sensation is experienced either when an act of stealing is carried out or when masturbation is practiced. In order to escape the pangs of his conscience, the thief abandons masturbation without giving up the anxiety-pleasure sensation that he derives from stealing. Thus stealing is frequently *compulsive* (neurotically conditioned *kleptomania*).

"What shall we do?", asks the greatly excited father. "Would not a good spanking be in order?"

"So as to discourage the boy!", the mother agrees.

"I most certainly do not want to excuse or belittle your son's misdeeds. But let us see first whether a punishment by spanking would really help your son; perhaps you have made certain mistakes in carrying out my recommendations!"

I succeeded in preventing a belated corporal punishment of the boy. It would hardly have promoted his further development, and would only have served the purpose of abreacting the parents' excited emotions.

Both parents have now realized that it has become necessary to take Caesar away from home for a longer period of time, placing him in a well-run special home for "nervous" children and adolescents.

Postscript: A year-and-a-half has passed since a "change of environment" was carried out. Caesar is doing well in his studies, and he has not stolen again. In addition to his school work, he builds models and works in the garden, or in the little forest that belongs to the home. He has made new friends, and has informed the director that he does not masturbate more than once a week now. Considering that at home he used to masturbate six and more times during the same time interval, this state of affairs may certainly be regarded as improvement. Progress has not been achieved by intimidation and force. Neither drugs (tranquilizers) nor actual psychotherapy have been employed—nothing but "educational methods," effecting reassurance. Education of this kind includes the fact that the total environment effects a comforting influence.

11. *Karl Kuhn,* 8 years old.

Mrs. Kuhn, a 38-year-old wife of a civil servant, brings her oldest son, Karl, 8 years old, for psychological counseling.

The problem is that the boy misbehaves; he is impolite, and aggressive toward his younger brother, who is 2 years his junior. On the other hand, he gets along well with his 2-year-old sister. Yet she cannot be entrusted to his care, for he might carelessly push her baby carriage right into the center of traffic.

In school, Karl does not get along well with his classmates. Perhaps they are to blame too, for they tease him about his red hair, and then he beats them up.

Karl's birth was normal. He had no unusual children's diseases; he did not have whooping cough. There is no adverse heredity and the family physician confirms the boy's good health.

Karl is of medium height; he is chubby and looks well-nourished; he is rosy-cheeked, alert. He does not look "unhappy," yet he is rather serious.

Mrs. Kuhn, who is a tall and beautiful woman, gives the impression of being worried, depressed, and disappointed. "One would like to do one's best for the children, to raise them properly. I do not understand Karl; I have the feeling that he eludes me. He is stubborn and he lies to me; for instance, when I call him and he claims not to have heard me, although he did hear me very well. The two other children are nice and do not present any problems in their upbringing. As parents, we try to treat them all exactly alike. Is it possible that Karl is jealous of his little brother? But in that case he should be jealous of his baby sister too; yet he is not! One does not know how to explain his ill manners, his negative traits. One also does not know whether or not one has made mistakes in raising him! The boy is a puzzle to me!" So says the mother, and her eyes have the look of a frightened deer. She is mistrustful and suspicious; at the same time, she is hoping to find help. She is resigned, rigid (and probably frigid).

The boy's manner is frank and he shows willingness. He finds a comfortable position when he sits down and stretches himself without embarrassment. He always seems glad when he has completed a test.

First the Zulliger Test, next the Bero, and finally the Duess Test (as a control test for the two others) are administered to Karl.

Zulliger Test

I.

An animal that has been taken
    apart .... FCh ➔ WF + A/anat; aggression
Clouds (left half, without AB 4/5) . ChF ➔ DF + cloud
Two horns (A 5/6) .... DF + Ad
of a bull, where the cows have
    their udders (meaning testicles)
    (FG 5/6) .... DdF + ad/sex

II.

"Oh!" (as he relinquishes the card.
    He does not remember having
    called out "oh!"; he denies it)
"This is more difficult!" (Pro-
    longed reaction time) .... shock!
c One half of a tree root (orange
    area) .... DCF pl
  A bone .... SF − obj/anat
a A bush that has not yet been cut
    (green area) .... DFC pl aggression
    or grass tufts .... DFC pl "or"
(Sighs). "Nothing more!"

III.

c A dragonfly, a red one; but such
    dragon-flies do not exist (red
    area, c) .... DF + A P obj criticism
d One half of a peacock (large upper
    dark part, portion extending
    from the "hand touching the

butterfly" to the "outstretched
arm"), one can see that he is
just spreading his tail .... DdF — Ad confabulation
Two witches raising their arm.
Their legs have .... WM + H P (O)
been torn off .... DF + Hd aggression
their children (outer red area)
are jumping around .... DM + H P O/individual
they wear odd hats, they act like
clowns because they are afraid .. DdF + obj
c A centipede with a tail (smaller
dark portion) crawling out from
the witch (laughs) .... DF ± A individual combination,
complex interpretation

Duration: 12 minutes

Bero

I.

c Cathedral steeples in Zürich
(center top portion, the
"squirrels") .... DF ± arch O
a Two bears standing there and
tearing something apart .... WM + A P aggression

II.

Two gnomes are dancing (red
inner area); the color is not right DM + H P obj criticism
Animal halves (dark area) .... DF ± Ad O aggression

III.

If this were still black (points to
the discontinued black portion),
these would be women .... WF + H (P) M repression
Two red sheep, jumping; but
sheep are not red (red area, c) .. DF ± A obj criticism
A baby (outer red area) .... DdF — H

IV.

A bell (gray center portion, lower
periphery) .... DdF + obj
A person taking a bath .... DdMs H P

V.

A flying swallow .... WF + A P

A worm crawling out of a hole
(outer left and right portions) .. DdF + A individual

A castle tower (top center portion,
the "head" of the "swallow") ... DF + arch

VI.

A fairytale cloud with a face; it
has a .... WChF cloud
terrible nose and an open mouth S → DF + Hd

A king in a robe .... WM + H O

VII.

Water squirts from faucets (top
portion) .... DdF + water O

A waterfall; a water spray crashes
over a rock wall into the valley
(left half portion) .... DF(C) nat O (S)

VIII.

c Two tigers (orange area) .... DFC A

Two animals (red area) .... DF + A P

Two pigs (yellow area) .... DF ± A (perhaps FC)

The head of an owl (gray area) ... DF − Ad

IX.

c A dragonfly with 4 wings (purple
and blue areas) .... DF + A

A bird (brown area) .... DF + A

A very tiny bird is sitting here
(orange area) .... DF + A

X.

"Well, the last one—thank you
very much!"

Two clouds (outer blue-gray area) . DCF clouds

Two animals shake hands with
each other (center orange area) . DMs A

Two green parrots (green center
area) .... DFC A

Two potatoes (brown area) ...... DCF pl/food

c-d A girl's face (within the blue area) . DdF + Hd

Duration: 16 minutes

370

Scores of the form-interpretation tests: Zulliger → Bero

W	= 2	5	F+	= 7	12	P	= 3	6
D	= 8	18	F—	= 2	2	O+	= 2	4
Dd	= 5	6	F±	= 1	4	H	= 2	5
S	= 1	(2)	M	= 2	3	Hd	= 1	2
F+%	= 75	77	Ms	= —	2	anat	= 2	—
A%	= 40	48	FC	= 2	2	sex	= 1	—
P%	= 20	20	CF	= 1	2	food	= —	1
O%	= 18	13	FCh	= 1	—	A	= 3	12
H%	= 40	27	ChF	= 1	1	Ad	= 3	2
			F(C)	= —	1	obj	= 2	1
						pl	= 3	(1)
Sequence:		orderly-loose		same		nat	= —	1
Experience balance:		2 M : 1½ C		3 : 3		cloud	= 1	2
Apperceptive type:		W—D—Dd—S		same		arch	= —	2
						water	= —	1

		Shocks = II	VIII and X
Time:	16/3	29/12	
Number of responses:	12 minutes	16 minutes	

In the Zulliger Test we find:
confabulation
individual interpretations, mother seen
  as a witch giving birth to a worm
"or"
In the Bero we find:
signs of fatigue,
  tendency to perseverations

In both tests we find:
aggression
object criticism
complex interpretations
M repression
a strong need for combination
good combinatory ability

Although the Zulliger Test is shorter than the Bero, it shows us the inner conflict that possesses the boy and causes him to misbehave, more graphically and clearly than the Bero does.

This should not be considered a depreciative statement with regard to the sensitivity of the Bero. It is possible that if the Bero had been used first and the Zulliger Test later, the Bero would have shown the subject's principal conflict more clearly, thus reversing the relationship.

However, the Zulliger Test's great sensitivity has become apparent once again.

Considering that the subject has produced both a direct (a bull's testicles) and an indirect (horns) sexual interpretation for the first card, we may draw the conclusion that sexual curiosity is present. From this point of view the very first interpretation becomes interesting, "an animal that has been taken apart." We assume that its contents contain fantasies centered around the mother's womb. We shall find out presently whether our assumption proves to be true. The very last response supplies us with this proof: "a centipede with a tail crawls out of the witch." Dream psychology has made us familiar with the usual meaning of "vermin"; it signifies siblings. The boy has been told about the facts of life: he knows that babies come out of the mother. In the Bero (Card V), "a worm comes out of a hole." This is a parallel interpretation to the last response on the Zulliger Test. Remembering also that Karl does not get along with his little brother, who is two years younger than he, and that consequently sibling rivalry is an obvious implication, we understand that vermin ("centipede with tail") and worm refer to the younger brother and that aggressive tendencies are at work in connection with the mother's womb ("What is in the mother's womb?" is the question, if we express emotional facts by verbal images and words).

But most revealing are some of the interpretations to Card III, succeeding the shock experienced in Card II: "Two witches raising their arm. Their legs have been torn off. Their children are jumping around. They wear odd hats, and act like clowns because they are afraid." Then follows the birth of a centipede with a tail, which represents a squirming male child.

Karl identifies himself with the two witch children who "act like clowns" because they are afraid. This really means that he himself is afraid and "acts" or plays the role of somebody he rather would not be ("clown"). In reality, this fully normal boy (see the test scores) "plays" at being mischievous, a problem child. He plays the role of being aggressively stubborn with his mother and he fights with his brother, in order to overcome his anxiety, which has been caused by his having been displaced by his brother from his position as the first-born and only child.

His misbehavior may thus be explained by his desire to become the focal point of his mother's interest, and he tries to achieve it by attacking his brother. The mother reacts by withdrawing her love from Karl ("the boy is a puzzle to me!"). She does not understand him and this makes him feel abandoned; the *complex d'abandon* thus becomes effective. It causes Karl to disobey anew and to become defiant. Thus, beginning with wanting her attention, Karl seeks to bind the mother to himself. A true *circulus vitiosus* is the result.

We realize that Karl is not alone to blame for his misbehavior, which he projects upon the school as well, by correlating the school situation with the home situation; there is also the mother who does not "understand" him, and thus forces him to take countermeasures.

It is readily apparent what our recommendation must be in this case. Before anything else, the mother and not her son, Karl, must submit to psychotherapeutic treatment. For as soon as her relationship with Karl has been set right, as soon as she "understands" Karl again, Karl will almost automatically change his attitude. His present incorrect "adaptation" is primarily a reaction to the mother who does not understand him.

When the mother learns to treat the boy more "normally," he too will behave differently, with more confidence and more naturally. He will be much less jealous of his brother than he is at present. His jealousy is mainly directed toward his brother, as the interpretation "a centipede with tail" clearly reveals. The boy is afraid that some more such "centipedes with tails" might crawl out of the "witch"; that is why he wants to know what is to be found in the mother's womb. In order for him to know, the womb must be "taken apart."

Why is Karl's jealousy less pronounced in his relationship to his little sister? Why does it manifest itself only when she is entrusted to his care? It is only when he is supposed to take care of her that he endangers her by carelessly exposing her to traffic.

One could suggest that Karl expends all his jealousy on his brother, so that there is hardly anything left for his sister. Moreover, he has made the observation that his little sister does not look like himself, that she is a female human being, like the mother whose womb is of such great interest to him. His little sister is for Karl an object that may serve to satisfy his sexual curiosity. Thus, she is "valuable" to him, he needs her; it is different with her than with his brother. Since he may benefit from his little sister, he hates her less than he does his male competitor, who is vying with him for the parents' love.

The Bero shows us Karl's relationship to his father more clearly than the Zulliger Test. The father is a "king in a robe" (Card VI), a "fairytale cloud with a face, a terrible nose, and an open mouth" (Card VI). Karl could hardly have projected more unmistakably his ambivalent attitude toward his father and the latter's remoteness with respect to himself. (The father is a lawyer; he does not stop talking, even when he is at home, and it almost appears as if the son had good reason to interpret a face with an open mouth.)

It has often been observed (and not only by myself) that the Zulliger Test stimulates complex and individual interpretations. In the case at hand, they are numerous. If one is capable of "seeing through them," one can understand that the boy's inner conflicts and his outward behavior as a "problem" child are the results of a child-parent conflict. A test lasting 12 minutes has brought us this striking revelation.

The Duess Test[6] confirms these results. Here the middle child is buried (Fable 4), and Karl's little brother is the middle child within the family. Defiance against the mother becomes apparent in Fables 1, 2, and 3, while the desires of which the mother is the object are revealed in Fable 9. Fables 5, 6, and 7 uncover the feelings of guilt and anxiety that beset the boy. His attitude toward his father is disclosed in Fable 8. The boy's acquiescence to his mother's desires—his being in part obedient and in part defiant—is expressed in Fable 7, as well as in Fable 3.

12. *Armin Halder,* 10½ years old.

The mother, Mrs. Halder, brings her 10½-year-old son to be examined, because he has been failing almost completely in his school work, has constant fights with his classmates (although he never defends himself, and acts "like a girl," despite his considerable physical prowess).

[6] This consists of 10 fables, which must be completed by the subject; the subject projects his conscious or unconscious conflicts onto the fables. They have been structured with that in mind.

Mrs. Halder would like to know:

What is Armin's intellectual ability?

Why is it that he gets into fights so much and why does he not defend himself? Why does he behave in such a passive manner?

What educational methods should be employed to affect a more "manly" behavior on Armin's part?

To begin with, we gather some anamnestic information. Armin is the first-born child in the Halder family. A brother was born two years after him. From the first, he got along excellently with his brother and has never shown any jealousy of him. Armin has never presented any educational problems. He has always been obedient, well-behaved, well-mannered; he was a "nice" boy, one never had to punish him. His birth was normal, and he was breast-fed for one year. Toilet-training was very easily effected. But Armin has always been short of stature and (even today) easily susceptible to illness. According to the doctor's certificate, he is completely healthy in every way—but he is short.

In passing, the mother mentions the following incident: "When Armin was two years old, he experienced a bomb attack. At that time, he was staying with his grandmother. She had just taken the little boy from his carriage when a bomb made a direct hit on the house. It was like a miracle; although an open cabinet fell on the grandmother, who was holding the child in her arms, both escaped injury. When the woman lifted the cabinet, she could see above her the sky; underneath, she was looking through smoke and fire into a big hole that extended to the basement. Only splinters remained of the crib; the bomb had fallen right through it. Both the grandmother and we, the parents, feel that Armin has received a second lease on life. That is why we feel that he must be given special care; as a result, we may have spoiled him a bit too much! Of course, we have always avoided speaking about this terrible incident in front of Armin. Since he was only two years old, he hardly realized what happened, although he screamed loudly at the time. At any rate, he has forgotten the occurrence and it could not have anything to do with his behavior!"

In the following, we record the scores of the Zulliger, the

Bero, and the Ro Tests. They were administered to the boy in rapid order so as to find out why he tires so easily (Table 10).

Let us first orient ourselves about Armin's *innate intelligence*.

TABLE 10

Armin Halder, 10½ years old
Scores of the three form interpretation tests: Zulliger Test ➔ Bero ➔ Ro

	Time:		4 minutes	11 minutes	8 minutes
	Number of responses:	16/4		42/16	30/13
DW	= 1	1	1	F = 13(—3) 28(—7) 18(—5)		
W	= 3	5	4	M = 1 1 2		
D	= 11	29	23	MC = — 1 —		
Dd	= 1	7	1	FC = (1) 2 3		
S	= (1)	(1)	—	CF = 2 6 7		
F+%	= 73	75	72	C = 1 1 —		
A%	= 55	59	53	FCh = 1 1 (1)		
P%	= 13	19	20	ChF = 1 1 —		
O%	= 5	4	3	Ch = 1 — —		
P	= 2	8	6	F(C) = 1 — —		
O	= 1	2	1			

Sequence:	orderly-loose, tendency to inversion	same	same
Experience balance:	1 M : 3½ C	2 : 8½	2 : 7½
Apperceptive type:	DW — W — D — Dd	same	same

Shocks	in Card II	II/VIII	II/VIII
	followed by CF (red)	"	"

H	= 1	1	1	A = 6	17	12
Hd	= —	2	1	Ad = 3	8	4
anat	= 1	2(6)	1(2)	obj = 2	1	3
blood	= —	1	1	pl = —	1	2
clothing	= —	—	—	nat = —	3	1
				geog = 2	2	1
				cloud = 2	2	3

Infantile abstractions and interpretations	"	"
Perseverations	"	"
Diminutives and double diminutives[7]	"	"
White as color	"	"
Descriptions	"	"
Last interpretation for Card III: "fire and smoke"	—	—

[7] For instance, III, Zulliger Test, red outer area: "Two small, small jumping boys."

The reaction time is greatly shortened. Armin takes considerable pleasure in expressing himself, but his statements are not based upon accurate observations and reasoning. On the contrary, he surrenders himself to his strong need to chatter. As represented in the test by DW, his confabulatory tendencies become apparent. The slightly loose sequence implies that Armin's thinking lacks discipline. The long content column proves that Armin has manifold and varied interests—too many, perhaps—and these prevent him from concentrating properly. It may be assumed that the boy is still—fully or in part—at the developmental level of early childhood. Taking into account the DW, their contents and the dainty diminutives, we are justified in inferring that the 10-year-old Armin is still at the "fairy-tale" level of three- to seven-year-old children. He has not yet reached the "reality age" of eight- to nine-year-old youngsters. Armin's tendency towards perseverations, along with the somewhat increased A%, indicate an inclination to laziness. However, this does not prevent the boy from possessing a certain intellectual ambition, expressed here by anat. On the other hand, anat may also suggest a certain attitude of anxiety. Inverse sequence indicates it, too. Since, as we have observed, Armin is a "chatterer," his anxiety and caution (anat and inverse sequence) are probably correlated with the emotional rather than with the intellectual area. If, in addition to an inverse sequence, the form-interpretation test contains anatomic responses, then the subjects have hypochondriacal traits. They are the people who see health hazards lurking everywhere.

With this, we have touched upon personality characteristics. Surveying the test, our attention is first of all attracted by Armin's supersensitivity. We see it when we examine the color column and find that he interprets white as color. If the dilation toward color, the many CF and C were taken into consideration, then we would come to the conclusion that Armin is a carefree and cheerful, egocentric, moody, excitable and motorically easily irritable boy. But the lack of S contradicts this. There are but slight traces of S, and the absence of S indicates that aggressiveness is inhibited (S and CF would be signs of aggression). Shocks also testify to the fact that inhibitions, impediments, and repressions exist, and lead us to believe that an infantile neurosis may be present. Since experience balance is clearly extratensive and since, each time following a color shock in Card II, a red blot is interpreted as CF, we may infer that Armin is inclined to a hysteria-like conversion of his anxieties. This could explain his susceptibility to sickness. Chiaroscuro responses disclose the forces that are inhibiting and diluting affectivity. They bestow a "seriousness" on Armin that has nothing childish about it; they are also related to his hypochondria, confirming it. Furthermore, Armin's tendency to dilute his emotions finds its expression in descriptions. In real life situations, subjects who substitute descriptions for interpretations are avoiding exposure to experience, by escaping into comtemplation in order not to become emotionally involved.

Since Armin interprets white as a color, we may suspect that he attempts to suppress his sensitivity (and aggression), that he tries to dissimulate it.

Thus, we see before us a boy of average ability. While he is still very childish for his age, he is alert and shows many interests, although he is not capable of concentrating too well and his mind is not well-disciplined. He is unaggressive, well-behaved, sensitive, and easily hurt. His affectivity has remained on an infantile level, alternating between impulsive cheerfulness and depressive "seriousness."

These are the data that we may establish by the test's technique. This much we are able to understand without any difficulty.

Yet our knowledge about the *dynamic structure* of the subject's personality traits, behavior forms, defects of character and positive qualities is still incomplete. We would like to comprehend all the complex relationships, the mutual interplay of forces, the effective causes, the control mechanisms, and the entire living structure (not only the wooden framework).

I shall attempt to attain such knowledge to the greatest possible extent.

Examining Armin Halder's test in order to determine his character traits, our attention had been attracted by his *hypersensitivity*. This quality is an innate one; it has been with him "from the cradle."

378

Innate potentialities may either grow in strength or else become inhibited, depending upon accidental and environmental influences; or they may be trained to remain "latent."

At any rate, as we may surmise in accordance with the mother's statements, development was not thwarted in Armin.

As a rule, hypersensitivity reflects an intensive need for *security* and *love*. In Armin's case, for many reasons this need has been sufficiently satisfied. Since the child was relatively small, special attention has been paid to his care. In addition, Armin has always been susceptible to illness—a susceptibility that probably originated in his being pampered by his mother, because he was her first-born child, as well as by his grandmother. Particularly after the bomb attack, the child has been coddled because he was seemingly reborn: he had been given life for a second time through a miracle performed by God, and this imposed upon those around him special duties toward him.

Being raised with overindulgence and pampering probably caused him to become *hypersensitive with regard to the possible loss of love*. In order to secure love, in order not to have to face the unpleasantness of losing it, the little boy early developed a tendency to please his grandmother, his mother, etc. How could he do it?

He could do it successfully by behaving in a manner expected of him. He made every effort to be well-behaved, well-mannered, and obedient; he catered to the wishes and decisions of those who were in charge of him. Thereby he could buy their love. In order to accomplish such a task, he had to suppress the impulses of defiance and aggression that every child possesses, and which he displays during his infancy and at some later stages. He had to keep these impulses from becoming manifest.

What happens if the tension level of needs is not reduced—in other words, if they cannot be discharged, because of motor innervation? The tension turns inward, it extends to one's own self; the ego, sensing this threatening danger, reacts with anxiety. It does this, in particular, whenever aggressive tendencies are turned inward, for these tendencies threaten one's existence to a degree that is hardly reached by anything else.

Furthermore, Armin repressed his aggression in order to avoid *guilt feelings* toward his undeniably kindly grandmother, and toward all the other people who raised him—especially his mother.

If inhibited aggression, anxiety, and impending guilt feelings endanger the ego, something must be done by the mental mechanism to control these forces. It is aggression that occupies the focal position. Once it is turned inward, its controlling nature is changed, so to speak. In a masochistic conversion, it now becomes *"pleasurable"; enjoyment of pain* results. As soon as an outlet into masochism has been constituted, aggression no longer triggers anxiety. It provides pleasure, since anxiety itself provides pleasure, and guilt feelings are now directly gratified by pain before they even develop. Thus they are no longer experienced.

The *crippling of Armin's "initiative,"* his passivity, and everything else that his mother calls "effeminate"—all this is rooted in his masochism.

As a rule, masochistic children are found out by their companions: they usually invite the aggression of their friends. "The weak are punished for their weakness." Thus we can understand why Armin quarrels all the time, and why he does not defend himself. He *cannot* defend himself, for secretly what he longs for are the pleasures of defeat.

Let us return to the bomb attack. Armin's mother assumes that it did not leave any traces on the little boy. However, his loud screaming after the falling of the bomb is proof that the incident frightened Armin very much indeed. Are we mistaken in assuming that the bomb attack not only moved the people who take care of Armin to greater affection and more loving attention toward him, but also increased the boy's own need for protection and love? Is it too far-fetched to think that the incident had a traumatic influence upon Armin? He has not absorbed it properly even yet. Could the last interpretation of the Zulliger Test, "fire and smoke," be a complex and individual response, indicating a faint recollection of the experience that once took place? Can this faint recollection be termed a breakthrough of a forgotten, "repressed" context?

If this is the case, then we have found the missing critical moment in Armin's developmental history. We may now assert that prior to the frightening experience the boy's development proceeded quite normally. Not until after this happened, did the increased and endangering coddling and overindulgence begin. It was at this point too that Armin's increased need for protection and love evolved and commenced to function.

Shortly after the bomb attack, the 2-year old had to face another event which probably affected the normal process of his development, the *birth of a baby brother.*

We know how first-born children normally react to later-born siblings: they are jealous of their "competitors." It is strange that Armin was able to reconcile himself immediately to his rival. We have to ask ourselves what could have happened in him at this moment. The answer is that Armin *identified* himself with his younger brother, in order to avoid being aggressive toward him. Because of this identification, an *arrest of development* took place, appearing in the tests as the (relative) "infantilism" that is so clearly observable in Armin. The identification with his younger brother manifests itself not only in the boy's physical retardation, but also in a mental and intellectual retardation of two to three years.

Finally, it is not surprising that Armin reacts in a hysterialike manner. Early in life he learned that, whenever he is sick, he is treated with special attention and loving care. Therefore, all he needs is to be ill, in order to invite increased attention and love; it is evident that "illness" is profitable for him. Moreover, hysterialike reactions are in accordance with his masochistic tendency: they produce an immediate autistic gain, which is attained by being sick.

Undoubtedly the boy needs psychotherapeutic treatment. It would probably help him to relive the frightening bomb-attack experience, as well as the birth of his younger brother, his appearance on the scene.

But the mother too needs psychotherapeutic treatment—for she must learn to handle Armin differently, more normally, without endangering him any further. She too has not properly integrated the bomb attack incident involving her eldest son. These then were the recommendations made to the mother.

18. Various Cases

A. VOCATIONAL GUIDANCE

Some time ago, *Joseph Thommen,* 17 years old (see Table 1), was able to enter junior high school without any difficulty. However, at that time he had been very well prepared for the examination by his elementary-school teacher. When the boy was attending the first grade of junior high school, he could not keep the same top position in the class that he had once held in elementary school, and he was disappointed—especially since his parents insisted that he should work constantly, and expected good grades and report cards from him. Later on, the boy succeeded in being promoted to the senior division of a public high school. Once there, however, he did even worse than in junior high school. The boy declared that school "stank"; the teachers complained that he was not industrious enough.

Consequently, his father enrolled Joseph in a private high school with only a few students. The father thought that in a smaller school the pupils were bound to be given individual attention in class, and that this would guarantee much better progress for each student. But Joseph had fallen in with companions who made it their aim to tease and irritate the teachers, and he took part in their mischief with childish pleasure. His school work deteriorated; when, at the end of his junior high school year, his report card specified that his promotion to the next grade was uncertain, his parents decided to take their Joseph out of school and let him have an extra year because they thought him still "immature." The boy was to study French and then choose some practical vocational training.

A place was found for Joseph in the vicinity of Lausanne. Commuting by bus from his place of work, he could easily attend the courses given by the city's commercial association.

However, although he was very big and strong, physical work proved very difficult for him. In the evening he was tired and sleepy; he frequently fell asleep during his evening classes, and both his teachers and fellow-students made fun of him. After three months, he suddenly appeared at his parents' house. He had run away, hitch-hiking home, and he did not not know what to do next. As far as he was concerned, he knew only that under no circumstances would he return to his job.

Apparently, he had no vocational aspirations.

The parents were disconcerted. A family dispute ensued. Since the father had a friend who was a horse trader, Joeseph was temporarily placed with him as a voluntary worker. He loved horses, and enjoyed taking care of them; yet he had no intention of spending his life being a horse-trader.

He was persuaded to resort to vocational guidance in order to establish his capabilities.

ANAMNESTIC DATA

Joseph's mother was already 40 years old when she married. Until then, she had spent her life holding a position as a secretary with an art firm. In addition, she had occupied herself writing. The father was a manager in a trade organization, and in good financial circumstances. He had been married once before, but his first wife had died young. They had had no children. For many years Mr. Thommen had led the life of a widower; he was 10 years older than his second wife. The marriage turned out well, and then Joseph came along and remained an only child.

For three years during his early childhood, Joseph was cared for exclusively by his mother. He was breast-fed for eight months. At the time of his weaning, Joseph reacted with feeding difficulties; he went on a hunger strike. The doctor recommended that he be permitted to go hungry, and very soon the feeding problem disappeared. Joseph developed to the full satisfaction of his parents. He was a bit whiny, perhaps, and willful. Also, if something did not go his way, he gave up quickly.

' When Joseph was three years old, his mother decided to take up her professional career again; since then, she has occupied an advanced position in a publishing house. Her son has been left in the care of a maid who loves him, and who has worked in the house ever since he was born.

Zulliger Test

The subject gives his responses hesitantly. From time to time, he looks at the examiner swiftly and with distrust.

Beginning: 2:30 P.M.

Card I.

An animal, some fur animal	FCh → WF + A
An X-ray	ChF → WF ± X-ray anat
A guinea pig full of food, sitting there, spreading itself out, crouching	WM + A O flexor kinesthesia individual interpretation
An old man with a long beard, seen from above, walks bent over a cane (darker area within gray area, left lower portion)	DM + H O flexor kinesthesia
b Part of a map, a shore landscape (2/3 D E F G)	DF — geog
a A tropical butterfly, a moth variety (center dark portion)	DFC A black as color

Card II.

(Hesitates for a long time. "Are all the cards in color from now on?")	shock
A meat-eating plant	WCF pl O aggression individual interpretation (particularizes)
on top, there is the flower (red area)	DCF pl
next to it are the leaves	DCF pl
on the bottom is the clump of soil in which the plant grows ...	DCF nat

384

The green could also be a cactus .. DFC pl
The red could also be two people,
women or men, kissing each
other .... DM + H O "or"

Card III.

Two men or women dancing with
each other .... WM + H P O "or" combinatory
                                           perseveration tendency
on the outside in one of their hands
they carry puppets or Teddybears DM + toy obj "or"
in the other hand they carry flower
bouquets .... DCF pl
c Two arms with open hands (top
portion) .... DF + Hd, tendency F(C)
                                                  End: 2:44 P.M.

In response to inquiry:
    I. "A moth, because it is black in color."
    II. "Meat-eating plant: well, it is somehow dangerous because of
        the impression it creates by its colors—threatening, suspicious."
    II. and III. "One does not know whether these are men or
        women, one only knows that they are affectionate toward each
        other."

                                     Beginning: 2:45 P.M.

Rorschach Test

I.

A kind of coat-of-arms, because of
the two eagles on its side ...... DWF — heraldry

II.

Two prize fighters, either at the be-
ginning or at the end of a fight WM + H aggression, "or"

III.

Two Negro women who want to
cook but the fire went out ...... WMFC H P O
c Two people back to back to each
other, they want to extend their
hands to each other over their
heads .... WM + H O individual
                                     interpretation

IV.

c A bat .... FCh → WF + A P
Two camel heads (outer portion) DF + Ad

V.

∧> ∨ <∧ .... Ch shock?
A hare (center portion) .... DF + A
                               (WF + AP is absent)

VI.

c A leaf .... DF + pl
On the bottom there is a small,
  frayed leaf .... DF + pl perseveration

VII.

Two girls with pony-tail hairdos are
  bowing to each other .... WM + H O flexor kinesthesia
Two men or women carrying some-
  thing heavy on their heads ..... MW + H O individual
                                interpretation "or" flexor
                                kinesthesia

VIII.

∧ > < ∧ (hesitates) .... color shock
c A colored shirt (red-orange center
  area) .... DFC clothing
d A cat (outer red area) .... DF + A P

IX.

A pale face looking out from behind a bush (S is the face) ..... SWCF Hd O

X.

Cave painting made by primitive
  men .... WCF painting O
Two of them have buds (gray area,
  a part of the center portion) .... DdF + pl

                                     End: 3:08 P.M.

In response to inquiry:

    II. "One does not know whether the prize fighters have started
      their fight or have just finished it; this is just an impression."
   III. "There is no fire; there is only something like a pot there."
      "These two people, they do not move naturally."
    V. "No, I cannot see a bat or a butterfly!" (in answer to the
      question of whether he had seen them).

   VII. "One does not know for sure whether these are men or women."

  VIII. "There are such men's shirts with many colors. I myself have a few of them. They could also be lady's blouses."

    IX. "As if hiding—perhaps it is somebody who did something wrong."

     X. "I have seen such pictures of cave paintings; my father brought home a book about them."

DISCUSSION OF THE TEST RESULTS

Zulliger Test

Prolonged reaction time	The subject does not enjoy oral expression too much.
In addition, many M High F+% A good W in Card II W type	A rather reserved, thoughtful individual who labors and absorbs inwardly. He is strongly introverted; his intellectual level is superior; his intelligence is quite high, and he has creative abilities. He is capable of organizing, has a pronounced talent for organization. He has an intense need for expansion and recognition.
W—M type High O% Anat and geog	He is generous and has intuition; his perception is accurate and he has many original ideas. He is inventive and has a certain amount of intellectual ambition.
Apperceptive type and M	His thinking is for the most part concrete. He is not a theoretician; it is difficult for him to think in the abstract; he "observes" more than he "thinks" (deduces); his thinking is of a kind that is characteristic of an individual with artistic ability. He is artistically talented.
D added	He is also gifted "practically"; he is good with his hands, and he must be an apperceptive type.
High F+% Detailed enumeration and toy interpretation "or"	On the one hand, he possesses the ability to judge reality accurately; on the other hand, he is still not completely grown up: he is infantile, immature, and somewhat play-

A% is too low

ful. Also, he is unsure of himself, slightly disoriented and uncertain in his judgments; he wants to escape from everything that is tying him down and wishes to keep the door open, in order not to commit himself, not to "bind" himself by his statements.

He is not altogether capable of forming stereotyped thought-processes. He suffers from a certain impairment of his powers of concentration, because he very quickly surrenders every train of thought, in order to take up new ideas.

Prolonged reaction time

These new ideas he then examines, considering them from all sides before formulating them. He hesitates when he makes statements (because of inner uncertainty).

Many W and relatively few responses

His qualitative ambition is much greater than his quantitative ambition.

Many H, high H%, and many pl

He is strongly attached to all that is human. He has a need for interhuman relationships, but he also has a strong feeling for nature.

M and H%

He seeks friendship, but is selective when it comes to making friends. Once he has found friends, however, he is loyal and warm. His friendships are permanent, not passing. His emotions are more intensive than extensive.

CF

But *intense* emotions and impulses also move him. They are not always objective; sometimes they are exaggerated and sudden.

M, CF, and FC in their relationship to abstract perceptions

He is definitely a *musing* individual; depressive impulses are familiar to him; he tends to

FCh
ChF

surrender to them passively, to let himself slide into depression. He

388

	does not offer enough active resistance to his depressive moods.
ChF and M	He is altogether "soft," lacking a certain necessary toughness, even with regard to himself. He tends to give up quickly, to quit in the face of difficulty; although he possesses
Aggression	aggressive properties in a sufficient measure,
Absence of S	he expresses his aggression by a rather passive defiance and by an indifference that is underlined by defiance, as well as by hidden criticism, rather than by open criticism—certainly not by blows. He escapes; a (defiant) flight reaction is typical of him rather than defense by a fist fight.
Perseveration tendency and M, flexor kinesthesias CF, FC	Furthermore, it is characteristic of this "soft," probably somewhat overindulged young man, that despite his high intelligence he travels along the road of least resistance because he is slightly "lazy."
	He is largely involved in himself and autistic. On the other hand, he is willing to adapt himself; he is skillful in adaptation, and readily capable of establishing contact with others.
Kinesthesias and colors	while he establishes contact easily, he preserves his distance.
F (C)	He has a sense for even slight subtleties. He is a visual type; his emotional reactions are quick and he feels acutely; he is sensible and sensitive.
Color shock and introversive experience balance	Neurotic repressions and mechanisms are probably in effect. A psychasthenic state may be present. A mixture of hysteric and compulsive symptoms could appear. These compulsive symptoms would then be found at the mental level rather than at the motoric level.

Neurosis and immaturity

We are probably dealing here with a puberty neurosis.

"Men or women being affectionate with each other"

The subject has not yet made up his mind as to his sex; he has a strong bisexual orientation. Emotionally, he still has strong homosexual traits.

Meat-eating plant is "dangerous, suspicious"

In considering the "meat-eating plant," we may suspect that the young man's development *could* take a sexually abnormal turn. There is danger of homosexuality and he seems to sense it, trying to ward it off. The youth's homosexual development is supported by his passive and effeminate attitude.

CF

These suggest that the subject is emotionally not well adapted. He may succumb to moods, as well as to sudden emotional breakthroughs.

And introversive experience balance

In general, his behavior is dominated by inner forces. He behaves calmly and with restraint. Introversion stabilizes his impulsive tendencies. Emotions are dealt with by imagination, instead of finding a release at the motility level.

Aggression

There is therefore hardly any breakthrough of aggression. But this is to be expected, for if aggression is prevented from becoming effective, enterprise and "initiative" become paralyzed. Thus, aggression turns inward, against one's own self, and passive and masochistic personality traits develop as a result.

W type and neurosis and individual interpretations, both of which are concerned with food

He has a strong oral fixation, and is therefore verbally gifted. His many M suggest language ability (a *sense for language*); because of CF, he also possesses *language* skills.

Individual interpretations only

Only people with original ideas produce them. If their forms are accurately perceived, then their thinking is creative; if their forms

390

are poorly perceived, then their thinking is aberrant. In Joseph's case, both individual interpretations are accurately perceived. Emotionally, he is not well enough adapted to reality, but his thinking is original.

High O% but too few P

Rorschach Test
Comparison with the Zulliger Test

The two tests agree:
in the Rorschach Test, the reaction time is prolonged, too;
the number of responses is small;
W type is well pronounced;
the number of M is large.
There are more CF than FC,
there is an FCh too;
F+% is exactly the same;
A% and P% are too low;
both O% and H% are high.
There is a marked color shock;
experience balance is introversive;
there is a rather large number of plant interpretations;
sequence remains orderly;
individual interpretations occur in both tests.

DIFFERENCES

In the Rorschach Test we see even more clearly than in the Zulliger Test that the subject turns his aggression inward. He incorporates the S into W; he "composes" it with the corresponding W, it does not appear separately.

We observe in the Zulliger Test that the subject's playful thinking is expressed by a toy interpretation. In the Ro, it is expressed by a DW (infantile, prelogical thinking).

Surprisingly, we encounter a Dd in the Ro. We must interpret its appearance as a symptom of fatigue, because several other signs that go in the same direction are present. Thus, the subject now needs 23 minutes for 16 responses, while in the Zulliger Test he has produced an equally large number of responses in 14 minutes. There are no anatomic and geographic responses any more in the Ro. What does all this mean? When the subject is tired, he can afford to be pedantic (Dd); his ap-

TABLE 1

Scoring
Subject: Joseph Thommen

	R		Z
DW	= 1		
SW	= 1	⎫ 9	
WS	= 7	⎭	
W	=		5
D	=		11
Dd	=		6
DdD	=		1
Do	=		
S	=		

F+%	= 87		87
A%	= 25		20 about
P%	= 18		6
O%	= 36		25
anat%	= −		6
H%	= 43		31

Sequence: orderly
Experience balance: 5 M : 6 C[1]
Apperceptive type: W — D
Remarks:

Z
orderly
particularization
individual response
perseveration tendency
toy

Time:	Number of responses:			
	Z		R	
F+	= 4 (−0.5)		8 (−1)	
F−	=			
F±	=			
M	= 5		4	⎫
MC	=		1	⎬ 5
MCh	=			⎭
Ms	=			
FC	= 2		1	
CF	= 5		2	
C	=			
FCh	= 1		1	
ChF	= 1			
Ch	=			
F(C)	= tendency			
CCh	=			
ChF	=			

R
orderly
5 : 2½
W — D

R
aggression
"or"
individual response
perseveration tendency
WFAP at V absent

Time:	14 minutes	23 minutes		
Number of responses:	16/6	16/5		
		Z		R
P	O =	1	=	3
	O =	4	=	6
H	=	3	=	5
Hd	=	1	=	1
anat	=		=	
sex	=		=	
scene	=		=	
blood	=		=	
clothing	=		=	1
food	=		=	
A	=	3	=	3
Ad	=	1	=	1
obj	=	1	=	
pl	=	5	=	4
nat	=	1	=	
geog	=	1	=	
others	=		=	2

		Z		R
Red shock	=	+		
Color shock	=	+	=	+
Chiaroscuro shock	=		=	?

individual response
"or" / aggression
perseveration tendency
WFAP at V absent

[1] Corrected experience balance = 5 M : 3 C (if one subtracts the 3 CF of particularization in Card II)

perceptive type may change and turn into a W—D type; he may take to seeing problems where there are none. As in the Zulliger Test, we again find neurotic brooding (its symptom is compulsive *thinking*, not compulsive *behavior*). Intellectual and school ambition (anat and geog) diminish when the subject is tired. All his interest in any subject decreases (although the testing time is prolonged, the same number of responses is produced as previously).

The comparison between the Zulliger Test and the Ro shows clearly that, mentally, the subject tires easily. It is difficult, frequently impossible, to establish this fact on the basis of just one form-interpretation test. Looking over Joseph's Zulliger Test, we see that the number of responses decreases in Card III, which is a sign of fatigue, too. The Ro confirms this finding.

Both F (C) and ChF, which occur in the Zulliger Test, are absent in the Ro. When Joseph is tired, he is less capable of experiencing slight emotional subtleties than when he is fresh and fully conscious of his experiences. One of Joseph's essential personality traits is not revealed in the Ro—namely, his letting himself go while in a depression, his unhindered gliding into a depression.

A *clothing* interpretation is found in the Ro. It is absent in the Zulliger Test. If male subjects produce clothing responses, we may usually conclude that they possess a certain vanity. This may consist in the subject's desire to appear "dapper"; or, if this trait has developed in the direction of a negativistic attitude, the subject may like to see himself as an unconventional character ["beatnik"]. At any rate, if a man produces clothing interpretations, that signifies that he wishes somehow to be conspicuous, to attract the attention of others. In Joseph's case, we observed that he was carelessly wearing a loud shirt with an open collar. His slacks were tight and made of flashy cloth; on his feet he wore open sandals. His hair was uncombed and too long, and his face was unshaven.

In the Ro, the subject's vanity is also expressed by his *heraldic* response produced in Card I. Heraldic interpretations are usually given by people who, no matter whether or not they find support in some accomplishment of their own, are proud of their heritage and strive to show it. Sometimes they do it by wearing different or striking clothes, sometimes by putting on "genteel" airs, sometimes by verbally pointing out that they are of noble birth or that they have noted relatives.

WF + A P ("bat" or "butterfly") is absent in Card V of the Ro. This, too, is a sign of fatigue. When Joseph is tired, he no longer sees the things that are closest at hand, and strays too far afield.

Oral phenomena are less apparent in the Ro than in the Zulliger Test. Still, "Negro women (Card III) want to *cook* something." Again, there are many W. It is interesting and revealing that the Negro women's "fire went out." This suggests an oral inhibition. The subject feels inhibited in his oral demands; for, in the manifestations of his fantasy, he voices facts that concern him, and that reach into the unconscious layers of his self.

As a memory trace, the interpretation of the "two Negro women who want to cook something but their fire went out," refers, perhaps, to the mother and the weaning trauma. At one time the mother was actually out of milk, and the infant produced a definite reaction to it: he went on a hunger strike.

In contrast with the Zulliger Test, the Ro's individual responses are not concerned with oral matters. "Two people back to back to each other; they want to extend their hands to each other over their heads" suggests Joseph's intense need for interhuman relations, and at the same time indicates that it is not quite proper, not quite "natural." Does this not again signify homosexual tendencies?

For, in the second individual interpretation: "Two *men or women* carrying something heavy on their heads," bi-sexuality is accentuated once more, with the additional suggestion that Joseph feels it to be a burden.

In general, we see that the Zulliger Test and the Ro are in agreement with each other here, and complement each other.

COUNSELING

Now we should like to return to our specific task, *vocational guidance*. It is to be based upon the material which the test has provided.

First we talked with Joseph in order to try to find out something about his vocational inclination. Often, one uses the most varied devices to keep this secret from one's blood relatives.

Little by little, Joseph reveals that he would like to work on a "newspaper.... But I am much too young for it! However, for myself I have already been writing short articles, sketches, poems, and such!"

I was convinced that he had a talent for drawing and painting. But talent alone is not enough; it must be supported by interest and cathected by libido, or else nothing can be done with it.

Joseph could utilize his artistic talents in journalism just as well. Many journalists or poets have been painters first—like *Gottfried Keller,* for instance. It is a well known fact that *Hermann Hesse* and many other writers paint. Furthermore, as we have established previously, Joseph definitely has a *gift for language.*

If a young person who comes to us for vocational guidance expresses a desire or shows an inclination for a profession, it becomes our task to scrutinize the test in order to establish whether anything in it runs counter to the subject's wishes. Furthermore, we must determine whether the young person's overall personality, character, behavior patterns—his entire "being" —make him suited for a specific profession. For under certain circumstances we must direct an individual candidate to another profession.

When we review Joseph's test results, we recognize that nothing stands in the way of journalism.

Joseph is linguistically gifted; he has creative and formative abilities; he is capable of establishing meaningful interhuman relationships; he is inclined to meditation, and yet sufficiently agile. He could invest all these capabilities in journalism.

Perhaps Joseph is sufficiently talented to become a poet. However, this we do not tell him, for we do not want to arouse expectations that later may not be fulfilled. If his "poetic gift" is strong enough, it will realize itself. Since Joseph is not yet fully mature, we are unable to make a definite statement at the present time.

However, there is no doubt in my mind that his capabilities are equal to the requirements of journalism. On the basis of my experiences I believe I can make such a statement.

B. A CASE OF HYSTERIA

Mrs. Lotte R., 34 years old, housewife (see Table 2).

Zulliger Individual Test

I.

The torso of a woman, cut open ..	ChF → WF — anat, aggression (sex)
A man with a leg cut off. He has a wooden leg (EFG 3/4/5)	DM + H O aggression
The udder of a cow (G 3)	DdF + Ad
A crater issuing lava (C 5/6)	ChF → DSF ± volcano

II.

Prolonged reaction time. "Oh my!"	shock!
Kidneys (dark red area)	DCF anat
Spine (large S within the red area) .	SF — anat
A flyer's insignia (upper small S within the red area)	SF + obj
A triangle (S within the green area)	SF ± geometry
Meat pieces (red area)	DCF food
A pile of sand seen from above (orange area)	DCF sand

III.

Two skeletons	ChF → WF ± anat (P)
c Butterfly	DF + A P
a A bird's head (gray area, G 4)	DdF + Ad
Shrunken kidneys [cirrhosis] (outer red area)	DCF anat O
The windpipe [trachea] and lungs (center red area)	DCF anat
b or a dog making a hump (outer red area)	DF + A "or"
The skeletons have masks in front of their faces (B 4 and 7)	DF + mask

Duration: 6 minutes

TABLE 2

Scoring
Subject: *Mrs. Lotte R.*

Time: 6 minutes
Number of responses: 17/6

Cd.	W	D	Dd	S	F+	F−	F±	M	FC	CF	ChF	P	O
I	1	1	1	1	1	1	1	1			2		1
II		3		3	1	1	1		3		1		1
III	1	5	1		4	1	1		2			2	
	2	9	2	4	6	2	3	1	5		3	2	2

F+%	= 68	H = 1	A = 2	obj = 1
A%	= 23	anat = 6	Ad = 2	geometry = 1

F+% = 68
A% = 23
P% = 12
O% = 12
H% = 53
anat% = 35

H = 1
anat = 6
sex = (1)
mask = 1
food = 1

A = 2
Ad = 2

obj = 1
geometry = 1
volcano = 1
sand = 1

shock = +

Corrected F+% (without anat) = 88%
"or"

Sequence: orderly
Experience balance: 1 M : 5 C
Apperceptive type: W—D—Dd—S

397

Displaying a definite extratensive experience balance, Mrs. Lotte R. produces a distinct color shock. She produces only CF, but no FC. In part, her CF approach pure color interpretations—as, for instance, in Card II: "Meat pieces" and "a pile of sand," and in Card III, "shrunken kidneys." Thus we may conclude that hysteria is present. In addition, anat = 35% is overly high. Therefore, the woman must have a strong intelligence complex and possess hypochondriacal traits.

The interpretation I/1 indicates a shift upwards (symbolically the torso that has been cut open signifies the female sex organ). Sadomasochistic traits appear, as, for instance, in interpretation I/2 ("a man with a leg cut off"). As a rule, such women are frigid. Or, if they do enjoy sexual activity, they have the unconscious desire to castrate the man during sexual intercourse (strong active castration complex).

Subjects producing "mask" responses, as Mrs. R. has, display a masklike, unnatural, and constrained attitude towards the outside world. Like Mrs. R., they attempt to succeed and to control themselves by intellectual means (corrected F +% is high; sequence is orderly-to-rigid; relative reaction time amounts to 1/3–1/2 minutes; number of responses is high; intellectual grasp (A%, P%, O%) is average-to-low; apperceptive type is not too broad). Moreover, they wish to shine by way of their intellectual accomplishments, and to impress others (high anat%). At the same time they would like to achieve more intellectually than they are inherently capable of achieving. "I am *nothing but a housewife*," they sigh, and they feel that, in being housewives, they are not occupying the right position, one that would bring them the gratification of their desire to dominate.

It is characteristic of such women that, whenever they find themselves in the company of others, they immediately direct the conversation to medical topics. They are familiar with all the complications of giving birth that may have occurred within the circle of their friends, speaking about them in a sugary-masochistic, plaintive tone of voice, as if they themselves had experienced them. They discuss accidents, illnesses, and operations, in the same way.

The medical diagnosis of Mrs. Lotte R. agreed in all points with that derived on the basis of the Zulliger Test. However, the physician added that she is constantly "on the warpath" with her husband, although this does not prevent the two of them from "loving each other violently." Probably we are dealing here with a mutual hate-love relationship, in which each of the two people has found a perfectly suitable neurotic partner. Yet if we had taken the subject's 5 CF and 4 S into consideration, this same hate-love relationship could have been established by the test's findings as well.

C. COMPULSIVE NEUROSIS

Mrs. Christine L., 28 years old, housewife ("a cleaning fiend")

Zulliger Individual Test

I.

Skull with eye socket and	S ➔ FCh ➔ DF + Hd/anat
a missing tooth (BC 5/6)	SF + missing tooth O (Hd)
A knife (A 5 and 6)	DdF + obj aggression
A woman's head (B 4)	Do ➔ DF + Hd
Butterfly (center dark area)	DF + A
Walking canes (FC 4/5 and 6/7) ..	DdF + obj aggression

II.

Prolonged reaction time	shock
A strange plant with a flower (S within red area)	SF + pl
The whole is really a flower arrangement	WCF pl O (DW tendency)

III.

Sitting children, with heads that are much too large	DM + H O (P) obj criticism
Roots like gnomes (EFG 3/4/5 and 6/7/8)	Ms ➔ DF + H/pl
A little pig tail (E 2 and 9) .. Do ➔	DdF + Ad Do = tendency
A giraffe (A 4 on the left side and 6 on the right side)	DdF + A
c Butterfly (inner red area)	DF + A P
b A bear (EF 9/10)	DF + A
a Two boys wearing red clothes are running to the gnomes (outer red area), they would like to beat them up	DM + H P aggression
A fluttering chicken (tiny Dd EF 3)	DdF + A

Duration: 18 minutes

TABLE 3

Scoring
Subject: *Mrs. Christine L.*

Time: 18 minutes
Number of responses: 16/2

Cd.	W	D	Dd	S	F+	F−	F±	M	Ms	FC	CF	FCh	P	O
I		3	2	1	6									1
II	1	5	3	1	1							(1)		1
III				6	6			2	tendency		1		2	1
	1	8	5	8	13			2			1	(1)	2	3

F+% = 100
A% = 38
P% = 13
O% = 18
H% = 38

H = 3
Hd = 3
anat = (1)

A = 5
Ad = 1

obj = 1
pl = 2(3)

tendency C (II/2)
tendency Do (I/4)
tendency DW (II/2)
aggression
shock = +

Sequence: orderly, tendency to inversion
Experience balance: 2 M : 1 C (1½ C)
Apperceptive type: W — D — Dd — S
$\qquad\qquad\qquad \overline{\underline{}}$

A definite color shock appears upon the presentation of Card II. The reaction time is prolonged, and the subject produces only 2 interpretations here, although she has managed to produce 6 responses to Card I and will produce 8 responses to Card III. In addition, Mrs. L.'s experience balance is ambiequal. With the support of the factors mentioned above, we make the diagnosis of a compulsive neurosis in which ceremonial acts play a marked part. The absence of FC points in the same direction. Many Dd and S lead us to expect a pedantic individual who is domineering (S) and stubborn, and who is aggressively nagging, thus compensating for her insecurity (tendency toward inverse sequence, Do added to an $F+\%=100$, and increased $A\%$). The subject is not capable of organizing, planning and assuming leadership (only one single W); she is unable to perform complex thought operations, she occupies herself mainly with small and unessential details (D—Dd—S type) and, especially since $H\%$ is high, she uses them in tyrannizing over the people closest to her. In accordance with the high $H\%=38$, the subject has the need to be with other human beings. Despite the absence of FC, the subject is not without empathy and sympathy. Thus, interhuman relationships play an important role for her.

However, since the subject is domineering and aggressively pedantic, it must be expected that although she seeks to establish human relationships within her environment, her behavior results in her quickly making enemies of everybody. She is egocentric and sentimental with regard to herself (CF only) as well as dull (few colors; the M are the usual MP). Thus, the woman can hardly be called creative. However, she would like to assert and to affirm herself everywhere. The subject is an industrious housewife, interested in trivia. Her intelligence is slightly higher than average ($F+\%$, $A\%$, $P\%$, and $O\%$, orderly sequence, the number of A is higher than that of Ad). At the same time she is also possessed by anxiety and caution (Do and inverse sequence). (See Table 3.)

Her husband describes her as a "cleaning fiend." She is governed by a craze for cleanliness. In discussions she always wants to be in the right. She tries to tyrannize over him as she does over her two children.

D. PHOBIA

(The Zulliger Test has been administered by a psychiatrist and has been sent to me for a blind diagnosis.)

Miss *Kaethe D.*, 31 years old, office secretary.

Zulliger Individual Test

I.

Pullover (center dark area)	DF + clothing
or also an ivy leaf	DF + pl "or"
A woman weighing a child. Her head is bent (BCD 2/3/4)	DM + H O
A man crawling out of a hole holding a spear in his hand (EFG 3/4/5)	FCh → DM + H O aggression
The whole is a sitting man holding up two daggers	WM + H O aggression

II.

"Well, well!" (Prolonged reaction time; turns the card immediately)	shock!
a Fighting cows (orange area) of the Simmenthal species	DFC A aggression
c Fans (D 5/6)	SF + obj
a Dwarfs with shield, wearing coats, walking with long steps (green area)	DM + H O

III.

Prolonged reaction time	after-effect of shock
Two men; both of them have lost one leg	M → WF + H (P) O masochistic; M repression ("castration complex")
c Two old men sitting at the grass's edge, smoking a pipe (CDE 5/4/3 and 8/7/6)	DM + H O Ms tendency
a And here there are two little boys playing a game (outer red area) .	DM + H P
There is a butterfly in the center; only there aren't any such red ones	DF + A P object criticism

Duration: 8 minutes

TABLE 4

Scoring
Subject: *Kaethe D.*

Time: 8 minutes
Number of responses: 12/3

Cd.	W	D	Dd	S	F+	F—	F±	M	Ms	FC	CF	FCh	P	O
I	1	4			2			3						3
II		2		1	1			1		1		1		1
III	1	3			1			2(3)	tendency	1			3	2
	2	9		1	4			6(7)	tendency	1		1	3	6

F+% = 100   H = 7   A = 2   obj = 1 = 1 shock = +
A% = 16   clothing = 1   pl = 1 = 1 M repression
P% = 25   object criticism
O% = 50   masochistic interpret.
H% = 66   aggression "or"
    stereotypes with H

Sequence: tendency to inversion, orderly-to-rigid
Experience balance: 6(7) M : ½ C
Apperceptive type: W — D (S)

Color shock becomes apparent in Cards II and III. Therefore, neurotic repression may be effective. Since experience balance is introversive, we are probably dealing here with an "introversive neurosis." However, a direct diagnosis cannot be made with regard to its symptomatic characteristics. Yet on the basis of the two factors, color shock and introversive experience balance, we must infer that anxiety phenomena exist in the form of psychasthenically transformed anxiety. Masochistic impulses may be observed (Card III/1) and sadistically aggressive impulses as well (Card I/4 and 5, Card II/1). The response in Card III/I is perhaps an "individual interpretation," illustrating the subject's strong castration complex. Card I/5 indicates phobic anxiety. Card I/4 probably suggests the same. This response contains a hidden phantasy as it is often produced by children, especially by girls: the sexual act is consummated in a dangerous attack, which produces physical injury. It is an assault executed by force. At the same time, a suppressed desire to be raped is suggested here. The high O% (50!) indicates that the subject loves to surrender to daydreams and that she enjoys them. Since M and flexor kinesthesias are numerous (Card I/3 and 4; Card III/2), and since the usual WMH P is absent (which indicates that M repression exists), anxiety may become converted into helpless paralysis (see Table 4).

In part, anxiety may be the result of the subject's inadequate professional choice. As a rule, office workers produce many more Dd. Since she produces too few color responses, Kaethe D. is probably inclined to depressive moods. She lacks gaiety, and her willingness to venture on new enterprises is frustrated by her anxiety neurosis. This is also proven by the fact that despite her good intelligence, she does not succeed in producing more than 12 responses. The avoidance of red in Card II suggests emotional shyness. The very high H% indicates that Kaethe D. possesses an extremely strong need for interhuman relationships. She would therefore be much better suited as a salesgirl than as a secretary.

E. A NEUROTIC THIEF WITH STRONG INTROVERSION

Zulliger Test

Blind diagnosis, "the subject is a thief"
Age of the subject: 15 years, female

Time:	35 minutes!
Number of responses:	14/3

I.

A summer bird (chiaroscuro tonali-
ty!) .... FCh ➔ WF + A
Clown .... WM + H O mask
Vine leaf (center area) .... DF + pl

II.

Two women putting their faces together (red area) .... DM + H O
c Two people swimming, clad in veil-
ing garments (orange area) .... DMFCh H O
b,d Two angels playing the flute (green
area) .... Ms ➔ DM + H O

III.

Two people arguing with each
other .... ⎱ WM + H P aggression
combinatory ⎰
Two goblins inciting them ...... DM + H P aggression
Summer bird (red area c) .... DF + A P
Snail without its shell .... DF + A
the little tail is unnecessary .... DdF + Ad object criticism
b A hill with a tree. The wind blows
through it (adjoining the "back"
of the "human figure," its
"stretched out hand") .... DF + nat O Ch tendency
a An old mill wheel with a pond (in
the same area) .... FCh ➔ DF ± nat O—
confabulation
Two people looking like devils
(already scored in III/1) ...... devils!
Evil spirits (EFG 3/4/5 and 8/7/6) DMFCh H O

W	= 3	F	= 7(—0.5)	H	= 7	P	= 3
D	= 10	M	= 5	Hd	=	O	= 7
Dd	= 1	FCh	= 2	A, Ad	= 4	F+%	= 93
S	=	FCh	= 2	obj	= 1	A%	= 38
				pl	= 1	P%	= 21
				nat	= 2	O%	= 50±
				mask	= (1)	H%	= 50
				devil	= (1)		

Sequence:	orderly	Color shock — ? (See number of
Experience balance:	7 M : O C	responses! = 14/3 and lack of
Apperceptive type:	W — D — Dd	color responses)

Need for combination	Pedantry and confabulation alternate
Confabulation	Phobic impulses and guilt feelings ("devil" —
Aggression	"goblins" — "arguing people" — "evil spirit")
Object criticism	

MFCh indicates a disturbance of the mind. The two nat suggest infantilism and regression, and a number of other responses point to guilt feelings. The too high F+% precludes the diagnosis of hebephrenia. Despite the absence of a definite color shock, we are probably dealing here with neurosis. Indeed, color shock may be supposed, on the basis of the number of responses. If we are not completely mistaken, stealing may be explained by a combination composed of a confused mind and misguided conscience reaction. The girl seeks punishment and unconsciously she attempts to force it upon herself by stealing (flexor kinesthesia).

Since "goblins incite people to argue," and since these people are "devils," while some others are "evil spirits" or "clowns," the thought readily occurs to us that the subject may be laboring under an intense parental conflict. She rejects her father ("clown"), and takes the side of one parent against the other ("arguing people incited by goblins"); that is how she creates guilt feelings in herself. The subject has assumed a masklike attitude ("mask") and has lost ground ("people swimming"). Despite her many M, she is unstable. Also, since all M are flexor kinesthesias, hebephrenia must again be ruled out. Her symptom corresponds with "compulsion" (kleptomania, *no* FC!).

F. A HEBEPHRENIC THIEF

Hermine T., 17 years old.

Zulliger Test   Time: 13 minutes

I.

There is a man sitting there	WM + H O flexor kinesthesia
He has two hideous white eyes . . .	SF + Hd white as color
His collar is in shreds	DdF + clothing
He wears a black vest with short sleeves	DFC clothing black as color
The shoes can be seen quite well (FG 5/6)	DdF ± clothing
This could also be the lung, exactly in the middle of the body (center dark area)	DF — anat/position
The whole could also be a lung, one can see the different parts .	ChF → WF — anat perseveration
A mother sitting with her little boy, bending down (BC 4)	DM + H O flexor kinesthesia
The whole could be death	WMCh H O death
c Flower (dark center area)	DF + pl
c Here is the pistil (large S)	SF±
c Below there is the flower bulb (B 5/6)	DF — pl confabulation

II.

Two Simmenthal cows attack each other. The color has come out rather too light (orange area) . .	DFC A aggression obj criticism
Two bears dancing with each other (red area)	DM + A O
b From a fairy tale: the two chickens that went up	DF + A ⎫
the Nuesberg (green area, the "chickens" are the uppermost large blot parts)	DCF nat ⎬ combinatory ⎭
b A shaggy dog with a white nose. He is lying down (upper green area and S)	DSF — A
b Shaped exactly like the "Jacob pasture" at home (lower green area) and it is just as green	DCF nat individual response
(smiles half gaily and half sadly)	homesickness reaction

407

b Our Savior walking upon the lake
in the glow of the evening (lower
orange area) .... DMC H O religion

a A pot with a magic plant (S) .... SF + pl
Butterfly wings (within the center
orange area, the dark, frayed
section) .... DdCF Ad

III. (Laughs)

Two prize fighters, one can
recognize the clumsy gloves
quite well. They are unfriendly
fellows! .... WM + H O aggression
DF + clothing

Two hobgoblins illuminated by
fire (outer red area; the
"fire!" = red center area) ...... DMC H O (P)

Or a butterfly (red center area) ... DF + A P "or"

A mouse raising its tail. It runs
after a beetle .... DF + A
on the other side ("beetle" =
small dark blot within the dark
blot on the bottom) .... DdF − A confabulation

A "piggy" (a portion of the dark
blot on the bottom) .... DF + A

The prize fighter on the right side
has a terribly big eye .... DdF + Hd *eye*

c This is a house (the contours) .... DWF − obj O− infantile
abstraction

c Somebody is sitting here on a
rocky slope .... DM + H O flexor kinesthesia

c A fir tree is hanging from the slope
(DC 1/2 and 9/10) .... DF − pl confabulation

c Two Socialist flags (center red
area) .... DCF obj O−

This is some kind of a snail, a sea
snail (the "hand" of the "human
figure") .... DF + A

408

Scoring

| | | | Time: | | 13 minutes |
| | | | Number of responses: | | 35/9 |

DW	= 1	F	= 20 (—8.5)	P	= 1
W	= 5	M	= 5	O	= 11(—3)
D	= 20	MC	= 1	religion	= 1
Dd	= 5	MCCh	= 1	H	= 1
DS	= 1	MCh	= 1	Hd	= 2
S	= 3	FC	= 2	anat	= 2
F+%	= 57	CF	= 4	clothing	= 6
A%	= 23	C	= 1	A	= 7
P%	= 10	shocks	= —	Ad	= 1
O%	= 31±			obj	= 2
H%	= 48			pl	= 5
anat%	= 6			nat	= 2
				fire	= 1

Sequence:	loose-irregular
Experience balance:	8 M : 4½ — 6 C
Apperceptive type:	(D) W — D — Dd — S
	= —

Flexor kinesthesia	Confabulations
White as color	Perseveration tendency
Black as color	Aggression
Position interpretation	"Evil eyes"
Combinations	Object criticism
Individual interpretations	Homesickness reaction
Infantile abstractions	

The entire record makes an unusual impression, partly because highly original interpretations alternate with trivial ones, and partly because, as far as the content is concerned, the substance of the thought processes changes aimlessly.

"Hideous white eyes" (Card I), the "unfriendly fellows—the prize fighters" (Card III) who also have "terribly big eyes" —all of this must be caused by ideas of persecution. People interpreting "eyes" observe themslves and try not to give themselves away to the outside world. They have guilt feelings. Frequently they see themselves observed by others and they believe that they are being observed. They feel "God's eye" upon themselves and the "sword of Damocles" above their heads.

The excessive number of flexor kinesthesias arouses our suspicion. It indicates intensified autism.

Furthermore, the following factors are suspicious:

white and black are seen as colors;

sharp object criticism changes into confabulation and accurately perceived generic concepts, as, for instance, in Card I "a man is sitting there," and then into infantile DWF interpretations, as in Card III, "this is a house";

perseveration with one interpretation and its confabulatory formulation: in Card I, for instance, a "flower" is interpreted first and then a flower bulb is added by confabulation. In Card I (interpretations 1-6) such perseveration had already become obvious;

the presence of MCH, which usually indicates that psychotic changes have occurred;

perseverations, position interpretations, absence of a genuine color shock;

the quite confused sequence and the low F+%.

Clinically, hebephrenia is established by the presence of all these factors.

Hermine T. grew up in the country and was transferred to the city after her graduation from school. She was supposed to attend a secondary school (a girl's high school) there. Very soon it was discovered that Hermine had committed a number of thefts. Neither her parents nor her teachers could understand the reason for these thefts. Hermine herself could supply them with only the most confusing information.

G. A MENTALLY RETARDED CHILD

Karl D., 10 years old, is an elementary-school student. He is the only child in a family of teachers residing in one of our small county towns. He has been brought in for a psychological examination because he is *unable to concentrate.* The school report cards that he brings home are progressively poorer and poorer; in addition, he presents a disciplinary problem. He is perpetually

410

restless and does not get along with his friends, either, because he always wants to "order" them about.

A certificate of the family physician states that Karl is physically well. In general, he has rarely been sick, never seriously, and until now he has never had any operations. The family is in good financial circumstances, and there is no adverse heredity. However, the boy's birth was difficult and forceps had to be used.

Zulliger Test	Time:	10 minutes
	Number of responses:	15, 5 of
	them to the colored Card II	

I.

An elephant; there on the bottom are the tusks (G 5/6)	DdWF — A O—
There is black in the middle	description; color naming
Legs (again 5/6)	DdF — Ad
Wings (D 2/9)	DdF — Ad
White follows black	description, color naming
Here on top are two cat eyes and a mouth (the three round inner white spaces on top)	Do → SF + Ad
And here is a belly-button (the lowest larger inner white space)	SF — Hd position
And here are two horns (A5 and 6)	DF + Ad

II.

Two beetles (brown area; Karl is unable to say whether color has helped in producing the interpretation)	DF + A; eventually FC
On top there are frogs because they are green	DCF A confabulation
The white are their eyes (within the green area)	SF — Ad
This is just hair (blob at the green blot)	DdF + Ad
A fire burns bright red (red area) ..	DC fire
One can see through (points to the inner white space between the red blots)	S tendency

411

III.

These are two black children. They are stretching their arms and jumping. They are wearing gray clothes	WM + H P
	FCh impression
Here is red and here is a butterfly	color naming, DF + A P
These are mice, because one can see their little tails (the "legs" of the "black children")	DF + A confabulatory tendency
This again is red (outer red area), two times, all in all three times (including inner red area)	color naming, counting
There are two boys here, they are racing with each other (outer red area)	DM + H P

Scoring

DdW = 1	F+	= 6	H	= 2	P	= 3
W = 1	F—	= 5	A	= 5	O	= 1(—1)
D = 7	M	= 2 (V)	Ad	= 7		
Dd = 3	FC	= tendency	fire	= 1	F+%	= 54
S = 3, tendency	CF	= 1			A%	= 80
	C	= 1			P%	= 21
	FCh	= tendency			O—%	= 7

Sequence:	loose to orderly	Position interpretation
Experience balance:	1 M : 2½ – 3 C	Color naming
Apperceptive type:	DW/W — D — Dd — S	Counting

EVALUATION:

The low percentage of good form-interpretations; the slightly irregular sequence; a definite confabulatory tendency; a much too high percentage of animal responses; a low percentage of original interpretations; more numerous Ad than A responses; color naming, enumeration, and position interpretations—these indicate without doubt that Karl is *mentally retarded*.

The pure C and CF imply egocentricity, moodiness, emotional excitability, and explosive and agitated motility. By correlating these factors with the strong S tendency, we may estimate the measure of Karl's aggressive personality traits.

Thus we arrive at the diagnosis of *erethic mental retardation*.

If D and Dd are correlated to M, it becomes clear that Karl's thinking is of the concrete kind. By relating them to his strong need for motor discharge (CF and C), we arrive, within the framework of the still existing intelligence, at the conclusion that Karl has a "practical manual" potential.

Karl's "inability to concentrate" and his disciplinary problems are symptoms of this particular form of mental retardation.

SUMMARY:

Since Karl is the son of honest, quiet, and well-educated parents, nobody has suspected that he is mentally retarded.

It was recommended to Karl's parents that they place him in a "special class." In such a class, instruction demands less theoretical thinking and offers many manual-skill exercises. After refusing at first, the parents finally agreed to follow this recommendation. They also tried to develop their son's capabilities, by supplying him with tools and a place where he could pursue model-building.

In order to promote Karl's social adjustment, it was recommended that he should be allowed to build his models together with his friends, and that the boys should be encouraged to work jointly. For instance, they were spurred on to construct a puppet theater from wood and cloth, carving the puppets from cardboard and then painting them. Later they all participated in play productions, to which other children were invited as an audience.

H. A MENTALLY RETARDED CHILD

Ludwig, 10 years old, is the last-born child in a family with 8 children. Of the older children, the youngest is 7 years his senior. The father operates a car-repair shop in Bern Canton village, and has been a councilman for many years. The mother is a housewife. Since Ludwig's birth she has frequently been ill. With the exception of Ludwig, all the children were able to attend a secondary school in a larger village nearby.

Ludwig had all the common children's diseases. During his early childhood, he was delicate, susceptible to illness, prone to running a fever. He has poor teeth (even now). Later his health

413

improved at a rapid rate and, since beginning school, he has never been sick again. The medical examination, carried out prior to the psychological examination upon the request of the psychologist, did not disclose anything unusual.

Ludwig is of medium height and somewhat chubby. He gives the impression of being a very quiet boy. In school, he has the reputation of being lazy and whiny, crying at the slightest reprimand.

When Ludwig was transferred into the fourth grade, he was promoted on a provisional basis. His parents and his older brothers and sisters, who had already finished their schooling, were very excited about it. They accused Ludwig's teacher of not paying enough attention to him and of letting him run the risk of having to repeat the grade.

Ludwig's oldest brother reproaches his parents for not being sufficiently strict with their youngest son, and for having over-indulged him and pampered him too much.

Upon the recommendation of the principal, and in agreement with the board of education, the parents permit their son to take a psychological examination. They are anxious to find out from some neutral source whether the boy's conditional promotion to the higher school grade had been justified.

Zulliger Test	Time: 16 minutes
	Number of responses: 13, 3
	of them produced for the
	colored Card II

I.

A calf that has been cut open.
   Here are the horns (A 5/6) and
   here is the head (B 5/6) .... DWF — Ad (anat)
And here are the bones (S 3/9) ... DdF ± Ad (anat)
The stomach is in the middle
   (darker blot in the center of
   the configuration) .... DF — Ad (anat) position

II.

Here again is some veal meat, two
   halves (red area), or human meat DCF meat (anat) perseveration
Next to the red there is two times
   green and two times brown .... color naming, counting

414

They have taken the liver out
(brown area) .... DCF Ad (anat)
And they have garnished it with
parsley (green area) .... DFC pl DW tendency food

III.

Two skeletons (upper dark blots) . DF — anat
b A "doggie" (outer red bottom
area) .... DF + A
a A butterfly (red center area) ..... DF + A P
Worms (smaller dark blots) ...... DF + A
Pincers of an earwig (the lower
portion of the small dark blot) .. DdF ± Ad
Or a mouse because of its little
tail (small dark blot) .... DF — A confabulation "or"
A hand with fingers (dark lateral
blot) .... DoF + Hd

Scoring:

DW =	1, tendency	F+ =	4	H	= —	P	= 1
W =	—	F— =	4	Hd	= 1	O	= minus
D =	9	F± =	2	anat	= 1		
Dd =	2	M =	—	A/anat	= 5	F+% =	50
Do =	1	FC =	1	A	= 4	A% =	70
S =	—	CF =	2	Ad	= 1	P% =	8
				(total Ad =	5)	O% =	minus
				pl	= 1	anat% =	48

Sequence:	loose to orderly	Confabulation
Experience balance:	O M : 2½ C	Position interpretation
Apperceptive type:	DW — D — Dd/Do	Perseveration, obsessions, (anat)
		Color naming, counting
		Food

We are dealing here with *mental retardation*. The following factors bear out this diagnosis:

low F+%;
occurrence of confabulatory DW, tendency toward confabulation;
absence of M;
number of Ad larger than number of A;
number of Hd larger than number of H;

415

poor (minus) originality;

low P%, attachment to the very first response, obsession and perseveration;

attachment to anatomic interpretations (anat $= 48\%$);

position response in Card I;

color naming;

enumerations.

Although CF predominate, Ludwig's retardation is probably of the unagitated type. The CF correspond with a poorly adapted, largely unadapted, egocentric affectivity; this lacks aggression and defiance, however, because no S have been produced.

Since reaction time is prolonged—on the average, one response should be produced in half a minute—the inference must be made that Ludwig is slow in thinking, as well as in his actions. Since M are absent and D are schematic, the boy lacks "practical ability." Nevertheless, he is relatively more suited for practical work, for tasks that require simple, standardized (high A%, high anat%) and schematic manual operations. He is the "handyman" type; he could perform simple work tasks on a farm or in a factory—as a weaver or a stamping machine operator, for example.

REPORT TO THE PARENTS:

Undoubtedly Ludwig is of inferior intellectual ability. Even if he makes every possible effort, and achieves as much as he is able to achieve, he would still hardly be able to follow instructions in an elementary school class. If it is not possible to place him in a "special" class, because there are no such classes in the village or in the vicinity of it, he will probably have to repeat one or two grades.

His conditional promotion to the fourth grade was well-grounded.

It would serve no purpose, nor would it be reasonable, to attempt to improve Ludwig's school work by treating him more strictly. It would only cause him unnecessary anguish.

On the other hand, what is indicated is to let him perform simple practical tasks, either by placing him with a farmer, or by permitting him to work in his father's shop.

One should be grateful for the boy's willingness and submissiveness; one should be glad that, in general, he gets along well with others, does not fight with his friends, and has a rather quiet temperament.

One must become reconciled to the fact that, intellectually, Ludwig is incapable of accomplishing much. However, within the framework of his ability, one must promote him as much as possible. He should be encouraged to perform practical manual work and simple tasks that are not beyond his capacities.

I. ERETHIC MENTAL RETARDATION

The 10½-year-old *Erwin Kunz* was sent for an examination by the school board because his teacher thought that he was mentally retarded. His parents did not believe that this was true. On the contrary, they felt that their son was capable of attending secondary school (lower middle school) and they supported their opinion by the fact that Erwin was quite able to weigh and sell groceries in his parents' grocery store. Also, he had been trading small animals (rabbits, hamsters, white mice, chickens, which he bred himself) and he was as skillful at it as if he were a "grown-up."

Erwin is his parents' only child. His birth was "normal" and quick. As an infant, he was breast-fed for 6 months. He was, however, a "lazy" milk drinker and it was only with some difficulty that he could maintain the weight expected for his age. Erwin began to walk when he was two, and to talk when he was three years old. He liked to talk, and talked a great deal and loudly. He grew into a healthy, strong boy. Except for measles and German measles, he has never been sick. Whooping cough and scarlet fever passed him by.

He is squat in his body build, well-nourished, and very lively.

Since his mother was busy in the store, Erwin was cared for during his early childhood by nursemaids who were changed frequently. His mother came home only then when she had to nurse the baby. At the time of his birth, the child was unwanted because his parents would have liked to be alone for a while longer, in order to devote themselves to their business. Erwin played well by himself. He had a large supply of toys (he still has them today); with other children, the boy played less well, nor did he get along with them when he started kindergarten. He had frequent fights with them, and could not adjust to the group. He grabbed toys away from his friends, always wanting to have the toy that another child had. At the end of his seventh year, both his kindergarten teacher and the school physician pronounced Erwin "ready for school."

Erwin Kunz, 10½ years old; elementary-school student, 4th grade.

Zulliger Individual Test

Beginning: 3:15 P.M.

I.

Points (A 5/6) (responds right away,
no initial shock) .... D F ± obj infantile abstraction
There are six points on the bottom Dd F ± obj
perseveration, counting
Kind of fog .... ChF → W F ± nat, fog

II.

Salad made from .... DW CF food O
  radishes (red area) ....⎫ D CF pl ⎫
  leaves (green area) and ....⎬ D CF pl ⎬ detailed enumeration
           combinatory⎪ D CF pl ⎭
  beets (orange area) ....⎭
A small house (red area) with ...
          combinatory⎧ DdD F ± arch ⎫ infantile
  a door (S within red area) ....⎩ S F − arch ⎭ abstraction
A green veil (green area) .... D CF clothing O−
A red veil (red area) .... D CF clothing; perseveration
A dirt heap (brown area) .... D CF nat; tendency to pure C
A white dove (upper S within red
  area) .... S FC A white as color

III.

Many points .... Dd F − obj perseveration
Butterfly .... D F + A P
Fog clouds .... ChF → W F ± clouds, perseveration
Shredded meat (outer red area) .. D CF food
Three red and two black .... color naming, counting
"Finished!"
End: 3:25 P.M.

Date: December 15, 1961

Scoring

Time: 10 minutes
Number of responses: 17, 10 of
which were produced for Card II

DW	=	1	F+	=	1	P	=	1
W	=	2	F−	=	2	O	=	2 (−1)
D	=	9	F±	=	5	clothing	=	2
DdD	=	1	FC	=	1	food	=	2
Dd	=	2	CF	=	8	A	=	2
S	=	2	C	=	tendency	obj	=	3
F+%	=	44	ChF	=	2	pl	=	3
A%	=	11				nat	=	2
P%	=	6				cloud	=	1
O%	=	11±				arch	=	2

F+ = 1, F− = 2, F± = 5 } 8 (−4.5)

Sequence: loose, tendency towards inversion
Experience balance: O M : 8½ C
Apperceptive type: DW W — D — Dd — S

Remarks:

Twice, infantile ab-stractions	Twice, combina-tions	Card I = 3 responses
Several persevera-tions	Color naming One SFC	Card II = 10 responses
Twice, counting	WM and DM are ab-sent in Card III	Card III = 4 responses
Detailed enumera-tion		

EVALUATION:

Reaction time, which should amount to one-third to one-half minute per response in the Zulliger Individual Test, is somewhat prolonged. A prolonged reaction time is observed in subjects who have few ideas, or else are cautious and timid, or inferior in intelligence. Since Erwin (see Card I) shows a tendency to an inverse sequence, the conclusion must be drawn that he is cautious and on guard. It is possible that, even though he did not produce an initial shock, he realized during the testing that he was in a test situation. When the colored Card II was presented to him, his ideas became more spontaneous and abundant, dwindling again with the red and black Card III. This leads us to infer that Erwin is most productive when he feels that he is being emotionally appealed to.

Erwin's low F+% indicates mental inferiority or even mental retardation. It leads us to suspect that Erwin has poor judgment and a deficient concept of all the obvious elements in his environment (poor judgment of reality); this is also borne out by DW and DdD, indicating that the boy still has not fully attained the level of "reality" thinking—in other words, the level of thinking that a 10½-year-old "normally" should have already reached. Erwin succumbs to illusions, believing that whatever he has imagined is true and real. Therefore, his thinking is not "neat" (not from a moral, but from a purely formal point of view); the loose sequence suggests that Erwin's thinking is erratic and unlogical. The logical function of his thinking is either unformed or defective; the too low A% indicates difficulties in concentrating. This is also supported by the relatively abundant content column in a variety of areas that form the basis for his ideas (clothing/food/A/obj/pl/anat/clouds/arch).

The complete absence of M, including the absence of even the common M in Card III, indicates that Erwin is incapable of absorbing impressions inwardly, as is usually expected of intelligent people. Although it has been proven by experience that mentally retarded (and epileptic or psychotic) subjects may produce M, their M, however, are inaccurately perceived. They are M—, as, for example, in Card II: "This is a crawling man. The red is his head, the green are his arms, and the brown his legs"; or, interpreting the dark blot in the center of Card I: "This is a sitting child with elbows extended."

An elementary-school student of 11 or 12 years of age who is expected to pass the entrance examination for a secondary school should display in the Zulliger Test an average reaction time of not quite ½ minute, an F+% of 80-85, an A% of 30-45, an orderly sequence, as P% of approximately 15, an O% of 5-12, several M, and one anatomic or at least one geographic response. P% permits us to estimate the adaptability of his thinking to that of other people (intellectual grasp, potential for empathy); O% establishes the ability to think originally in a positive way (O+), as well as to think and to conceive independently; M indicate the capacity for "inner life."

We are forced to come to the conclusion that Erwin K. is mentally retarded. Yet how does this diagnosis tally with the parents' observation that Erwin weighs grocery items correctly in the store, counts the money without making mistakes, and is a skillful, even a "shrewd" (the father's expression) trader of small livestock?

Mentally retarded people often possess some single ability. It is possible that Erwin may be endowed with a talent for simple, practically applied arithmetical operations (according to his teacher's statement, he did not especially "shine" in school in arithmetic). Most likely Erwin is cunning, in addition to being "stupid." The concept of "cunning stupidity" is well known. Cunning is not at all a sign of intelligence, however, even though some people are deceived by it, and believe that cunning people are also intellectually superior.

As experience has taught us, people with a real talent for mathematics almost always have a gift for grammar. This does not hold true in Erwin's case. In form-interpretation tests, subjects with mathematical ability always present an orderly-to-rigid sequence and several M.

Let us now turn our attention to the other test results.

Erwin's experience balance is O M : $8\frac{1}{2}$ C. The C are composed of 1 FC and 8 CF, of which 1 CF approaches a pure C. FC are the criteria of adapted and adaptable affectivity. Erwin has very little of this. CF indicate the presence of moods, and an egocentric and impulsive affectivity. The absence of M means that there are hardly any forces in Erwin that would control his impulsivity. He is probably quite unstable, and tends to abreact stimuli instantly, and without any inhibition. On the basis of the 8 CF, we can assume that he is probably a restless individual, a boy who is incapable of sitting still in school and is beset with intense motile needs. However, his teacher has stated that, as far as his initial restlessness is concerned, the boy has markedly improved. This too finds expression in one of the test's signs, the 2 ChF. Individuals who produce few ChF, not more than 1-2 in approximately 20 responses, in addition to producing CF but no pure Ch, are not depressive. To a large extent, they have "adapted" themselves by deliberate consideration based on experience. Theirs is not an authentic emotional adaptation, but an adaptation through shrewdness in accordance with the saying: "One learns by experience!" With his 8 CF, Erwin is indeed a very sensitive human being. Moreover, his SFC indicates that he is hypersensitive and irritable.

Erwin's insincerity in interhuman relationships is proven by the fact that he does not produce any H and Hd.

Summarizing, we now see that we are forced to regard Erwin not only as mentally retarded, but also as an irritable, restless child. Since he does not possess any impulse-controlling forces (absence of M), he is compelled to follow all his sudden impulses. Thus, we arrive at a picture of erethic mental retardation.

Erwin's apperceptive type is characterized by D. D types are usually manual workers with a certain "practical" aptitude. Numerous color interpretations, as well as the fact that Erwin produces most of his responses for Card II (colored card), lead us to the conclusion that he is endowed practically.

COUNSELING OF THE PARENTS:

We must inform you that your son's intellectual ability is actually not high enough to permit him to do satisfactory school work or engage in other intellectual pursuits. You must accept this fact even though it may be "difficult" for you. It would be torture for Erwin if it were demanded that he follow lessons in a secondary school. It must be anticipated that he would have to repeat some grades or that, after the customary probation period, he would be transferred back to elementary school. Such an experience would be extremely painful for the hypersensitive boy. One should avoid inflicting this kind of suffering upon him. His having to repeat some grades, or being expelled from secondary school (and it is highly dubious that he would pass the entrance examination, even if he were drilled for it by private tutoring), would also be very unpleasant for the parents. Therefore it would be better for all concerned if Erwin were to give up all attempts to enter a secondary school.

J. PSEUDO MENTAL RETARDATION

Annelies R., 10 years old, is a city child. She is the middle child in a family, with one brother four years older and another two years younger than herself. The father holds a job in a warehouse of a hardware firm; the mother devotes herself to the children and the house, from time to time helping out as a saleswoman. (This used to be her profession, but she gave it up when her first child was born.) The family's financial circumstances are average.

Both boys seem intellectually alert and well endowed. The older boy attends junior high school, having been admitted without an examination. The younger boy attends the second grade of the elementary school; he is at the top of his class.

Annelies, on the other hand, receives average-to-poor school marks. Her parents would have liked to send her to secondary school. Her teacher maintains, however, that Annelies will not be able to pass the entrance examination. Although she is quite good in arithmetic, she is poor in essay-writing, and she makes a great many spelling mistakes. She is forgetful and anxious, frequently excited, and she lacks gaiety and initiative (school reports, report cards).

Since an uncle on the mother's side of the family is mentally retarded, the parents fear that Annelies may be equally afflicted; they have therefore sent the girl for a psychological examination.

Annelies has never had any unusual illnesses: her birth was easy, and according to the physician's report, a physical examination has indicated normal good health.

The little girl is tall and slender. She is rather thin, has a boyish figure, and a serious "old" face. She looks worried, shy, and embarrassed. When the examiner attempts to engage her in some small talk, she becomes a little more at ease, but only after she has been offered a peach.

This cannot possibly be a retarded girl! Her $F+\%$ is too high, her innate ability for intellectual adaptation is too superior ($A\% = 40$, $F\% = 20$); her diligence—21 responses in 11 minutes—is too great, her quality ambition ($F+\%$, $O\%$) too

Zulliger Test   Time: 11 minutes
                                         Number of responses: 21, 7 of which
I.   are produced for the colored Card II

A squashed beetle .... FCh → WF + A P defective
A girl with a feather on her head
   holding a doll on her lap (BC
   4 and 7) .... DM + H O+
Ivy leaf (center portion) .... DF + pl
A small deer jumping away (D 2
   and 9) .... DdF + A
The head of a man with a beard
   and a peaked cap (EF 2/3) ..... DdF + obj
Just sticks (G 4/5 and 6/7) ...... DdF ± obj
b The index finger (G 3 and 8) .... DdF ± Hd

II.

Oh, there are colors here! .... color shock!
Moles (brown area) .... DFC A
Dog or fox heads (outer brown
   area) .... DoF + Ad "or"
Bushes (green area) .... DFC pl
Smeared blood (red area) .... DCF blood
Bean stalks (within red area) ..... SF + pl
An eagle (within red and brown
   areas) .... SF ± A
A man with a beard and a long
   nose; only his head, which has
   been cut off (green blots, outer
   upper area) .... DdF + Hd defective

III.

Girls whose legs have been cut off
   in a driving accident .... (W) → DF + H O (P) defective
A butterfly (center red area) ..... DM + H P
Running boys (outer red area) ... DM + H P
Snakes (on the top of the "head"
   of the "girls," the long blob
   towards the center line) .... DdF − A
b A little dog with a hump. It is
   mutilated (outer red area, lower
   configuration) .... DF + A O defective
A doll with a peaked cap (smaller
   dark blot) .... DF + H (obj)
"This is so cloudy!" (points to the
   upper dark blot) .... Ch impression DCh cloud

424

Scoring

W	=	1 to 2	F+	= 11	H	= 4	P	= 4
D	= 11		F−	= 1 to 2	Hd	= 3	O	= 3
Dd	= 7		F±	= 3	blood	= 1		
Do	= 1		M	= 2	A	= 7	F+%	= 80 – 83
S	= 2		FC	= 2	Ad	= 1	A%	= 40
			CF	= 1	obj	= 1	P%	= 20
			FCh	= 1	pl	= 3	O%	= 15+
			Ch	= 1	cloud	= 1		

Sequence:	orderly to loose	Ch impressions
Experience balance:	2 M : 2 C	Color shock!
Apperceptive type:	W — D — Dd — S/Do	Cut-off or run-off Hd!

strong, her quantity ambition, patience and endurance (21 responses) too extensive.

According to her *innate* intelligence, Annelies ought to be at least an average student and to have succeeded in increasing her achievements by diligent effort. She ought to be able to work conscientiously (Dd) and with self-criticism (M : S), and she should not find it difficult to participate in the work of a secondary school.

It is obvious that Annelies cannot bring her intellectual capacities to full realization *because her intelligence is inhibited.* Since a pronounced color shock has occurred in her test, the conclusion must be drawn that a neurosis exists and, since the red color has been interpreted as "blood," the presence of anxiety must be inferred. "Anxiety makes people stupid," says Heinrich Meng.

The most revealing interpretation was produced in Card III: "Girls whose legs have been cut off in a driving accident." This interpretation leads us to suspect intense castration anxiety; it probably represents a self-description too. Equally suspicious are the men's heads, which have been "cut off" (Card II), and the "snakes" (Card III), which are direct sex symbols. They are placed upon the girl's head and they probably correspond with Annelies' unconscious wish-fantasy.

Furthermore, it is undoubtedly correct to say that she is suffering from anxiety and tries to compensate for it. If a shock is produced and the red blots are interpreted as "blood" in one of the form-interpretation test's cards, it is quite certain that anxiety is present. It may assume the form either of manifest anxiety or of anxiety equivalents.

The extent to which Annelies' anxiety causes depressive ill-humor may be seen in the Ch impression produced in Card III: "This is so cloudy." People producing pure Ch are helpless against their depressions. They are paralyzed and their helpless inactivity assumes panic-like proportions. Paralysis does not remain solely at the motility level (where the purpose of anxiety is defense by escape), but is carried over to the intellectual level as well. Anxiety then corresponds to a so-called "deathlike" reaction.

Annelies' seeming "mental retardation" is a *pseudo debility.*

RECOMMENDATION TO THE PARENTS:

Annelies urgently needs psychotherapeutic treatment. Such treatment will undertake the task of dissolving the anxiety that paralyzes the girl's good intellectual ability.

At home, Annelies must be treated with equanimity. It would be out of place to reproach her for her scanty intellectual achievements. The girl does not lack good intentions; it is her inner inhibitions that have prevented her from developing her perfectly adequate intellectual capacities.

Annelies must have time. She should not apply for the entrance examination to the secondary school this spring, but should wait until next year. By then her treatment will be terminated, and Annelies will be quite capable of passing the examination. If she took the examination now, she would become even more confused and inwardly disoriented by her (probable) failure; as a result, she would be even less capable of achieving.

FOLLOW-UP REPORT:

Annelies began psychotherapeutic treatment; it lasted for about six months. Then she entered a private school, from which she passed the entrance examination to a junior high school, and joined a class corresponding to her age group. At the present time she is a good student at this school.

K. PSEUDO MENTAL RETARDATION

Sixteen-year-old *Denis Lambert* is the first-born son of a veterinary doctor. The family lives in one of the larger villages.

Denis' father brings his son for vocational counseling. He believes that, since Denis is mentally retarded, vocational counseling will be difficult in his case.

Life history (anamnesis): Denis' birth was absolutely normal. Denis was breast-fed for six months, and he has been in good health. Because his mother, a former teacher, assisted her husband in the laboratory and in the pharmacy, a nurse was engaged for Denis. Weaning and toilet training presented no difficulties. When Denis was 1½ years old, Mrs. Lambert gave birth to another child, a girl. Even before the birth of this child, the mother became ill and went to the hospital. Later, she had to recuperate for nine months. For this, she went to a rest home in the mountains, taking her second child with her. Denis, on the other hand, was placed in a foster family with the sister-in-law of the nurse who had taken care of him. The boy remained there for about one year, and everything seemed perfectly all right. Afterwards, however, it became known that Denis had been treated with extreme strictness: he was screamed at if he did not keep quiet, and corporal punishment was used in order to force him to obey; he was tied to his crib, which made it impossible for him to move. They thus succeeded in converting the child into an extremely submissive little boy. When he finally returned to his family, he was "well-trained"; from then on, he never presented any educational problems, even obeying his little sister, who tyrannized over him.

The Lambert family is in good health. With regard to Denis' ancestry, nothing unusual is to be noted, either on the parental or on the maternal side.

Denis has always been a healthy child. Except for measles, he has had no diseases; he never had whooping cough. He was quiet, dreamy, and lazy and he liked best playing by himself with blocks or some other toys. He never had any childhood fears, and allegedly had no phobias of any sort. He seemed to become somewhat indolent, at an early age.

When Denis was seven years old, he entered the village school. In school, he was very quiet and obedient, but he never volunteered to speak and was extremely slow, maintaining that he could not take part in the work or solve any of the problems, because he did not understand them. Toward the end of the school year, his parents took him out of school and placed him in a home for slow learners. Two years later, he was transferred to yet another school. This time he was enrolled in an educational institution for mentally retarded children, where he made friends with a boy who was a year older and whose parents lived in France. After three years, Denis' friend, Clement, was taken home by his parents, a private tutor having now been engaged to instruct him. Denis was permitted to accompany Clement. He thus went to live in a small French town and, in a very short time, he had mastered the French language to the great surprise of both Clement's parents and his own. A year later, after Denis had become 14 years old, he had to return to Switzerland, where he entered an institution in Waadtland. Here he took English as well as Latin, and both languages presented no difficulties to him. In all other subjects Denis did less well, however. It seemed that his gifts were one-sided, as one often observes in the mentally retarded. He was quite skillful at manual work, but slow. Since Denis' teacher maintained that Denis must be mentally retarded, he was examined by the school psychologist at the end of the first school year. The latter confirmed the teacher's diagnosis and recommended that Denis be placed in a so-called "special" class. Being extremely grieved and ashamed to have a child of inferior ability, his parents chose instead to send him away from the village, and to enter him in the above-mentioned home. Under the circumstances, they were overjoyed with their second child, Anna, who was intellectually very gifted, and who passed the high-school entrance examination without any difficulty. Anna was their consolation.

Denis is very friendly, polite, willing, and pleasant. He is instantly ready to submit to the tests, recollecting that, when he was six years old, he had been given similar tests by the school guidance counselor (at that time the Binet-Simon test had shown an intelligence quotient of 58).

First the Zulliger Individual Test is administered to Denis. Since even a cursory scrutiny of this test shows that Denis could not possibly be mentally retarded, he was in addition tested with the Rorschach Test, the Behn-Rorschach Test, the Duess Fables Test, and the Tree Test, for we wished to obtain comparative material in order to arrive at a more reliable evaluation (see Table 5).

| *Zulliger Individual Test* | Beginning: 2:45 P.M. |

Card I.

The skull of a monkey (upper center portion)	DF + Ad/anat H repression
with white eye sockets: one can see through them	SFC eyes
c Two cat heads (center dark area, upper part)	DdF + Ad
b Italy (outermost lower part)	DF ± geog
c A harlequin (at the right outer top portion); one sees only the head with a peaked cap	DdF + Hd *pars pro toto*
a A mutilated human being sitting, with wooden legs. He is hiding behind something	WM + H O mutilation "hidden"

Card II.

(Prolonged reaction time; turns the card back and forth hesitantly. Sighs, shakes his head) ..	shock
b Fishes (green area)	DF + A
a Brown beetles, larvae	DFC A P
An X-ray of a reddish tinge, a section through the spine or something similar	DCFChF X-ray "or"

Card III.

| (Prolonged reaction time, turning the card back and forth indecisively) .... | shock |

429

a A hand with revolver (inner center
   portion) .... DoF + Hd/weapon
  Butterfly (center red area) .... DF + A P
b A dog (lower red portion) .... DF + A
c Greece, the spits of land (laterally,
   the "fists" of the whole configuration) .... DF ± geog
a Two dwarfs are dancing (outer
   red area) .... DM + H P
  or running away .... "or"
  (Laughs): Two figures riding, in
  old-fashioned clothes, trying
  to lift something .... WM + H P

                    End: 2:54 P.M.

Rorschach Test   Beginning: 3:00 P.M.

I.

A headless woman raises her hands
   high up (center portion) ...... DM + H mutilation
b An imaginary animal with wings
   (upper part of the picture) ..... DF + A O
a A building in a foreign land. It is
  Chinese and it has odd windows . WSF + arch

II.

(Prolonged reaction time. Turns
   the card back and forth for a
   long time) .... shock
a A small fir tree (center portion) .. DF + pl
b A dog (upper part of the picture,
   dark area) .... DF + A
  (Turns the card back and forth)
  A dancer on her toes, in a white
  dress. She stretches her arms
  high up .... SMFC H O white as color
c Sunset (center red area) .... DCF nat

III.

c (Turns the card)
a A tree branch (small dark configuration) .... DF + pl
  Or, this way, it is a leg with foot .. DoF + Hd "or"

c A young crow just about to fly off
(center portion of the larger
dark configuration) .... DdF + A

c Monkeys looking down (outer red
area) .... DM + A

IV.

A snake's head and neck (outer
portion) .... DF + Ad P

b A stooping man carrying a load
(right upper portion) .... DM + H

A speckled ornament such as one
sees on nut-wood furniture .... WFCh ornament O

V.

A bat .... WF + A P

Pincers (bottom center portion) .. DF + obj

VI.

A fur rug .... (FCh) → WF + AP

A cat's head (top portion) .... DF + Ad

c A small wrought table leg (bottom
center line) .... DdF + obj

VII.

Atoll island .... WF ± geog

A head mask (center portion) .... DF + Hd/mask

VIII.

(Prolonged reaction time, hesitant
turning of the card) .... shock

a Butterfly with delicate colors
(orange-red area) .... DFC A

c A stag's head (gray area) .... DF ± Ad

IX.

d A witch grabbing a fleeing child
by the hair (green area; upper
half of the picture) .... DM + H O

X.

Spiders (outer blue portion) ..... DF + A P

c A lyra (green center area) .... DF + obj

a Caterpillars (center green area) .. DFC A

End: 3:14 P.M.

Behn-Rorschach Test   Beginning: 3:20 P.M.

I.

Two bears .... DF + A P

c Two sitting squirrels (upper center portion) .... DF + A

II.

Two dogs .... DF + A P

Two little devils dancing (center
   red inner area) .... DM + H P

Pelvis (upper red portion) .... DSF — anat

c A hand pointing (top portion) ... DF + Hd

c A young corn plant (red inner
   area) .... DF + pl

III.

(Prolonged reaction time, turns
   the card back and forth) ...... shock

a A man pushing a small car (dark
   black area within the dark configuration on the right side) .... DdMs scene O

b The helmet of a papal Swiss guard
   (a part of the upper larger dark
   figure) .... DF + obj O

a A head with a pointed beard ..... DoF + Hd

The whole are men pointing to
   something .... WM + H P

IV.

a c Skiers who fell on their backsides
   (center upper periphery) ...... DdMs H P

Butterfly .... WF + A P

Or a masked figure, spreading its
   arms, like a Ku Klux Klan man . WM + H O "or"

V.

A jet plane .... WF + obj

Or a dancer turning with great
   speed .... WM + H O "or"

VI.

a c A boat anchor (dark center portion) .... DF + obj

432

c A spade, a garden tool (lowest S) .. SF + obj
b A sitting woman (the S within the
    center upper part) .... SM + H O

VII.

a c Two heads of old men with beards
    (top portion) .... DoF + Hd
a A crow's head (uppermost portion) DdF + Ad

VIII.

(Prolonged reaction time)
a c Two hen-like birds (orange area) . DFC A P
    Little fishes (blue area) .... DF + A
    Chameleon (red area) .... DF + A P

IX.

a c A bird of prey (blue area) .... DF + A P
    Two squirrels (orange area) ...... DFC A
b A chicken (upper brown area) .... DF + A
c An owl (center light-blue area) ... DF + A

X.

An aviary .... WCF obj A O
On top there are two green parrots DFC A
    underneath two reddish ones .. DFC A
A badger (outer blue area, upper
    portion) .... DF + A
A peacock (inner blue area, the
    lower configuration) .... DF + A

According to the test results (see Table 5), Denis cannot possibly be mentally retarded. Rather, his innate intelligence indicates that his mental ability is of a superior level (a relatively short reaction time with a high F+%; orderly sequence; adequate admixture of M; normal percentage column; the number of A is larger than the number of Ad; the number of H is larger than the number of Hd; the apperceptive type has a wide range, yet it is not too wide; there is an adequate quantity of O). Even in the Behn-Rorschach Test, F+% as well as concentration ability (the variability of contents is not too large) remain high, despite fatigue (sequence remains orderly).

TABLE 5

Subject: Denis Lambert
Psychograms
(The numbers refer to the Zulliger Individual Test, the Rorschach Test, and the Behn-Rorschach Test)

	Zulliger Individual Test	Rorschach Test	Behn-Rorschach Test
Time:	9 minutes	14 minutes	13 minutes
Number of responses:	15/3	27/6	31/12
WS	—		
W	2	4	6
D	9	18	19
Dd	2	2	2
Do	1	1	2
S	1	1	3
F	9 (−1)	17 (−1)	21 (−0.5)
M	3	5	5
Ms	—	—	2
FC	2	3	4
CF	tendency	1	1
FCh	—	1	—
CCh	1	—	—
F+%	88	94	98
A%	40	44	48
P%	26	15	24
O%	13	15	18
H%	46	35	33
Red shock		+	+
Color shock		+	+
Ch-shock		—	—
Sequence:	orderly, tend. to inversion	same	same
Experience balance:	3 M : 1½ C	5 : 2½	5 : 3
Apperceptive type:	W — D — Dd/Do — S	same	same
P	4		7
O	2		6
H	3		6
Hd	3		3
anat	1		1
scene	—		1
A	4		15
Ad	2		1
obj	—		5
pl	—		1
nat	—		—
arch	1		—
geog	2		1
ornament	—		1
Remarks:	"eyes" / "hidden" / "or" / H = repression / white as color / perspective / pars pro toto / mutilation / mask	white as color / mutilation / mask	"or" / mask / one W in Card XI

434

Thus, innate intelligence level is high, yet it has been prevented from developing. Color shocks indicate that neurotic inhibitions exist; red shocks as well as Do lead us to the conclusion that anxiety is present. Considering the rather introversive experience balance, psychasthenic symptoms may be expected. Nevertheless, colors still exist, for in addition to the FC there is one CF in both the Ro and the Bero. Experience balance approaches ambiequality with a preponderance of M. Consequently, compulsions may be expected. Since M prevail, they are effective at the psychic rather than at the motility level. Most probably compulsive thinking, rather than compulsive neurotic rituals, etc., is present.

"Mask" interpretations have been produced in all three tests. This leads us to the conclusion that Denis acquired a "mask," hiding behind it (like the "mutilated human being" in the Zulliger Test, last response to Card I). A subject producing "eye" responses feels that he is being observed and controlled, and he observes and restrains himself. And people producing "mutilations" in their interpretations feel that they themselves are somehow "mutilated." White is seen as a color by individuals who are extremely sensitive, and who attempt to dissimulate their hypersensitivity, which is correlated with their being easily hurt. Inner uncertainty is often expressed by two interpretations connected by an "or." People who reverse their sequence (as Denis does) are affectively—as well as with regard to their intellectual expression, their judgments, and their verbal formulations—cautiously anxious. The interhuman relationships of subjects who "repress" H (in other words, who interpret an A where other subjects usually produce an H) are in some way impaired. However, since Denis's H% is overly high (in the Zulliger Individual Test the norm is approximately 20-25%; in the Ro and Bero, it is about 12%), he is nonetheless greatly dependent upon such interhuman relationships. In his case one can suppose a disappointment in somebody very close to him, a disappointment that he experienced during his early childhood, and which left a traumatic effect on him that lasted throughout his entire life. In the Zulliger Individual Test, Denis's tendency to repression is clearly revealed when he interprets a whole human being, even though he has seen only a human head (*pars pro toto*). This is also seen in his using perspective in one of his interpretations (Card I, first response). Most of Denis's flexor kinesthesias are found in the Zulliger Individual Test—which leads us to the conclusion that Denis escapes from the outer world into the world of autistic phantasies, turning away from his environment.

Both Ro and Bero confirm the results of the Zulliger Individual Test (a subject capable of producing a well-conceived W in Card X of the Bero is certainly not mentally retarded!) "Losing one's head"—in other words, intellectual inhibition—is very aptly described in the first interpretation of the Ro ("a headless woman").

Thus, our conclusion must be that we are dealing here with *"pseudo mental retardation,"* which has developed on the basis of a neurosis and inadequately mastered anxiety. In terms of his innate ability, Denis should be quite capable of attending high school.

This could not be established by *intelligence tests,* since they merely indicate *manifest intelligence* (as when Denis was tested by the school psychologist). On the other hand, the Zulliger Test, the Ro, and the Bero show his *innate* intelligence, and at the same time disclose why his innate ability has been prevented from developing.

Assisted by anamnesis, we may now state: Denis is still trying to escape from the "witch who grabs a fleeing child by the hair" (Ro, Card IX). The "witch" is probably the nurse who took care of the little boy while his mother was away, and who treated him with inhuman strictness.

The disappointment mentioned above concerns this "witch," but it also concerns the mother who "abandoned" her little son when she went away to give birth to his little sister and then stayed away in order to recuperate.

The Ro's response to Card IX (Ro) is as much an individual and complex response as is the interpretation that produced a "mutilated" human being (Zulliger Test I and Ro I).

Since all the various tests that have been performed yield the same results, confirming and supplementing one another, we may state with a high degree of certainty: Denis is not really a mentally retarded individual. However, because of neurotic complications, he is at present incapable of developing his superior innate intelligence. Inner factors are "preventing" him from doing it.

At present, Denis does not need vocational training but rather psychotherapeutic treatment, which will release his intellectual inhibitions; later, Denis will be able to catch up with his high-school work, and subsequently embark on a course of studies.

Since he is a D type (Zulliger Test, Ro, Bero), and has produced many M, he is not suited for a purely scientific profession. He ought to be permitted to use his hands. Thus, he should become a physician rather than a minister or a lawyer; he might study architecture, or some other profession that is taught at a Technical Institute.

If his professional training were to entail nothing else but language ability, his manual talents would not be used to good advantage. Therefore a profession based solely upon his language skills could neither fully satisfy him nor "make him happy" (for instance, if he were to become a translator or an interpreter).

The Lambert parents are advised to leave Denis temporarily at the home, while making it possible for him at the same time to have psychotherapeutic treatment. Later, Denis ought to attend a private high school and obtain a high school diploma; only then should he decide about his vocational training.

This recommendation was made in 1952, and the parents accepted it. In the fall of 1954, Denis passed the entrance examination for a high school. The work proved easy for him, and later on, he decided to study chemistry.

L. SCHIZOPHRENIC EPISODE

Charles de P., who is 18 years old and comes from a wealthy family, is a junior at the public high school in L. He is believed to be extremely bright: his teachers say that he will pass his final examinations, not merely satisfactorily but easily and with excellent grades. One day, however, he declared that he was utterly tired of school. He wanted to leave school, continue his education by teaching himself, and then apply for a Swiss Confederation examination, in order to obtain a high-school diploma. He was well aware of the fact that such an examination is more difficult than the one at the public high school, yet this did not worry him. He wanted to work at gaining time and he maintained that, if he were allowed to work by himself, he would be prepared to apply for and to pass the examination within six months. He was even convinced that if he were permitted to do as he wished, he could gain an entire school year.

More than one of his teachers believed it possible that the highly intelligent youth would reach his goal sooner by teaching himself than by remaining in high school.

However, to the parents, their son's wish seemed somewhat strange, at least unusual; before granting their permission, they wanted to submit Charles to a psychological examination. They have made some observations regarding Charles which alarm them. In the attic of his parents' home Charles has furnished a study room all by himself. He maintains that in the attic he is undisturbed by others. He locks the door whenever he is there and he has wired the lock for electricity—"as a warning against possible intruders." During his vacation, he buried himself in the attic; sometimes he did not even come down for meals, neglected his outer appearance, did not wash or shave any more. All this was accompanied by the assertion that these matters are unessential and that it was more important for him to study and to contemplate himself. He also neglected his numerous former friends, as well as all those sports in which he had previously engaged eagerly.

Charles is an only child. During a rather lengthy conversation with the parents, it was revealed that the child had been unwanted at the time of his birth. The pregnancy took the mother by surprise; when it was definitely established, she flew into a rage and cried. The woman had wanted to remain without children for a few more years. She was ashamed to become "shapeless"; when Charles was born, she did not even want to nurse him. Charles was raised from birth on baby cereals, and at first he reacted with stomach trouble and by being underweight. A special diet prescribed by the doctor helped to overcome these difficulties. Until he was approximately one-and-a-half years old, the child was cared for by baby nurses. Then, discovering how pretty he was, the mother began to devote herself more intensely to little Charles and to spoil him. During his early childhood, he was prone to illness. After a tonsillectomy during the third year of his life, his health improved; since then, Charles has never had any serious diseases.

The boy's high intelligence showed itself early. He became toilet-trained very early, and he walked and talked early. He liked to play by himself, and did not seem to need others to play with. In kindergarten he was submissive and shy at first, but then he frequently brought playmates home with him and, while watching them at play, he would put all his many toys at their disposal. Later, in school, he was almost always at the head of his class. Subsequently, he expressed a desire to study law and to embark upon a diplomatic career. The father is an attorney and is considered well-known as a lawyer; he is a high officer in the Swiss Army.

Charles came only once to the psychological examination. When he was supposed to come for a second time, he was sick in bed with a sore throat. Instead of Charles, his father came, in order to obtain advice as to what should best be done with his son.

Zulliger Individual Test

	Time:	20 minutes
	Number of responses:	40/10

I.

A beetle	W F+ A P	
c Looked at from here, it is also an insect	W F+ A	
At the outline—like something geographical—yes, it is a continent	DW F± geog	
a It is symmetrical	stress on symmetry	
and yet not entirely symmetrical (points to the "head" in upper center)	irritated by inexact symmetry	
c Bagpipes, one can clearly see the individual parts (EFG 3/4)	D F(C) obj O+	

439

a Here, in the middle: lungs; they
   are in the middle (darker blot)   D F— anat position responses
   Cats whose .... D F Ad *pars pro toto*
   eyes shine at night (upper center
   portion) .... S FC eyes
d An attack (points to EFG 6/7/8/9)
   (To the question "Why?" the
   subject shrugs his shoulders: "I
   do not know; that is just my im-
   pression!") .... D F± abstraction aggression
   Here, then, are cannons and armor
   (G 6/7 and FG 8) .... Dd F+ obj aggression
   The caricature of a lady (D 9) .... Dd F+ H O+, dehumanization
                                            M repression
   It could be the picture of a woman
   centaur (D 8/9) .... D Ms H O+
a The head of a Mongolian with eyes
   (FG 3) .... S → Dd F+ Hd, eyes
c This way it is also a head .... Dd F+ Hd, tendency to
                                            perseveration

II.

   (Laughs!) An anatomical experi-
   ment, torn (red area and S) . S → D CF anat, defect
   Two imaginary animals (brown
   area) (the color plays no part in
   the response) .... D F+ A
   Fishes, imaginary fishes, aquarium
   fishes (green area) .... D F+ A
   The head of a duck coming up
   from the mud (B 5/6, upper part
   of S, one half of it) .... S F— Ad O—
c Heads of comedians (red area,
   outer periphery, upper portion,
   BC 7 and 4) .... Dd F+ Hd
d Cuttlefish (green area) .... D F+ A
b Part of a modern picture: a Negro
   head looking into space, the hair
   is distinctly set off (F 6) .... Do F(C) Hd, M repression
b A ham (EFG 7/6) .... Dd CF food
a Two heads and hands of some
   gossiping women, just statues
   (upper red portion) .... Do F+ Hd, M repression
a A white tie, a so-called "fancy" one
   (upper S) .... S FC clothing, white as color

440

III.

Two ghosts, witches dancing
   around a ..... combinatory { W MCh H O+ P
   butterfly ...... { D F+ A P
Running children (outer red area) D M H P
They wear pointed Sicilian helmets Dd F+ obj
This picture too is not completely
   symmetrical (points to tiny details within the red center por-
   tion) .... symmetry accentuation and
      criticism

At the right, it is rather a little
   devil, even the color is well
   chosen (red outer area) .... D MFC devil (P)
b A stag looking out from behind
   something (larger dark blot, on
   top) .... D F± A
a Two prize fighters who stopped
   moving (the "prize fighters" are
   seen against the border of the
   card), as if they had wanted to
   run away and hesitated suddenly W M H O
Here, flies are swarming across the
   hand and underneath is one, too
   (dots) .... Dd F± A
c A young prince with three hands,
   holding the thumb of one of
   them in his mouth (CDE 7) .... D M H O+
A strong man arriving during a
   storm, liberating himself from
   something (CDE 4/3/2) .... D M H O+, individual
      interpretation

The whole is something eaten away,
   something that has been fouled W ChC defective O−
The cut-off hand of a robot (small
   dark blot) .... D F+ Md dehumanized O−
   with a broken cable rope (E 2) Dd F+ obj
d Zeus, hidden behind a morning
   cloud (red area EF 10) .... D CF mythology O Ms tendency
a An elongated horse's head (C 4) Dd F+ Ad
a Dwarfs who have lost their balance
   and are falling backward (small
   dark figure) .... D M H O+
Gorgon heads ("heads" on top)
            Do → D F+ Hd

441

Scoring:

			Time:	20 minutes
			Number of responses:	40/10

DW	= 1	F+	= 18	H		= 9
W	= 5	F−	= 2	Hd		= 7
D	= 19	F±	= 4	A		= 8
Dd	= 10	M	= 6	Ad		= 4
Do	= 2 (3)	MCh	= 1	obj		= 4
S	= 3 (5)	FC	= 2	anat		= 2
F+%	= 83	CF	= 3	clothing		= 1
A%	= 30	ChC	= 1	food		= 1
H%	= 45	F(C)	= 2	eyes		= (2 times)
anat%	= 5	P	= 5	geog		= 1
P%	= 12	O	= 13 (−4)	mythology		= 1
O%	= 32±			abstraction		= 2

Sequence: orderly-loose
Experience balance: 7 M : 5 C
Apperceptive type: DW : W : D : Dd : Do : S

Remarks:

Symmetry accentuation and   M repression
symmetry criticism   MCh
Position response   White as color
Pars pro toto interpretation   "Devil"
Defect interpretations   Abstractions
Dehumanization

EVALUATION:

I suspect that Charles is schizophrenic, on the following grounds:

1. Since the red blots are interpreted in the first response to Card II, it is hardly possible to speak of neurosis. At the same time, this interpretation is a "defect" one ("torn").

2. The "attack" interpretation: (Card I/8) approaches a contamination (being followed by the interpretations of "armor" and "cannons"); besides, abstractions are often seen in schizophrenics.

3. Also, it is frequently found that schizophrenics stress symmetry. These subjects have the uncanny feeling that they are "coming apart" and therefore they search for a central and centralizing force that will give them support. In addition, Charles is irritated by the fact that symmetry is not always and not every-

where adhered to ([Card I]: "and yet not entirely symmetrical.") See also Card II/5. Hermann Rorschach had earlier stated that such "pedantries" are reason for suspecting schizophrenia.

4. Where other, normal subjects give the interpretation of human figures, Charles produces dehumanized figures, as in Card I/10, Card II/9, and Card III/16.

5. The sequence is rather orderly in Card I. In Card II it is already quite loose and in Card III—although not to a large extent—it is nevertheless irregular. In schizophrenics, one quite often observes this increasing loosening of sequence.

6. Especially the Dd are irregular. Sometimes one Dd is selected within the inner part of the picture, sometimes the borders of the picture are searched for Dd. On the occasion of discussing his test before the Swiss Association for Psychoanalysis, Rorschach stated that such a fluctuation in the selection of Dd leads to a suspicion of schizophrenia.

7. A number of further "defect" interpretations are found in the test, as in Card III/12 and 13. The entire record makes a very strange impression.

8. The two eye interpretations, I/12 and I/7, indicate paranoid impulses. These are even more apparent in the MCh response in Card III/1, as well as by the H%, which is too high in proportion to the other test factors.

9. Primarily, the position interpretation in Card I/5 must be evaluated as a very pathognomonic one, in relation to the other factors that have been mentioned above.

10. Intellectual adaptation to the environment is poor: the P%; the fact that both experience balance and apperceptive type are too broad, that the sequence becomes increasingly loose, that O% is too high and contains several O—, and that there are relatively too few D. It is more difficult to evaluate the existing introversion, as indicated by the mere number of M, because there are several original M responses. All of this points to a tendency toward highly subjective and autistic thinking.

ADVICE TO THE FATHER:

It was reported to the father that it might well be that his son was the victim of a schizophrenic episode. Under no circumstances should he be allowed to lose contact with his schoolmates. Therefore it was not advisable for him to leave school. First of all, the father was instructed that an examination by a psychiatrist was absolutely necessary.

This recommendation was not followed.

Charles was permitted to leave school and to continue studying by teaching himself. Thereupon the boy withdrew completely from other people, and even refused to appear at the family table. The food had to be brought up to him to his study. He became more and more disorderly, confused, and negligent. Ultimately, he ate nothing but rolls with ham, and drank tea; he lost so much weight that he finally looked like a ghost.

The psychiatrist, who was consulted only then, ordered that he should be immediately admitted to a private mental hospital. There Charles was submitted to an insulin shock treatment. The diagnosis was: paranoid schizophrenia. The treatment proved successful, and he was able to be dismissed. He then continued his studies at a private high school and began to study law at a university. From 1958 until 1962, he did not have a relapse; he is now well.

M. SCHIZOPHRENIA—BLIND DIAGNOSIS

A doctor who is a friend of mine sends me the record of a Zulliger Test—and nothing else—and then calls me up: he has examined an 18-year-old young man, has found the right diagnosis, and has also administered the Zulliger Test to him. In the doctor's opinion, the test does not show anything. He asks me whether I can find anything in the record and what it may be.

I did not see the subject, nor did I know anything else about him: all I had was the record. It follows:

Duration of the test: 8 minutes, 7 of which are spent on Card I.

I.

This is a cloud-devil! He wants to
  get at me (= he "threatens me") WMCh devil O contamination;
                                   self-reference

444

II.

Also devilish .... perseveration

III.

(grins mischievously) I do not let
    myself be caught! .... self-reference

One may interpret boldly when one deals with a doctor who is also a friend. I therefore asked him: "Isn't the young man a schizophrenic, a paranoiac one?"

It was actually true.

How, then, could the "suspected" diagnosis be established on the basis of one single response—the response to Card I?

The contamination leads to the assumption that schizophrenia is present; this assumption is strengthened by both self-reference and perseveration. The subject has labored for seven minutes over Card I and has then become convinced that it represents the devil, perhaps also a cloud; on this basis the 18-year-old young man reaches the formulation "cloud-devil," which is very similar to the contaminations that are typical of certain schizophrenias. After he has once conceived the idea that the picture represents a devil, it becomes a "fixed idea"; thus, he also identifies Cards II and III as devils who wish to tempt, to "catch" him —he is no longer capable of seeing anything else in the cards but threatening devils; he confabulates devils everywhere. This leads us to suspect schizophrenia. The fact that we are dealing here with a paranoiac is obvious because the patient feels himself threatened both by the pictures and by the doctor who examines him and who, in his self-reference, appears as a menace or a "seducer" to him. This is the reason why he grins mischievously when he talks to the examiner saying (Card III): "I do not let myself be caught!"

I have included this small example in order to show that scanty responses may frequently lead one to suspect certain diseases. It may indeed seem presumptuous, even impermissible to entertain suspicions on the basis of a single or very few interpretations. However, if one has repeatedly had similar experiences, one becomes more sure of oneself; in any case, the "blind diagnosis" made under the conditions I have described—in other words, not delivered to the patient himself but to his physician, who is able to verify it with the help of other means—serves only as a comparison with findings derived by other test methods.

N. SCHIZOPHRENIA—BLIND DIAGNOSIS

I should like to present yet another blind diagnosis, which was also made for a physician, a psychotherapist. The problem had been raised whether 20-year-old *Lore F.,* who was very efficient in her profession but somewhat "strange" in her dealings with other people, was neurotic or schizophrenic. The form-interpretation test should help to decide which of the two hypotheses was the more probable one.

Zulliger Test

Time: 33 minutes
Number of responses: 17, 7 of which were given to Card II

I.

1. A beetle that had worn a black mask before; now it has taken it off, and it is holding it in front of its mouth .... WF + A P
DFC mask, humanization

   (The "black mask" is the darker spot, in the center) .... black as color
unreal combination
Ms tendency

2. On top, there is a bird; actually there are two birds, confronting each other (B 4/A 5; A 6/B 7) .. DF — A
uncertainty
self-correction

3. (The patient turns the card around in such a way that whatever was on the bottom is now on top)
Sideways (BC 3/4; BC 7/8), there are two mountains and a man with a weapon is just climbing up; the two men are just confronting each other (AB 4/5 – 6/7) .... F(C) → DMW + H O

446

4. Holding the card again in an
   upright position)
   This way, it is suddenly uni-
   lateral. Prometheus is looking
   down from a mountain
   ("Prometheus" = AB 4/5,
   everything else is the mountain. The head of "Prometheus" is accurately seen. His
   body, as well as the "mountain," are added by confabulation) .... DWMCh — H O

II.

1. A figure standing in a colored
   forest (the "figure" is the inner
   white space within the red
   axis; the red area is the
   "forest") .... SF — H
   combines with DCF forest

2. (Turning the card into the
   reverse position)
   Two animals approaching
   each other (brown area), wanting to eat the red and fighting
   about it. It is a dish from which
   both of them would like to eat,
   and both of them would like
   to come down .... M → DFC A
   combines with C and
   S → DF — obj

3. (Holding the card again in an
   upright position)
   A fungus at the bottom of a
   forest ("fungus" is the red blot,
   the "bottom of the forest" is
   the orange area), Iceland moss
   (points to the green portion) .. DF + pl
   DWCF forest O
   DCF pl

447

III.

1. Two birds (dark portion) flying
   through red evening clouds.
   They are bending their necks,
   as they usually do while flying . confabulation
                                      DWF — A, M tendency
                                      DCF clouds

2. Two children playing and
   throwing something again and
   again behind them (the "children" are the dark blots, the
   something that they are throwing behind them is the red;
   they take hold of it within the
   red center picture area and
   throw it behind them, red
   outer area) .... WM + H P (O)
                                  combinatory tendency

3. The entire black portion is a
   belt buckle. If one were to
   squeeze it together, it would
   close .... WF — obj clothing O—

4. (Placing the card on its right
   narrow edge)
   A landscape with a tower and a
   cloud (red area) that is re-
   flected (upper dark blot) ..... DWChF nature observation O—

5. (Turning the card to a reverse
   position)
   Two caterpillars (larger dark
   blots), and there on top is
   another one, creeping over
   their shoulders (smaller dark
   blot) .... DWF — A
                                  DF + A

6. (Placing the card again into an
   upright position)
   The shadow image made with
   white paper (inner white space
   above the center red blot) de-
   picts a cactus; the black around
   it is the background .... SWF + pl
                                 → white as color
                                 → black as color

448

TABLE 6

Scoring:
Subject: *Lore F.*

Cd.	DW	SW	W	D	S	M	MCh	Ms	FC	CF	C	F(C)	FCh	ChF	P	O
I	3	—	1	2	—	1	1	(1)	1	—	—	(1)	—	—	1	2
II	—	—	—	5	1(2)	(1)	—	—	1	3	(1)	—	—	—	—	—
III	.5	1	—	2	—	1(1)	—	—	—	1	—	—	—	1	1	3(—2)
Total	8	1	1	9	1(2)	2(2)	1	(1)	2	4	(1)	(1)	—	1	2	5(—2)

F+ = 4
F— = 6
F+% = 40
A% = 32
P% = 10
O% = about 20±
H% = 26
H = 4
mask = 1
A = 6
obj = 2
pl = 3
forest, nat = 3
cloud = 1

Sequence: loose, tendency to inversion
Experience balance: 3 and more M : 4 – 5 C
Apperceptive type: DW — SW — W — D — S
confused!

Black as color
White as color
Irrational combinations
Extremely strong combinatory tendency, together
with confabulations
Since sequence is inversed in Card II, color shock
probably exists

449

Short evaluation for the physician:

Test factors:	Corresponding to:
Testing time/number of responses	Does not like to express herself; is rather reserved.
Sw and S and confabulation	Is somehow not satisfied with her role in life; has the tendency to take things seriously; if a situation is partly disagreeable to her, the patient immediately rejects the entire situation.
S : M and colors; self-criticism ..	She is critical toward herself as well as toward her environment; mistrusts herself, corrects herself.
W tendency and self-criticism; number of responses	Ideality; a will to achieve; quality ambition and tenacious quantity ambition; diligence.
Flexor kinesthesias	Highly autistic; instead of being acted upon, matters are dealt with by imagination.
Several MCh or M—, for instance "Prometheus" in Card I	Autistic fantasies extend into the realm of the fantastic.
MCh and tendency to MC (Card II/2)	Intuitions, "visions"; since there exists a tendency to produce pure C, and since some CF are almost C, it is possible for the patient to experience ecstatic states.
Preponderance of CF	Affectivity is partly unadapted; sensibility, sensitivity, emotionalism.
White as color	Dissimulates her supersensitivity.
"Mask" (Card I) and Ch tendency	Shows a pseudo adapted attitude to the outer world, which is not quite genuine; it is rigid, forced; it is the result of having been "well brought up" and does not derive from an inner affective equilibrium.

M in general for the case on hand .... Strongly introversive; has creative ideas that are frequently "strange," however; "egocentricities." Imagination and fantasies are stronger than her sense of reality.

DWM .... Illusions of strongly intrapsychic quality; self-deceit with regard to reality.

Nature observations, tendency to Ms .... To some extent, she conducts herself with naive-infantile playfulness.

ChF .... Depressive moods are not controlled and mastered by the intellect any more; the patient "succumbs" helplessly to her depressions.

ChF, FC, S, and a high H% ..... Longs for attachment, but is disappointed by other people; feels herself "misunderstood"; rejects other people (regarding SW); withdraws from them.

Innate intelligence .... Very high innate intelligence, strongly influenced by artistic ability.

W tendency
combination ability .... Need for combinatory thinking; need for organization; need for order.

M as creative ability
F+%; DW .... Her arrangements are, however, unworldly, unusual, unreal.

Apperceptive type .... Thinking is (abnormally) disturbed.

F+ alternates with F—, MCh, M— in their relationship to CF and C .... Suspicion of strong psychic disturbances; states of confusion.

Color shock and experience balance .... Compulsive phenomena, compulsive acts; possibly compulsion neurosis, which may be covering some even more serious disturbances.

General impression .... Strong suspicion of schizophrenia, covered up by a compulsion neurosis.

451

FACTORS THAT OCCASION SUSPICION OF SCHIZOPHRENIA:

MCh, M—, irregular apperceptive type; change from very sharply conceived to completely inaccurate or confabulated F and M. In a compulsion neurosis, F+% would have been high, experience balance more strongly coarctated, sequence rigid, apperceptive type more concentrated. Thus we are not dealing here with a compulsion neurosis.

The results of the Zulliger Test that has been administered to the patient therefore confirm the physician's suspicion of schizophrenia (see Table 6).

O. SCHIZOPHRENIA—BLIND DIAGNOSIS

This case provides an example of double presentation of the test according to Salomon.[2]

A psychiatrist has sent me the following record. It was neither scored nor evaluated. He asked me what I could make of it, for he would like to compare his clinical diagnosis with my test diagnosis. Except for the sex and age of the subject, no anamnestic data were given.

Johann Schwander, 46 years old.

1. Presentation

Time: 9 minutes
Number of responses: 21

I.

A spider monster	W ChC "monster," A O—
A ghost or a spirit approaching threateningly	W MCh H O, ghost
A rotten meat-eating plant	W ChC pl, defect O—
c A nude woman is lying there (EFG 3-8)	SDd M — H, sex O—
A soldier with a rifle and a rucksack (B-G 6-8)	D M H, itemized
d Italy (D 2)	D F± geog

[2] Fritz Salomon, *Ego and Libido Diagnosis in the Zulliger Test* (translation in preparation).

452

II.

A female sex organ (red area and S) DS CF sex
Eyes with nerves (green area) .... SD F— eyes, anat
Feces (brown area) .... D C nat
b Brush (green area) .... D CF pl
c A monkey's head (red area CB 7) Dd F± Ad
Snakes (green area, C 8) .... Dd F+ A

III.

A robot or people from Mars (outer
    red area) .... D M H P "or"
                                   dehumanization tendency

The large figures are women wear-
    ing slacks and high-heeled shoes W M H P O combinatory
they are pursued by men (outer red
    area) .... D M H P
the women are wearing a bloody
    piece of underwear (red center
    area) .... D CF obj/blood
b A pig (EF 2/3) .... D F+ A
c An animal's denture, a jaw, one can
    see the teeth; on top its uvula DW F— Ad
    (red center area) .... D CF anat
and next to it the tonsils (red outer
    area) .... D CF anat
                                   combination, confabulation
                                   position response
c It could also be the heart (red
    center area) .... D CF anat

2. Presentation

Time: 6 minutes
Number of responses: 9

I.

Cloud-witches' dance .... W MCh scene O—, witches
c A nude woman is lying there (EFG
    3-8) .... SDd M— H sex repetition
d Italy (D 2) .... D F± geog repetition

II.

Simply color spots, two red ones,
    two brown ones, two green ones W C color naming, color counting
A nature heart (subsequent inquiry
    reveals; red area is the heart, all
    the other colors are "nature") ... W CF contamination

453

III.

b A dog (lower red area) .... D F+ A
b On top there is a wild sow
      (FEDCBA 4-2) .... D F+ A
b and a duck (EDC 4-1) .... D F+ A
      and the whole is really a zoo ....
                              DW → W F± P O—

EVALUATION:

Even the first presentation produces a very unusual test, which leads us to suspect mental disease (see Table 7).

The very first response, "spider monster," could be a contamination. We cannot be sure, however, because a healthy child could also produce such an interpretation. The second response is a WMCh, and such a response is never produced by completely healthy subjects. The third response, a "rotten meat-eating plant," WChC, a defect interpretation, is again strange. It is almost as if it were a symbolic interpretation of a disease process that exists in the subject. The fourth response, a "nude woman is lying there," reveals a strong sexual conflict. Now, suddenly, after these "abnormal" and unusual interpretations, there follow a sharply conceived M+ and a geographic response that is relatively accurately seen and not too rarely produced. One has the impression that the subject, after having been confused, has suddenly taken hold of himself again. Nevertheless, no P is produced for Card I, such as, perhaps, "crayfish," "crab," "bedbug," etc.

Without hesitation, a sex interpretation is produced again in Card II: the red color of the blot and the intermediate form have provoked it. Whatever has been stated regarding the sex interpretation in Card I becomes confirmed here: the subject is in the throes of a strong sexual conflict; there may exist an extraordinarily intense castration complex. I believe that the subject is a man who has not reached the genital stage sexually as yet, and has remained at the stage of a *voyeur*. He may be a homosexual; he is afraid to look at female genitalia, even though he is drawn to them as if by a magnet.

Scoring:
Subject: *Johann Schwander*

TABLE 7

	1. pr	2. pr	1 + 2 pr
DW =	1	↑	1(↑)
W =	4	4	8
D =	11	4	15
Dd =	2		2
DS =	1		1
SD =	2	1	3
P =	3		3
O =	5(—3)	2(—2)	7(—5)
Time =	9	6	15
Number of responses =	21	9	30

Sequence: orderly-loose
Experience balance: 6 M : 9½ C; 8 M : 12 C
Apperceptive type: DW : W : D : Dd : DS

Remarks:
"Monster-ghost-spirit"
Defect interpretation
SDdM—
Itemizing

	1. pr	2. pr	1 + 2 pr
F+ =	2	3	5
F— =	2		2
F± =	2	2	4
M =	5(—1)	1(—1)	6(—2)
MCh =	1	1	2
CF =	6	1	7
C =	1	1	2
ChC =	2		2
F+% =	50		64
A% =	24		30
H% =	29		23
P% =	14		10
O% =	24(∓)		23(∓)

"Or"
Repetitions
Color naming
color counting

	1. pr	2. pr	1 + 2 pr
H =	6	1	7
Hd =			
A =	3	4	7
Ad =	2		2
anat =	3		3
sex =	1(1)	(1)	1(3)
blood =			(1)
scene =	1		1
eyes =	1		1
obj =	1		1
pl =	2		2
nat =	1		1
geog =	1	1	2
contam. =		1	1
{ color / naming =	1		1

Position response
Mixture of combinations
 and confabulations
Contaminations

People who produce "eye" responses (Card II, second response) are inclined to paranoid self-control, and may also feel themselves outwardly observed (paranoid). In any case, MCh interpretations (Card I/2, and Card I/1 upon the repetition of the test) indicate that paranoid traits exist. The third response, "feces," a pure C response, is suspicious too, as are all pure C responses. They suggest a tendency toward drive eruptions, even though M may counterbalance C in the experience balance.

And now, strangely enough, the subject produces suddenly some "ordinary" responses once more: a "bush," a "monkey's head," "snakes" (the last-mentioned response could be a disguised sex interpretation, insinuating male genitalia this time). But again the impression is gained that the subject has collected his wits, regained his control.

This does not apply any longer when Card III is presented to the subject. His responses become more and more confused. First a combinatory-confabulatory W response is produced: "women in slacks and high-heeled shoes pursued by men; the women are wearing a bloody piece of underwear." No doubt, this is a "complex and individual interpretation." The subject probably identifies himself with women (homosexuality), and feels that he is being persecuted. The "bloody piece of underwear" is a pure color confabulation;[3] mentally normal subjects do not produce such responses. Our subject produces some more color confabulations: "uvula," "tonsils," "heart," which are probably at the same time position interpretations. All this leads us to suspect schizophrenia.

Considering that the subject has managed to produce at least one very pronounced confabulation response (Card III, first presentation: "an animal's denture, one can see the teeth"), as well as one with strong confabulatory traits, ("a nude woman lying there," Card I, both presentations), and considering that 7 CF and 2 C but no FC have been produced, that the sequence is orderly-to-loose, and that the F+% is quite low, it must be inferred that the subject has stealing impulses and a tendency to lie.

[3] According to Salomon, *loc. cit.*

The diagnosis becomes certain at the second presentation. For here we encounter responses that are most certainly contaminations; the "cloud witches' dance" (Card I) could be one of them. Undoubtedly the "nature heart" is such an interpretation (Card II), and the "zoo" (Card III) also come close to it. In addition, there is color naming, color counting, repetitions of interpretations which have already been produced at the first presentation and which the subject obviously does not remember any longer. Thus, he suffers memory lapses (in schizophrenics, these are usually based on somatopsychopathology, and are the result of physical brain damage).

The originally high intelligence of the subject is in the process of deterioration. This explains the fluctuation between sharply seen and (rather) "ordinary" interpretations and the odd ones. Some O are partly O—, O% is too high, P% is too low, the sequence is not stable enough (it is still orderly in Card I, becoming loose to confused in the later text).

On the basis of the test one must conclude that schizophrenia exists, with paranoid and erotomanic traits. There are also strong homosexual tendencies.

Later report of the physician: The subject, who has previously been a conscientious worker, has gradually become eccentric and has stolen money, spending it on himself. He came to the psychiatric examination upon the request of the business company. Since he had formerly been a faithful servant of the company, and especially since he had compensated for the damages, it did not merely dismiss him.

Medical diagnosis: Latent homosexual paranoiac. Should be subjected to insulin treatment and psychotherapy.

P. EPILEPSY

Marguerite B., 14 years old.

Zulliger Test: Time = 14 minutes

I.

Bat	....	FCh → WF + A
An open human body	....	FCh → WF − anat
Eyes	....	SF + Hd

c This is also a bat .... WF — A perseveration
A lady with a doll, but knees are
  not like these .... DM + H O pedantic accuracy, obj
                          criticism
A bent man who holds a cane .... DM + H O
  (at the left lower side of the
  picture; subject imitates the
  movement before interpreting)
"This is the first time I am doing
  this!"
"Did you do all this?"
A hand (gray figure over the center
  dark blot) .... DdF ± Hd
(counts the fingers:) one, two,
  three, four, five fingers .... DdF + Hd counting
"When I am at home I call myself
  Wagnière!"

II.

The cross of a church .... SF — obj O—
These are branches (green area) .. DCF pl
A brown sheep .... DFC A
Red .... D C color naming
A house (red area) .... DF — obj
  (points to the cards: "Does one
  have to pay for these?")
A heart (inner red area, the darker
  one) .... DCF anat
c Again a cross (the whole S between
  the brown and red areas) ...... SF + obj perseveration

III.

A mouse which is going to eat (the
  "leg" of the W figure) .... DF + A
A little dwarf (outer red area) .... DM + H P
A butterfly (red c) .... DF + A P
c Two cats, which want to catch the
  mice (larger dark blot) .... WF ± A confabulation
a Two men, one cannot see their
  legs (upper dark blot) .... M? → DF + H (P)

Subject: *Marguerite B.,* 14 years old
Scoring:

Time: 14 minutes
Number of responses: 20/7

DW	=		F+	=	7	P	=	2
SW	=		F−	=	4	O	=	3
WS	=		F±	=	2	H	=	4
W	=	4	M	=	3 – 4	Hd	=	3
D	=	11	Ms	=		anat	=	2
Dd	=	2	FC	=	1	blood	=	
Do	=		CF	=	2	sex	=	
S	=	3	C	=	1	scene	=	
F+%	=	61	FCh	=		clothing	=	
A%	=	30	ChF	=		A	=	6
P%	=	10	CCh	=	±	Ad	=	
O%	=	15	F(C)	=		obj	=	3
H%	=	45				pl	=	1
anat%	=	10				C	=	1

Sequence: loose-orderly
Experience balance: 3 – 4 M : 4 C
Apperceptive type: W — D — S

Remarks:

Perseveration	Counting	Confabulation
Pedantic accuracy	Personal remarks	
Object criticism	Infantile abstractions	

If a physician had asked me for my comment on this diagnosis, I would certainly have inferred that *epilepsy is present* in this case. The intelligence factors are bad; there is perseveration, in addition to fanatic accuracy; there is counting, inclusion of personal matters, confabulation, a pure C, a low A%, the imitation of movement. All these point to epilepsy, as do the blurred affectivity, the strong egocentricity, the relatively numerous M, and the flexor kinesthesias.

I do not believe that the F+% = 50 signifies that Marguerite suffers from "epileptic mental deterioration." I am rather of the opinion that the girl's innate intellectual ability is generally low.

Extremely accurately perceived F+ are usually found side by side with F− in epileptics with mental deterioration.

In Marguerite, the rather good M are surprising.

459

Because some of the abstractions are typically infantile, I suspect that her mental retardation is innate and not acquired through epilepsy.

Since her ability is mostly "practical," the girl might, with the help of habit formation, just be able to perform simple manual work in order to make her own living (basket weaving, broom binding, knitting, perhaps, plain needlework, etc.).

Q. EPILEPSY

Olga R., 17½ years old.

Zulliger Test: Time = 14 minutes

I.

Head with eyes	S → DF + Hd
Arms (AB 4/5 and 6/7)	Do → D + Hd
The mouth (round S)	SF + Hd
The feet (FG 3/4 and 7/8)	DdF + Hd (has probably seen W)
"I always cough!" (coughs)	
Here it again looks as if it were a foot (bottom "sticks")	Dd ± Hd
And this also (center, F 5/6)	DdF − Hd perseveration
This too (Dd next to it)	DdF − Hd perseveration
c Here it also looks like two legs (on the bottom, the sickles)	Dd − Hd perseveration/ confabulation
Here too (small detail at the periphery)	DdF + Hd perseveration
b Here too (somewhat lower at the bottom)	DdF − Hd perseveration
c The white (laughs slyly) "I do not know whether it is this here below at the abdomen" (shows upon herself)	SF − sex upside-down response

II.

A cross (small S at the top)	SF ± obj
A little bird (red area, places which come in contact with the green part)	DdF − A
Arms (upper red area)	DoF + Hd
Here too are arms (a part of the S)	SF + Hd perseveration
This here is the body (S underneath the arms)	SF + Hd position
Moss (green area)	DC pl

460

A white stone in the moss .... SCF obj white as color O
An animal, a cow with brown spots DFC A
Here too (on the opposite side) ... DFC A

III.

A girl, she wants to take something
   (larger dark outer right blot) ... DM + H (P)
A mouse (part of the "leg" of the
   W) (left) .... DF + A
Half a doll (larger dark blot at the
   left) .... DF + Hd (obj) (P) (O!)
A butterfly (red area, c) .... DF + A P
This again is also like a girl (outer
   left red area) .... DM + H (P)
Again half a doll (right black area) DF + Hd (obj) perseveration
Again a mouse (part of the "leg"
   at the right) .... DF + A

Subject: *Olga R.*, 17½ years old

Scoring:

Time: 14 minutes
Number of responses: 27/9

DW	= tendency	F+	= 13	P	=	3
SW	=	F—	= 6	O	=	3
WS	=	F±	= 2	H	=	2
W	= tendency	M	= 2	Hd	=	15
D	= 15	Ms	=	anat	=	
Dd	= 5	FC	= 2	blood	=	
Do	= 1	CF	= 1	sex	=	1
S	= 7	C	= 1	scene	=	
F+%	= 66	FCh	=	clothing	=	
A%	= 22	ChF	=	A	=	6
P%	= 11	CCh	=	Ad	=	
O%	= 7	F(C)	=	obj	=	2
H%	= 63			pl	=	1
anat%	= —			C	=	

Sequence: loose
Experience balance: 2 M : 3½ C
Apperceptive type: D — Dd/Do — S

Remarks:
Perseveration
Position
Individual interpretations
Does not see symmetry

461

OLGA R.:

In this case it is primarily the perseveration, the position interpretation, the confabulation, the pure C and aggression (many S in addition to CF and C), the "*half* doll," and the digression into personal matters ("I always cough!") which lead us to suspect epilepsy. Also, the upside-down response in Card I.

Since there are so many perseverations and since the sex response is given without restraint, I ask myself whether Olga R.'s mental deterioration might be the result of epilepsy. Olga R. does not produce such fine and well perceived M as did Marguerite B. Yet on the other hand she produces numerous Hd, and this too suggests that we may be dealing here with epileptically caused mental deterioration.

As far as the character picture is concerned, aggressiveness should be more noticeable in Marguerite B., while Olga R., on the other hand, who has produced two FC, is more adaptable (affectively) than Marguerite B. Olga R. is the more restless, the more irritable, and the more easily hurt of these two subjects (white interpreted as color!).

When offended, she will react with greater irritability and she will be more readily inclined to hit back than the younger Marguerite B.

Therefore she should find an occupation where she could be aggressive.

R. EPILEPSY

Manfred L., 10 years old.

Manfred L. comes from a poor background. His father works occasionally as a farmhand and has a bad reputation, because he is a habitual drunkard. His mother is a hard-working washerwoman who supports her family—there are five children, of whom Manfred is the fourth—almost entirely by herself.

Manfred is believed to be feeble-minded. He is hot-tempered, obstinate, aggressive toward those who are weaker, while sneaking away from those who are stronger than he. He is obsequiously friendly toward his teachers. He has already repeated one grade, and it has been suggested that he should again repeat a grade. His father is strongly against it, but agrees to let Manfred have a psychological examination.

The physical examination by the school physician does not show anything unusual, except that Manfred is short-sighted and has bad teeth. The school reports state that the boy "dreams" instead of following the lessons, that he is "absent-minded," never knowing where to start when he is called upon, and that he could do better work if only he would apply himself.

As far as it can be established, there is no adverse heredity. When he was a little boy, Manfred once fell from a low stool and lost consciousness for a short time. He soon recovered, however.

Zulliger Test

Time: 9 minutes
Number of responses: 19, 8 of
which are produced for the
colored Card II

I.

(Stretches, holds arms with the fingers spread out wide, pulls his legs up as in a crouching position)

This is a monkey and he has pulled his legs up and stretches his hands away from himself; they have cut his belly open, through the center, and here one sees the guts (EF 3/4/5/6/7) .... DWMCh — A (anat) O—

(Looks at my ball-point pen: "How much does such a pen cost?" In reply to the question: "Don't you see any more?":)

There is a heart in the center (darker spot in the center) ..... DF — anat position

Here there are holes (white inner spaces) .... SF ± abstraction

Here there is a small fir tree (tiny detail at D 2) .... DdF + pl

And here there is a cow udder (FG 3/4; FG 7/8) .... DdF ± Ad/sex

463

II.

This is a flower in a pot . . . . DWCF pl

Or no, these too are the guts of a
human being . . . . DWCF anat O— perseveration "or"

The flesh (outer red area) . . . . D CF anat

The heart (inner dark-red area) . . DCF anat/position

The spine (between the red areas) SF — anat

The liver (orange area) . . . . DCF anat

and the green here—I do not know
what it is—

Or the green is the liver . . . . DCF anat perseveration "or"

And the brown are the kidneys,
that's what they are! . . . . DCF anat perseveration

("Have the pictures been especially
made for me?") . . . . self reference

III.

Here there are two "clowns"
dressed in red who are fooling
around (outer red area) . . . . . . DMC H P

("Does your watch show the correct
time? Should I wind it?")

(Examiner: "As soon as we are
finished with the pictures, I will
let you wind it!—What else do
you see?")

A bloody fly in the middle . . . . D FC A

("Do you also have children? Do Familiarity
they behave well, are they good
in school?" Smiles at me. Examiner: "What else do you see?")

Here there are men shooting at
each other, wanting to hurt each
other . . . . WH + H P aggression

Their legs are cut off . . . . DF + Hd

Snakes are coming out from their
belly . . . . DdF ± A

They also have snakes in their
hands . . . . DdF ± A perseveration

("Is it 4 o'clock and 9 minutes now,
am I right?—May I wind the
watch now?" He does it immediately, without waiting for my an-
swer) . . . . impudence

TABLE 8

Scoring:

Subject: *Manfred R.*

DW = 3	F+	= 3		H	= 2	
W = 1	F–	= 1		Hd	= 1	
D = 9	F±	= 4		anat	= 10	
Dd = 4	M	= 2		A	= 2	
S = 2	MCh	= 1 (–)		Ad	= 1	
	FC	= 2		pl	= 2	
	CF	= 7		abstraction	= 1	

P	= 2
O	= a few minus
F+%	= 62
A%	= 15
P%	= 10
O%	= large, minus
anat%	= 50

Sequence: orderly in the first two cards, then irregular

Experience balance: 3 M : 8 C

Apperceptive type: DW — W — D — Dd — S

Two position responses

Perseveration with anat and "snakes"

Self-reference

Familiarity and impudence

Lolling into secondary M

Even if we disregard Manfred's side-remarks, which we have recorded, his test arouses suspicion of epilepsy (see Table 8).

The following factors support this diagnosis:

strongly extratensive experience balance;

almost entirely pure C (Card II) occurring in various responses;

DWMCh;

perseveration;

position responses (not only the color, but also the central position of the red blot incites the subject to produce the "heart" interpretation);

relatively easy-flowing productivity and short reaction time;

relatively low A%;

high anat% and perseveration with anat, strong viscosity;

naive self-reference;

added factors are Manfred's casual and at the same time impudent behavior and his stretching into kinesthesias.

Since epileptic convulsions, falling down, and *grand mal* have never been observed in Manfred, however, we must be dealing in his case with a form of epilepsy in which only short absences and short losses of consciousness occur. In all probability, the states which the school reports have designated as "sleep" and "dreaming" are *petit mal* epileptic attacks, while his "retardation" is due to epileptic mental deterioration.

REPORT TO THE AUTHORITIES AND THE PARENTS:

Manfred L.'s mental retardation is not a simple form of intellectual disability. He is probably suffering from a certain variety of epilepsy. This must be further investigated by a specialist.

FOLLOW-UP REPORT:

After a prolonged clinical observation, the psychiatrist confirmed the suspicion of epilepsy. Manfred is the victim of a genuine, larvated epilepsy and must be treated.

S. EPILEPSY

Paul K., 11½ years old.

The subject, a boy of 11½ years, is the first child in a family of an official. He has a younger sister, 2 years his junior, with whom he does not get along at all. It is difficult to discipline him. In kindergarten, there were already disciplinary difficulties; later, also in school.

Upon the request of the elementary school teacher, he was brought to the school counselor. She recommended that they take the boy away from the city and place him with a family in the country, feeling that the country environment would calm him.

Instead, the parents undertook a change of their domicile. The boy had to change classes, he went to another school and now had a male teacher. The parents hoped that this teacher might be able to discipline the unruly boy. Their hope was not fulfilled.

Before the parents decided to send their son away from the family, they submitted him to an examination by a private vocational guidance agency.

Anamnesis and development showed nothing unusual. The boy's birth had been normal, and he did not have any of the more serious children's diseases (except for the common ones).

He is tall and strong for his age and gives the impression of being in good health. The family physician believed him to be healthy, and implied that the boy should be treated more strictly at home. It is primarily the father who is too lenient with him and, as a result, other people have to suffer.

On the basis of the Zulliger Test, I recommended a special neurological-medical examination, including possibly an electroencephalogram. For the test was unusual and led me to suspect epilepsy.

The test follows:

Beginning: 2:30 P.M.

   Card I.

This is a beetle	WF + A P
These all around are leaves, because there below are leaf-stems. It sits on top of them	DWF ± pl
It has built a nest in a leaf; it is black, and in the middle the beetle has crept out of it	DWF − pl confabulation color naming perspective

Here on the outside there are
spikes, the wings of a bird; here
too (on the opposite side) (D 2/3
and 8/9) .... DF + Ad
This is a white water spot in the
middle .... SCF nat
Here there are two bear paws (B 4
and 7) .... DF + Ad
And here there are two horns (A 5
and 6) of cows .... DdF + Ad
The beetle has white eyes .... SFC Ad, eyes
It wears a tie (center BC 5/6) .... DdF + obj/clothing
Here there is just a line (the thin
line AB 6) .... DdF ± abstraction

II.

A cockchafer (the whole red blot) . DF − A perseveration
Or a caterpillar, because of the color DCF A "or"
This is just white stuff in the belly
of the beetle .... SF − Ad
This could be a larva (red area) .. DF − A, confabulation
A water animal from the sea or the
aquarium (green area) .... DF + A
An old tree leaf which they (water
animals and larvae) are climbing
(brown area) .... DCF pl combinatory W tendency
The green on the right side is
lighter than the one on the left criticism of the colors, color naming
Some white spots in the green .... SCF spot white as color
One green is on one side, the other
on the other .... description

III.

A butterfly .... DF + A P
c A mouse, because of the little tail
and (EF 2/3) .... DF + A
a cat in front of it (FG 3/4) ..... DdF − A, confabulation
c Human bones (CD 1/2) .... DF − anat
c It looks like a circle; the mice chase
each other, running around it .. DWF − abstraction O−
a Human head (AB 3/4) .... DoF + Hd (P)
A hand with four fingers (CD 9/10) DoF + Hd (P) counting
A tail (whole small dark blot) .... DF − Ad

End: 2:41 P.M.

Scoring:

<table>
<tr><td></td><td></td><td>Time:</td><td>11 minutes</td></tr>
<tr><td></td><td></td><td>Number of responses:</td><td>25/7</td></tr>
</table>

DW	=	3	} 4	F+	=	10	Hd	=	2
W	=	1 - 2		F−	=	9	anat	=	1
D	=	11		F±	=	1	clothing	=	(1)
Dd	=			FC	=	1	A	=	8
Do	=	2		CF	=	3	Ad	=	6
S	=	4		C	=	1	obj	=	1
F+%	=	52		P	=	4	pl	=	3
A%	=	52		O	=	1 (−1)	nat	=	1
P%	=	16					spot	=	1
O%	=	4					abstraction	=	2
H%	=	12 (−)							
anat%	=	4							

Sequence:	loose	Red shock:	—
Experience balance:	0 M : 5 C	Color shock:	—
Apperceptive type:	DW — W — D — Dd — Do — S	Ch-shock:	—

Remarks: confabulation, combination, color naming, perspective, criticism, counting, description, WMHP III absent.

Peculiarities in this test include:

extensive confabulation (DW);

attachment to a response that has been produced and completion of it by further and possibly combinatory-confabulatory responses;

pronounced aggression (S - CF - C);

in contradiction, Do, which usually mean anxiety but here rather indicate pedantry, as, for instance, the sixth and last responses to Card II;

unadapted, excitable, egocentric, and sticky affectivity (colors, no M);

low F+%, indicating inferior intelligence;

too high A%, suggesting laziness;

O−%, pointing to eccentric ideas;

too low H% which, together with the single FC, the 3 CF and the pure C, suggests a poor ability to form interhuman relationships, the loose sequence is suspicious; confusion of ideas is opposed to the above-mentioned viscosity;

lack of concentration, expressed by an experience balance that is too large;

shocks are missing, which means that the boy's condition is not a form of neurosis.

The counselor implies that he must be endogenically conditioned and makes his recommendations accordingly.

The result of the medical examination by a specialist:

"From the medical and neurological point of view, the patient's state does not provoke any misgivings. On the other hand, after hyperventilation, the EEG showed the presence of typical centrocephalic forms (waves and spikes), which clinically go hand in hand with absences. We are dealing here with epilepsy (*petit mal*). The abnormal personality traits are in agreement with this finding."

T. EPILEPSY

Jacob Keller, 9 years old.

Mrs. Keller brings her 9-year-old son to the office. She would like him to have psychotherapeutic treatment.

He is failing in school, although from time to time he gives brilliant answers, which proves that he is not stupid. In his class, he ranks on the borderline between the first and second thirds. Both his parents are college graduates, and they would like to see Jacob enter a lower middle school. He is their only child, born after they had been married for six years.

The teacher does not complain as much about his intellectual performance as about the boy's not being able to sit still on some days. Only with great difficulty was she able to induce him not to run constantly about the classroom. Finally, he has now become used to sitting, but he keeps moving his chair back and forth, and frequently making rhythmic movements with his arms and body; he dangles his feet, makes funny faces to draw his classmates' attention to himself and provoke their laughter. She just about hopes to put him through the examination, which will take place in approximately one year, but she is not certain of it. Undoubtedly, there has been progress in learning and discipline, but the pupil's "nervousness" worries her. She demands that something definite be done about it.

The family physician, who knows the family since the beginning of the marriage, believes the boy to be healthy; he does not think that the teacher's complaints are to be taken too seriously. Jacob is a "wild one" and needs a great deal of physical activity. The fact that, during his three school years, the boy has become somewhat quieter than he had been at the beginning, is a hopeful sign, indicating that he may become even calmer during the course of this year. He interprets the motoric as well as the learning difficulties as being the result of emotional causes, and has no objection to Jacob's psychotherapeutic treatment. Nevertheless, he prescribes tranquilizers for him.

Jacob is a lively little boy, indeed. He is somewhat too tall. He is easy to talk to, for he is talkative, and does not seem to be stupid.

A scrutiny of the anamnesis does not produce anything out of the ordinary. It is true that Jacob has been susceptible to colds during his early childhood, but this disappeared after he lost his milk teeth. He has had no serious diseases and no operations. He is sociable and pleasant; every effort has been made to bring him up well. He walked and talked at the proper time, and he is quite able to play either by himself or with his friends. But among his friends he likes to be the leader and to dominate.

After the examiner has chatted with him for a while, in order to make him feel at ease, he is given the Zulliger Individual Test.

First of all, the child psychotherapist would like to obtain information about Jacob's "nervousness." He would like to know whether Jacob is actually suffering from a psychogenic disorder, or, perhaps, a physiologically conditioned disturbance. In addition, he is anxious to find out about his intellectual ability, wondering whether the demands made upon him by wanting to place him among the students of a middle school are too great. Under certain circumstances, Jacob's psychological treatment could become a failure: it would fail if Jacob's "being different from the others" has an endogenic cause.

471

The psychotherapist must beware of incorrect treatment. Also, he must protect the patient against it. This is the reason he gives Mrs. Keller in explaining the test examination. She would have preferred him to begin treatment immediately.

Zulliger Individual Test

Subject: *Jacob Keller,* 9 years old   Beginning: 2:30 P.M.

I.

This is inside in the belly; here
there is a piece of white intestine
(center dark area) .... SWCF anat O— white as color
c A tree leaf (center dark area) .... DF + pl
a Here there is a head—with (upper
center area) .... DF + Hd
two eyes .... SF + Hd, eyes
This is a devil who spreads out his
arms .... DM + H O aggression
and wants to seize something ... tendency to MCh
A gray color .... WChC color naming

II.

a A heart (red area) .... DCF anat
seen upside down
a These are human bones (white
space within red area) .... SF — anat
c Perhaps this is a flower (red area) DCF pl
I can think of nothing here (points
to the green area) .... green shock
Two green dots at the sides ...... DCF color description
They could be grass tufts .... DFC pl
c Somebody is swimming and he is
going to .... DM + H O
collide with somebody else (brown
area) .... inverted response

III.

c A butterfly (red center area) ..... DF + A P
a Here there are two arms, which he
holds in this manner (he shows
how) (CD 1/2 and 9/10) .... DoM + Hd (P)
c A mouse (EF 7/8) .... DF + A

a Blood (outer red area) .... DC blood
c Bones (EG 2/3/4 and 6/7/8) .... DF — anat
                                   tendency to perseveration
c This must be inside a human being WF — anat, perseveration
                                        End: 2:39 P.M.

> *Remark:* In interpretation "heart" in Card II: "This is the tip!" and
> the subject points to the upper portion of the red area, while
> holding the card in an upright position.

Scoring:

			Time:	9 minutes
			Number of responses:	18/6

SW	=	1 ⎫ 4	ChC	=	1	ChC	=	1
W	=	3 ⎭	F+	=	5 ⎫ 8 (−3)	P	=	2
D	=	11	F−	=	3 ⎭	O	=	3 (−1)
Do	=	1	M	=	3	H	=	2
S	=	2	MCh	=	tendency	Hd	=	3
F+%	= 62		FC	=	1	anat	=	5
A%	= 11		CF	=	4	blood	=	1
P%	= 11		C	=	1	A	=	2
O%	= 18±					pl	=	3
H%	= 27					color	=	2
anat%	= 27						

Sequence:	orderly-loose,		
	tendency to inversion	Red shock:	—
Experience balance:	3 M : 7 C	C-shock:	green shock
Apperceptive type:	W — D — (Do) — S	Ch-shock:	—

> *Remarks:* aggressive traits, color naming, inverse responses (twice), tend-
> ency to perseveration.

EVALUATION:

Not only because J. stereotypes with H and not with A, but
also because he produces such a high O%, his test deviates markedly from the norm. The color relationships are unusual too;
one of the 4 CF is almost a pure C ("two green dots at
the sides"); in addition, there is another pure C ("blood"),
and color naming, "a gray color." Furthermore, it is strange that
J., who does not produce either a red or a general color shock,
produces a green shock.

The relationship of the number of responses to reaction time is normal. The relationship of W : D : Do: S is also normal, although there are slightly too many S.

The F+% corresponds with that of an elementary-school student, who is a borderline case of mental retardation. However, since it is primarily produced by perseveration of anat interpretations, we must not give it too much weight in evaluating innate intelligence. The relatively high number of W does not indicate high intellectual ability either, because one of them is a confabulated SW. The too low P% leads us to expect difficulties in intellectual grasp; the too high O% bears this out too (normally, a 9-year-old does not yet think in such a highly original and independent manner); in addition, one of the O is an O—; thus, there are some odd traits in his thinking: an "eccentric's" ideas might emerge in conjunction with some surprisingly good, captivating ones. Again, the DoM is somewhat puzzling. One might ask why it is that Jacob does not see the usual M in Card III. It is possible that he has indeed seen one M, but he produces the moving arm only, which he has already produced in the M of Card I.

Whoever produces more than one anat is usually motivated by a strong intellectual ambition, or suffers from hypochondriacal ideas. It is possible that Jacob has developed a strong intellectual ambition: his parents are college graduates, and they expect him to gain entrance into a lower middle school. It is quite certain that this has been discussed in his presence and he has let himself be influenced accordingly. We cannot be completely sure, however.

Yet a further suspicion forces itself upon us. Experience has taught us that subjects who produce responses such as "inside of the belly," "intestines," and similar interpretations are really referring to the brain. In their interpretations they symbolically describe the brain, thus projectively betraying a brain lesion. And it does not matter whether or not they themselves know about it.

In addition, Jacob has produced two inverted interpretations.

The meaning of an "inverted interpretation" may be most easily explained through Card III. Card III is presented to a subject. The subject immediately puts it into the c-position and then produces the interpretation: "Two men are standing here wearing high-heeled shoes." Thus the subject sees the men in an upside-down position, as if the top were the bottom. The subject sees the men standing on their heads, but he does not, however, take note of the fact that they are standing on their heads.

It is similar with the red blot in Card II. In an upright position, it is not rarely interpreted as "two women kissing each other," "two women arguing with each other," etc. However, if such an interpretation occurs while the card is held in a c-position, it must be called an inverted interpretation.

Occasionally, while the patient is holding Card II in a c-position, a response is produced in which the red blot is designated as a "heart." In that case, form is inaccurately perceived, and it is chiefly the red color that has contributed to the interpretation. Sometimes the S too is involved, and then the interpretation may be "the two heart ventricles."

Our subject, Jacob, also interprets the red blot in Card II as a "heart," but he is holding the card in an a-position. Jacob has seen the "heart" inversely.

In Card II he produces another upside-down response. It is the last one: "somebody is swimming and he is going to collide with somebody else." In the card's a-position, this interpretation is produced not too infrequently, but not in the c-position. One might think, of course, that Jacob has perceived the figures as swimming on their backs. However, he explains, in response to inquiry: "they are swimming on their stomachs." Thus, he has seen them inversely.

In 1944, Arnold Weber[4] drew our attention to the occurrence of inverse interpretations in the Rorschach Test. According to his observation, these occur in children from time to time. In a special study, Fritz Salomon[5] investigated their diagnostic significance in detail, and came to the general conclusion that they are characteristic of simple or more severe brain damage; they

[4] A. Weber: "Der Rorschach'sche Formdeuttest bei Kindern," in *Psychiatrie und Rorschach'scher Formdeutversuch,* Art. Institut Orell Fuessli, A. G. Zuerich 1944.
[5] Verbal communication, 1952. Now in: F. Salomon, *Ego and Libido Diagnosis in the Zulliger Test.* (Translation in preparation.)

occur most frequently, however, in epileptics and epileptoid patients, sometimes even in cases where the EEG would not permit us to diagnose organic brain damage. He does not exclude the possibility that there may be epilepsies who do not exhibit inverse interpretations in the test. Moreover, he pointed out that they occur not only in children, but in adults as well and that, from a diagnostic point of view, they are much more suspicious in adults. He has arrived at his conclusions on the basis of extensive statistical material.

One might ask why it is that this "epilepsy sign" was not discovered earlier. The following reason may be given for it: not enough attention has been paid to inverse interpretations. Either they were not considered important, or, if they were noticed, their diagnostic significance was not investigated. They were not even registered in the test record as something specific.

I have re-examined Salomon's findings and on the basis of my own experience, I have reached the following conclusions during the course of many years:

1. If *young* children—those 3-6 years of age—produce inverse interpretations, these do not signify anything in particular. The children may be epileptics or epileptoids, or they may be normal. The fact that inverse interpretations have been produced does *not mean anything definite in terms of differential diagnosis.*

2. If *6-8-year-old children* produce inverse interpretations, they are *"retarded"* (as long as they are not epileptoid as shown by other methods).

3. If subjects who are older than 8 years produce inverse interpretations, then one is justified in suspecting epileptoid changes, and a further medical examination is indicated.

4. If *subjects whose milk teeth have already been replaced,* produce inverse interpretations, however, *brain damage* must be suspected; it is betrayed in the personality of these persons by disturbances that assume "epileptic forms." In each one of these cases, the cause does not necessarily have to be epilepsy; it may be something else (brain hemorrhage, poliomyelitis, severe fever, etc.).

Let us return to Jacob Keller once again.

476

Primarily on the basis of the two inverse responses and the anatomy response to Card I, the mother was advised to submit her son to an examination by a specialist, for there was ground for suspicion that the boy might be suffering from brain damage.

This recommendation did not appeal to the mother. Jacob was given extensive tutoring. In view of the pending examination, his parents believed this to be more important. They thought that, in the spring, he would be able to pass the examination for the higher school. Two years later, his performance became so poor that the teaching staff was of the opinion that he should repeat a grade. The parents took Jacob out of the school and enrolled him in a private boarding school, where he was also given tutoring.

After three years at the boarding school, Jacob reached puberty. His personality changed: he became violent, hot-tempered, obstinate, and greatly sentimental about himself. In addition, his school performance deteriorated frightfully. He was in a much worse condition than he had been at the time when he was attending elementary school. All the usual educational measures were tried in order to calm the boy, but they were of no avail.

Now, five years after the psychological examination, the parents decided to accept the recommendation, and to let a specialist examine Jacob. He discovered that Jacob's brain was quite severely damaged. The damage had been caused by a hemorrhage, which had resulted from his having been delivered by forceps at birth (this also explains the presence of green shock in his test); according to Salomon (*Ego and Libido Diagnosis in the Zulliger Test*), it indicates an emotionally experienced trauma during the early oral phase. The parents had forgotten about it and had not mentioned it to the psychologist at the time when the anamnesis was being discussed. It was not until now—when the medical specialist inquired about it—that they remembered.

Anyone who thinks that what I have wanted to prove here is that abnormalities resulting from brain damage can always be determined with the Zulliger Test or any other form-interpretation test, is mistaken. It has been mentioned before that people with brain damage do not *always* produce inverse interpretations.

There still is no method that would be completely reliable; even the electro-encephalogram can be deceptive.

In 1960, a 10-year-old was brought to me because of difficulties in school. He produced three inverse interpretations in the Zulliger Test and I insisted that he should be examined by a specialist for possible brain damage. An EEG was administered to him. It was negative; no pathological condition could be found. But half a year later the boy suffered an epileptic attack (*grand mal* with foaming, urinating and bowel movement, and convulsions).

U. PSEUDO (HYSTERO) EPILEPSY—BLIND DIAGNOSIS

A physician sent me for evaluation the following record of *Irma B.*, a 14-year-old elementary-school student. He would like to know whether anything could be found in it that would indicate epilepsy.

Since the age of five Irma has had attacks, which became more frequent when she was 11 years old; she had been treated with drugs for epilepsy for the previous three years, after a specialist had examined her because of her attacks and had diagnosed them as being epileptic.

The doctor who had administered the Zulliger Test expressed his doubts that this was a "genuine" epilepsy.

Zulliger Individual Test   Time: 12 minutes

I.

The wounded head of a human
   being (upper center area) ..... S ➜ FCh ➜ DF + Hd
Butterfly (dark center area) ..... DF + A
d A mouse (BCDEFG 8/7/6) with a
   long tail .... DF + A
a A cow's udder (FG 4) .... DdF + Ad

II.

"Here I cannot say anything!"
   (wants to relinquish the card.
   After some encouragement, she
   begins turning the card back and
   forth) .... shock!

478

A white dove (AB 5/6) .... SFC A white as color
Blood (red area) .... DC blood
Kidneys (inner red area) .... DCF anat
"Nothing more!"

III.

Two evil women arguing (large
   dark blot) .... DM + H (P) aggression
A glider pilot (red inner area) .... DF — obj
Smeared blood (all red areas),
   blood spots .... DCF blood, tendency C
A mushroom (in between the large
   dark figure) .... SF + pl
A branch; a branch of a cherry tree
   (small dark blot) .... DF — pl
b An evil animal, a dragon (EDC
   3/4) .... DF + A
b Little snakes (A 3/4) .... DdF ± A
b A bird's head (CD 1/2) .... DF + Ad

REPORT (TO THE DOCTOR WHO HAS RECORDED THE TEST):

Except for the anat and blood interpretations (the C and CF), there is nothing in the test that would arouse the suspicion that epilepsy is present. But in real epilepsies I have never yet found a genuine color shock (see Table 9).

Since Irma B. produces a color shock, followed by an S and then by a "blood" interpretation, and furthermore, since her experience balance is clearly extratensive, I would be inclined to suspect the existence of a *hysteria*—namely, an *anxiety hysteria*. All test factors tally with this suspicion.

The following factors negate the possible existence of epilepsy:

color shock;
absence of M—, of confabulated or secondary M;
absence of self-referring interpretations or side remarks, self-
   references;
absence of DW;
absence of typical O—;
absence of "chummy" side-remarks;
absence of typical position interpretations;

TABLE 9

Scoring:
Subject: *Irma B.*

Time: 12 minutes
Number of responses: 15/3

Cd.	W	D	Dd	S	F+	F−	F±	M	FC	CF	C	Ch	P	O
I	—	2	2	1	4							1		
II	—	2		1			1		1	1	1 tend.		1	
III	—	6	1	1	3	2	1	1	1	2	1–2	1	1	
	—	10	3	3	7									aggression

F+% = 75   H = 1   A = 5   obj = 1
A% = 46   Hd = 1   Ad = 2   pl = 2
P% = 6   blood = 2
O% = —   anat = 1   color shock = very pronounced
H% = 13

Sequence: orderly
Experience balance: 1 M : 4 – 5½ C
Apperceptive type: $\underline{D} - Dd - \underline{S}$

absence of perseverations;

a small number of anat;

average A%, no stereotyping with anat or other contents;

average H%;

orderly sequence;

absence of inverse responses;

absence of the typical epileptic forms of nagging, which would alternate with an equally characteristic epileptoid, meaningless "generosity."

In addition, the entire record, including its neurotic traits, makes a completely "normal" impression. Although no W are produced and although the F+% does not amount to more than 75, one cannot speak of "mental deterioration." Characteristically epileptics produce *silly* F—; these are not found in Irma.

REPORT OF THE PHYSICIAN:

He too is of the opinion that Irma B.'s attacks are caused by hysteria. The girl needs psychotherapeutic, not medical treatment. By sending the record for an appraisal, he had merely wanted to assure himself that his own opinion was correct; he wanted to get information about the test. From the first, the fact that Irma B. remembered her absences had been suspicious to him, as well as the fact that she usually remembered the stereotype "dream" that occurred at the same time (as the girl herself stated).

PART III

The Zulliger Group Test

19. Editor's Introduction to the Zulliger Group Test

In 1948, in the first edition of his book on the group test, Zulliger reported only on his own experiences, gathered within the framework of the Swiss Army. At that time he still believed that the test was not suitable for anything but the detection of those people in a group whose range deviates from the norm. These subjects—primarily, the ones who were suspected of psychopathology—were then submitted to an individual psychological examination. According to a personal communication, Zulliger soon gained the impression that this testing technique also made possible relatively far-reaching characterological conclusions. He remained reserved, however, in his writings because he had not yet been able to collect enough material to be able to carry out a comparison with non-military subjects.

The short diagnoses that he had published, and which had been checked and partly supplemented by other psychologists who worked with other tests, were for the most part suitable enough for the intended military selection. Moreover, he was frequently in a position to check them, by observing the candidates' performance during the course of several years. These military qualification reports, which were based upon active duty lasting 1-3 years, showed a relatively high percentage of agreement between the diagnoses of the army psychological service and the observations made during military service, although these two were arrived at independently of each other (the correspondence was 80-90%). Of course, this kind of checking helped Zulliger to improve his test technique. Cases that were later submitted to an individual psychological examination gave him the opportunity to check his thinking further. Ordinarily, such cases amounted to $1/4$ to $1/5$ of the candidates among the applicants for officers' training.

Only some of the army tests are published here since, from a practical point of view, they belong to a technically obsolete era. As early as 1955, in the second edition of his book, Zulliger published some samples of psychopathological cases for which, as control, he had obtained, in addition to the test, the psychiatric diagnoses as well. A number of cases taken from special publications, along with some tests that were especially prepared for this American edition, are published here.

The non-military tests demonstrate especially well the scope of psychological conclusions and clinical diagnoses that can be drawn from the group test. They hardly fall short of those that may be obtained by using the Zulliger Individual Test or even the Rorschach. To arrive at similar diagnostic results, presupposes, of course, great familiarity and extensive experience with the Rorschach technique in general, and with the Zulliger Test in particular. Whether other scoring methods would lead to comparable results, I am in no position to judge.

In addition, Zulliger rightly foresaw that the group test would prove its great positive value with regard to other, non-military groups, and even for schools. At the present time, there are a number of publications, in the form of books and articles, that clearly establish this to be true. To refer to just one example, the test has proven to be an excellent aid for teachers who, upon taking over a new class, would like to orient themselves quickly about the innate intelligence of their students, their emotionally caused inhibitions, and their personalities. (For further information, consult the bibliography of this book.)

One further remark seems important, with regard to the reliability of the Zulliger Group Test. The psychologist who uses it does not ordinarily have any direct contact with the subjects, either before or after the administration of the test. Thus, the diagnosis worked out by him is practically equal to a blind diagnosis. The numerous positive comments that have been written in many different countries, especially in Europe, will certainly contribute to the test's rapidly gaining many friends in the U.S. as well.

20. Author's Preface

Since the first publication of this small volume, standardization studies have been carried out in various locales, among others in Paris by Fritz Salomon. There too it has been shown that the results of the Zulliger Test agree with those obtained with the Ro- and Bero-series.

The usefulness of the Zulliger Group Test has been demonstrated in selecting applicants for the police force, teachers for special schools, so-called "displaced persons," etc. Similar experiences have been published by Dr. V. Bacci of the Department of Labor in Genoa; A. Friedemann, M.D., Director of the Institute of Social Hygiene in Biel (Switzerland); Hildegard Hiltmann, M.D., of the Institute of Psychology at the University of Freiburg in Breisgau; Dr. A. Linares Maza, Trabajo del Laboratorio de psicotecnica del Institución sindical de formación profesional in Malaga, and especially by F. Salomon in Paris and W. Traenkle, M.D., in Marburg-Lahn. It is possible that others, whose studies are not known to me, have conducted similar researches with the test.

Dr. Bacci in Genoa, who has tested Sardinian workers among others, offered them a contour picture of the exposed slide drawn in India ink. On it, the interpreted spots could be framed with a pencil. This "technique" replaced the one that used designations on a watch dial. However, this method prolongs testing time by approximately 10-15 minutes.

A few additional records, along with some short or more detailed diagnoses based upon them, have been included in the second edition. Among them are a number of records of medically and clinically diagnosed mental patients.

Furthermore, an index of studies on the Zulliger Group Test has been included.

May 1955   H. ZULLIGER

21. The Administration of the
Zulliger Group Test

The administration of the group test takes place in a darkened room, in which 30 to 60 subjects may be seated. The subjects should not be placed either too far from or too close to the screen upon which the three pictures are projected in successive order. Care should also be taken that those subjects who sit at the extreme corners of the first few rows should not be seated at too sharp an angle to the projection screen, because then they would see the pictures distortedly. The projected picture should be about 40 to 50 inches large. At each place, there is a sheet of paper upon which the subjects themselves write down their responses. At the upper part of this sheet, space is provided for the recording of the name, age, sex, etc., according to the special needs of the various groups to be tested. At the right hand corner, there is a margin of about 2 inches separated by a vertical line from the rest of the sheet.

The examiner's instructions are approximately the following: "I shall project three pictures upon this screen, one after another. You are asked to write down on the sheet before you what you think these pictures mean. You may interpret the whole picture or only its parts. Of course, you may also do both; the manner and the order in which you proceed is up to you. The pictures do not have any particular meaning; different people see different things in them. Therefore, *all* answers are "correct." Please give as many responses as you can.

490

"Later, I would like to know where you saw the things that you have interpreted. If you interpret the whole picture, please write down at the end of your response in parentheses (W), indicating that the whole picture is meant. If you interpret a part of the picture, designate the location of that part according to an imaginary dial (do this also at the end of your response). For instance, 12 means upper center, 3 the right part, 6 the low center part, etc." (It has been found useful to indicate the various locations with a stick on the still empty picture screen in order to avoid later errors as much as possible.) "Please write your responses underneath one another. You may also number them. Write a Roman I in the center above the responses to the first picture. Then, when you are finished with the first picture, draw a horizontal line below your responses, and put a Roman II underneath it for the second picture and, correspondingly, a Roman III for the third picture.

"I am going to project each picture upon the screen for about 15 seconds while the room is completely dark, so that you may look at it closely. Afterward, when I have provided you with some light, write your responses on the sheet. At the same time, I shall leave the picture upon the screen in order that you may orient yourselves again as you like. After a certain time" (about 3 minutes, according to whether or not any of the subjects are still writing), "I shall again turn off the light in the room, in order to give you another opportunity to see the picture more accurately. Again, write only when I turn on the light. I shall proceed in exactly the same manner with each of the three pictures."

As soon as the examiner believes that everybody is finished writing, he asks whether he may show the next picture. Many experiments have shown that it is better to leave the picture upon the screen when the light is turned on, because otherwise the subjects may become worried about having forgotten something they saw earlier. Moreover, if this is not done, the subjects may have difficulty pointing out the localization of their interpretations. The lighting required for writing should not be too bright, in order that the projected picture may not appear too blurred.

"If anything is still not clear to you, you may ask me now, before starting the test." Any kind of suggestion should be avoided in answering questions. To begin with, it is imperative that the instructions be given in a quiet tone of voice, and that the formulation of the instructions be confined to essentials, as I have demonstrated here. Sometimes there is a certain restlessness and nervousness prior to the taking of the test. This is especially evident in children and adolescents, but it is often found in adults, too. Fritz Salomon has pointed out to me that this can best be avoided by administering a simple drawing test directly before the administration of the real test—as, for instance, letting the subjects draw a tree or a human being. In this case, a sheet of paper should be provided in advance. Immediately following this, the Zulliger Test may then be performed. The test instructions are, of course, not given until the drawing-test papers have been collected. In the case of adults, smoking may be permitted, in order to relax the candidates.

The entire test procedure takes about 15-20 minutes.

As soon as the psychologist has become somewhat more experienced with the group test, he will become almost independent of the subjects' localizations. This is especially important when one is dealing with children, or even adolescents, who either forget localizations or do not indicate them well enough. The group test is shown only in the cards' regular position. Thus the pictures are not turned, as is possible and customary in the individual test.

22. Scoring of the Responses

The scoring is performed in the same way as in the Zulliger Individual Test. In order to become more familiar with it, some beginners may discuss the first 100 group tests with the subjects, following the administration of the test, just as is done with the individual test. It is best to show the location sheets in order that the subjects may be able to orient themselves to them, because they rarely remember the picture as they have seen it before. As I have mentioned previously elsewhere in this book, the scores are not always exactly the same for the group test and the individual test. In the following, I list the most frequent responses and their scores.

Scoring Table

Slide 1

Bedbug, louse, crab, beetle		W F+ A P
A bee		W F+ A
A microscopic picture or an enlargement of a crab, a bedbug, a plant-louse, a beetle	FCh ➜	W F+ A P
Petrification of a beetle, crab	FCh ➜	W F+ A P
Enlarged head of an insect	FCh ➜	W F+ Ad
X-ray of a water animal ...	FCh ➜	W F+ A
A basket		W F± object
A bat	FCh ➜	W F± A

A rotten tree leaf .... ChF → W F± plant
Rotten tree trunk and roots ......
                     ChF → W F± plant
Fog formation .... ChF → W F± fog
Clouds .... ChF → W F± clouds
Clouds with gaps .... ChF → WS F± clouds
A corpse; the heart is in the middle
    (tendency : position) ... ChF → W F± anatomy
Torn clothes .... ChF → W F± clothing
A grotto .... ChF → W F± nature
A cave .... ChF → W F± cave
Hell .... ChF → W F± hell O—
Lungs .... FCh → W F— anatomy
Coat of arms .... W F— coat of arms
Map .... WS → W F— geog
Smoke .... Ch → W F— smoke
Fog .... Ch → W F— fog
A standing human being .... W M H O+
A human being with raised arms .. ⎰ W M H O+
             combinatory ⎱ D F+ Hd
A cowering anthropoid ape ...... W M A O+
An advancing bent monster ...... W MCh H O+
Threatening fog ghost .... W MCh H O+
There is a frozen person lying there W MCh H O+
A dried-out blood puddle . ChF → W CF blood
A squashed animal, all bloody ....
                 ChF → W CF A/blood
A female sex organ ...... ChF → SW F— sex O—
A leafy plant .... DW F± plant
Skeleton clad in a veil (proceeding
    from 12) .... FCh → DW F± anatomy
The skeleton of a sea animal .....
                FCh → DW F± A/anatomy
A potato with sprouts .... DW F— plant
A dog, an elephant .... DW F— A
It looks like a divided animal skull
                 ChF → DW F— Ad/anatomy
A human head (12) Do → D S → D F+ Hd
An animal head .... SW → D F+ Ad
A human head in profile (1 and 11) D F± Hd
A fist with a knife (1 and 11) Do → D F+ Hd
A plant leaf (c) .... D F+ plant
A lady's blouse (c) .... D F+ clothing
Butterfly (c) .... D F+ A

Heart or lungs in the center (c) ...	D F— anatomy/position
A black spot (c)	D CF description
An Indian with a feather on his head, kissing his squaw (1-2 and 10-11)	D M H O+
A woman carrying a small child (1-2 and 10-11)	D M H O+
A leaping chamois (3 and 9)	Dd F+ A
A fir tree branch (3 and 9)	Dd F+ plant
A scorpion (3 and 9)	Dd F± A
Sickles, knives, daggers (1 and 11)	Dd F+ object, aggression
The pincers of an insect, on top (1 and 11) .... Do →	Dd F+ Ad
Testicles (6)	Dd F— sex
Eyes and mouth (underneath 12) .. Do →	DS F+ Hd
A mask with eyes (12)	DS F+ mask
An insect's larva (above 6)	S F+ A, possibly FC
Four holes	S F± infantile description
Vagina (above 6)	S F— sex

Slide 2

Stage setting by a theater designer; two women greet each other amidst bushes	W FC object O+
A Chinese picture of a landscape with a pagoda	W CF object O+
The palette of a painter with color blots; a painting experiment ...	W CF object
An Indian burial place	W CF object
A flower ornament	W CF ornament/plant
The bottom of a sea with plants, shells and strange fishes	W CF A/nature
An old map	W CF geog
Plant parts, flower leaves, cup-shaped leaves and various other leaves	W CF plant
A human being who has been cut open	W CF anatomy O—
Smeared colors	W C color
The symbol of life	W C abstraction
A garden	DW CF plant
Various colors	DW C color

The Holy Ghost comes down to earth in the form of a white dove (small S in the upper red area) on a pink cloud		SW CF scene O+
Cuttings from a silhouette drawing (red area)		D F+ object
Horse-shoe (red area)		D F± object
Shell (red area)		D F— A
Butterfly (red area)		D F— A
A house (red area)		DdD F— architecture
Two women hugging each other (red area)		D M H O+
Two bears standing up (red area)		D M A/H repression
Flower petals (red area)		D CF plant
Lobsters (red area)		D CF A
Chops (red area)		D CF food
Lungs (red area)		D CF anatomy
Embryos		D CF H/anatomy/sex
Heart ventricles		D CF anatomy
Blood spots (red area)		D CF blood
Blood (red area)		D C blood
Fire (red area)		D C fire
Mask (red area and S)		DS CF mask
Chest and spine (red area and S) ..		DS CF anatomy
Mask (light red at the borderline)		Dd F— mask
Human heads (upper dark red) ...		Do F + Hd
Insects, beetles (brown area)		D F + A
A centipede (brown area)		D F± A
Two people are lying there	" "	D M H O
Moles pushing against each other	" "	D FC A aggression
Two cows, bulls	" "	D FC A P
Two foxes; their heads are pointing toward the outside	" "	D FC A
Prehistoric cave-painting	" "	D FC painting O+
Salmon slices	" "	D FC food
Meat pieces	" "	D CF food
Clouds in the evening glow	" "	D CF clouds
Rocks	" "	D CF nature
Earth clods	" "	D CF nature
Liver and intestines	" "	
	ChF →	D CF anatomy

Earth	(brown area)	D C earth
Feces	" "	D C feces
Blood	" "	D C blood
Fox heads (outer brown area)		Do F+ Ad
Bull heads (inner brown area) ...		Do F+ Ad
A butterfly (brown area and S in-between)		DS CF A
Mask of a human head (inside brown)		Dd F+ Hd/mask
Shells, fishes, crabs, scorpion	(green area)	D F+ A
Ship, canoe	" "	D F+ object
Two dwarfs approaching each other	" "	D M H O+
Horses standing on their hind legs with riders	" "	D Ms scene O+
Parsley	" "	D FC plant/food
Tree root	" "	D FC plant
Shrubbery	" "	D FC plant
Grass tuft	" "	D FC plant
Moss	" "	D CF plant
A puddle	" "	D CF nature
Lawns	" "	D C plant
Water		D C water
Eyes (green area and S)		DS F— eye
Bean stalk (S within red area)		S F+ plant
Ornament " " " "		S F+ ornament
Totem pole " " " "		S F+ object
Plant " " " "		S F+ plant
Chinese inscription (S within red area)		S F+ inscription O+
Vertebrae, spine (S within red area)		S F— anatomy
Road sign (S within red area)		S F— object
A cardinal's head, crown (upper part of S within red area)		S F+ object
A female dancer (lower part of S within red area) .... FC →		S Ms H O+
Bird (small S underneath 12)		S F+ A
A flyer's insignia (small S underneath 12)		S F+ object
Bird (S between red and brown areas)		S F+ A
A bull's head, inverse interpretation		WS CF Ad

Slide 3

Two persons; men, women	W M H P
Fighting people, attacking each other	W M H P/aggression
Men falling toward the outside ...	W M H P
Two figures followed by running children are .... reaching for a butterfly (this is simultaneously P and O+ because the manner of composition is original and therefore more valuable than the usual P)	W M H O+, P D M H P D F + A P *combinatory*
Men with Janus heads	W M H P O+
A fire dance by primitive priests ..	W MC H/scene O+
Halloween dance	W MC scene O+
Ghost dance .... ChF ➔	W M H O+
A silhouette .... ChF ➔	W F± shadow
Two statues	W F+ object (H) dehumanization
Human parts	W F— anatomy
Windblown trees (all dark parts) .. FCh ➔	W F± plant
Something burnt .... ChF ➔	W CF burnt object
India ink blots	W CF blots
Various animals or animal parts ..	DW F± A, Ad
Bulls (all dark blots)	DW F— A
A blood puddle	DW CF ChF blood
A fantastic cloud formation before a thunderstorm	DW ChF CF clouds
A woman lying; her abdomen is uncovered .... CF ➔	W M— H/sex O—
Two old-fashioned aunts (upper part of the dark area)	D F+ H
A torn or corroded tree leaf (upper dark part)	D F— plant, defect
A root piece (the "feet" of the "men")	D F+ plant
Gnomes " " " " "	D F+ H
Caterpillars " " " " "	D F+ A
Centipedes " " " " "	D F± A
Worm, snake " " " " "	D F— A

Butterfly (red center area)			D F+ A P
A flyer's insignia (red center area)			D F± object
Running children (red outer area)			D M H P
A leaping bear	"	"	" D M A (P) H repression
Rabbits, a standing			
dog	"	"	" D F+ A
A doll	"	"	"
		Ms →	D F+ object/(H repression)
Bird	"	"	" D F± A
A flying duck	"	"	" D F— A
A devil's mask	"	"	"
		(FC)	D F+ mask
Blood spots (usually all red blots)			D CF blood
Blood	"	"	" D C blood
Fire (red center area)			D C fire
A hand (outer dark area) ... Do →			Dd F+ Hd
A spider " " "			Dd F± A
A fir tree branch at the outside			
(dark outer area)			Dd F— plant
Pincers of a crab (the light part of			
the lower dark area) ..... Do →			Dd F+ Ad
Pliers (light part of the lower dark			
area)			Dd F— object
A head (on top, if no human figure			
has been seen before)			Do F+ Hd
Snakes (above the head on top) ...			Dd F+ A

23. The Average Number of Factors per 100 Tests

The average computation presented in the following table is based upon rather extensive test material. In a way, this material is one-sided, however, because it deals primarily with military personnel. The 2,000 subjects are composed of 1,600 army men ranging in age from 20 to 25 years, and 400 non-military persons, 18 to 40 years of age. The test material of civilians as compared with that of military personnel is still too small. In addition, we have to take into account the fact that the military material that has been used here originated with people living within the very definite confines of a collective. It is obvious that people who live in a *differently organized collective* (for instance, inmates of an institution, workers in a factory, members of some other professional or spiritual group, with a corresponding emotional "deformation"), or those who do *not belong to a collective* at all, will show *different averages*.

In general, the color factors are intensified in tests performed with military personnel (the extratensive factor is strongly stressed, motility is greater, physical and sportive needs are prominent). On the other hand, a decrease of M (coarctation of inner life, introversive factors, imaginative creativeness, meditation) may be observed. The number of Ch responses is increased correspondingly with the formal adaptation—that is to say, the regimented military external behavior. The number of

TABLE 1

Card	SW	DW	W	D	Dd	Do	S	M	Ms	FC	CF	C	FCh	ChF	Ch
I	3	2.5	150	95	35	2	10	18	—	—	—	—	70	19	2
II	1	1	45	230	10	—	50	5	—	90	95	2.5	—	—	—
III	—	—	85	165	50	2.5	5	62	25	5	10	—	5	6	—
Total	4	3-4	280	490	95	4.5	65	85	25	95	105	2.5	75	25	2

F+ = 485
F− = 80
F± = 70

P = 255
O = 90

H = 150
Hd = 50
anat = 50
blood = 5
A = 350
Ad = 100
obj = 130
pl = 100
nat = 20
geog = 15
others = 30

Number of responses = approximately 1,000

A increases too, and the A% is relatively higher, in accordance with the strongly stereotyped thinking, the search for routine, for a model. Generally, the number of responses is smaller than it is for civilians. Within the military material itself, certain differences have been found to be related to the special formations. Although they were not significant, they were conspicuous enough. Here it became apparent that, throughout the years and at various schools, the averages remained constant, as did the differences between the diverse branches of service in the armed forces. Thus, specific qualification for a particular branch of service could be determined on the basis of the Zulliger Test alone.

Table 1 is based upon approximately 2,000 tests. As comparison material for other groups and ages, we are inserting at this point two tables compiled by Salomon on the basis of his material in Paris. Table 2, which is also based on roughly 2,000 tests, originated with the applicants for work in a large factory that produces electrical appliances. The material deals with people between 20 and 45 years of age, mostly technicians and engineers, but also persons seeking positions in the administrative branch of the enterprise. The number of male and female subjects is approximately the same. In this case, too, a grouping according to the various professional categories produced some rather significant differences.

Table 3 is based upon a publication by Salomon, dealing with Jewish North-African adolescents who, in preparation for their later immigration to Israel, lived for a period of time in special children's homes in France. The averages per 100 cases are computed from test material comprising 1,000 tests. The number of male and female adolescents is approximately equal. They range in age from 13 to 17 years.

Other publications, which have reported on the use of the group test in psychosociological research, for which it has proven to be especially well suited, have arrived at different averages, in accordance with the groups used for the testing. This too points to the fact that the test has possibilities for fine differentiation, although the total number of responses to the group test does not amount to more than an average of

TABLE 2

Computed on the basis of 2,000 tests of work applicants in a factory for electrical appliances

WS	DW	W	D	Dd	Do	S	M	Ms	FC	CF	C	FCh	ChF	Ch
23	16	300	695	216	46	229	201	11	77	158	8	61	41	1

$F+$ = 802
$F\pm$ = 155
$F-$ = 119
$\overline{P}$ = 282

$F+\%$ = number	
86 – 100 =	44
80 – 85 =	18
75 – 79 =	15
70 – 74 =	8
less than 70 =	15

H	= 189
Hd	= 87
A	= 447
Ad	= 173
pl	= 147
obj	= 168
anat	= 77
nat	= 29
others	= 208

Total number of responses = 1,525

TABLE 3

Computed on the basis of about 1,000 tests of Jewish North-African adolescents

WS	DW	W	D	Dd	Do	S	M	Ms	FC	CF	C	FCh	ChF	Ch
—	1	131	680	231	31	134	141	12	80	95	15	39	12	1

F+ = 654
F± = 43
F— = 175
P = 210

H   = 188
Hd   = 63
A   = 393
Ad   = 163
pl   = 69
obj   = 109
anat = 11
blood = 11
nat   = 38
others = 71

Total number of responses = 1,208

10-17. Moreover, Heinz Schmid, in Bern, has demonstrated that the average number of responses is the same for both the individual and the group tests. This corresponds with my own experience. Salomon has reported that, in his studies with the material of the above mentioned factory, he has obtained a larger average, and even a larger absolute, number of responses in the group test than in the individual test. The inmates of a psychiatric hospital, who were almost all psychotic, produced more responses in the individual than in the group test. According to Salomon, the psychological explanation for the fact that so-called normal subjects—at any rate, subjects who are not seriously pathological—produce the same number of responses in both the group and the individual tests, or even a larger one in the group test, and that this relationship is reversed with psychotic patients, is to be found in the different object relations and the different capacity for transference in the two groups.

In any given case, it has proven useful to turn to the following average numerical results.

Averages of One Test

W	=	$2-4$	M	=	$2-3$	H	=	$2-3$
D	=	$5-8$	FC	=	$1-2$	Hd	=	$1-2$
Dd	=	$1-2$	CF	=	$1-2$	A	=	$4-5$
S	=	$1-2$	C	=	0	Ad	=	$1-2$
			FCh	=	1	obj	=	$1-2$
			ChF	=	$0-1$	pl	=	$1-2$
			Ch	=	0	anat	=	$0-1$
						nat	=	$0-1$
						others	=	$1-$

$F+\% = 75-90-95$
$H\% = 15-25$
$A\% = 35-55$
$\overline{P \quad = \quad 3-5}$

Total number of responses $= 10-17$

24. The Group Test in Use

A. THE EVALUATION OF THE FACTORS FOR THE SHORT ARMY DIAGNOSIS

1. As has already been indicated, the Zulliger Group Test was first used by the army for the sole purpose of *screening candidates roughly from large groups*. If the Zulliger Group Test deviated too much from the average, then the respective subject's name was immediately earmarked for an individual test.

2. It was our aim to investigate quickly the following aspects:

a. Does the candidate possess enough intelligence? If so, what is the character of his intelligence? Is he more capable of theoretical or of practical thinking?

b. Does the candidate possess any talent for organization and leadership?

c. Is the candidate capable of human contact?

d. Are there any symptoms indicating that the candidate may not be mentally and intellectually completely healthy?

Intelligence as well as affectivity and personality factors should be considered and information about them should be given in telegram-like abbreviations.

With some experience this can be accomplished in a relatively short time.

3. Not too rarely, however, the commanding officers requested short diagnoses of people whom we did not think it necessary to examine individually because we believed them to be "average."

TABLE 1

Scoring:
Subject: *Corporal A.*

Date: Oct. 23, 1943
File No. 37

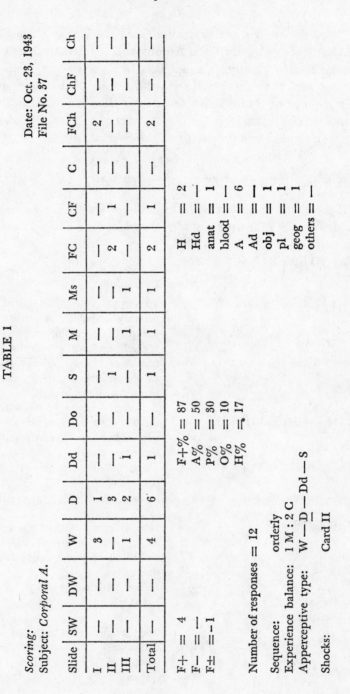

Slide	SW	DW	W	D	Dd	Do	S	M	Ms	FC	CF	C	FCh	ChF	Ch
I	—	—	3	1	—	—	—	—	—	—	—	—	2	—	—
II	—	—	—	3	—	—	1	—	—	2	1	—	—	—	—
III	—	—	1	2	1	—	—	1	1	—	—	—	—	—	—
Total	—	—	4	6	1	—	1	1	1	2	1	—	2	—	—

F+ = 4
F— = |
F± = −1

F+% = 87
A% = 50
P% = 30
O% = 10
H% = 17

H	= 2
Hd	= —
anat	= 1
blood	= —
A	= 6
Ad	= —
obj	= 1
pl	= 1
geog	= 1
others	= —

Number of responses = 12

Sequence: orderly
Experience balance: 1 M : 2 C
Apperceptive type: W — D — Dd — S
Shocks: Card II

The requested short diagnoses were worked out instead on the basis of the group tests. Among the other materials, everything that the Zulliger Group Test had shown was used. The results were then compared with the results of the other group tests, in a joint conference attended by all those working in the army psychological services. The short diagnosis that was finally presented was the result of these joint efforts.

B. SHORT EXAMPLES FROM THE MILITARY SERVICE

Example 1: In his test with the Zulliger Group Test, *Corporal A.* yielded the following numerical results (see also Table 1).

EVALUATION:

Factor	*Evaluation*
4 W, none in Card II	average organizational talent; sufficiently capable of structuring; has qualitative ambition.
6 D	is chiefly endowed practically.
1 Dd and 1 S	can be accurate; is critical, but not to excess; however, he possesses the power to assert himself.
S and M	is also critical toward himself.
M and Ms and O	occasionally he is not without some good ideas; good plans suddenly occur to him.
Color (FC, CF)	well-adjusted; capable of human contact.
Colors and M	is impulsive (CF), but restrained (M);
FCh	behaves in a "well-brought-up fashion"; possesses formal adaptation ability; is not completely without shrewdness.
%-column	innate intelligence is high average.
1 anat	has intellectual ambition.
Geography	is not free from a schoolboy's attitude; when facing authority, he is occasionally embarrassed like a schoolboy; he is still somewhat "immature."

Number of responses 4 : 4 : 4 = 12	ability to work and to become fatigued are normal; he also has diligence, and is steadily industrious.
Sequence	he has common sense.
Experience balance	within the surroundings in which he has been placed (practical), he is versatile, attentive; is probably good at sports.
Apperceptive type	good intellectual grasp; an accurate observer (S and F+%).
Shock, S at the end of Card II	he is still developing; his inhibitions are fading away ("development neurosis").

This evaluation, as we carried it out above, was perfectly adequate for the conference of the examiners (if a short diagnosis was desired).

An examiner who has more experience with the handling of the Zulliger Group Test takes in the scoring table at a glance. In addition, since he knows by heart the significance of the factors, the factors' groupings, and the factors' relationships, he does not have to revert to a written evaluation prior to the conference. For he is capable of weighing the factors against each other directly without written notes.

2. The case of *Corporal B.* is an example which outlines the process of the examiner's reasoning as he evaluates the scores (see Table 2).

EVALUATION:

The large number of W, the F+% of 100, the almost rigid sequence, and the large apperceptive type indicate very good innate intelligence; since a W response is produced for Card II, the combinatory ability is high; the fact that the subject possesses a pronounced ability for combination and a need for organization is further confirmed by the SW in Card I, as well as by the W in Card III, which encloses not only the dark blot but also the center red blot ("two men are tearing a fire apart" = WMC H O). The subject is also quite capable of abstracting; the three W in the Cards I and II are perceived abstractly; the F+% of 100 suggests accuracy of observation and reliable

TABLE 2

Scoring:
Subject: *Corporal B.*

Slide	SW	DW	W	D	Dd	Do	S	M	Ms	FC	CF	C	FCh	ChF	Ch
I	1	—	2	1	1	—	—	—	—	—	—	—	2	—	—
II	—	—	1	—	—	—	2	—	—	—	1	—	—	—	—
III	—	—	1	—	2	—	—	1	—	—	—	1	—	—	—
Total	1	—	4	1	3	—	2	1	—	—	1	1	2	—	—

F+ = 7
F− = —
F± = —

F+% = 100
A% = 20
P% = 10
O% = 40
H% = 9

H = 1
Hd = —
anat = 3
A = 2
Ad = —
obj = 3
pl = 1
geog = 2

Responses: 11
Sequence: orderly
Experience balance: 1 M : 2½ C
Apperceptive type: W — (D) — Dd — S
Shocks: $\overline{\text{Card II}}$

formulation, and implies reliability in general. The relatively large number of DdF+, a sign of exactness, points in the same direction; on the other hand, there are too few D; thus, practical thinking will not be the subject's strong point. The small number of A and P confirms this personality trait; his thinking is somewhat eccentric and not exactly well adapted to that of his fellow-human beings, for the originality of thinking expressed by a high O% is an impediment to adaptation; also, taken with the high O%, the P% is too low (the latter is an indicator for the adaptation of the subject's thinking to that of others).

The subject has produced a relatively large number of W, too few D, too many Dd, and too many S. From this it is clear that he alternates between generosity and pedantic criticism; the joint occurrence of a large number of W and S suggests that the subject indulges in a critical view of problems; he has a tendency to contradiction and to the questioning of everything. On the other hand, he possesses strong intellectual ambition (anat), and a tendency to objectivity (3 obj); also, the subject is not free from a schoolboy's concepts (geog). Affectivity is controlled by the intellect, a fact that is indicated by the two FCh and, in general, by his entire innate intelligence. However, the affects remain egocentric, and may suddenly break through violently (no FC, 1 CF and 1 C); violence is stressed by the occurrence of more than one S. The subject tries to camouflage his opposing tendencies, which are a permanent condition with him rather than spontaneous occasional phenomena (SW). He does not always succeed, however. This is supported by all the other S; if the S are considered together with the subject's egocentric affectivity (experience balance) and C (representing explosive, impressionable, and impulsive qualities), then the subject may be expected to be strongly aggressive by nature. Since his innate intelligence is so high, this means that the subject prefers discussing things violently and stubbornly to dealing out blows (as might be the case, if his innate intelligence were more primitive). The subject may be very easily influenced by suggestion (CF, C), yet extensively (experience balance) rather than intensively; he also reacts readily with opposition to suggestions (suggestibility in connection with S); his contact with his environment is impeded (no FC, the form of innate intelligence). Violence and abruptness are mitigated by quite formal (conventional) behavior, and adaptation is established as an expression of having been well brought up (FCh) as well as by repression of affects (color shock).

These reflections result in the following synopsis (*short diagnosis*):

Corporal B. possesses a very good innate intelligence which is rather theoretical, geared to the solving of problems, and marked by a strong tendency to criticism. He is able to organize, and his ability to observe accurately stands him in good stead. Yet the subject finds it difficult to adapt himself to the thinking of others; he is somewhat unworldly in his thinking, so that often a theoretical problem may interest him more than life. He is an "intellectual" at the expense of his emotional expressiveness, which is either neglected or erupts impulsively. His ability to establish contact is somewhat impeded, although this is mitigated by a rather formal adaptation. The subject's behavior is uncorrupted and fair when he is dealing with others. In addition, since he is intellectually ambitious, he is not entirely free from a schoolboy's submissiveness.

3. *Corporal C.* (see Table 3)

Slide I.	Record
A typical picture of a crab	WF + A P
One observes the tentacles in front like arms	DdF + Ad itemizing
in front and in back for moving forward	DdF + Ad
It could also very well be the enlargement of a beetle	FCh ➔ WF + A P

Slide II.	
The red color represents a human torso that has been cut open	DCF anat
The green color: fishes of foreign lands	DF + A
Brown: a crab (lobster) seen from the side	DFC A
or two dead foxes	DFC A "or"

Slide III.

The outer red colors: a jumping
    Jack ....   DF + obj/H P
Center red color: a butterfly ......   DF + A P
Black color: two devils approach-
    ing each other ....   WM + H P educational level?

EVALUATION:

Low educational level, although intelligence is good. He is more practically endowed than he is theoretically; is an accurate observer; possesses intellectual ambition. He is cautious, and not without shrewdness.

He is impulsive, yet able to have contact with others; diligent, exact; makes an effort. He is reproductive, but without creative imagination, and therefore remains subordinate.

As a candidate for officers' training: his educational level makes this questionable.

Proposal: examination of educational background and of manifest intelligence.

4. *Corporal D.* (see Table 4)

Slide I.   *Record*

A beetle, enlarged, dim ....   FCh → WF + A P
There is a chestnut leaf in the
    center ....   DF + pl
A dog's head, on top ....   DF + Ad

Slide II.

A horseshoe form from a mountain
    path (red area) ....   DF + obj
South Sea fishes (green area) .....   DF + A
A cutting from a silhouette draw-
    ing (red area) ....   DF + obj O+

Slide III.

Butterfly ....   DF + A P
Caterpillars (small dark parts) ....   DF + A
Spiders, outer black area ....   DdF + A
Two dolls, outer area ....   DF + obj

TABLE 3

Scoring:
Subject: *Corporal C.*

Slide	SW	DW	W	D	Dd	Do	S	M	Ms	FC	CF	C	FCh	ChF	Ch
I	—	—	2	—	2	—	—	—	—	—	—	—	1	—	—
II	—	—	—	4	—	—	—	—	—	2	1	—	—	—	—
III	—	—	1	2	—	—	—	1	—	—	—	—	—	—	—
Total	—	—	3	6	2	—	—	1	—	2	1	—	1	—	—

F+ = 7
F− = —
F± = —

Responses: 12
Sequence: orderly
Tendency to inversion
Experience balance: 1 M : 2 C
Apperceptive type: W — D — Dd
Shocks: —

F+% = 100
A% = 67
P% = 42
O% = —
H% = 17

H = 2
Hd = —
anat = 1
A = 6
Ad = 2
obj = 1
pl = —
nat = —
geog = 1
others = —

514

TABLE 4

Scoring:
Subject: *Corporal D.*

Slide	SW	DW	W	D	Dd	Do	S	M	Ms	FCh	ChF	Ch	FC	CF	C
I	—	—	1	2	—	—	—	—	—	—	1	—	—	—	—
II	—	—	—	3	—	—	—	—	—	—	—	—	—	—	—
III	—	—	—	3	1	—	—	—	—	—	—	—	—	—	—
Total	—	—	1	8	1	—	—	—	—	—	1	—	—	—	—

$F+ = 10$ $F+\% = 100$ H = —
$F- = |$ $A\% = 60$ A = 5
$F\pm = |$ $P\% = 20$ Ad = 1
          $O\% = 10$ obj = 3
                              pl = 1

Responses: 10
Sequence: orderly
Experience balance: 0 M : 0 C
Apperceptive type: W — D — Dd
Shocks: —

EVALUATION:

A practical, accurate worker, with an average capacity for work.

Serious, with tendency toward depressed moods. Inclined to separate himself from others, likes nature better than people, enjoys the solitude of nature more than its colors (did not give any color responses). His adaptation to others is somewhat arid and rather formal.

Proposal: Should be tested individually in order that his apparently strong depressive tendencies may be looked into.

5. *Corporal E.* (see Table 5)

Slide I.	*Record*
A bent advancing monster	WMFCh + H O+
An enlarged spider	FCh → WF + A P
A small crab	WF + A P

Slide II.	
Colored wallpaper pattern	WCF obj
Flower petals, red area	DFC pl
Grass tufts, green area	DFC pl
Two girls kissing each other (dark red area)	DM + H O+

Slide III.	
Two masked people	WM + H P
Two running Indians	DM H P
A butterfly	DF + A P
A piece of root (small dark area) ..	DF + pl

EVALUATION:

The subject has both technical and theoretical abilities. He has many different talents, is gifted in many areas, and has creative ideas of his own.

He is gentle rather than rough, yet he is not without impulsivity. However, the latter is controlled by a rich inner life. He is quite capable of contact with others, and his formal adaptation is good. He is lively, sportive without exaggeration. He is exact without being pedantic; rather generous, yet not "sloppy."

Type: a good troop-leader, with a talent for organization and the ability to arrange things quickly.

TABLE 5

Scoring:
Subject: Corporal E.

Slide	SW	DW	W	D	Dd	Do	S	M	Ms	FC	CF	C	FCh	ChF	Ch
I	—	—	3	—	!	—	—	1	—	—	—	—	2	—	—
II	—	—	1	3	—	—	—	1	—	2	1	—	—	—	—
III	—	—	1	2	1	—	—	2	—	1	—	—	—	—	—
Total	—	—	5	5	1	—	—	4	—	2	1	—	2	—	—

F+ = 5
F− = 1
F± = 1

F+% = 100
A% = 27
P% = 50
O% = 20
H% = 36

H = 4
Hd = 1
A = 3
obj = 1
pl = 3

Responses: 11
Sequence: orderly
Experience balance: 4 M : 2 C
Apperceptive type: $\dfrac{\text{W — D — Dd}}{}$
Shocks:

6. *Corporal F.* (see Table 6)

Slide I.	*Record*
Clouds with gaps in them	ChF → WSF ± clouds
Potatoes with sprouts	DWF − pl

Slide II.

Smeared colors	WC color
Chops (red area)	DCF food
with parsley (green area)	DFC pl/food
on the bottom there is some fried meat	DCF food, perseveration tendency
Crab (green area)	DF + A
These could also be shells	DF + A

Slide III.

India-ink spots	WCF spots
Smeared blood (red area)	DCF blood
Centipede, on the bottom, dark area	DF ± A
Two men without legs	DF + H
A butterfly	DF + A P

EVALUATION:

The subject is capable of being easy-going and "generously sloppy," and he loves to act in this manner. But he can also be accurate; he is capable of conscious effort and diligence. In general, his thinking is not very well disciplined. His powers of empathy are reduced; both his intellectual and his emotional adaptation are impeded. He seeks to adapt himself in a more formal way. He is greatly impulsive and yet not without endurance. He is good at sports (the CF types are motile). His inner life is meager; he lives and experiences externally, and is strongly influenced by suggestions. On the one hand, he has illusions; on the other hand, his interests are rather trivial, as is typical of spoiled people with a good family background.

Although he is a good soldier, Corporal F.'s personality is still not stable enough.

Proposal: Individual examination is recommended in order to find out whether Corporal F. should perhaps be deferred for another year (candidates' school) and observed, because of his lack of maturity.

TABLE 6

Scoring:
Subject: *Corporal F.*

Slide	SW	DW	W	D	Dd	Do	S	M	Ms	FC	CF	C	FCh	ChF	Ch
I	1	1	—	—	—	—	—	—	—	—	1	—	—	1	—
II	—	—	1	5	—	—	—	—	—	1	2	1	—	—	—
III	—	—	1	4	—	—	—	—	—	—	2	—	—	—	—
Total	1	1	2	9	—	—	—	—	—	1	4	1	—	1	—

F+ = 4
F— = 1
F± = 2

F+% = 70, circa
A% = 30
P% = 8
O% = —
H% = 8

H = 1
Hd = —
A = 4
Ad = —
obj = —
pl = 2
blood = 1
blood stains = 2
food = 2 to 3
clouds = 1
tendency to persevera-tion
combination and con-fabulation

Responses: 13
Sequence: orderly-loose
Experience balance: 0 M : 6 C
Apperceptive type: (DW) — W — D
Shocks: —

7. *Corporal G.* (see Table 7)

Slide I.	*Record*
Ascetic priest clad in a floating garb, striding along	WMCh H O
An ivy leaf	DF + pl

Slide II.	
People bowing to each other	DM + H O
Bushes	DFC + pl
The baton of command of a primitive chieftain	SF + obj O
Moles, very plastic	FCh → DFC A

Slide III.	
Two men	WM + H P
followed by dwarfs ...... (Ms →)	DM H P
There is a butterfly in the center ..	DF + A P
The whole could also be a silhouette drawing	ChF → WF ± obj

EVALUATION:

This is a person who is sensitive to everything that is refined and delicate, and whose emotional approach is rich in nuances. He is gentle and artistically gifted, and his intelligence level is very high. His is a broad horizon; he is well educated. His thinking is self-critical and original. He is capable of organizing and combining; he is emotionally and intellectually adaptable; he establishes contact easily. At the same time, he is selective in making friends, but his friendships are long-lasting.

Because he is good-hearted, he can be too kind and may be deceived.

He has hardly any interest in sports; his interests are rather of a more intellectual kind.

As a candidate for officership, he should be somewhat more hardened; he should have military training with this in mind.

TABLE 7

Scoring:
Subject: *Corporal G.*

Slide	SW	DW	W	D	Dd	Do	S	M	Ms	FC	CF	C	FCh	ChF	Ch
I	—	—	1	1	—	—	—	1	—	—	—	—	1	—	—
II	—	—	—	3	—	—	1	1	—	2	—	—	1	—	—
III	—	—	2	2	—	—	—	2	(1)	—	—	—	—	1	—
Total	—	—	3	6	—	—	1	4	(1)	2	—	—	2	1	—

F+ = 5
F− = —
F± = 1

F+% = circa 90
A% = 20
P% = 30
O% = 30
H% = 40

H = 4
Hd = 1
A = 2
Ad = 1
obj = 2
pl = 2

Responses: 10
Sequence: orderly
Experience balance: 4 M : 1 C
Apperceptive type: W —D
—
Shocks:

The MCh in Card I has been computed as an M and as an FCh at the same time

521

8. *Fusilier H.* (see Table 8)

Slide I.	*Record*
A leafy plant	DWF — pl

Slide II.

Various colors	DWC colors
Various animal parts of crabs and beetles	DF + Ad

Slide III.

Larva faces	DoF + Hd
Halloween	M? — WCF scene O
Again various animals or animal parts	DWF ± A

EVALUATION:

This is a man who is egocentric; who reacts in an erethic manner, is stubborn, and intellectually not very gifted. He is sometimes quite indifferent, and at times anxious, not seeing the forest for the trees. For instinctual reasons, he is probably dishonest, and could steal.

Proposal: Individual examination, in order to clarify the level of suspected mental retardation; possibly referral to the psychiatrist for a discharge. He is not a good soldier, nor a good comrade.

9. *Fusilier I.* (see Table 9)

Slide I.	*Record*
Silly stuff	rejection!
A skull	DF + anat

Slide II.

Blood spots	DCF blood
A bean stalk (within red area)	SF + pl
A flyer's insignia (within red area)	SF + obj

Slide III.

A butterfly	DF + A P
People whose legs have been torn off	WF + H
Blood	DC blood
On top, trees shot down	DdF — pl

TABLE 8

Scoring:
Subject: *Fusilier H.*

Slide	SW	DW	W	D	Dd	Do	S	M	Ms	FC	CF	C	FCh	ChF	Ch
I	—	1	—	—	—	—	—	—	—	—	—	—	—	—	—
II	—	1	—	2	—	—	—	—	—	—	—	1	—	—	—
III	—	1	1	—	—	1	—	—	—	—	1	—	—	—	—
Total	—	3	1	2	—	1	—	—	—	—	1	1	—	—	—

F+ = 3
F— = 1
F± = 1

F+% = 70
A% = 43
P% = —
O% = 14
H% = 14

H = 1
Hd = 1
scene = 1
A = 1
Ad = 2
pl = 1
C = 1
DW and tendency to perseveration

Responses: 7
Sequence: ?
Experience balance: 0 M : 1½ C
Apperceptive type: DW — D — (Do)
Shock: —

TABLE 9

Scoring:
Subject: *Fusilier I.*

Card	SW	DW	W	D	Dd	Do	S	M	Ms	FC	CF	C	FCh	ChF	Ch
I	—	—	—	1	—	—	—	—	—	—	—	—	—	—	—
II	—	—	—	1	—	—	2	—	—	—	1	—	—	—	—
III	—	—	1	3	—	—	1	—	—	—	—	1	—	—	—
Total	—	—	1	5	—	—	2	—	—	—	1	1	—	—	—

F+ = 5
F− = 1
F± = —

F+% = 83
A% = 13
P% = 13
O% = —
H% = 13

H = 1
anat = 1
blood = 2
A = 1
obj = 1
pl = 2

Responses: 8
Sequence: loose
Experience balance: 0 M : 2½ C
Apperceptive type: W — D — Dd — S
Shock: —

EVALUATION:

Very instinct-ridden and aggressive; could be tainted by adverse heredity (child of alcoholic parents?). He has a tendency to quarrelsome behavior, which can lead to sudden and unexpected fights. He has a negative attitude toward the outside world; he is obstinate and emotionally unadapted. His intelligence is average; it is more practical than theoretical. He has fantasies of violence and is not capable of comradeship. He is intellectually ambitious; he believes himself to be brighter than he really is. He does not have a great deal of sympathy for others, and no capacity at all for empathy and contact with others; he is egocentric, but submits easily to suggestions.

Advice: Should be used as a manager in the warehouse. There he should be further observed; should perhaps have a psychiatric examination, because there is reason for suspicion that he may be a psychopath.

10. *Fusilier J.* (see Table 10)

Slide I.	*Record*
A corpse, in the center there is the heart	ChF → WF ± anat O
	DF — Hd, position
Slide II.	
Lungs and spine	DCF anat
	SF — anat
Liver and intestines	DF — anat
	DCF anat
Slide III.	
Parts of a human body	WF — anat
in the center there is the heart	DCF Hd, position

EVALUATION:

(Preliminary remark: Fusilier J. was the victim of a serious accident.)

The subject's innate intelligence is of a rather practical kind, but considerable emotional changes have taken place. Fusilier J. suffers from a severe hypochondria which is, perhaps, the result of his accident (accident neurosis?). He is overwhelmed by gloomy thoughts.

TABLE 10

Scoring:
Subject: *Fusilier J.*

Slide	SW	DW	W	D	Dd	Do	S	M	Ms	FC	CF	C	FCh	ChF	Ch
I	—	—	1	1	—	—	—	—	—	—	—	—	—	1	—
II	—	—	—	3	—	—	1	—	—	—	—	2	—	—	—
III	—	—	1	1	—	—	—	—	—	—	—	1	—	—	—
Total	—	—	2	5	—	—	1	—	—	—	3	—	—	1	—

F+ = —   F+% = low   H = —
F— = 4   A% = —   Hd = 2
F± = 1   P% = —   anat = 6
    O% = 13   position interpretations
    H% = 25   perseveration with anat!
    anat% = 75!

Responses: 8
Sequence: orderly
Experience balance: 0 M : 3 C
Apperceptive type: W — D — S
Shock: Card II?

526

He is no longer within the range of "normalcy." He must be sent to a psychiatrist to be treated, or possibly discharged from the army.

11. *Sapper K.*

Slide I.	*Record*
Hell	ChF ➜ WF ± hell O—

Slide II.	
A garden	DWCF O+

Slide III.	
The Middle Ages	ChF ➜ WF ± nat O—/impression

EVALUATION:

A man who is strongly given to fantasies. He has unworldly ideas, and is undoubtedly eccentric. He has a strong need for unification.

The results of the Zulliger Group Test are insufficient. Individual tests should be administered.

12. *Gunner L.* (see Table 11)

Slide I.	*Record*
On top there are the pincers of an insect	Do ➜ DdF + Ad
Maple leaf	DF + pl
An enlarged plant louse	FCh ➜ WF + A

Slide II.	
Flower petals (red area)	DCF pl
Moss plants (green area)	DFC pl
Farm soil (brown area)	DCF soil
The whole could be a child's effort at painting	WCF obj O

Slide III.	
Two boys	DF + H P
A red butterfly	DFC A P
Centipedes	DF ± A
Two old-fashioned fighters	WM + H P

TABLE 11

Scoring:
Subject: Gunner L.

Slide	SW	DW	W	D	Dd	Do	S	M	Ms	FC	CF	C	FCh	ChF	Ch
I	—	—	1	1	1	(1)	—	—	—	—	—	—	1	—	—
II	—	—	1	3	—	—	—	1	—	1	3	—	—	—	—
III	—	—	1	3	—	—	—	—	—	1	—	—	—	—	—
Total	—	—	3	7	1	(1)	—	1	—	2	3	—	1	—	—

F+ = 5
F— = 1
F± = 1

F+% = 90
A% = 36
P% = 30
O% = 10
H% = 18

H = 2
A = 3
Ad = 1
obj = 1
pl = 3
earth = 1

Responses: 11
Sequence: inverse
Experience balance: 1 M : 4 C
Apperceptive type: W — D — Dd (Do)
Shock: —

EVALUATION:

L.'s behavior strikes us as having slight overtones of anxiety and as being cautious. This impedes his capability for making decisions. His intelligence is practical, but he is also capable of understanding larger relationships—provided he has time enough to think. His hesitant behavior prevents him from being a dashing soldier. He is exact and conscientious, however, and although he lacks courage, and does not come easily to grips with new situations, he is capable of human contact. He is impulsive by nature, but inhibited.

He could easily try the patience of a superior. If he is treated impatiently or reproachfully, L. will be pushed even further into an anxious, cautious, and hesitant attitude, and become even more confused.

He needs warm praise and encouragement. If he is treated incorrectly, he will undoubtedly prove to be a "bad" soldier; but if he is treated correctly, his performance will be average. He should be entrusted with a certain degree of responsibility (for instance, that of a mailman, cook, etc.), and his conscientious efforts should on occasion be praised. Since he is the type of person who is dependent upon others, he will then make every effort, even though he may be doing it just out of gratitude.

The "problems" of this "difficult soldier" originate in a misunderstanding of his specific personality; there is no real need for candidate L. to be a "difficult soldier." His superior officer must treat him as an individual, in terms of his individuality. Then his "difficulty" will cease to be effective.

13. *Soldier M.* (see Table 12)

Slide I.	*Record*
Some animal	WF + A
Four holes in the black	SF ± description infantile

Slide II.	
Blood	DC blood
Dirt	DC obj
There is a plant in the center	SF + pl
A triangular hole in the green	SF ± description infantile

Slide III.

A water-nymph in the center ..... DF + A
A worm .... DF + A
On the outside, there is a fir tree
    branch .... DdF — pl
On top there is a head .... DoF + Hd

EVALUATION:

M. is an easily excitable, argumentative, and rude person. He is impulsive and unpredictable like a child, he tends to be obstinate and scheming. His ability to establish contact with others is poor, and he is not a good comrade. He is a "lone wolf," ill-bred and superficial. He is pedantic toward others. His intelligence is average: he has the intelligence of an odd-jobber. He is obstinate, sentimental about himself, and poorly disciplined; his inner self has degenerated, and he may be psychotic.

Military strictness is good for him; it may discipline him. Severity is appropriate for him, for he takes advantage of kindness, which only makes him more demanding.

Proposal: Individual testing for further clarification.

14. *Karl B.*, 20 years old, had to be discharged from the training school for recruits because of mental retardation (see Table 13). "He is a headstrong eccentric" (remark of the instruction officer).

Zulliger Group Test

Slide I.

A dog .... DWF — A
or an elephant .... DWF — A "or"
Ibexes (9 and 3) .... DdF + A

Slide II.

A human being cut open .... WCF anat, O—
Eyes of a cat (within the green
    area) .... SF — Ad
A cat's lungs (red area) .... DCF Ad, perseveration
Cats (brown area) .... DF — A, perseveration

Slide III.

A butterfly (red inner area) ...... DF + A P
Bears (red outer area) .... DF + A
Bulls (dark area) .... DWF — A, perseveration
Spiders (9 and 3) .... Dd — A
Crabs (small dark area) .... DdDF — A

TABLE 12

Scoring:
Subject: Soldier M.

Slide	SW	DW	W	D	Dd	Do	S	M	Ms	FC	CF	C	FCh	ChF	Ch
I	—	—	1	—	—	—	1	—	—	—	—	—	—	—	—
II	—	—	—	2	—	—	2	—	—	—	—	2	—	—	—
III	—	—	—	2	1	1	—	—	—	—	—	1	—	—	—
Total	—	—	1	4	1	1	3	—	—	—	—	2	—	—	—

F+ = 5
F− = 1
F± = 2

F+% = 70
A% = 30
P% = —
O% = —
H% = 10

H = —
Hd = 1
blood = 1
A = 3
obj = 1
pl = 2
descrip = 2
infantile abstractions

Responses: 10
Sequence: orderly
Experience balance: O M : 2 C
Apperceptive type: W — D — Dd — Do — S
Shock: —

TABLE 13

Scoring:
Subject: *Karl B.*

Card	DW	W	D	DdD	Dd	S	F+	F—	M	CF	P	O
I	2				1		1	2				
II		1	2			1		2		2	1	1—
III	1		2	1	1		2	3				
Total	3	1	4	1	2	1	3	7	—	2	1	1—

F+% = 30   H = —

A% = 92   anat = 1

P% = 8   A = 9

O% = 8—   Ad = 2

Sequence: loose
Experience balance: O M : 2 C
Apperceptive type: DW — W — D — DdD — Dd — S
Shock: —
Remarks: perseveration with A

Responses: 12/4

EVALUATION:

The low F+%, the high A%, the perseveration tendency show clearly that the subject is mentally retarded. The absence of M and FC indicate that this is an "erethic" form of mental retardation; considering the CF and S, the assumption must be made that Karl B. is inclined to aggression; the anat suggests that Karl believes himself to be more intelligent than he really is ("intelligence complex"). In connection with the absence of FC, and because of the above-mentioned tendency to aggression, the lack of H and Hd leads to the assumption that Karl B. is not suitable.

C. OTHER EXAMPLES OF RAPID DIAGNOSIS

1. *Alfred X.,* 45 years old, writer (see Table 14)

Zulliger Group Test

Slide I.

A beggar is sitting here with his
arms raised .... FCh → WM + H O+
demandingly, pressing his head
into his neck .... DF + Hd
Apparently he is a disabled war
veteran and .... S → DF + Hd
he has put his crutches in front
of him .... DdF + obj
his clothes are torn and dirty ..... ChF → W ± clothing

Slide II.

A dream image in delicate colors:
spring. Two .... WCF image O+
people kissing each other in the
(dark red area) .... DM + H
morning light .... C impression
there are some young shrubs close
to them .... DFC pl
the street is white, it is illuminated
by lights .... SCF nat, white as color
and below there are the clods of a
freshly plowed field .... DCF nat

Slide III.

This is funny: here some wildly
gesturing Italians are bargaining
about something .... WM + H P O+
perhaps about a piece of strangely
shaped cloth; filled with curiosity, two small .... DFC obj
boys come running, away from a
game of Indians .... DM + H P
that they are playing—for they
are wearing
feathers on their heads and they are
clad in .... DdF + Ad
colored garments .... DFC clothing

EVALUATION:

It is typical for a writer to replace the A% by H%: everything
is given life, everything becomes humanized. Creative imagination (M), introversive forces, and originality play an essential
role. Contemplation becomes apparent in the first interpretation: it is simultaneously a flexor and an extensor kinesthesia.
The fact that the writer is also capable of bringing out his inner
images becomes clear not only in that he produces extensor kinesthesias, but also because of his color interpretations as well.
Introversive factors are balanced with extratensive ones (experience balance). Since, in addition to FC, he also produces
CF, it may be said of Alfred X. that he is high-spirited, but capable of keeping his high spirits in check (in other words, they
do not run away with him). His gifts for forming, organizing,
and arranging become further obvious when we consider his
W and his F+%. Because of them, we may infer that Alfred
X.'s intelligence is at least within the average range of the
highly intelligent. In addition, Alfred X. is an ambiequal type;
these are usually people with many talents. He is probably interested in painting, too; his color impression bears this out. He
is slightly vain, perhaps (clothing interpretations), but in his
case this should be "taken in stride." Because of the CF, and
since white has been interpreted as a color, we must infer that
Alfred X. is sensitive. Sensitivity is close to sensibility: subjects

TABLE 14

Scoring:
Subject: *Alfred X.*

Essentially, only three scenes have been interpreted, one for each of the cards. However, in this case it should be wise to separate the scenes into their parts. In this manner we not only obtain 14 responses (instead of three), but we are also able to evaluate the test results much more thoroughly.

Slide	W	D	Dd	S	F+	F±	M	FC	CF	FCh	ChF	P	O
I	2	2	1	1	3	1	1	1		1	1		1
II	1	3		1			1	1	3				1
III	1	3	1		1		2	2		1	1	2	1
Total	4	8	2	2	4	1	4	3	3	1	1	2	3

F+% = 90
A% = 7
P% = 13
O% = 20+
H% = 40

H = 4
Hd = 2
clothing = 2
Ad = 1
obj = 2
pl = 1
nat = 2
image = 1

Sequence: orderly
Experience balance: 4 M : 4½ C
Apperceptive type: W — D — Dd — S
Shock: —
Color impression
Responses: (3) 15/5

who interpret white as a color are easily hurt, but are trying to dissimulate it.

Alfred X. does not show any neurotic traits; he is capable of expressing his conflicts creatively, thus "getting them out of himself." The two S show that he has conflicts, indeed. When we relate the two S to the total record, we realize that irony and self-irony are not alien to him (presence of CF = irony toward the outer world; presence of M = irony toward the self—always in connection with the S). This too supplies him with a weapon against neurotic repressions.

2. *Julius Y.*, 36 years old, painter (Table 15)

Zulliger Group Test

Slide I.

Weather-beaten Buddha figure,
    obese, squat .... WM + H O+ object criticism
If one disregards the offshoots, it
    could also be a cloud figure .... ChF → WF ± cloud

Slide II.

The colors are delicate; it is almost
    as if it were Japanese .... C-impression
A strange flower (red area) ...... DCF pl
strange cup-like petals (green area) DFC pl
and on the bottom there are earth
    clods (brown area) .... DCF earth
In the center there is something
    like a bean-stalk, wilted .... SFC pl white as color

Slide III.

Dancing people in costumes; the
    ones in front are clad in black .. WMC H O+ (P)
the ones in the background are clad
    in red .... DMC H P
They are moving about in a kind of
    contredanse and are carrying
    something in their hands that
    looks like a butterfly .... DF + A P
The legs of the black people look
    like those of a mandrake ...... DF + Hd/pl O

TABLE 15

Scoring:
Subject: *Julius Y.*

Slide	W	D	S	F+	F±	M	MC	FC	CF	ChF	P	O
I	2		1		1	1				1		1
II		3					2	2 (2)	2		3	2
III	1	3		2	1							
Total	3	6	1	2	1	1	2	4	2	1	3	3

F+% = 83
A% = 10
P% = 30
O% = 30
H% = 40
pl% = 30 – 40

H = 4 – 3
A = 1
pl = 3 – 4
cloud = 1
earth = 1

Sequence: orderly
Experience balance: 3 M : 4 – 5 C
Apperceptive type: W — D — S
Shock: —?
Responses: 10/4
Color impression
White as color

EVALUATION:

The talent for painting may be recognized in the numerous color responses; the creativeness in the M, which are primarily MC, indicate intuition. We are dealing here with a generous (W-type) and probably many-gifted (ambiequal experience type) person, who is very touchy, sensitive and sensible, and easily offended. He tries, however, to hide his sensibility and sensitivity behind a "rough exterior" (white as color plus W-type).

His paintings are very colorful, well composed. From time to time Mr. Y. creates charcoal drawings (the MChF could point in this direction). His contexts are landscapes, portraits. In this connection, it may be interesting to note that he does not stereotype with A but rather with H and pl in the test. If the first response to slide II, the color impression, is considered an index of a slight color shock, then there is something neurotic to be found in Y. This may be confirmed by the quite rigid sequence. In painters, one usually finds a rather loose sequence. In real life, Mr. Y. is strict with himself. It takes a long time until he is satisfied with his creative efforts; he is self-critical, but also critical of the outer world (S : M : colors).

D. EXAMPLES OF TESTING FOR GUIDANCE COUNSELING

1. *Huber, Franz,* 30 years old, blacksmith, an applicant for the job of a foreman in a large mechanical factory.

Zulliger Group Test

I.

A crab	W F+ A P
A grape leaf (center area)	D F+ pl
A human head (upper center area)	
Do → S → D F+ Hd	
The branch of a fir tree (3 and 9)	Dd F+ pl
An owl (12 and center dark area)	D F+ A
A sitting woman with an infant	
(left side, upper part)	D M H O+

II.

Spine and ribs and (S within red area)	S F— anat
combinatory	
lungs (red area)	D CF anat
Sea-fishes, cuttle fishes (green area)	D F+ A
Two bulls pushing against each other with their heads (brown area)	D FC A P aggression
Fir tree bushes (green area)	D FC pl
Cactus-like formations (green area)	D FC pl
Two girls kissing each other (red area)	D M H O

III.

A Halloween scene, people in black and red clothes ... combinatory	W MC scene O (P)
A butterfly	D F+ A P
Puppets (red outer area)	D Ms H/game P
Caterpillars (5 and 7)	D F+ A
An animal face licking something (5 and 7 inside)	D F+ Ad
An old rusty can opener (small dark blots, 5 and 7)	D F+ object tendency to F(C) and FCh

Scoring: Number of responses: 19/7

W	= 2	F+	= 10	H	= 3		P	=	5
D	= 15	F—	= 1	Hd	= 1		O	=	3
Dd	= 1	M	= 2	A	= 6				
Do	= (1)	MC	= 1	Ad	= 1				
S	= 1 (2)	FC	= 3	anat	= 2				
F+%	= 90	CF	= 1	scene	= 1				
A%	= 37	FCh	= tendency	obj	= 1				
P%	= 26	F(C)	= tendency	pl	= 4				
O%	= 16								
H%	= 21								
anat%	= 10								

Sequence: orderly
Experience balance: 3 M : 3 C
Apperceptive type: W — D — (Do) — S

Remarks:
Aggression
Combination
Playfulness

EVALUATION:

This is a clever man ($F+\% = 90$; orderly sequence; more A than Ad; more H than Hd; optimum A%; P% and O% average-to-optimum), his capabilities are rather technical (D-type with three M, one of which is an MC). He might be capable of making some small inventions, because he has intuition (MC). He is not generous (only two W), but he is also not petty (only one Dd, the number of A is larger than the number of Ad, there are more H than Hd). He has imagination and he thinks mainly in a combinatory and constructive manner (response I/1). He is endowed with what is usually called "common sense" (the "practical" D type). He is not "learned and well-educated," although he does not lack the ambition for education (S). He is critical (S and colors) and also self-critical (S, M, and, in addition, Do), and somewhat shy (Do). He is certainly not an assertive person. He is not only endowed with a gift for handicraft, but he is also quite a model-builder (experience balance). In general, he is a "nice" person; if he is a father, he ought to be a good playmate to his children (II, last interpretation, III/1 and 3 responses). He is cheerful (3 F and 1 CF); his impulsivity is controlled; (M and CF); he has a sense for nuances (tendency to FCh and F (C)). He is not arrogant (FC and FCh), but rather too modest, despite his obvious technical ability (Do).

It is desirable that he should be installed as a foreman, for in impressing his subordinates by his technical skill and his kind "human" approach, he will be able to lead a team well.

2. A mechanic—an applicant for technical training: *Strahm, Hermann,* 16 years old, second-year high-school student.

Zulliger Group Test

I.

A lobster	W F+ A P
Or a crab	W F+ A P "or"
An ivy leaf (center area)	D F+ pl
Or a sleeveless sweater	D F+ clothing "or"
A dog's head (center upper area)	S → D F+ Ad
A dancing couple (right upper outer area)	D M H O

II.

The diagram of a flower (red area
  and center S) . . . . S → D CF pl
Rearing horses (both green areas)
  Ms → D F+ A
Strange fishes, aquarium fishes
  (green area) . . . . D F+ A
A crab variety (brown area) . . . . . . D FC A
Or fighting cows (brown area) . . . . D FC A "or" aggression
Two dwarfs with shields striding to-
  ward each other (green area) . . . D Ms H O
Baked fish filets (brown area) . . . . D FC food O
An airplane (upper portion within
  red area, white area) . . . . S F+ object
An elephant or a tapir head (red
  right outer area, 2) . . . . Dd F+ Ad "or"

III.

Two men attacking each other with { W M+ H P
  pistols . . . . combinatory   { Dd F+ object/weapon
A butterfly (red center area) . . . . . D F+ A P
A profile with a thick nose (red
  outer area, towards the inside) . . Dd F+ Hd
Indian boys running (red outer
  area) . . . . Ms → D M H P
Snakes (small dark blots at the
  bottom) . . . . D D± A
The Walen Lake (small dark blots
  at the bottom) . . . . D F+ geog
The small heads of a devil (upper
  inner area, towards 12) . . . . Dd F+ Hd/"devil"
A cannon (next to it) . . . . Dd F± object

Scoring: Number of responses: 23/9

W	= 3	F+	= 13	H	= 4	P = 6
D	= 14	F±	= 3	Hd	= 2	O = 3
Dd	= 5	M	= 3	A	= 7	
S	= 1 (3)	Ms	= 1 (3)	Ad	= 2	

F+% = 91   FC = 1
A% = 39
H% = 26
P% = 26
O% = 13

obj = 3
pl = 2
clothing = 1
food = 1
geog = 1

Sequence: orderly
Experience balance: 3 M : 2 C
Apperceptive type: C : D : Dd : S
                           $=$ $=$

Remarks:
"or"
aggressive
combinatory
weapon
Small heads of devils

EVALUATION:

This is an intelligent youth (F+% = 90, orderly sequence; optimum A%, P%, and O%; more A than Ad and more H than Hd; 3 M) and a very industrious (23 responses) as well as a technically gifted one (D — Dd type). He is critical and self-critical (S and colors, S and M, "or"), although still somewhat uncertain ("or"). But he is "bright," and he thinks in the abstract, as well as in a combinatory fashion. Also, he is already quite "mature." He has left his "childhood shortcomings" far behind him (no typically infantile interpretations), and the "devil's *small head*" suggests a sense of humor and not (phobic) anxiety remnants. His impulsivity is kept under control (3 M : 1 C); he is emotionally well-adapted and adaptable (experience balance); he is probably a nice and loyal (M) friend, with humorous ideas (Ms). He pays attention to obvious essentials, but at the same time he does not neglect the smaller details either (D and Dd). He also has it in him to become a specialized precision-tool worker, a tool maker, an electro-mechanic (there is a sufficiently large number of Dd, in addition to the D).

3. An applicant for training as a manager of a supermarket: *Mueller, Herta,* 22 years old.

Zulliger Group Test

I.

A decorative pattern of a cork or
turnip rubber stamp for wall-
paper .... ChF → W FC ornament O+ "or"
The leaf of a maple tree (center
dark area) .... D F+ pl
The whole picture could represent
a tree .... ChF → W F± pl
A bird, an eagle owl with big
feathers wanting to spread its
wings .... S → W F+ A
A robber approaching, bending
down, ... W M H O+
threatening with knives .... Dd F+ object/aggression

II.

Fishes (green area) .... D F+ A
A flower bud (red area) .... D CF pl
A bull fight (brown area) .... D FC A P/aggression
Salmon slices (brown area) ...... D FC food
A flyer (upper center white area) .. S F+ object
A rocket (white area between the
red area) .... S F+ object
Two ambitious women discussing
something (dark red area) ..... D M H O+

III.

Two dancers .... W M H P
Modern art, a picture .... W FC object/art
Two dancing hares (red outer area) D Ms A (P) humanization;
fairytale at the same time;
H repression
A butterfly (red center area) ..... D F+ A P
A Halloween scene .... W MCF scene O

543

Scoring: Number of responses: 18/7

W	= 7	F+	= 7	H	= 3	P =	3 (4)
D	= 8	F±	= 1	A	= 5	O =	4
Dd	= 1	M	= 3	obj	= 4		
S	= 2 (3)	MCF	= 1	pl	= 3		

F+%	= 94	Ms = 1
A%	= 28	FC = 3
P%	= 17 (22)	CF = 1
O%	= 22	ChF = 1
H%	= 17	ChFFC = 1

scene = 1
food = 1
ornament = 1

Sequence:	orderly
Experience balance:	4 M : 4 C
Apperceptive type:	W — D — S

Remarks:
Aggressive interpretations
Humanization
Fairy-tale motif

EVALUATION:

This "ambitious" young lady—she is describing herself in Card II, last response—who, despite the fact that she is only 22 years old, would already like to manage a shopping center— is most probably talented. It seems that she knows it, too. Intellectually, she belongs in the highest average category. Her 18 responses indicate diligence; the F+% = 94 indicates an accurate perception of reality and clear thinking; orderly sequence points to an ability to think consistently (logically); the relatively large number of W suggests comprehensive thinking and generosity, which is also borne out by the absence of Hd and Ad; since P% is 17 (22), we may infer that her ability for empathy and her power of intellectual grasp are satisfactory; the relatively high O% = 22 and the MCF indicate an ability to think originally and intuitively. The subject is capable of organizing and arranging, yet remaining critical (S and colors) and also self-critical (S and M). At the same time, she has a sense for nice (Ms) and decorative things ("dancing hares," "a Halloween scene," "a decorative pattern for wallpaper"). Therefore she could become a shop-window decorator instead of working in a grocery. In addition to her justified drive to create and to occupy a leading position, she is also amiable and uncomplicated (H%, more FC than CF) with regard to human contact, especially if she is not personally involved. It is easy for her to take advantage of her slightly juvenile traits (fairy-tale thinking, Ms) in this respect, as well as of her artistic interests (ornament, MCF, picture) and of her intuitive nature. Despite her excellent intelligence, she is by no means an intellectual.

On the basis of her 2-3 S, brought into relationship with the CF as an incentive to impulsive acts, as well as on the basis of the 2 ChF, she has a tendency to give up in the face of resistance when she encounters it, or in the case of "defeat." This is because she is sensitive (CF) and also because she tends to submit to depressive moods (1 ChF FC and ChF). She is inclined to short-circuit reactions, although in principle she has a gay disposition (3 FC, 3 M, and 1 MCF). It is partly because of her youth and slight immaturity that she is likely to see things as either white or black, without paying any attention to the simultaneous nuances that cause her to act impetuously at times and irritate her. At present, this is the "danger" threatening her, although she is capable of recovering quickly after having experienced shocks. Thus, she first "escapes" into the green in Card II, then immediately interprets the red; finally, she manages to interpret a lively scene by using the red blots and projecting herself into them. The course of action that she is considering and which will bring her into association chiefly with men who will be her co-workers, should lead her to further inner maturity, security and adjustment. In the above statement, we have already indicated implicitly that we recommend her for this career and for further professional advancement.

4. Applicant for the position of a supermarket manager: *Petersen, Paul*, 26 years old.

Zulliger Group Test

I.

A black butterfly on a	D FC A black as color
combinatory	
wilted autumn leaf	W ChF CF pl
The leaf is—it won't stay on much	
longer and it will fall off soon ..	"just talk," DW tendency
The butterfly cannot be described	
in more detail, because it is in	
shade .... Ch ➜	W F— shade/nature

545

II.

Shell animals from the depths of
the sea, with sharp points like
corals .... W CF A/nature   itemized,
                                           tendency to DW

Two brown bulls in a fight against
each other .... D FC A P, aggression
Two animals (upper read area)
flirting with each other .... D F+ A H repression
               combinatory tendency to sexual responses
to the left and to the right of
them two small horses, rearing on their hind feet. They
are "climbing" upon each
other   D Ms scene O+

III.

Two big devils assisted by a .... W M H P
little helper, they are fighting about
  the ....(D M H P O
          combinatory
possession of a reddish dragon-fly .(D FC A P

Scoring: Number of responses: 10/4

DW	= tendency	F+	= 1	H = 2	P	= 4
W	= 4	F−	= 1	A = 6	O	= 1
D	= 6	M	= 3	pl = 1		
F+%	= ?[1]	FC	= 3	nat = 1		
A%	= 60	CF	= 1	sex = (1)		
P%	= 40	ChFCF	= 1			
O%	= 10	Ch	= 1			
H%	= 20					

Sequence: orderly – tendency to inversion
Experience balance: 3 M : 3½ C
Apperceptive type: W — D

[1] *Editor's note:* In the rare cases in which a relatively small number of pure
form-M responses is produced, F+% must be evaluated by taking into account
the good M responses, FC, etc. Consequently, in this particular case, it must be
considered to be relatively good. However, the insufficient number of pure form
responses proves that the subject is not sufficiently controlled by his intellectual
functions.

EVALUATION:

Innate intelligence corresponds with intelligence that is found in above-average subjects (orderly sequence; W — D apperceptive type; 3 M; good P% and O%). However, the insufficient number of pure F responses indicates inadequate intellectual control of thinking and behavior. The subject is quite uncritical (absence of S, and S in its relationship to colors) and uncritical of himself (S in relationship to M). Sometimes he does not think very clearly and then he likes to "get over the hump" by talking a great deal (idle talk). He is not exactly industrious (only 10 responses). Primarily, his thinking is combinatory and constructive (combinations, mainly in Cards II and III); this leads him to broad concepts. Consequently he undoubtedly has a talent for arranging and organizing. If things go wrong, or if he encounters obstacles, he may lose himself in depressive moods (pure Ch and ChFCF). If this occurs, he finds it difficult to take hold of himself again and not to just "put his hands into his lap," for he is somewhat lazy (A% = 60). He becomes easily and quickly used to routine (A%), and tends to depend on it.

Despite the H% = 20 and the 2 FC, his ability for interhuman contact is disturbed, because he is not capable of satisfactory intellectual control (an insufficient number of form-responses, as well as absence of S). For these very reasons, he lacks leadership ability. Certain other insecurities become apparent also, as remnants of former childhood anxieties ("devil"). In addition, it seems that he has not yet been able to cope with his own sexuality. This becomes quite clear in his combinatory third response to Card II: "Two animals flirting with each other." He seems to fight his sexual feelings and thoughts, for apparently he simply has not yet outgrown his puberty. The entire test gives the impression of a relatively still immature person (DW tendency; idle talk; absence of S; a too high A%; a certain infantile awkwardness, which is expressed in a correspondingly small number of responses, despite the above-average innate intelligence). Outwardly, he gives the impression of being self-confident (apperceptive type = W : D) and quite sure of himself (no "or" responses, no S). He succeeds in "impressing" people (W type). Inwardly, however, he is vulnerable, still quite unstable and easily irritated (3 FC : 1 CF : 1

ChFCF : Ch). He tends to illusions (in the first response, DW tendency), and correspondingly to self-deceit. His experience balance indicates that he is capable of becoming more mature.

We can recommend him with great reservations only, for he is still too immature as a person. In the absence of psychotherapeutic treatment, his further development cannot be predicted with any degree of certainty.

5. An applicant for technical training: *Binder, Ulrich,* 15½ years old.

Zulliger Group Test

I.

The lungs (center part)	D F— anat/tendency to position response
On top there is the head of a beetle (upper center area) . Do → S →	D F+ Ad
The lower half—thunder storm clouds .... ChF →	D F± clouds
The rear part of a butterfly (5-6-7) Do →	Dd F+ Ad
This could also be the human heart because it is situated in the center (center dark area)	D F— anat/position response

II.

The chest cavity of a human being (white area within red area)	S F— anat white as color
The red is the heart	D CF anat/position response?
Birds (green area, at the left and at the right)	D F± A
Abdominal muscles (brown area)	D CF anat
It could also be just earth (brown area)	D C nature

III.

Again there is the heart in the center (red area)	D CF anat/position response
People carrying a	W M H/scene P O
bag and a (outer red area)	D F— object, confabulation
combinatory	
suitcase (inner red area)	D F— object, confabulation
Blood spots (all red blots), three altogether	D CF blood/counting

Scoring: Number of responses: 15/5

W	=	1	F+	=	2	H	=	1	P	=	1
D	=	12	F−	=	5	A	=	1	O	=	1
Dd	=	1	F±	=	2	Ad	=	2		
Do	=	(2)	M	=	1	anat	=	6		
S	=	1 (2)	CF	=	4	blood	=	1		

F+% = 33
A% = 20
P% = 7
O% = 7
H% = 7
anat% = 40

C = 1   scene = (1)
ChF = (1)   obj = 2
             nat = 1
             cloud = 1

Sequence: loose
Experience balance: 1 M : 5½ C
Apperceptive type: (W) — D — Dd — Do — S
                            =

Remarks:
Several position
   interpretations
Perseveration with
   anat
Combination and
   confabulation
Counting

EVALUATION:

In aggregate, the several position responses, the perseveration with anatomical responses, the counting, the loose sequence, the very low F+%, the confabulation, the too small P%—these make us suspicious; they give the impression that the youth is not quite normal. He is probably a psychopath or even a latent psychotic. At any rate, a psychiatric examination is strongly recommended.

The applicant's affectivity is also suspicious; the unadapted affectivity (4 CF), the egocentric, wild affectivity, which tends to short-cut actions, are checked only by a single M (in Slide III), which is at that a confabulatory and combinatory one. This sole inhibiting factor is not at all sufficient to prevent unexpected outbreaks. The subject's possibilities for establishing satisfactory interhuman relationships are poor; he produces only one single H (Slide III), and his interest in people tends to be merely theoretical and anatomical. The fact that he produces a score of anatomy interpretations indicates that he is probably a hypochondriac. At the same time, he is an eccentric.

Since he possesses the intelligence of a student who is attending a special school (F+% = 33, loose sequence, Do (anxiety), blood (confirms anxiety), more Ad than A), and since, on the other hand, he possesses intense intellectual ambition (anatomy)—which is, however, not based upon corresponding abilities, and is therefore unjustified—he is not capable of taming his morbid affectivity by intellectual means.

He would be best suited for the job of a factory worker, occupied at an assembly line, where the rate of work speed would be prescribed for him (the fact that he has no more than 15 interpretations indicates that his thinking is slow). Such work hardly requires much intelligence. It would also force the subject to acquire a sense of routine (which he does not possess inherently, for his A% is 20) and would discipline him. If he were to go into training as a mechanic, he could scarcely follow the instructions necessary for learning the trade, although he does have "technical" ability (D — Dd type). The boy's vocational aspirations are "above his head."

The psychiatric diagnosis notes: he is an acting-out psychopath.

6. Applicant for the position of a manager in a branch store of a grocery firm: *Steiner, Franz*, 27 years old, until now warehouse manager in a branch store.

Zulliger Group Test

I.

This is a rocky wall with a cave in
the center .... ChF → W F± nat O—
The flame of a candle (center
lower S) .... D FC fiame white as color
The rocky wall is situated amidst
snow and it has some snow spots
(all of the white space) .... SW CF nat white as color
It could also be an insect .... W F+ A
It has evil eyes (center upper area) . S F+ Ad/eyes

II.

This is Christmas .... W CF scene O+ religion,
color impression
Decorative trees (green left and
right) .... D FC pl

A snow-covered fir tree stands in
the center (white space) .... S CF pl

The whole thing is to tell you the
truth, during the winter .... SW C impression

There are two red, two green and
two brown .... D C color naming   counting

III.

There are two soldiers in the snow . {W M H P perseveration
      combinatory {S C nat snow

Their hands are bleeding .... D CF blood   C tendency

Two dogs, standing on their hind
legs (outer red area) ..... Ms → D F+ A, H and M repression

A butterfly (red center area) ..... D F+ A P

It would interest me to know why
the pictures of all three slides
are amidst snow; it makes them
cold .... impression

Scoring: Number of responses: 15/5

SW	= 2	F+	= 4	H	= 1	P = 2
W	= 4	F±	= 1	A	= 3	O = 2
D	= 6	M	= 1	Ad	= 1	
S	= 3	Ms	= tendency	scene	= 1	
F+%	= 90	FC	= 2	blood	= 1	
A%	= 27	CF	= 5	eyes	= (1)	
P%	= 13	C	= 2 (3)	pl	= 2	
O%	= 13	ChF	= 1	nat	= 3	
H%	= 7			color naming	= 1	
anat%	= 0			flame	= 1	
				impression	= 1	

Sequence: orderly   *Remarks:*   H and M
Experience balance: 1 M : 9 C   Religion   repression
Apperceptive type: SW — W — D — S   Color impression Counting
                      ⎯⎯   ⎯   = Color naming   Combination
                                    White as color   Perseveration

EVALUATION:

Although under certain circumstances—for example, when
he thinks he has been provoked—he may use confabulation and
react in a paranoid manner (SW), inclined "to reject the good
together with the bad," he is intelligent (F+% = 90, orderly

sequence, 15 responses, 1 M, a relatively high O%). His apperceptive type reveals a person who finds problems everywhere, and who is hard-hearted: his interhuman relationships are unsatisfactory (H% amounts to only 7, there is H and M repression and 2–3 pure C). He is capable of "walking over corpses" for the sake of solving a problem. He has the traits of a tyrant, and is thus poorly suited to "lead" and to supervise other people.

On the other hand, he is capable of comprehending complex relationships; he is able to arrange and to organize, to find a synopsis and to create one (6 W and F+%). He tends to ill-tempered short-cut reactions (5 CF, 2–3 C and, in addition, the ChF), and he is altogether a very impulsive human being. He is moody and hypersensitive (CF and C; he interprets white as color, and he also interprets the entire white card space. According to my experience, this frequently indicates paranoid sensitivity as well). Despite his 2 M, he is egocentric and selfish and wants to carry through his opinion (S and color interpretations). He is indeed religious, but rather in the sense of a fanatic and a member of some sect (religion and CF and C).

Color impressions, color naming, and counting indicate that the subject has an "epileptoid personality." Consequently, the man is not suited to lead a team; he might be capable instead of handling objects, and he would therefore be correctly placed as a warehouse manager.

He should be told of his being rejected in a cautious and pleasant manner; if at all possible, by way of personal discussion and not by letter; since the subject has produced pure C and a ChF, he could become suicidal.

E. EXAMPLES OF PSYCHOPATHOLOGY

1. Applicant for the position of a supermarket manager: *Herren, Daniel,* 38 years old.

Zulliger Group Test

I.

An old tree trunk just about to fall
apart .... W ChF CF pl O— defective

A pullet seen from the back, one
can see its rear end, the wings,
and the legs. It is even of the
right color .... DW ChF CF food

The entrance to a cave in a rock ..
                           F(C) → W ChF CF nat O— perspective

A cross-section of a rotten fish .... W ChF CF food

A living creature's rotten piece of
skin .... W ChF CF Ad O—

The cross-section of a nut .... W ChF CF food

A sea animal that has not yet been
discovered .... W F± A

A wilted flower .... W ChF CF pl

Weather-beaten decomposed rock   W ChF CF nat

II.

India-ink blots .... DW CF blot

A painting of a modern painter ... W CF picture, obj O+

There is red and white in it; it is a
carved "martyr pole" of a primi-
tive tribe. It is ....⎛ D CF object
            combinatory ⎬
illuminated by the evening ⎪
sun ....⎝ S F+ ornament

The spine of a cow (white space
within red area) .... S F± Ad animal anatomy
                              white as color

Human lungs (red area) .... D CF anatomy

Sea animals (green area) .... D F+ A

A watchman guarding against intruders upon ....⎛ D Ms H O+
            combinatory ⎬
(green area) the precious red ⎪
stone ....⎝ D CF obj

Frayed piece of cloth .... DW CF obj

A fight of crabs (brown area) .... D FC A aggression

A bull fight (brown area) .... D FC A P aggression

A picture on a map; a narrow pass
between two mountain ranges
(brown areas and white space between them) .... DS CF geog

III.

A fight between two people	W M H P aggression
People carrying a jewelry box combinatory	W M H P
	CF → D F— obj
Two men fighting over a piece of meat	W M H P aggression
combinatory	D CF food
A lady getting dressed for the evening in front of a mirror	W M H P O+
	mirror reflection
A ballet dance	W MCF H P
Stones for monuments in the process of being manufactured	W F± obj
Sea island on a map	DW F± geog
A decayed skull of a cow .. ChF →	DW F— Ad animal anat O—
A set of human teeth that has been pulled out of the earth	W ChF CF Hd O—

Scoring: Number of responses: 33/13

DW	= 5	F+	= 2	H	= 6	P =	6
W	= 16	F—	= 2	Hd	= 1	O =	9 (—5)
D	= 9	F±	= 4	A	= 4		
DS	= 1	M	= 5	Ad	= 3		
S	= 2	Ms	= 1	anat	= 1 (3)		
F+%	= 50	FC	= 2	food	= 4		
A%	= 21	CF	= 9 (18)	obj	= 6		
P%	= 18	ChF	= 1	pl	= 2		
O%	= 27∓	ChF CF =	9	nat	= 2		
H%	= 21	F (C)	= (1)	geog	= 2		
anat%	= 3 (9)			blots	= 1		
				ornament	= 1		

Sequence: orderly
Experience balance: 5 M : 10 (19) C
Apperceptive type: DW — W — D — S

Remarks:
Defects
Perspective   Variations of the same interpretation and
Combinations   sticking to the same blot portion
Aggressive interpretations   Reflection (women!)

554

EVALUATION:

An extraordinary record!

First of all, the very large number of W is striking (21 W, 5 of which are DW). These indicate a strong claim for leadership and a desire to dominate. When we consider them more closely (in their contents), we discover that they are variations of the first interpretation produced for each slide, that this man remains "glued" to the same part of a blot. The D responses are also an indication for this. It is as though a child were playing with a toy, taking it apart and constructing something similar with it. Some of the variations seem flimsy; they are O—, and suggest that the applicant may be approaching hebephrenia. D. H. produces his variations, not because he is doubtful (indications for it would be the connection of two responses with an "or" and Do responses, as well as an inverse sequence); on the contrary, this man is self-assured and does not doubt himself with regard to his interpretations. He is extremely industrious (33 responses), and believes himself to be a good organizer (W type) and administrator. Furthermore, he accepts his confabulations (DW) as real, true to reality, "actual." Thus, he submits to self-deceit and to illusions. His thinking is "generous"; at the same time, it is "eccentric" and unrealistic (DW and variations of W and D). In addition, he has concentration difficulties (A% is only 21; the contents column is too large). Psychopathological disturbances of a more serious nature are suggested when a subject produces responses that indicate defects, as occurs repeatedly in this case: Slide I: "An old tree trunk just about to fall apart," "A cross-section of a rotten fish," "A living creature's rotten piece of skin," "Wilted flower"; Slide II: "Frayed piece of cloth"; Slide III: "A decayed skull of a cow," "A set of human teeth that has been pulled out of the earth."

D. H.'s thinking is not precise (F+% = 50), his ideas bubble over, he is afflicted with a "diarrhea of ideas": before he has managed to convert one of his ideas into reality, another one appears that he believes to be better. He is almost incapable of selecting one idea from the abundance of all his varying ideas, and to form it correctly according to reality, to carry it out on a practical scale. He has a poor sense of reality; although he has inventive ideas, he does not put them to practical use. He is not even capable of thinking them out to their logical end, because one idea is always being replaced by another.

Although D. H. produces an average H% (21), his interhuman relationships are somehow impeded, for as compared with the 9 CF (which indicate unadapted, moody, impulsive, egocentric affectivity), he produces only 2 FC (participation of the affectively adaptable and adapted emotionality). In addition to the numerous CF responses, the reflection interpretation in Slide III: "A lady dressing for the evening in front of a mirror" indicates that D. H. is sexually not quite normal (prevailing voyeur and exhibitionist impulses, as well as difficulties in both the selection of an object and attachment to that object because of too intense narcissistic needs [Salomon, 1962]). Undoubtedly he must be struggling with strong homosexual tendencies (Slide II: "A map: a narrow pass between two mountain ranges" [brown blots]).

Also, in addition to the too numerous CF, we discover that the number of ChFCF responses is too large as well. This leads us to the conclusion that H. D. oscillates between a strong (egocentric) hypermanic inclination toward impulsive ventures and depressive moods. This must be disadvantageous to him in his relationship with others, and especially in his attempts to lead a team, although he does not lack the desire for friendship and love (H%).

The test conveys the definite impression that in this case a formerly quite high and even original intelligence has become involved in a schizophrenic deterioration process.

On the basis of all the above-mentioned psychological defects and difficulties, D. H. is absolutely unqualified for the position of a supermarket manager.

In a town, recruits for the police force were to be selected. Sixty men had applied for the job, but only 20 could be considered. These applicants were men who had already finished their vocational training and wanted to change their position.

2. The only information given about this particular applicant

was his age. He was 24 years old. Neither his name nor anything else was given, just "X," (see Table 16).

Zulliger Test Record

I.

Dried blood puddle	ChF ➔ WCF blood O— black as color
A bat	WF + A P
The backbone of an animal (dark center area).	DF — A anat
On top there is a skull (upper center portion)	S ➔ DF + anat
An animal that has been squashed, it has been compressed	ChF ➔ WCF A O—/defect
Spine (white space within red area)	SF — anat color shock!
Lungs (red area)	DCF anat a red CF interpretation following a color shock!
Two bird wings, separated from each other (orange area)	DFC Ad
Green paint, splashed on a window frame (green and white colors are included)	DC color SDC obj O— white as color
A brown fish with a severed head (brown area)	DFC Ad
The whole: the head of an animal, a bull, turned upside down	WSCF Ad O figure-ground fusion/inverse response
A fox head (the whole card)	WSCF Ad perseveration

III.

A blood puddle	ChF ➔ DWCF blood O— perseveration
A human head (upper dark portion), turned toward the outside	DoF + Hd (P)
A bear standing on one leg (outer red portion)	DM + A
The arms of a human being (outer area)	DoF + Hd (P)

A cap. I saw one like that in Ober- land (at the top, upon the "head of the men")	DdF + clothing Ego reference
Mouse (the back and side portions of the small black configuration)	DF + A
The shape of a squashed arm (small dark blot)	FCh → DF + Hd defect
A human head (seen toward the inner part)	DoF + Hd (P)
An eye (a part of the portion in- terpreted above)	DoF + Hd eye
Something burnt (the whole card) .	WCCh ashes O

EVALUATION:

Since F+% is slightly over 70, sequence is orderly to loose, A% is somewhat too small, P% is greatly reduced, O% is overly high and includes bad O (O—), and if we take into account the subject's tendencies to confabulation and perseveration, the almost complete absence of M, and the ratios H : Hd and A : Ad, we must classify X's innate intelligence as not especially high, but on the other hand as not especially low; it corresponds to a low average intelligence. Considering the relationship of W : D, we cannot help doubting whether the subject is in fact a "practical" man; either he takes things in one big lump (W), alternating between being generous and superficial (DW), or else he complains (S) and finds problems everywhere (W : S). He lacks intellectual courage, however (Do); he is likely to find a flaw in everything (S and Do), and he would like to be more intelligent, to appear more intelligent, than he really is (anat indicate an "intelligence complex" and hypochondriacal traits). He does not lack a conscious and purposeful tendency toward intellectual adaptation—a tendency that is calculating because of his anxiety (Do, combinatory W at the end of some cards, FCh). From time to time the originality of his perception is surprising (O). He tries to hide (WS) his obstinacy (S, CF and C)—of which he has a certain amount—and to incorporate his strong criticism into concessions and pacifying actions (WS). X.'s intelligence is rather reproductive in kind (lack of M), which does not prevent him, however, from succumbing to "dreamy" illusions (DW, SD).

TABLE 16

Scoring:
Subject: X

Card	WS	DW	W	D	Dd	Do	S	F+	F−	F±	M	FC	CF	C	FCh	ChF	Ch	CCh	P	O
I			3	2			1	2	1	2			2			2				1—
II	2	1	1	4			2		1			2	4	1	1	1				2±
III			1	2	1	4		5			1		1		1	1	1	1	3	2±
Total	2	1	4	8	1	4	3	7	2	2	1	2	7	1	1	4	1	1	3	5±

Number of responses: 23/8

F+% = 72
A% = 34
P% = 13
O% = 21
H% = 20

H = —1
Hd = 4—5
anat = 4
blood = 2
A = 4
Ad = 4

color = 1
obj = 1
ashes = 1
clothing = 1

1— tendency to confabulations
2± white and black as colors
2± tendency toward perseveration
5± Figure-ground fusions

Sequence: orderly – loose
Experience balance: 1 M : 8½ C
Apperceptive type: W(S) — W — D — Dd — Do — S

If the subject is provoked by some external provocation—in other words, if his tendency to opposition and aggression is stirred up (strong S tendency)—he will be on guard against expressing his feelings, because he tends to make compromises and to be intentionally friendly. His aggression is discharged by daydreaming (WS, SD), and does not reach the level of motility; this is borne out by the color shocks (in Cards II and III, where the usual M does not appear), and further by the defect interpretations, which correspond to hypochondriacal expectancy ideas. Thus we may conclude that neurosis is present and estimate that it serves to convert this inherently primitive and impulsive human being (CF and C) into a social one by constricting him. Actually, if we take into account his many S and his strong egocentricity (extratensive experience balance, preponderance of CF and C as compared to FC), he should react thoughtlessly and impulsively, and be inclined to impulsive and short-cut acts. In addition to intellectual circumspection (caution) and neurotic countercathexes, what prevents the subject's affective outbreaks, however, or makes them ineffective, is his marked tendency to depressive moods and ill humor (FCh, ChF, CCh, Ch).

By making an extraordinarily diligent effort (23 responses), the subject tries to counteract his inability to function and his depressive tendencies.

Since, on the one hand, we have established that the subject has a strong vitality and extratensive traits (color responses) that force him to seek motoric discharge; since, on the other hand, we have discovered that he is inhibited (shocks and strong depressive tendencies); finally, in the light of the fact that X. has produced a pure C as an expression of explosive affectivity—through all these, we become aware of the intensity of the inner tensions that rule this man. Furthermore, it becomes clear to us that these tensions are released in impulsive outbreaks, that in such instances X. is prone to paniclike reactions and that, in addition to all this, he is probably in danger of becoming suicidal (C : Ch, CCh). The aggression that is inhibited and controlled must turn inward, against the person himself. This thought also occurs to us because of the fact that the man is hypersensitive and inwardly very vulnerable. This is indicated in the test by his using white as a color;—it is usually characteristic of people who use white as a color in the form-interpretation test that they behave in the manner discussed above. They generally attempt to disguise their attitude by outward "roughness." X. is hypersensitive; he reacts quickly and is easily offended. At the same time, he makes an effort to dissimulate all this.

It seems very clear that a sado-masochistic tendency exists in X.'s personality. It nourishes his imagination, and that is why he produces the many "heads," "blood puddles," as well as the engrams of "squashed," "squeezed," "torn off," and "severed" parts of the body. Masochistic tendencies also become evident in the relatively numerous anatomical interpretations contained in the test; as we have already indicated, these suggest the co-existence of hypochondriacal traits.

Responses such as "green paint splashed on a window frame" and "something burnt" are unusual. Both these responses are "individual interpretations," in other words, interpretations that very likely would not be produced by anybody but this particular subject. For the most part, they correspond to direct projections. In the given case, something dark, gloomy, morbid, and suspicious is described, as has been brought out by many analogies with similar individual interpretations and corresponding clinical observations; the "blood puddles" are part of the same set of circumstances referred to above.

Taking into account the fact that X. immediately produces a color shock when Card II is presented to him (escaping into the interpretation of the white inner space), and then a CF and anat, and considering that his experience balance is markedly extratensive, we should expect the subject to manifest neurotically converted anxiety and anxiety symptoms.

We have realized all along that X. is not qualified to become a policeman. Because of his egocentricity (predominance of CF and C within the experience balance), he would project his own inner threats upon other people, combatting them in others—just as, for instance, he is fighting his own aggression, which has been at least partly "prevented" from becoming effective. In reactive acts he could thus discharge his aggression by the use of (seemingly) "legal means," because the profession furnishes him with certain "powers" over other people.

A light has now been shed upon X.'s "vocational choice." He would like to become a policeman in order thereby to fight his own aggression—or, strictly speaking, his own latent criminality —by projecting it onto others. As a policeman, he would see other people who were evil, and deserved to be prosecuted, while in fact all this is what is troubling *him* deeply. He might even persecute others who were innocent (as in the fable of the sack that is beaten instead of the donkey).

It is not our intention to judge X. unfairly, and it should therefore be pointed out that he possesses some good qualities, too. We have already determined previously that he is tenaciously industrious. Also, his tendency to arrive at W reveals an ability to make plans and to organize, while the S show his critical conscientiousness. If he is placed correctly, he will be a good worker and his friendliness and conciliatoriness will be found to be pleasing, even though they are nothing but "exercises" for him, and do not really "come from the heart."

He should do the sort of work which, while it prevented him from projecting his sadomasochistic impulses and conflicts onto other people, would nevertheless permit him to project them onto objects; some occupation that would allow him to discharge his aggression directly, by applying it to a useful purpose, would be appropriate for him. He could, perhaps, find employment in the wholesale meat business, as a meat-cutter or a salesman. It would not be advisable, however, to use him as a butcher for the slaughtering of animals: he should have *nothing to do with living creatures*. It would therefore seem best if he were to work in an enterprise that was engaged in the demolishing or building of houses. He could be employed as the operator of a caterpillar tractor, a crane, or an excavation machine; in this line of work, he could abreact his aggression by exercising it against "inanimate matter," and by exercising command over machines. Thereby, he would be using his aggression "profitably," and within a socially accepted pattern. Undoubtedly, his diligence, conscientiousness, and "seriousness" will be appreciated by his employer. Moreover, under such circumstances he would be able to carry out his work with relative "independence," which would fulfill the requirements of his total mentality extremely well.

Although all these thoughts and deductions require a great deal of space when they are written down, a test specialist actually arrives at them within a very short span of time. By surveying the scoring and the record, he knows in a few minutes what the outcome will be, and he is able to submit something like the following short diagnosis:

"This man is not qualified; he is too neurotic and egocentric. He tends to succumb to panic-like reactions and, if he is ever provoked, his aggressive and destructive impulses will break through proportionately.

"Since he is industrious, serious, and critically conscientious, and since he is not without talent for organizing and abstracting, he would be extremely well qualified for working as an excavation-machine operator, a steam-roller machinist, etc. It is urgently recommended that he be not just rejected but advised!"

Other specialists examined the tests that were performed with X., their results did not reveal anything contrary to those arrived at with the Zulliger Test. Aggression was even more evident in the Color Pyramid Test, while X's inner isolation could be observed more clearly in the Tree Test. In general, all test results were quite unequivocal.

SOME FINAL REPORTS

We saw in X. a man who wished to become a policeman in order to combat his own aggressive impulses by projecting them onto others. His "vocational choice" was based upon a tendency that had originated in neurotic motives.

That is why X. is not qualified for the profession for which he was seeking training.

However, the examination has proved that this man would be extremely well qualified for working within other vocational categories, and he had to be told about it. For such information would be useful not only for his own purposes, but also (if he followed the recommendations) for the enterprise that would employ him.

It has been shown plainly here that the presence of a neurosis may have a socializing effect. In all probability, this occurs quite frequently, even though one might hardly ever expect it to be so.

3. *Gertrud G.*, 14 years old, student at a special school for the retarded (see Table 17).

Zulliger Group Test

I.

A devil	S → DWF ± devil
Horns (upper portion)	DF + Ad
Horns (lower portion)	DdF — Ad, perseveration
Horns (outer portion)	DdF — Ad, perseveration
A blouse (center portion)	DF + clothing

II.

A red dress	DdDFC clothing O—
A caterpillar (green area)	DCF A
A caterpillar (brown area)	DF — A, perseveration
Horns (adjacent to the green area)	DdF — Ad
Horns (adjacent to the brown bottom area)	DdF — Ad, perseveration
Small horns (S within the outer green area)	SF — Ad, perseveration

III.

A butterfly (inner red area)	DF + A P
Horns (upper area)	DdF — Ad, perseveration
Claws (5 and 7)	DF + Ad
Horns at the red (red outer area) ..	DdF + Ad

EVALUATION:

The degree of mental retardation can be recognized here in the perseveration and the monotonous repetition, rather than in the F+% alone: the stronger and more monotonous the perseveration, the higher is the degree of mental retardation (if, at the same time, F+% is low).

The large number of "horns" in the test also have the significance of sex symbolism. Taking into account the CF and the 2 S, we may conclude that aggression is present. The clothing interpretations prove that vanity exists. The very first response—"a devil"—leads us to expect phobic anxiety or at least phobic ideas.

TABLE 17

Number of responses: 15/6

Scoring:
Subject: Gertrud G.

Slide	DW	D	DdD	Dd	S	F+	F—	F±	FC	CF	P	O
I	1	2		2	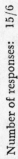	2	2	1				
II		2	1	2	1		4		1	1		
III		2		2		3	1		1		1	
Total	1	6	1	6	1,↑	5	7	1	1	1	1	

devil = 1
clothing = 2
A = 3
Ad = 9

F+% = 42
A% = 80
P% = 8
O% = minus

Sequence: loose
Experience balance: O M : 1½ C
Apperceptive type: DW — D — DdD — Dd — S
Shock: —

Remarks:
Perseveration with "horns"

565

Next to mental retardation, the clinical examination was marked by a certain phobic fearfulness (being afraid of the dark), in addition to egocentric impudence, aggression toward boys, which is a special form of sexual aggression, and vanity.

4. Mrs. *Anna L.*, 26 years old, has been admitted to a private mental hospital because she is constantly sick, although clinically a diagnosis cannot be established. In addition, she is extremely aggressive, even "impossible" in her behavior. Both her personality and her "diseases" have been recognized as hysteric phenomena (see Table 18).

Zulliger Group Test

I.

An X-ray picture of a human
   being .... Ch → WF± X-ray
One can see the lungs shining
   through (dark center area) ..... DF — anat
and the navel (white bottom area) . SF — Hd position response
This person has wooden legs .... DdF + Hd
The eyes are looking in an un-
   friendly manner .... SF + Hd, impression

II.

This is ugly in its color combination .... shock!
Spine and (white area) .... SF — anat
lungs (red area) .... DCF anat
                    W
The green could be the gall
   bladder .... DCF anat
and the brown the kidneys, perhaps perseveration

III.

Men who have been squashed .... FCh → WF + H (P) O
                    sadistic fantasy
Blood stains .... DCF blood tendency to C
Finished!

EVALUATION:

From the standpoint of the form-interpretation test, this is actually a "classic" example of hysteria: we see here a very pronounced color shock and a markedly extratensive experience

TABLE 18

Scoring:
Subject: Mrs. Anna L.

Number of responses: 11/4

Slide	W	D	Dd	S	F+	F−	F±	M	FC	CF	C	FCh	ChF	P	O
I	1	1	1	2	2	2	1						1		
II	tendency	3 1		1		1			— —	3 1	tendency	1		1	1
III	1	1	1		1	3	1	—	—			1	1	1	1
Total	2 →	5	1	3	3	3	1	—	—	4	tendency	1	1	1	1

F+% = 50
A% = —
P% = 9
O% = 9+
H% = 36
anat% = 50

H = 1
Hd = 3
anat = 5
X-Ray = 1
blood = 1

Sequence: orderly
Experience balance: O M : 4 C
Apperceptive type: W — D — Dd — S
Shock: $\frac{-}{+}$

Remarks:
Perseveration with anat
Sadistic fantasy toward "men"

567

balance, two symptoms that indicate (according to Hermann Rorschach) phenomena of a conversion hysteria.

The form percentage should not be evaluated "numerically"; it must be corrected. It has become so small because the subject has produced such a large number of anat. If it were calculated without the anat, it would increase to 100%. The fact that the subject is capable of producing a W in Card II suggests that her intelligence is higher than one might expect from merely considering the calculated 50% of accurately perceived forms. This would be our explanation: "Since the subject already has an 'intelligence complex' (anat% = 50), and since she is a hypochondriac (high anat%, aggression toward 'men'), she partly destroys the manifestation of her intelligence."

In all probability, Mrs. L. has never become reconciled to her sexual role. Her sexual development is retarded; it has remained infantile. In terms of sex, this woman is still at the stage of a pre-adolescent girl, a time when girls would prefer to be boys and, since they know that they are not boys, reject the entire male sex. In view of this emotional attitude, the development of infantile sexuality towards the genital phase has been prevented. Such women usually remain frigid.

The aggressive elements, evident in the ratio of 4 CF : 3 S : O M, turn against the "men," who are "squashed" (in the subject's imagination).

The subject's interest in other people is merely a rather theoretical one (most of the responses are anat or X-rays or blood); above all, there are no FC as indicators of adaptable and adapted affectivity. Since she gives free play to her egocentric emotions, insofar as they are not inhibited by neurotic mechanisms, a woman who is unadaptable to such a great extent will obviously behave in an "impossible" fashion.

Since some aggression is neurotically inhibited (converted), it turns against the woman's own inner self and brings about (in a masochistic sense) conversion-hysteric reactions. The repressed aggression changes into masochism, a state in which pleasure is derived from one's own suffering. By means of her "suffering," the woman succeeds in tyrannizing over her environment.

5. Miss *Ursula A.*, 27 years old, office worker. Compulsion neurosis. The subject sought the help of a psychotherapist because, despite her diligence and intelligence, she cannot make any headway in her work: she must constantly check her work, in order to find out whether she has perhaps made a mistake. She doubts everything, and suffers from insomnia because of her brooding (see Table 19).

Zulliger Group Test

I.

A mask with terrible eyes .... S → DF + mask
at the right it is mutilated (12) ... symmetry and object criticism
A butterfly (dark center area) .... DF + A
Icicles (bottom area) .... FCh → Dd F+ ice
The whole is an ice picture on the
    window .... ChF → WF ± ice

II.

A spine (center area) .... SF − anat
Decorative fish (green area) ...... DF + A
Or shrubs .... DFC pl "or"
Larvae (brown area) .... DFC A
Or small earth clods .... DFC nat "or"

III.

Again, masks or Janus heads ...... DoF + masks, O, "or"
    self-correction
A butterfly .... DF + A P
A hobgoblin .... DM + H P
Hands with pistols .... { DoF + Hd
                             { DdF + obj
On the outside there are also hands,
    arms .... DoF + Hd
As a matter of fact, the black blots
    are two men having an argu-
    ment; they threaten each other   WM + H P, aggression

EVALUATION:

Color shock, when it occurs together with ambiequal experience balance, indicates compulsion neurosis, says Hermann Rorschach. This combination of factors is found in Miss Ursula A. Furthermore, she produces Do, which usually correspond with

TABLE 19

Scoring:
Subject: *Miss Ursula A.*

Number of responses: 16/5

Slide	W	D	Dd	Do	S	F+	F—	F±	M	FC	CF	FCh	ChF	P	O
I	1	2	1		1	3		1					1		
II		4			1	1	1			2	1	1			
III	1	2	1	3		5			2					3	1
Total	2	8	2	3	2	9	1	1	2	2	1	1	1	3	1

F+% = 85   H = 2
A% = 25   Hd = 2
P% = 20   anat = 1
H% = 25   mask = 2
O% = 7   A = 4
anat% = 7 obj = 1
           pl = 1
           ice = 2
           nat = 1

Sequence: inverse
Experience balance: 2 M : 2 C
Apperceptive type: W — D — Dd — Do — S
Shock: +

Remarks:
Object criticism
Symmetry
"Or"
Aggression

a compulsive-neurotic lack of self-confidence and intellectual courage. S; self-correction expressed by "or"; the tendency to notice flaws in symmetry; the relatively numerous responses with greatly varying content—and, in addition, a large apperceptive type—show an impairment of intelligence and poor concentration ability, as well as diligence (16 responses). Self-correction; S in relationship to M; inverse sequence—these suggest self-doubts and brooding accentuated by anxiety. In the end, an interpretation is produced that points to aggressive impulses, even though they seem to have been rather obliterated. Thus, aggression must have been repressed. The "terrible eyes" (Slide I) leads us to expect that the subject believes herself to be observed. The high F+% would point to good innate intelligence. However, the subject's intelligence is neurotically impaired because:

a. the subject is incapable of summarizing large concepts; she is not able to abstract, to classify, to organize, and to plan;

b. as has already been mentioned, the subject's concentration ability has been affected;

c. the ability to form stereotyped thought processes is inhibited;

d. her intellectual grasp is impeded.

The subject feels insecure, threatened by cold (ice interpretations), and tries anxiously to replace, by diligence and good intentions, all that the disease has taken away from her. She seeks to make amends for her inadequate qualitative performance by substituting a quantitative one; she has acquired a stiff, mask-like attitude.

F. ORGANIC BRAIN DAMAGE

ZULLIGER GROUP TEST

Marliese Kaster was tested along with her school class of 11 to 12-year-old children, by means of the Zulliger Group Test. Even before the test was administered, the teacher had noticed that she was unable to sit still; she was subject to nervous jerky twitching, seemed very distracted, and could not follow the lessons with any degree of uniform attention. Sometimes she gave the impression of being "lost in thought." The girl's parents, who were informed about all this by the teacher, were of the opinion that Marliese simply did not try to get hold of herself, that she "let herself go" and did not make any effort to follow class instructions. They urged the use of stricter handling, and even reproached the teacher for being too lenient with the child. However, since the teacher suspected that other and more serious causes were producing the girl's behavior, he sent me the following test record for a blind diagnosis.

6. *Kaster, Marliese,* 12 years old.

Zulliger Group Test

I.

The face of a dog (12) .... S →	D F+ Ad
Two sticks (bottom portion)	Dd F+ object
A man's head with a peaked cap (bottom outer area)	Dd F+ Hd/inverse response
A fir tree branch (3 and 9)	Dd F+ pl
The udder of a calf (6)	Dd F+ Ad
An ivy leaf (dark center area)	D F± pl

II.

A Chinese sitting there wearing
bright clothes .... ⎰ DW M— H O
           combinatory ⎱
Face and body (red and white area) ⎰ SD F— Hd
           and ⎱
Sleeves (green area) of the dress .. ⎰ D CF clothing
           confabulatory ⎱
Legs (brown area), they are sun-
tanned .... ⎱ D CF Hd

Six colors, one red, two green, two brown, and one white	W C color-naming and color-counting
A man falls from above on top of another	D M H O/inverse response

III.

Three times blood	D C blood/counting red attraction
A beautiful red butterfly (red center area)	D FC A P

Islands on a geography map ...... DW F± geog
Pistols (3 and 9 within inner area) . Dd F+ obj/weapon
A cactus in a flower pot (center
    white area) .... S F+ pl
A fat woman without head (center
    white area) .... S F+ O+

Scoring: Number of responses: 18/6

DW	= 2	F+	= 8	H	= 2	P = 1
W	= 1	F−	= 1	Hd	= 4	O = 3 (1−)
D	= 7	F±	= 2	A	= 1	
Dd	= 5	M	= 2 (1 M−)	Ad	= 2	
S	= 3 (1)	FC	= 1	obj	= 2	
F+%	= 82	CF	= 2	pl	= 3	
A%	= 17	C	= 2	blood	= 1	
P%	= 6			clothing	= 1	
O%	= 16 (±)			geog	= 1	
H%	= 33			color-naming	= 1	
				weapon	= (1)	

Sequence: orderly – loose
Experience balance: 2 M : 5½ C
Apperceptive type: DW — W — D — Dd — S

Remarks:

2 inverse interpretations	Red attraction
1 M−	Weapon
Combination and confabulation	Absence of W M H P and D M H P
Color-naming and color-counting	in Card III

EVALUATION:

When a girl of 12 produces 18 responses with a F+% = 82, it can hardly be assumed that she is not industrious and uninterested in class instruction. However, since she produces 2 DW, her thinking is not realistic: she lives for the most part in magic and animistic thoughts; she is at the "age of fairy tales," and "dreams" are more important to her existence than reality. She enjoys her daydreams and believes them to be real. These reveries lure her with a force that she cannot resist, compelling her to give herself to them. They distract her from observing reality and from "paying attention" in school.

From another point of view, however, the test is even more informative. Mariliese produces two inversely perceived interpretations; she does not see the usual M H P in Card III, but produces instead an M— in Card II; she counts and names the colors. All these factors indicate that the girl is probably suffering from organic brain damage. In this connection, the two pure C bear this out, too. Her being "absent-minded" in class, her persistence in remaining at the confabulatory thinking level, her nervous behavior and the uncoordinated muscle movements, her muscular restlessness—all these are probably the result of brain damage. We are dealing here with phenomena that point to a condition similar to epilepsy. This too is borne out by the test factors, and with a rather high degree of certainty. It would therefore be completely inappropriate to treat the girl with greater strictness. Her reactions in school are not based upon carelessness, indifference or such motives. It is absolutely necessary that a medical specialist examine her, in order to establish clinically whether the girl is actually suffering from brain damage, and in order to investigate the nature of the damage.

Follow-up remark: The medical examination revealed the presence of genuine brain damage, with epileptoid symptoms but without true epileptic attacks.

7. *Ernst H.*, 20½ years old, inmate of an institution. Genuine epilepsy (see Table 20, p. 576).

Zulliger Group Test

I.

This is a crooked corpse .... WMCh H O
At the right side the forehead is
   poorly drawn .... object criticism
                                       remark about symmetry
One can see the lungs (c) .... DF — anat
The legs are already decayed down
   to the bone .... Dd + anat
The eye sockets are too round .... SF + Hd, object criticism pedantry

II.

Lungs (red area)	DCF anat
The heart (dark-red area)	DCF anat/position
The gall bladder (green area)	DCF anat; confabulation
The spinal cord (he means the spine) (white area)	SF — anat
Smeared blood (brown area), my blood is even darker	DCF blood ego-reference

III.

Again corpses with legs that have been run over	FCh → WF + M (P) O sadism, perseveration
and blood stains	DCF blood
they have shot themselves[2]	Dd + obj

EVALUATION:

The diagnosis of "epilepsy" is obvious. The symptoms are:

1. The strongly extratensive experience balance;

2. The tendency to pure C ("blood stains");

3. The MCh;

4. The admixture of confabulation;

5. The perseveration tendency: after having produced an anat once, the subject remains glued to anat interpretations; furthermore, his entire affectivity is "sticky";

6. Tendency to position interpretations;

7. Replacement of A% by stereotypy with anat;

8. The "sadistic" interpretation; tendency to sadistic interpretations finds its expression as early as in Card I ("corpse," "legs decaying away");

9. The tendency to pedantic criticism in contrast to the tendency to confabulation;

10. The tendency to self-reference;

11. Absence of a color shock;

12. Mental capacity has greatly deteriorated (epileptic mental deterioration)—the accuracy of perception is reduced (F+% is low), the adaptability of thinking to that of others in the subject's environment is impaired (low P%).

[2] Based on the protrusions, which are often interpreted as "pistols." (Note of the recording physician.)

TABLE 20

Number of responses: 12/5

Scoring:
Subject: *Ernst H.*

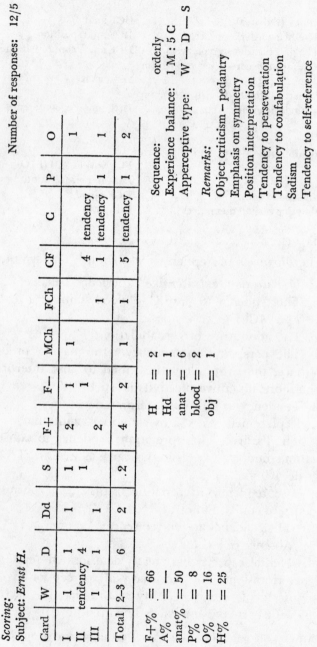

Card	W	D	Dd	S	F+	F—	MCh	FCh	CF	C	P	O
I	1	1	1	1	2	1	1					1
II	tendency	4		1		1			4	tendency		
III	1	1	1		2			1	1	tendency	1	1
Total	2–3	6	2	.2	4	2	1	1	5	tendency	1	2

F+% = 66
A% = —
anat% = 50
P% = 8
O% = 16
H% = 25

H = 2
Hd = 1
anat = 6
blood = 2
obj = 1

Sequence: orderly
Experience balance: 1 M : 5 C
Apperceptive type: W — D — S

Remarks:
Object criticism – pedantry
Emphasis on symmetry
Position interpretation
Tendency to perseveration
Tendency to confabulation
Sadism
Tendency to self-reference

8. Miss *Emma R.*, 23 years old, inmate of an institution. Epilepsy (see Table 21).

Zulliger Group Test

I.

A skull (12)	S → DF + anat
Fists with knives (11 and 1)	DF + Hd, aggression
A blouse (c)	DF + clothing
Sticks (5 and 7)	DdF + obj
Cloud devil	WMCh H O

II.

Meat pieces (red area)	DCF food
Bones (white area)	SF − anat
Kidneys (green area)	DCF anat, perseveration
Dirt (brown area)	DC nat
All these are parts of the insides of a human being	WCF anat

III.

A butterfly (red area)	DF + A P
Running boys (red outer area) ...	DM H P
It could also be blood stains	DCF blood, tendency to C
Caterpillars (5 and 7)	DF + A
Masks (11 and 1)	DoF + Hd (P)
Men fighting with each other	WM + H P aggression
it really is only their shadows	ChF → WF± H/shadow

EVALUATION:

Comparing the results with those obtained in the case of Ernst H., we find considerable differences. The diagnosis of "epilepsy" is much less obvious.

Nevertheless there are these symptoms:

1. The experience balance is markedly extratensive;
2. The affectivity is "sticky." There is a tendency to pure C;
3. Presence of one MCh;
4. The perseveration tendency with anat is evident;
5. The A% is too low, the anat% is too high;
6. Tendency towards aggression is indicated;
7. Color shock and chiaroscuro shock are absent.

577

TABLE 21

Scoring:
Subject: Miss Emma R.

Number of responses: 17/5

Slide	W	D	Dd	Do	S	F+	F±	F−	MCh	M	CF	C	ChF	P	O
I	1	3	1		1	4			1						1
II	1	3			1			1		1	3	1	1	3	
III	2	4		1		3	1			1	1	tendency	1	3	
Total	4	10	1	1	2	7	1	1	1	1	4	tendency	1	3	1

F+% = 80
A% = 12
anat% = 23 – 30*
P% = ca. 20
O% = 6
H% = 35

H = 4
Hd = 2
anat = 4
blood = 1
food = 1

clothing = 1
A = 2
obj = 1
nat = 1

* counting "blood,"
anat% = 30

Sequence: orderly, tendency to inversion
Experience balance: 2 M : 5½ C
Apperceptive type: W — D — Dd — Do — S

Remarks:
Tendency towards aggression
Tendency to perseveration
  with anat
Tendency to pure C
"Mask"

All these signs would force us to arrive at the conclusion that we are dealing here with an "epileptoid personality" even if the clinical diagnosis were unknown to us and in spite of the fact that the subject's mental ability is not as much impaired as it was in Ernst H.

The appearance of an inverse sequence and the mask interpretations are interesting. There is a tendency towards caution and pretense. In the sense of the behavior pattern of the personality, they contribute, perhaps, to the concealment of epileptic traits.

9. *Emil B.*, 47 years old, inmate of a mental institution. Schizophrenia (catatonia).

Zulliger Group Test

I.
A spider nest .... DdWF ± A O—
A frozen man with .... WMCh H O—
staring eyes .... SF + Hd/eyes

II.
Love's heaven .... M → WCF heaven O impression

III.
A dance of the ghosts .... Ch → WM + H (P) O

The interpretation "spider nest" has come about because the subject has interpreted the small splashes at the periphery of the dark blot as caterpillars.

The "frozen man with staring eyes" interpretation could be a self-description.

The "love's heaven" interpretation has been probably arrived at on the basis of the color impression and by observing the "couple" (red area). An artistically talented person could have produced it too, for one senses the intuition here. At the same time, however, it approaches a contamination.

Taken separately, the "dance of the ghosts" interpretation could also have been produced by an artistically gifted person. However, in connection with the entire record, it becomes suspicious.

A human being with so many O and M, of which one is certainly, and another one most probably an MCh, is definitely no longer "normal." Nevertheless, he must once have been highly intelligent and he must have had artistic abilities. Even if I had seen nothing but the test and did not know anything about the clinical diagnosis, I would have suspected schizophrenia, because of the MCh and on the basis of the total impression conveyed by the test. The suspicion that we are dealing here with a catatonic (catatonics are inwardly productive people, even though they remain outwardly rigid) is readily aroused by the many M and O and, by taking into account the second interpretation in Slide I. The S and the "eye" interpretations lead us to assume that paranoid ideas may be present. By relating them to the one single color interpretation (Slide II), we could infer that, occasionally, agitated states (S + CF) —characterized by aggression—may break through.

10. Miss *Klara C.*, 24 years old, inmate of a mental institution. Schizophrenia (see Table 22).

Zulliger Group Test

I.

A knife	DdF + obj, aggression
A white spot in the center	SCF spot white as color
A Friesian lagoon (5 and 7)	S → DdF ± geog
A head with	S → DF + Hd
little snakes next to it	DdF + A
A snake tamer	DW → WM + H O contamination

II.

Flower petals (red area)	DCF pl
A snake nest (green area)	DdDF ± A
I see snakes down below also (brown area, lower periphery) ..	DdF ± A, perseveration
There is a flower in the center	SF + pl

III.

Clouds	ChF → WF± clouds
On top there are snakes	DdF + A
at the right and at the left there are snakes (3 and 9)	DdF − A
on the bottom there is a little snake (probably adjacent to the small dark blot towards the large one)	DdF + A, perseveration
Dancing Medusas	WM + H O (P)

580

TABLE 22

Number of responses: 15/4

Scoring:
Subject: *Miss Klara C.*

Card	W	D	Dd	S	F+	F−	F±	M	CF	ChF	P	O
I	1	1	3	3	3		1	1	1			1
II		1	2	1	1		2		1		1	
III	2		3		2	1	1	1		1	1	1
Total	3	2	8	4	6	1	4	2	2	1	1	2

F+% = 73
A% = 40
P% = 6
O% = 13
H% = 33

H = 2
Hd = 1
A = 6
obj = 1
pl = 2
spot = 1
clouds = 1
geog = 1

Sequence: loose – confused,
Sequence: tendency to inversion
Experience balance: 2 M : 2 C
Apperceptive type: W — D — Dd — S
Shock: —

Remarks:
Perseveration with "snakes"
Tendency: contamination
Tendency: DW

EVALUATION:

Schizophrenic factors are immediately evident in this test. The following factors lead us to suspect that the subject is not normal:

contamination probable;

the loose-to-irregular sequence;

the perseveration with snakes;

the selection of the picture parts for interpretation (sometimes at the center, sometimes at the periphery);

in addition to perseveration, the confusion prevailing with regard to content;

the contrast of the "dancing Medusas" interpretation (which could be produced only by an intelligent person) with the intelligence factors;

absence of a color shock;

the DW tendency.

25. Observation of Group Psychological Phenomena in the Zulliger Group Test

The results of the Zulliger Test, as well as those of other tests, differ in some points, depending on whether we test a subject while he is aware of being an *independent individual* or after he has lived for a time within a group as a *"member of a collective."*

This was most markedly revealed in tests carried out with military personnel: here certain differences were positively striking. However, they were found by chance. For the experiments that drew our attention to the fact that the emotional makeup of an individual differs according to whether he finds himself in the position of being a free individual, or a member of a group with definite characteristics, were originally not performed for the sake of science; they had an immediate practical aim.

Some young people had been admitted to a school for recruits. A few days after school started, they were asked whether anybody among them would like to become an officer later on. From among the 600 men, 60 applied; these men were at once subjected to a number of examinations, one of which was the Zulliger Group Test. Later, the examination results were to be compared with those intended to establish a purely military qualification, such as physical endurance, withstanding of exhaustion, etc. They were to be submitted to the chief of the respective branch of service as a further aid in the process of selecting soldiers, whenever he might be confronted with the task of naming the candidates for officers' training.

After the first selection, which we have referred to above, 40 men were found to be "qualified," out of the group of 60 men who had applied.

After having finished their basic training and served on field duty for some time, they were admitted to a school for non-commissioned officers. While attending this school, they were re-tested. Some of the groups were even tested for a third time, even though they were already in the school for officers.

And now the differences that I should like to discuss here became evident.

The first tests were carried out at a time when the recruits had just reported for military service; they were still "civilians," and not yet "soldiers." This situation is well-known in the army, where it is said maliciously about the men that they are "still wearing a civilian's sweater under their military uniform." After a few days or weeks, they are said to take off the sweater that they brought from home and "send it back to their mother." This may be the outward sign of the fact that they have now found the path from a "civilian" to a "military" existence. An emotional re-adjustment has taken place; somehow their "mentality" has become different from what it was before.

The tests carried out at a later date testify to this new adaptation.

As regards the Zulliger Group Test, I noticed first of all that the *experience balance* of some of the recruits appeared to be changed:

a. After having been in military service for some time, 13-15 recruits presented an *introversive* experience balance, out of 100 recruits who had previously shown an *extratensive* experience balance.

b. Out of 100 recruits who had been *introversive* before, 10-12 recruits had since become *extratensive*.

c. Out of 100 recruits who had originally been ambiequal, about 66 recruits became *extratensive* and the remainder changed to *introversive;* strictly speaking, two thirds of the men acquired an extratensive ambiequal experience balance, while one third attained an introversive ambiequal one.

Group (a) consisted of people who did not succeed in finding their way "inwardly," although on the surface they had adapted themselves to military service. Usually they performed their military duties just as everybody else did; yet at times they were likely to harbor in secret an increasing antagonism. Frequently they expressed themselves as being "sick and tired" of the army, or else they withdrew. Among their comrades, they occupied a special position, very often a respected one; whenever the others needed good advice, they came to them; they were regarded as the "reasonable ones," as people who had a "level head on their shoulders," who did not lose their temper and who did not become frightened easily, or excited right away. They were less "dashing,"and it was usually difficult for them to win the appreciation of their superiors (if indeed they wanted to). In terms of their physical makeup, they were thought of as being awkward and sometimes even as "weaklings"; nevertheless, in certain precarious situations, they proved themselves, as for instance, when one of their comrades "got the shakes" (a panic-like state) while at a remote post and had to be "straightened out," or when they were sent together with others, on a patrol that proved to be difficult, where one could not afford to "lose one's head" if one wished to come through safely. They were the unperturbed planners.

This expresses averages and rather general values. Among the introversive men there were naturally some eccentrics, some defiant ones, and some with a tendency to obstinacy; others were poor soldiers and poor comrades, for whom military service was a torture, although in civilian life they had felt at ease and had not been at all noticeable.

Group (b) and the group that included extratensive ambiequal men comprised people who adapted themselves best. These were the first to "take off the civilian's sweater," both actually and symbolically. Since they were agile physically as well as mentally, they immediately became accustomed to "life according to army regimentation," submitting to military requirements with apparent ease and often with grim humor, and taking nothing seriously. They were especially well suited for the ventures of assault troops; they were frequently "dare-devils." In addition, the group of the ambiequal-extratensive soldiers proved inventive in small practical matters. For the most part, these men were easy-going, and not inclined to be as exuberant as their more markedly extratensive comrades. In general, they were what is called "good soldiers."

The ambiequal-introversive men did not differ from them to any great extent; they were somewhat quieter and were usually excellent corporal material or, later on, higher non-commissioned officer or officer material. Their troops respected them greatly, because they never became "nervous" in their dealings with some particular situation (as did their more extratensive comrades). The "good leaders" were recruited from their ranks.

In addition to the various small groups mentioned above, there were the much larger ones that remained unchanged in their experience balance under the influence of military service:

about 85% of the men who had been extratensive in civilian life remained so;

about 90% of the men who had formerly been introversive remained so;

and the greatest fluctuations of experience balance were exhibited by the ambiequal men. These fluctuations were never very significant, however, and presented approximately the following picture:

I. Examination *II. Examination*
Experience Balance

I. Examination (shortly after entering the school for recruits) | II. Examination (after the service had lasted for a longer period of time)

Recruit A.
$3 M : 3 FC + 1 CF = 3 : 2\frac{1}{2}$ $2 M : 1 FC + 1 CF = 2 : 1\frac{1}{2}$
Recruit B.
$2 M : 3 FC = 2 : 1\frac{1}{2}$ $1 M : 1 FC + 1 CF = 1 : 1\frac{1}{2}$
Recruit C.
$3 M : 4 FC + 1 CF = 3 : 3$ $2 M : 2 FC + 2 CF = 2 : 3$

Recruit D.

$4 M : 4 FC + 2 CF = 4 : 4$ $2 M : 1 FC + 2 CF = 2 : 2\frac{1}{2}$

Recruit E.

$3 M : 3 FC + 2 CF = 3 : 3\frac{1}{2}$ $2 M : 1 FC + 2 CF = 2 : 2\frac{1}{2}$

Recruit F.

$4 M : 4 FC + 2 CF + 4 : 4$ $3 M : 3 FC + 1 CF = 2 : 2\frac{1}{2}$

Usually, under the influence of military service

1. experience balance became coarctated;
2. the number of W decreased;
3. the number of D, Dd, and S increased;
4. occasionally Do were produced where there had been none previously;
5. the A% became higher;
6. the P% became higher, at the expense of the O%, but in cases where M increased, the O% increased as well;
7. as a rule, the F+% became higher;
8. the Ms largely disappeared;
9. individual interpretations disappeared; the total record became more monotonous; the content column became limited to a few H, A, obj, and pl; the obj interpretations sometimes referred chiefly to military objects, such as "cannon shafts," "bayonets," etc.
10. Generally, the CF increased while the FC decreased.

A *déformation professionelle* appears, related to military matters. In military language, this is often called "service stupidity." However, we are not dealing here with actual mental deterioration, but with the adaptation and partial submission to all the mental and intellectual requirements of the army routine. A soldier needs restrictions in order to get along with this particular life situation and to feel happy in it.

By surveying the ten factors that change, sometimes more, sometimes less markedly, it becomes evident that in a collective the individual's

a. mind is brought into line to a certain degree,
b. total mentality becomes quasi-"uniform," and
c. his personal peculiarities become partly obliterated.

It should be expected that young people who undergo *vocational training* within the confines of some *collective*—I think in this connection of *policemen*, for instance, or of people engaged in working as *custom officials*—and those who attend special *vocational schools*, will show phenomena similar to those observed in the army recruits. Changes must also become noticeable in the *inmates of an institution*, the pupils of a *detention home, prisoners*, etc. Both intellect and attitude become transformed according to circumstances, and adapt themselves to the framework of the given conditions.[1]

Déformation professionelle appears in other areas too. Its symptoms exist in people of the most varied *professional groups*. In the Zulliger Test, a mild form of it is evidenced, too: medical men frequently see atomic images in it; technicians, some special technical objects; craftsmen, objects and tools that they see and use daily. In such cases we speak of *"shop-talk interpretations."* It is not our intention to deride them; we merely wish to indicate that the respective subjects are hardly capable of thinking in any other than a "professional" fashion. Subjects with strong religious feelings, as well as clergymen, often see the upper white space form (inner white blot within the red area) in Card II of the Zulliger Test as a "white dove" or "the Holy Ghost," and the parts underneath as a human head, upon which the Holy Ghost alights in the shape of a white dove.

Student and *student-type subjects* produce map responses, geometric abstractions, plant and flower diagrams, and sometimes (poorly perceived) anatomic interpretations as well.

Children of school age not infrequently assume that they are taking an *examination* while they are being tested. If this is the case, then they too are apt to display a kind of a *déformation professionelle* or "professional stupidity": the flow of their associations becomes slow; instead of W they produce Do; the number of responses decreases, or else it is increased by conscious industrious effort; experience balance becomes markedly

[1] A young thief who was tested while he was still free produced an experience balance of 1 M : 1 FC + 2 CF + 1 C = 1 : 4; after spending about six months in a detention home, he was tested again and presented an experience balance of 4 M : 1 CF = 4 : 1. The "captivity" had made him more introversive.

coarctated (even in otherwise lively, impulsive subjects); the $F+\%$ becomes relatively increased (because the child produces, or rather mentions, only those interpretations that he considers to be absolutely "correct"), thinking in terms of the "school's" system is expressed by an increased $A\%$; S are presented in increased number, as a sign of mistrust and self-doubts. The entire record is "falsified," inasmuch as it does not correspond with the true personality of the particular child but rather with the student's "*mask*." It depends greatly on the attitude of the tester whether children respond in such a manner or whether their way of responding is really in adequate agreement with their personality.

According to whether we are testing a subject as a "free" individual or as a member of a collective, different mental characteristics find their corresponding forms of expression. In the latter instance, a human being is easily influenced by very strongly marked suggestions that have been imprinted on him by the *collective life and experience,* forcing all the of the subject's more individual traits into the background. Aside from the fact that a human being is "never a shrewdly puzzled-out book," as Konrad Ferdinand Meyer has put it, but just a "person with all his contradictions," he does not appear the same as he would under ordinary circumstances whenever he is made part of a "collective group" (Freud, Le Bon).

From this point of view, a scarcely touched field unfolds here for psychological testing in terms of *social psychology*. Conversely, social psychology could probably gain enrichment and a great many suggestions from test psychology.

BIBLIOGRAPHY

Bacci, V. (1949), Prime considerazione sull' Applicazione in Italia del reattivo di Zulliger. *Riv. Psicol.*, 45:138-142.

—— (1950), Statische italiane del reattivo di Zulliger. *Riv. Psicol.*, 46:26-38.

—— (1951), Nuove considerazione sul reattivo di Zulliger. Rome: Atti IX Congresso Psicologi Italiani.

—— (1954), L'impotenza del reattivo di Zulliger. Chianciamo: Atti X Congresso Psicologi Italiani.

Battaglia, U. and Cruciani, G. (1956), Constanza del test di Zulliger in un esperimento di test-retest. *Schweiz. Z. Psychol.*, 34:394-396.

Burger, R. (1963), *Eignungs- und Erziehungsdiagnosen für höhere Schulen mit dem Diapositiv-Z-Test.* Bern/Stuttgart: Huber/Klett.

Cenestrari, R. and Mingizzi, G. F. (1956), Z.-test e percezione sociale. *Z. Diagnost. Psychol.*, 4:261-270.

Durand de Bousingen, M. R., Nevers, J., and Schmidt, O. (1956), Comparison entre le test Rorschach et le test Z chez les malades mentaux. Bordeaux: Comptes Rendus du Congrès des Médecins Aliénistes de Neurologistes.

Eble, S. J., Fernald, D. J., Jr., and Graziano, A. M. (1963), The Comparability of quantitative Rorschach and Z-Test data. *J. Project. Tech.*, 27(2).

Friedemann, A. (1957), Erfahrungen mit dem Zulliger-Test. *Schweiz. Z. Psychol. Anwend.*, 16:127-130.

Giuliani, C. (1949), Il reattivo di Zulliger nell'indagine psicologica. Parma: Atti del X Congresso di Medicina Legale e delle Assicurazione.

Gladston, E. R. and Amado-Haguenauer, G. (1960), A note on the Z-test results of 37 schizophrenics. *Rorschach Newslet., J. Brit. Rorschach Forum,* 5(2):23-24.

Hagenbuchner, K. and Thurner, E. (1956), Ueber die Brauchbarkeit des Diapositiv-Z-Tests in der klinischen Psychiatrie. *Z. Diagnost. Psychol.*, 4:331-343.

Hiltmann, H. (1953), Anwendung des Z-Test unter Prüfungsdruck. In: *Untersuchungen zum Z-Test. Studien zur Diagnostischen Psychologie.* Biel: Institut für Psychohygiene, pp. 11-16.

Ichimura, J. (1959), Comparability of the plates-Z-test and the Rorschach. *Jap. J. Psychol.*, 29:396-398.

Jaur, J. M. (1953), Etude expérimentalle sur le test de Zulliger. *Arch. Psicol. Neurol. Psychiat.*, 14:159-166.

Maza, A. L. (1952), Primeras investigaciones con el dia-Z-test en sujetos espanoles. *Riv. Psicol. Gen. Appl.*, 21.

Meistermann-Seeger, E. (1962), Sozialpsychologische Aspekte eines psychodiagnostischen Tests (Z-Test). *Kölner Z. Soziol. Sozialpsychol.*, 14:175-197.

Misiti, R. and Nencini, R. (1956), Rassegna delle applicazione dello Z-Tests in Italia. *Schweiz. Z. Psychol.*, 34:372-377.

Morali-Daninos, A. and Canivet, N. (1953), Le test "Z," technique collective. *Bull. Groupement Français du Rorschach,* 4:1-4.

Bibliography

———— ———— and Thierry, B. (1952), Le (dia) Z-test en psychotechnique. *Travail Humain*, 15:277-291.

Pfister, O. (1925), Ergebnisse des Rorschachen Versuches bei Oligophrenen. *Allg. Z. Psychiat.*: 82:198-223.

Riquier, M. (1964), Contribution à l'étude de l' inadaptation scolaire. Apport du test-Z-collectif de Zulliger. *Rev. Psychol. Appl.*, 14(2):97-118.

Salomon, F. (1953), The Rorschach test in criminology. *Int. Crim. Police Rev.*, No. 72.

———— (1954), Erfahrungen mit dem Z-diapositiv-test. *Z. Diagnost. Psychol.*, 2(1).

———— (1955), Le test-Z-collectif en filmologie. Contrôle des modifications émotives dans la situation cinématographique. Paris: *Rap. Imp. Congrès Intern. de Filmologie.*

———— (1956), Diagnostic des mécanismes de défense dans le test-Z-individuel et collectif. *Schweiz. Z. Psychol.*, 34:286-296.

———— (1958), Les problèmes affectifs en sélection professionnelle. Recherche à l'aide du test Z. *Schweiz. Z. Psychol.*, 40:164-169.

———— (1959), Fixations, régression et homosexualité dans les tests de type Rorschach. *Rev. Franç. Psychanal.*, 2:235-282.

———— (1961), Die symbolische Bedeutung der formalen Rorschach-Faktoren. *Schweiz. Z. Psychol.*, 45:163-174.

———— (1962), *Ich-Diagnostik im Zulliger-Test*. Bern/Stuttgart: Hans Huber.

Schmid, H. R. (1965), *Der Zulliger Test in der Berufsberatung. Mit einem Persönlichkeitsprofil für die Berufsberatung*. Bern/Stuttgart: Hans Huber.

Spitznagel, A. (1953), Senile Demenz im Z-Test. In: *Untersuchungen zum Z-Test. Studien zur Diagnostischen Psychologie*. Biel: Institut für Psychohygiene, pp. 41-75.

Tränkle, W. (1954), Herz- und Kreislaufkranke im Dia-Z-Test. Vortrag auf der 21. *Tagung der Mittelrheinischen Studiengesellschaft für Balneologie und Klimatologie in Bad Soden.*

Van der Meulen, E. E. C. (1959), Vulgär Deutungen bij de Z-Test in Indonesia. *Ned. Tijidschr. Psychol.*, 14:218-231.

Vogel, H. (1953), Der Z-Test bei Normalen Schulkindern. In: *Untersuchungen zum Z-Test. Studien zur Diagnostischen Psychologie*. Biel: Institut für Psychohygiene, pp. 17-39.

———— (1956), Ein Beitrag zur Frage des Aufforderungscharakters des Tafeln-Z-Tests. *Schweiz. Z. Psychol.*, 34:351-360.

Zulliger, H. (1948), *Der Z-Test. Ein Formdeut-Verfahren zur psychologischen Untersuchung von Gruppen*. Bern: Hans Huber.

———— (1952a), Über die Verwendbarkeit des Z-Tests. *Psych. Rundschau*, 3(4):249-264.

———— (1952b), Ein Ablösungs-Konflikt. *Psyche*, 6(3):210-218.

———— (1953a), Z-Test und Eignungspruefung. *Industrielle Organisation*, 22(10).

———— (1953b), Die Empfindlichkeit des Zulliger Testes. In: *Untersuchungen zum Z-Test. Studien zur Diagnostischen Psychologie*. Biel: Institut für Psychohygiene, pp. 5-10.

———— (1953c), Möglichkeiten und Grenzen der Diagnostik mit dem Formdeut-Test. *Psyche*, 7(2):140-149.

———— (1953d), Spiegelung Kollektivpsychologischer Phänomene im Z-Test. *Psyche*, 7(6):387-392.

———— (1953e), *Symbolische Diebsaehle bei Kindern und Jugendlichen.* Biel: Institut für Psychohygiene.

———— (1954a), *Der Tafeln-Z-Test.* Bern/Stuttgart: Hans Huber.

———— (1954b), Angst in der Spiegelung des Tafeln-Z-Tests. *Z. Diagnost. Psychol.,* 2:55-63.

———— (1954c), Imbezillität in der Spiegelung des Tafeln-Z-Tests. *Z. Diagnost. Psychol.,* 2:321-329.

———— (1955a), Der Diapositiv-Z-Test. Bern/Stuttgart: Hans Huber.

———— (1955b), "Kleine Psychotherapie" an Hand eines Tafeln-Z-Tests. *Z. Psychother. med. Psychol.,* 5(1):11-18.

———— (1955c), Warum stiehlt Jolande? Hergang einer testpsychologischen Begutachtung. *Z. Diagnost. Psychol.,* 3/4:344-359.

———— (1956a), "Complexe d'Abandon" im Tafeln-Z-Test. *Prax. Kinderpsychol. Kinderpsychiat.,* 5(5-6):114-118.

———— (1956b), Un cas de pseudo-débilité. *Rev. Psychol. Appliquée,* 6(3):161-177.

———— (1957), Projektive Tests und "Kleine Psychotherapie." *Psyche,* 10(10):610-629.

———— (1958), Praxis mit einer kleinen Testbatterie. *Prax. Kinderpsychol. Kinderpsychiat.,* 7(11-12): 273-277.

———— (1960), Berufsberatung anhand eines Tafeln-Z-Tests und Rorschachtests. *Schweiz. Z. Psychol.,* 19.

———— (1962a), *Der Zulliger-Tafeln-Test.* Bern/Stuttgart: Hans Huber.

———— (1962b), Der Zulliger-Tafeln-Test im Dienste der Diagnostizierbarkeit von Hirnschaeden. *Schweiz. Z. Psychol.,* 21(2):126-136.

———— (1963), Falldarstellung einer erethischen Debilität mit dem Zulliger-Tafeln-Test. *Diagnostica,* 9(3):125-132.

———— Die "doppelte Darbietung" des Zulliger-Testes.